Advances in Computer Vision and Pattern Recognition

More information about this series at http://www.springer.com/series/4205

Branislav Kisačanin · Margrit Gelautz
Editors

Advances in Embedded Computer Vision

Springer

Editors
Branislav Kisačanin
Interphase Corporation
Plano, TX
USA

Margrit Gelautz
Vienna University of Technology
Vienna
Austria

ISSN 2191-6586 ISSN 2191-6594 (electronic)
Advances in Computer Vision and Pattern Recognition
ISBN 978-3-319-35788-1 ISBN 978-3-319-09387-1 (eBook)
DOI 10.1007/978-3-319-09387-1

Springer Cham Heidelberg New York Dordrecht London

Softcover reprint of the hardcover 1st edition 2014

Printed on acid-free paper

Springer International Publishing AG Switzerland is part of Springer Science+Business Media (www.springer.com)

To Saška, Milena, and Nikola

BK

To Jürgen, Karina, and Laurenz

MG

Preface

Advances in Embedded Computer Vision

This book offers a fresh look at the advances that the field of embedded computer vision has made in recent years. It is similar in structure to the similarly named book, *Embedded Computer Vision*, published in 2008 also by Springer, but the content is all new.

What Is Embedded Computer Vision?

If you are new to this field, think of *Embedded Computer Vision* as the art of doing *computer vision*, with its complex algorithms and high computational and data bandwidth requirements, on processing platforms with serious constraints in terms of power, size, and cost, what we typically call *embedded systems*. These constraints come from specific requirements in which such systems are used: mobile devices (such as smart phones and tablets), robots, cars, micro air vehicles, remote cameras, etc.

Can It Be Done?

Oh, yes, it can be done! It is not easy, and that is why our field is still dominated by, in the language of *The LEGO Movie,* master builders. In Part I we present a number of success stories, in Part II we have descriptions of recent developments in our field, and in Part III we take a look at what the future challenges might be.

Target Audience

This book is meant for researchers, both in academia and industry, practitioners, and innovation managers interested in embedded computer vision. It offers insights at a variety of different levels: historical perspective, markets, technologies, systems, algorithms, embedded implementation, tools, and future developments.

The book can be used in academic teaching and research in various ways. It could be used as reading material for specialized advanced courses, for example, to introduce students of a computer vision course into state-of-the-art problems and applications of embedded vision technologies. To help with that, the chapters in the book are self-contained and could be assigned to students as individual reading material in seminar courses. The book may also provide an inspiring source of information for students and supervisors who are looking for promising and industry-relevant topics for Master and Ph.D. theses in the field of embedded vision.

Organization of the Book

Each chapter is a self-contained unit describing a particular topic. The chapters are grouped into three parts:

Part I: Success Stories—with detailed descriptions of three major success stories in our field—the optical mouse, robotic vision, and vision for automotive safety.

Part II: State of the Art—with seven chapters on the recent work in embedded 3D vision, unmanned aerial vehicles, automotive vision, mobile vision, and augmented reality.

Part III: Future Challenges—with three chapters that provide a peek into some of the future research directions.

Overview of Chapters

Before we briefly describe each chapter in the book, we would like to emphasize two areas of research that experienced a significant growth in the last few years.

The embedded realization of 3D vision technologies is of high relevance for a variety of applications including robotics and automotive safety, and it is currently receiving increased attention with the growing availability of stereo cameras on mobile devices such as tablets and smart phones. Especially in outdoor scenarios, with bright sunlight and varying imaging distances, stereo cameras offer advantages compared to other 3D sensors such as Microsoft's Kinect or time-of-flight sensors. The importance of embedded stereo matching algorithms that enable the computation of high-quality depth maps in real-time on resource-limited systems is well reflected by several contributions in the book.

A recent trend towards the development of small unmanned aerial vehicles (UAVs) increases the demand for light-weight and low-power sensors and processing units that can be used on-board the moving platform. The embedded implementation of image and video processing algorithms for fast and reliable self-localization, collision avoidance, and object recognition is a basic requirement for envisioned applications such as search and rescue tasks.

Part I: Success Stories

- In Chap. 1, "The Optical Mouse: Early Biomimetic Embedded Vision," Dick Lyon recalls his 1980 work on the development of the Xerox optical mouse integrated circuit. He emphasizes the mouse's bio-mimetic vision architecture and connections to other things going on in the vision and integrated circuit fields at the time.
- In Chap. 2, "Consumer Robotics: A Platform for Embedding Computer Vision in Everyday Life," authors Mario E. Munich, Phil Fong, Jason Meltzer, and Ethan Eade describe their work in robotic vision. They present a graph-based SLAM approach designed to operate on computationally constrained platforms using monocular vision and odometry.
- In Chap. 3, "Embedded Vision in Advanced Driver Assistance Systems," Zoran Nikolić tells us about applications of computer vision in advanced driver assistance systems—automotive vision.

Part II: State of the Art

- In Chap. 4, "Computer Vision for Micro Air Vehicles," authors Roland Brockers, Martin Humenberger, Yoshi Kuwata, Larry Matthies, and Stephan Weiss show us how their autonomous flight navigation framework for micro air vehicles addresses the challenges of low-power, small size solution for navigation in cluttered environments where these small unmanned aerial vehicles have to operate.
- In Chap. 5, "Stereo Vision Algorithms Suited to Constrained FPGA Cameras," Stefano Mattoccia reviews stereo vision algorithms suited for FPGA-based cameras. In particular, this chapter deals with the implementation of such algorithms on embedded camera systems with constrained hardware resources.
- In Chap. 6, "Plane Sweeping in Eye-gaze Corrected, Tele-immersive 3D Video Conferencing," authors Maarten Dumont, Patrik Goorts, and Gauthier Lafruit extend the stereo disparity estimation towards multiple cameras. Targeting high-quality image post-processing applications, they describe a view interpolation system, synthesizing new intermediate viewpoints for application in tele-immersive 3D video conferencing.
- In Chap. 7, "Challenges in Embedded Vision for Augmented Reality," authors Rajesh Narasimha, Norbert Stöffler, Darko Stanimirović, Peter Meier, and Markus Tremmel give us a broad overview of augmented reality applications.

- In Chap. 8, "Tic-Tac-Tandroid: A Tic-Tac-Toe Mobile Vision App," authors Milena Djordjević-Kisačanin, Vinjai Vale, and Branislav Kisačanin present an 8th grade science fair project in which an Android app was created for smart phones that can play the game of tic-tac-toe by "seeing" a hand-drawn board, and "thinking" of the next best move.
- In Chap. 9, "Vehicle Detection Onboard Small Unmanned Aircraft," authors Mathias Kölsch and Robert Zaborowski present their work on ground vehicle detection from a small flight platform.
- In Chap. 10, "Vision-based Lane Analysis: Exploration of Issues and Approaches for Embedded Realization," authors Ravi Kumar Satzoda and Mohan M. Trivedi give us insight into their latest algorithmic approaches for efficient automotive vision.

Part III: Future Challenges

- In Chap. 11, "Distributed Smart Cameras in the Age of Cloud Computing and the Internet-of-Things," Marilyn Wolf surveys development in embedded computer vision systems related to the Internet of Things. The chapter considers algorithms, software architectures, and hardware platforms.
- In Chap. 12, "Data-driven Stream Mining Systems for Computer Vision," authors Shuvra S. Bhattacharyya, Mihaela van der Schaar, Onur Atan, Cem Tekin, and Kishan Sudusinghe discuss their ideas about how the huge volumes of image data coming from networks with large numbers of cameras can be processed in a systematic and efficient framework.
- In Chap. 13, "Designing Vision Systems that See Better," authors Sek Chai, Sehoon Lim, and David Zhang present a summary of their work on computational sensing. This chapter introduces the reader to a branch of computer vision that deals with computationally improving captured imagery by fundamentally changing how light is sensed, captured, and processed.

How This Book Came About

As organizers of the ninth Embedded Vision Workshop in 2013 (these workshops have been held almost every year at IEEE CVPR conferences), we were in a unique position to help satisfy the need for a focused, comprehensive overview of recent developments in embedded computer vision. We invited a number of authors who contributed to recent Embedded Vision Workshops and the result of that collaboration is in front of you!

Plano, TX, USA, August 2014 — Branislav Kisačanin
Vienna, Austria — Margrit Gelautz

Acknowledgments

First and foremost, the editors are grateful to the authors of the chapters in this book for a dedicated effort to share their valuable experiences and complete their chapters under very ambitious publishing schedule for the book. They further helped improve the quality and relevance of the book by agreeing to review other chapters.

Furthermore, we greatly appreciate the work of our Springer editors, Wayne Wheeler and Simon Rees, who expertly guided us through the book production process.

Contents

Contributors

Onur Atan University of California, Los Angeles, CA, USA

Shuvra S. Bhattacharyya University of Maryland, College Park, MD, USA

Roland Brockers Jet Propulsion Laboratory, California Institute of Technology, Pasadena, CA, USA

Sek Chai SRI International, Menlo Park, CA, USA

Milena Djordjević-Kisačanin Fermat School of Math and Science, Plano, TX, USA

Maarten Dumont Expertise Centre for Digital Media, Hasselt University—TUL—IMinds, Diepenbeek, Hasselt, Belgium

Ethan Eade Microsoft Research, Redmond, WA, USA

Phil Fong iRobot, Pasadena, CA, USA

Patrik Goorts Expertise Centre for Digital Media, Hasselt University—TUL—IMinds, Diepenbeek, Hasselt, Belgium

Martin Humenberger AIT Austrian Institute of Technology, Seibersdorf, Austria

Branislav Kisačanin Fermat School of Math and Science, Plano, TX, USA

Mathias Kölsch Naval Postgraduate School, Monterey, CA, USA

Yoshi Kuwata Jet Propulsion Laboratory, California Institute of Technology, Pasadena, CA, USA

Gauthier Lafruit Expertise Centre for Digital Media, Hasselt University—TUL—IMinds, Diepenbeek, Hasselt, Belgium

Sehoon Lim SRI International, Menlo Park, CA, USA

Richard F. Lyon Google Inc., Mountain View, CA, USA

Larry Matthies Jet Propulsion Laboratory, California Institute of Technology, Pasadena, CA, USA

Stefano Mattoccia Department of Computer Science and Engineering, University of Bologna, Bologna, Italy

Peter Meier Metaio GmbH, Munich, Germany

Jason Meltzer iRobot, Pasadena, CA, USA

Mario E. Munich iRobot, Pasadena, CA, USA

Rajesh Narasimha Metaio GmbH, Munich, Germany

Zoran Nikolić Texas Instruments, Inc., Houston, TX, USA

Ravi Kumar Satzoda Laboratory of Intelligent and Safe Automobiles, University of California San Diego, CA, USA

Mihaela van der Schaar University of California, Los Angeles, CA, USA

Darko Stanimirovic Metaio GmbH, Munich, Germany

Norbert Stöffler Metaio GmbH, Munich, Germany

Kishan Sudusinghe University of Maryland, College Park, MD, USA

Cem Tekin University of California, Los Angeles, CA, USA

Markus Tremmel Metaio GmbH, Munich, Germany

Mohan M. Trivedi Laboratory of Intelligent and Safe Automobiles, University of California San Diego, CA, USA

Vinjai Vale Fermat School of Math and Science, Plano, TX, USA

Stephan Weiss Jet Propulsion Laboratory, California Institute of Technology, Pasadena, CA, USA

Marilyn Wolf Georgia Institute of Technology, Atlanta, GA, USA

Robert Zaborowski Naval Postgraduate School, Monterey, CA, USA

David Zhang SRI International, Menlo Park, CA, USA

Part I
Success Stories

Chapter 1
The Optical Mouse: Early Biomimetic Embedded Vision

Richard F. Lyon

Abstract The 1980 Xerox optical mouse invention, and subsequent product, was a successful deployment of embedded vision, as well as of the Mead–Conway VLSI design methodology that we developed at Xerox PARC in the late 1970s. The design incorporated an interpretation of visual lateral inhibition, essentially mimicking biology to achieve a wide dynamic range, or light-level-independent operation. Conceived in the context of a research group developing VLSI design methodologies, the optical mouse chip represented an approach to self-timed semi-digital design, with the analog image-sensing nodes connecting directly to otherwise digital logic using a switch-network methodology. Using only a few hundred gates and pass transistors in 5μ nMOS technology, the optical mouse chip tracked the motion of light dots in its field of view, and reported motion with a pair of 2-bit Gray codes for *x* and *y* relative position—just like the mechanical mice of the time. Besides the chip, the only other electronic components in the mouse were the LED illuminators.

1.1 Early Mice

At Xerox PARC, wheel mice and ball mice went through several generations in the 1970s, and when Xerox first delivered their commercial workstation product—the Xerox "Star" 8010 Information System—in the early 1980s, it shipped with a ball mouse. But the optical mouse that I first designed in 1980 made it to product a few years later, and displaced the ball mouse in favor of this less expensive and more reliable technology based on a single-chip VLSI sensor with logic (see the chip photo, Fig. 1.1).

The early mechanical mice worked well when they were clean, but tended to gum up over time. They did not have removable balls like the later Apple Macintosh mice, so had to be disassembled and cleaned by a technician. Due to these difficulties, several researchers at PARC had worked on developing no-moving-part optical alternatives. I had the advantage of being able to review several different previous

R.F. Lyon (✉)
Google Inc., Mountain View, CA, USA
e-mail: dicklyon@acm.org

B. Kisačanin and M. Gelautz (eds.), *Advances in Embedded Computer Vision*, Advances in Computer Vision and Pattern Recognition,
DOI 10.1007/978-3-319-09387-1_1

Fig. 1.1 The Xerox optical mouse chip in its injection-molded dual-inline package (DIP) of clear plastic, with pins stuck into a conductive packaging foam. The bond wires connecting the chip's pads to the lead frame are (barely) visible

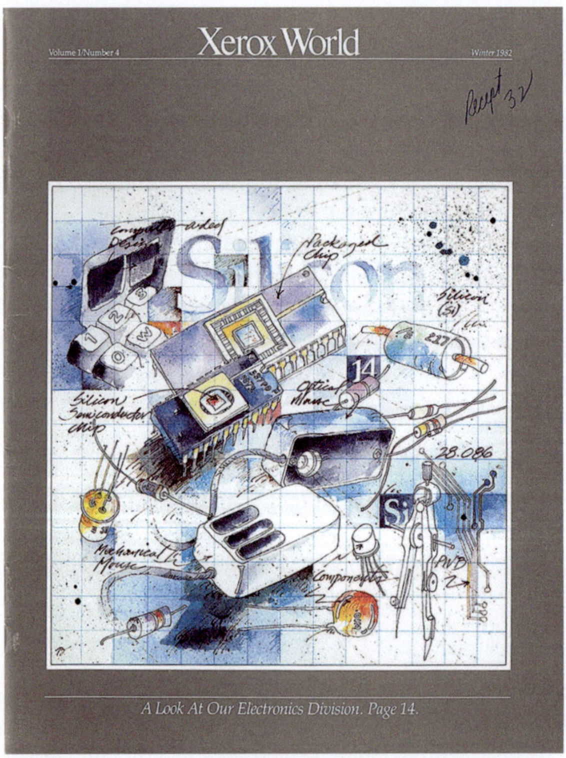

Fig. 1.2 The Winter 1982 Xerox World internal magazine cover featuring the Electronics Division and their three-button mechanical and optical mouse developments, among other electronic developments. The three-button mouse shipped on SmallTalk and Lisp machines, but the 8010 and 6085 office systems used a two-button version [18]

Fig. 1.3 This 1985 product brochure shows the two-button Xerox optical mouse on its special mouse pad. The corner of the mouse pad not shown in this image is detailed in Fig. 1.4

attempts that had resulted in the filing of invention proposals, but no prototypes or patents, as well as the advantage of having the new custom VLSI chip prototyping system available (we had developed this capability in Lynn Conway's VLSI Systems Group). The previous optical mouse attempts were based on good concepts for one-dimensional motion sensing, but the attempted extensions to 2D were not workable.

At the same time as my optical mouse chip, Steve Kirsch independently invented a way to make two one-dimensional trackers work together, using two different LED colors and a mouse pad with special colors of orthogonal stripes. In this design, the mouse's coordinate system was in the gridded pad; for this reason, Jack Hawley, maker of the X063X ball mouse for Xerox, called Kirsch's devices "pseudo mice" [28]. My design that Xerox pursued was truly two-dimensional, with coordinates relative to the mouse body, like a mechanical mouse.

Kirsch's mouse was a big success, being adopted for early Sun workstations, but was not really an embedded vision system; it had a few photosensors, but no imaging array. The Xerox mouse, on the other hand, had a 2D imaging array (4×4 pixels) with simple correlation-based spot tracking, and was an embedded vision system in

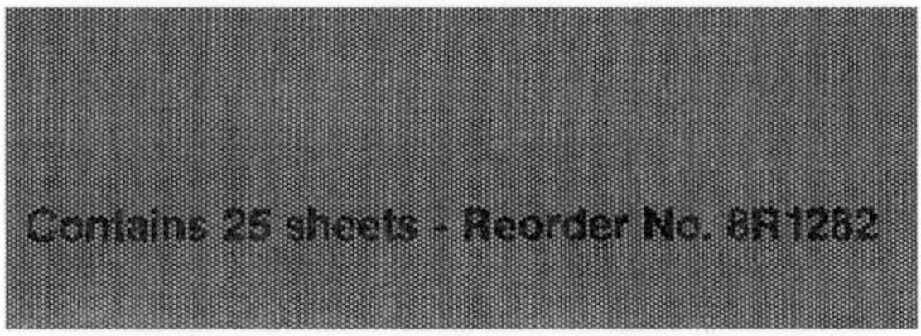

Fig. 1.4 The mouse pad was paper, sold in packs of 25 sheets. The pattern was a hexagonal array of light dots in a dark field, shown here at approximately actual size. Effective mouse pads could be made by a copier

that sense. Further, it was specifically neuromorphic and biomimetic in the way it incorporated lateral inhibition in its imager.

Xerox's optical mouse development was celebrated on the cover of their internal Xerox World magazine in 1982, as shown in Fig. 1.2. The Xerox optical mouse was sold with a range of office workstations, such as the 6085 shown in Fig. 1.3, as well as with Xerox Lisp machines, Tektronics SmallTalk machines, and high-end copier/duplicator products—none of which were high-volume products. Xerox was not successful in their attempts to sell licenses to their optical mouse patents, even after the market for mice exploded on the introduction of the Apple Macintosh with its low-cost ball mouse in 1984.

This chapter reviews the ideas that went into the optical mouse's very application-specific embedded vision system.

1.2 Image Sensing with Lateral Inhibition

The elementary light detector in an nMOS process is a PN photodiode, with the P region being the substrate and the N region being a diffusion region, as shown in Fig. 1.5 (a "green" area as we taught it in the red/green/blue/black scheme at the time). As shown in Fig. 1.6, a reset transistor back-biases the photodiode to an initial high voltage, and the voltage decays as the diode collects photoelectrons. The photodiode voltage can be used as an input to digital logic (shown in the figure as an inverter), provided the logic is designed to tolerate the intermediate analog values that the voltage will necessarily go through slowly.

The imaging strategy in the optical mouse relies heavily on an engineering interpretation of lateral inhibition as a nonlinear scheme for arriving at a stable image, independent of light level. In the simplest example, as shown in Fig. 1.7, a two-pixel imager uses mutual inhibition in a form that forces the system to decide which one of the two pixels receives more light than the other.

In systems of more than two pixels, each pixel can inhibit, and be inhibited by, pixels within some radius. For example, in the four-pixel imager of Fig. 1.8, pixels at distance 1 and 2 mutually inhibit, but the end pixels, at a distance of 3, do not inhibit each other. This radius-of-inhibition idea has an obvious extension into two dimensions.

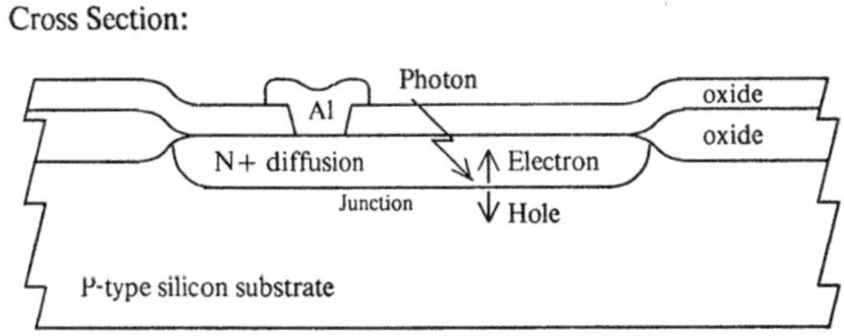

Fig. 1.5 The photodiode is an *n*-type region in an nMOS process. These and other diagrams are scanned from my 1981 PARC optical mouse report [24]

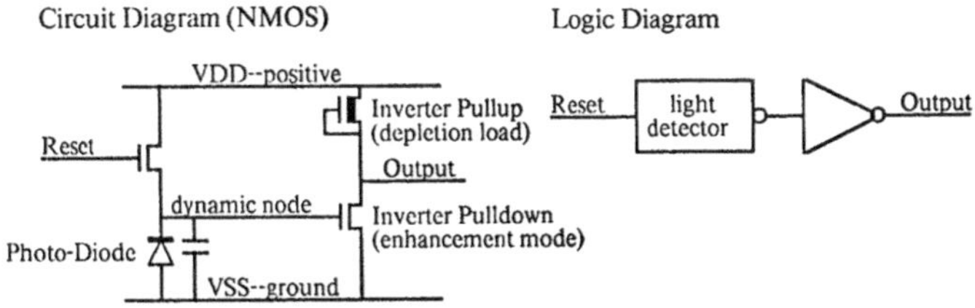

Fig. 1.6 The photodiode was incorporated as a dynamic node, going directly into a logic gate, just as other switched dynamic nodes were used in the methodology we had been teaching [9, 10]

The stable images from the four-pixel imager, that is, images where no more pixels can change from "dark" to "light," are just three: 1001, 0100, 0010. These patterns are ideally suited to imaging and tracking light lines spaced at about 3 pixels, in a dark background, as shown in Fig. 1.9. Figure 1.8 also shows logic for comparing successive images, by local binary cross-correlation, and keeping track of position by a counter, under control of the timing logic of Fig. 1.10.

When I studied the literature on lateral inhibition in the 1970s, based mostly on the compound eye of the horseshoe crab *Limulus*, it seemed to be based mostly on a linear systems view, with subtraction from neighboring sensor elements resulting in a bandpass or highpass filtering effect. In his 1967 book *Sensory Inhibition*, von Békésy [36] explored the effects of lateral inhibition in various sensory systems, including vision, hearing, touch, and taste, in essentially linear systems terms, for "sharpening" the response to stimuli. Papers argued that the effect could be very accurately modeled as linear. For example, while Knight et al. [19] noted that crab eye was quite compressive, with a "graded response to a wide range of light intensities (to a factor of about 10^7 in intensities for *Limulus*)," they also said that "the response to an intensity decrement is the close mirror image of the response to the corresponding increment. This suggests that we are dealing with a so-called 'time-invariant linear' system." In most subsequent analysis, the locally short-time approximately linear filtering behavior was modeled as if it were accurate, and the extremely nonlinear large-scale long-time adaptive behavior was ignored, so the important property of lateral inhibition as a strategy for normalizing the response across a wide dynamic range was missed. Barlow finally forcefully explained why lateral inhibition is a key

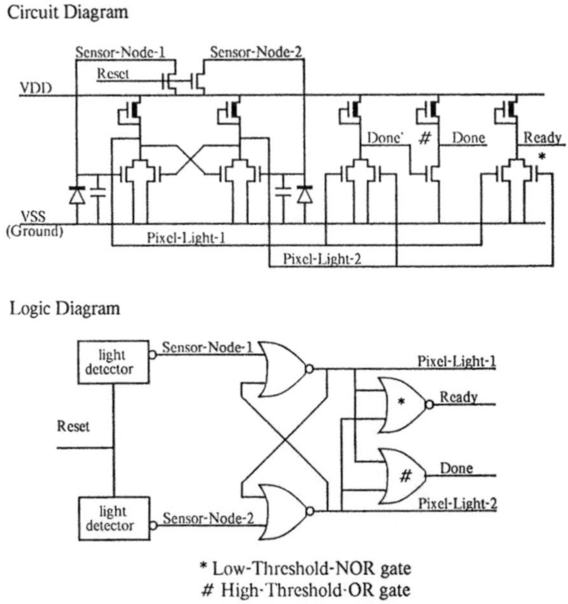

Fig. 1.7 The circuit and logic diagrams for a two-pixel imager. Through the cross-coupled feedback, each pixel inhibits the other. It is essentially a flip-flop, with two known stable states, that can hang for a while in an unstable all-dark state after being reset to that state (like an RS flip-flop with both set and reset asserted at the same time). The gates on the right detect "Ready" when the "Reset" signal has put the imager into the unstable state (Pixel-Light-1 and Pixel-Light-2 both low), and "Done" when light discharging one or both photodiodes has allowed the flip-flop to commit to one of the stable states (Pixel-Light-1 or Pixel-Light-2 high)

part of the strategy for wide dynamic range vision [3]: "If critical limiting factors are emphasized one says that lateral inhibition, color opponency, and the gain changes of light and dark adaptation, are necessary to transmit information about the light intensities in subdivisions of the visual image, because the available information has a much wider dynamic range than can be transmitted directly down a nerve fiber in a reasonable time interval." It may be that I had already inferred that from some of his pre-1981 writings, though they were not as clear on this point.

My original chip layout, done "by hand" on a Xerox Alto with a mouse and the ICARUS IC editor [14], is shown in Fig. 1.11. I had no idea how much light would be needed, or what the contrast ratio of the imaged surface would be, so I used lateral inhibition to make the logical function independent of overall light level. I did no calculations of photodiode capacitance, photon flux, noise margins, or any of the things that I had to learn about decades later, designing image sensors at Foveon. I just wanted to make sure it would work, and generate trackable binary patterns, at any light level. It was very clear that a linearly responding sensor system would be useless, but I saw the way to use the well-studied networks of lateral inhibition for their nonlinear normalizing effects. This approach is now more common, in concepts

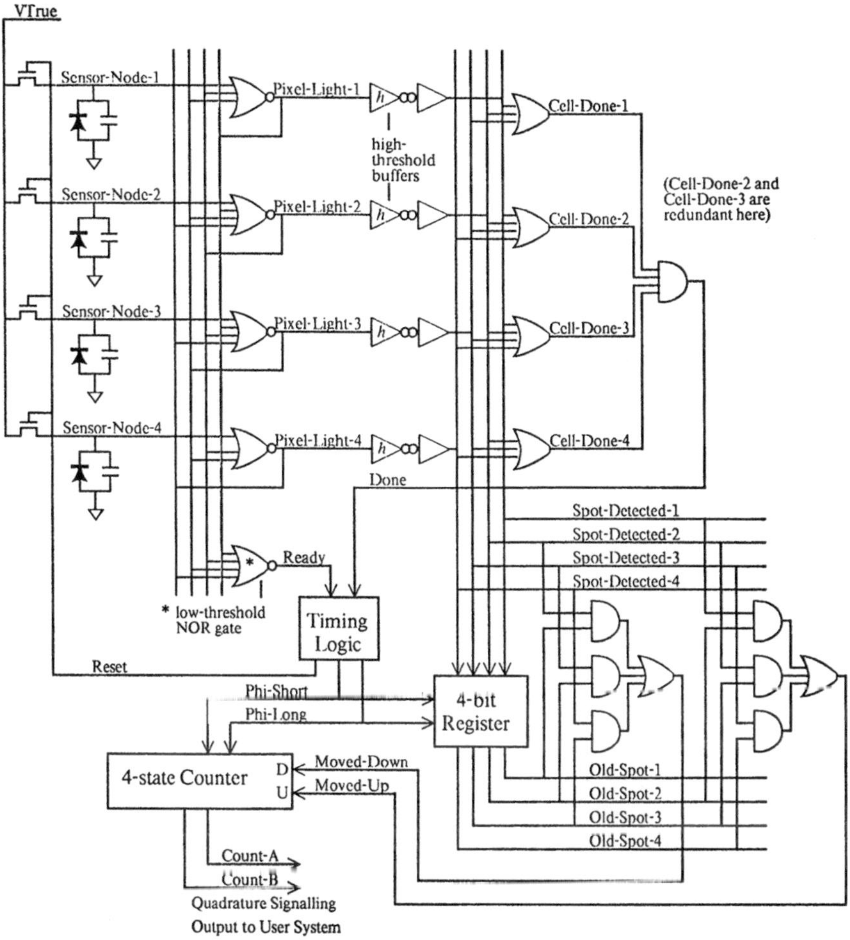

Fig. 1.8 A four-pixel version of the imager scheme of Fig. 1.7, with timing and motion detection logic. This linear imaging array has each pixel inhibiting neighbors up to two pixels away, but the extreme end pixels do not inhibit each other, illustrating the idea of a radius of inhibition. The done-detection logic is looking for every pixel to either be indicating light, or be inhibited by one that is light; such states are stable

such as "contrast gain control"—an idea proposed in 1978 by Shapley and Victor [34] for better modeling the cat retina. It is sometimes implemented as "divisive gain control," dividing by a neighborhood average as a way to control the local gain [32]. In the mouse sensor, the lateral inhibition implements a source of a *race* in time; the first sensor channel to get enough signal inhibits its neighbors, and if there is a near tie, they inhibit each other in a positive feedback loop until one wins.

I initially investigated lateral inhibition for robust automatic gain control in hearing models, starting at Xerox before the optical mouse work; I have continued to use the

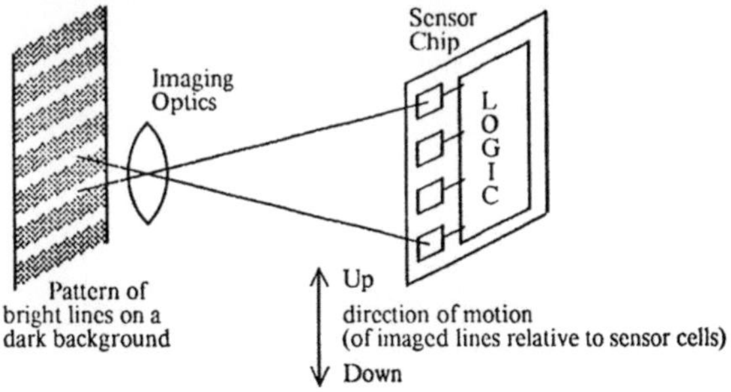

Fig. 1.9 *Light lines* in a dark background can be imaged as shown here, and tracked using a linear array of just four pixels, using the circuit of Fig. 1.8

concept this way in my current work on machine hearing [22]. Another interpretation of nonlinear lateral inhibition, rather than as gain control, is as sparse coding—which is essentially what the mouse sensor does. To arrive at most outputs being zero due to inhibition, and only one or a few outputs being active, a competitive or comparative dynamic process operates on initially small differences, resulting in a *winner-take-all* effect. This concept was later used in the silicon retina [21]. Variations on sparse coding and winner-take-all coding have become popular in computer vision in recent decades.

1.3 Symmetric Mutual Inhibition

The two-pixel and four-pixel examples show symmetric patterns of mutual inhibition: if pixel A inhibits pixel B, then pixel B inhibits pixel A. This is not the only kind of logical inhibition pattern that can be built, but it has the useful property that it leads to a set of stable states that are easy to enumerate, and it is easy to build logic to determine when a stable state has been reached.

Networks with symmetric inhibitory connections came to be known as Hopfield networks, and were valued for these properties [1]. I recognized the value of the final states being stable, and of being able to predict, enumerate, and detect stable states, when working on extending the one-dimensional tracking idea to two dimensions. In this sense, I was building both a Hopfield network, though not of the scale or application envisioned by John Hopfield [16], and also a silicon retina, though not of the scale or generality envisioned by Carver Mead [29]. The imager with lateral inhibition was a nonlinear dynamical system, before that concept was popularized with the notion of chaotic attractors; but the attractors in the mouse imager are stable by design, not chaotic or periodic.

In Fig. 1.8, the column of four NOR gates on the left, with feedback from their outputs to the inputs of others, is the Hopfield network. The rest of the circuitry is for resetting it, determining when it is reset, determining when it reaches a stable state, repeating that sequence indefinitely, and tracking the motion implied by the successive states. Comparable lateral inhibitory connections of limited range are

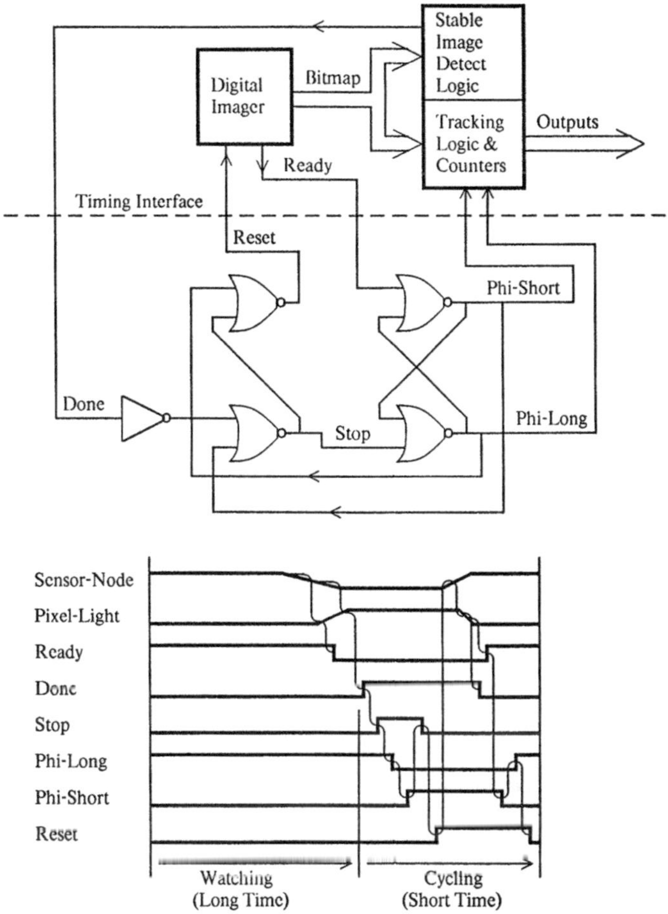

Fig. 1.10 The "Ready" and "Done" signals from an imaging array with lateral inhibition, such as that in Fig. 1.8, cooperate with this nonoverlapping-clock generation circuit to yield a free-running self-timed imaging system. The synchronous digital logic parts of the system use the two-phase nonoverlapping clocking methodology that we were teaching for digital system design as part of the Mead–Conway VLSI design revolution [30]. The duration of the "long" clock phase would be whatever time was needed for the imager to reach a stable binary state—faster at high light levels, slower at low light levels

found in real retinas, involving horizontal cells and amacrine cells [11], and in silicon retinas [13].

1.4 Metastability

The ability of the Hopfield network to fall into a stable state depends on positive feedback. A multi-stable system also has metastable states, or saddle points, where it can hang for a long time before deciding which side to fall toward. The mouse's

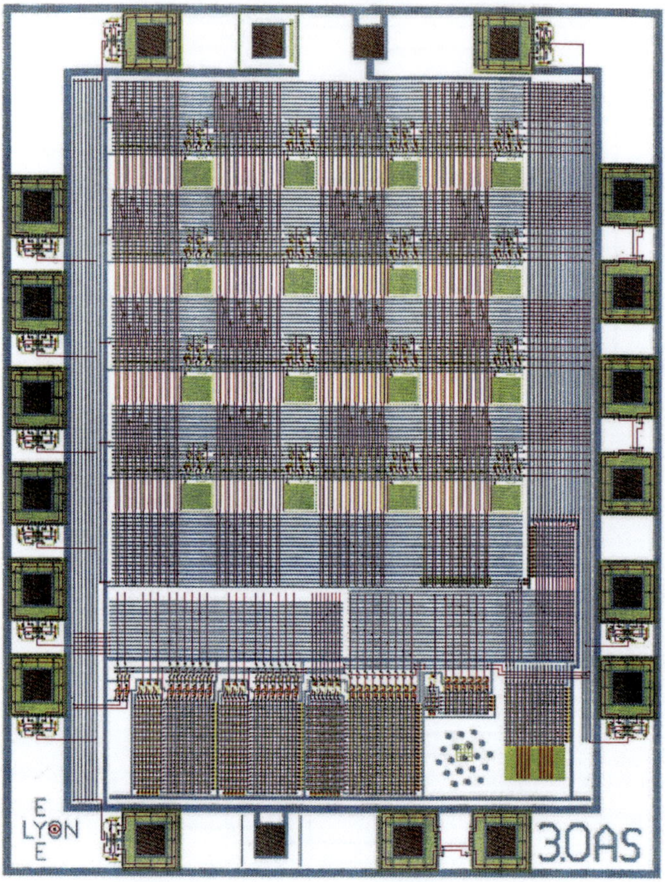

Fig. 1.11 The layout of the first-generation Xerox optical mouse chip, which I did quickly toward the end of 1980, had the lateral inhibition, done-detection, and image storage logic distributed in the pixel cell array, along with image cross-correlation logic. The arrays at the bottom were essentially programmed logic arrays (PLAs), programmed as the timing generator, the counters, and the logic that converted the sensed move directions, or image cross-correlations, to counter increments. Six of the bond pads are cross-coupled inverter pairs, to debounce the SPDT switch contacts of the three mouse buttons. Of the eleven output pads, four are for the motion encoding and seven are for observing internal timing signals

done-detection logic waits to see when it has committed, but this strategy only works if the metastable states are static, not oscillatory.

Oscillatory metastable states were well known to us in the 1970s, having been reported by Chaney and Molnar [7], who showed the oscillatory metastable behavior of a pair of cross-coupled TTL logic gates; Fig. 1.12 shows random samples of a flip-flop output being put into and exiting its metastable state. Charlie Molnar had worked with us at Caltech during the early VLSI developments, and was influential in

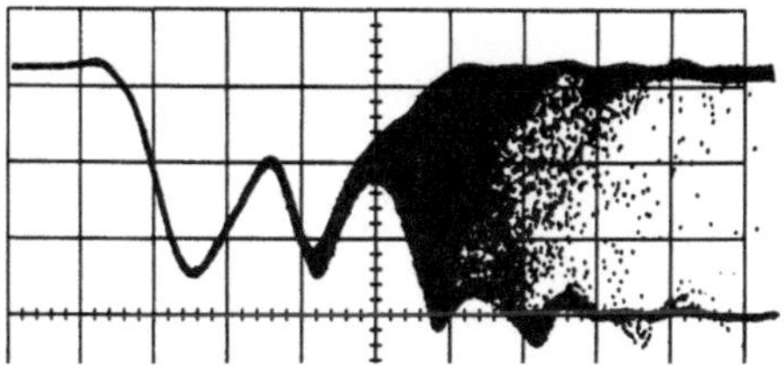

Fig. 1.12 Chaney and Molnar showed in 1973 that a pair of cross-coupled TTL NAND gates had an oscillatory metastable state

Fig. 1.13 Chaney and Rosenberger showed, at the 1979 Caltech Conference on VLSI, that cross-coupled nMOS NOR gates would exit the metastable point via a simple exponential divergence

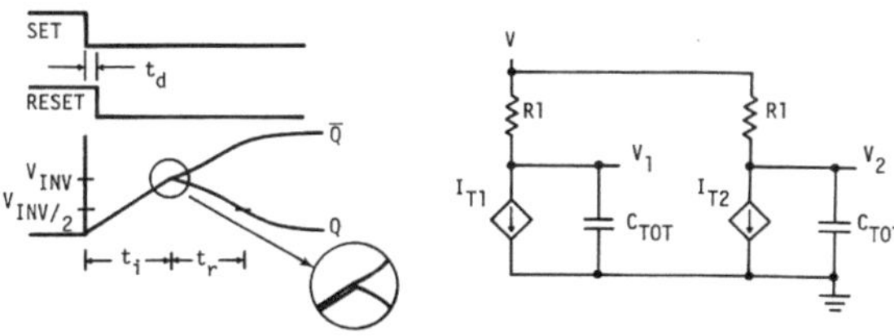

TYPICAL WAVEFORMS FOR t_d SMALL AND POSITIVE

FIGURE 3

EQUIVALENT CIRCUIT FOR FLIP FLOP IN THE METASTABLE REGION

FIGURE 4

If the circuit has voltages $V_1 = V_{INV} - \Delta V$ and $V_2 = V_{INV} + \Delta V$ at time t_i, then the voltage V_1 as a function of time is given by

$$V_1 = V_{INV} - \Delta V \cdot \exp[p(A-1)(t-t_i)] \qquad t \geq t_i \qquad (8)$$

where $p = \dfrac{C_0 \cdot \mu(V_{INV} - V_{DD} - V_{TPU})}{C_{TOT} \cdot L^2 \cdot k}$ = the bandwidth of one inverter stage of the Flip Flop

$A = k \cdot \dfrac{V_{INV} - V_{TPD}}{V_{INV} - V_{DD} - V_{TPU}}$ = magnitude of the low frequency gain of one inverter stage

thus the τ_r defined in Section II is given by

$$\boxed{\tau_r = \frac{1}{p(A-1)} = \frac{C_{TOT}\, L^2}{C_0\, \mu} \cdot \frac{k}{k(V_{INV} - V_{TPD}) - (V_{INV} - V_{DD} - V_{TPU})}} \qquad (9)$$

$$\text{and} \quad V_1 = V_{INV} - \Delta V \cdot \exp \frac{t-t_i}{\tau_r} \qquad (10)$$

$$V_2 = V_{INV} + \Delta V \cdot \exp \frac{t-t_i}{\tau_r} \qquad (11)$$

our thinking about system timing, as described in Chuck Seitz's chapter in the Mead–Conway book [33]. In my initial report, I credited Seitz for the done-detection idea:

> Note that we do not use the inhibition NOR gate output itself for done-detection, but a buffered version of it after a high threshold buffer (inverter pair); this is the easiest way to prevent false done-detection during a metastable condition (Seitz 1980). The buffered signal is not used for inhibition, since that would make it participate in the metastable condition, and because the extra delay would cause oscillatory metastable states.

Chaney and Rosenberger had shown that the metastable state of a pair of cross-coupled nMOS NOR gates, like that of the two-pixel imager of Fig. 1.7, would be a simple unstable equilibrium, which would diverge exponentially toward a stable state, without oscillation [8]; Fig. 1.13 shows their model and analysis from the 1979 Caltech Conference on VLSI. This was the behavior I needed, and I had reasoned that with one capacitance per node, a multinode generalization, such as the one in Fig. 1.8, or the larger one in the full 2D imager, would have similar dynamics in exiting its metastable states. Yet I had no proof.

Hopfield showed in 1984 that with symmetric interconnection weights, such a network can be characterized by an energy function, and that any state change reduces the energy, until it settles into a stable state, a local minimum [17]. Hopfield's differential equation formulation with one state variable per node exactly describes the network of interconnected nMOS NOR gates in the optical mouse imager, so we can be sure, in retrospect, that the metastable states of that circuit are nonoscillatory. The cross-coupled TTL gates that Chaney and Molnar analyzed had extra internal (not symmetrically interconnected) nodes with their own state and delay, which is why the metastable states in that case could be oscillatory.

1.5 Two Dimensions

The idea of a 1D line tracker such as that of Fig. 1.9 has various possible extensions into two dimensions. Extensions that use axis-aligned patterns of lines or dots have problems when the mouse is rotated, which is why pre-1980 attempts at PARC did not get very far. Using the idea of a radius of inhibition in two dimensions, I set about finding a way to track less rigid patterns of light dots in a dark field. An ideal pattern seemed to be a close-packed hexagonal array of dots, allowing the imager at arbitrary angles to treat the dots as being randomly arrayed, with a characteristic distance between them.

After evaluating various radii of inhibition and imager sizes, I found that a 4×4 array with a "3.0 special" radius of inhibition would yield a set of stable images containing either one light dot in the central 2×2 area, or two light dots on opposite edges—a total of 30 possible state binary images, as shown in Fig. 1.14. Here "special" means that pixels at a distance of exactly 3.0 pixel spaces will inhibit each other if they are corners, but not otherwise; this scheme eliminates patterns of 3 and 4 dots, but allows patterns of dots on opposite edges, so that motion can be detected, much as with the lines on opposite ends of the linear array of 4. In the 2D case, a pattern of light dots in a hexagonal array, as shown in Fig. 1.15, works well.

When the radius of inhibition exceeds $2\sqrt{2}$, a light spot in an image cannot be adjacent or diagonally adjacent to two different spots in a previous or subsequent image, so we will not have any ambiguity of which direction a spot moved. Furthermore, with the 3.0 special inhibition pattern, since there can only be at most two spots (as shown in Fig. 1.14), there will be at most two motion directions involved in a correlation of one image with the next. Computing the average of two moves is easy, using a half-step bit in a position counter: when an old image and a new image each have two spots, with different apparent move directions, their average can still be represented in terms of half steps. The logic to drive the half and full steps

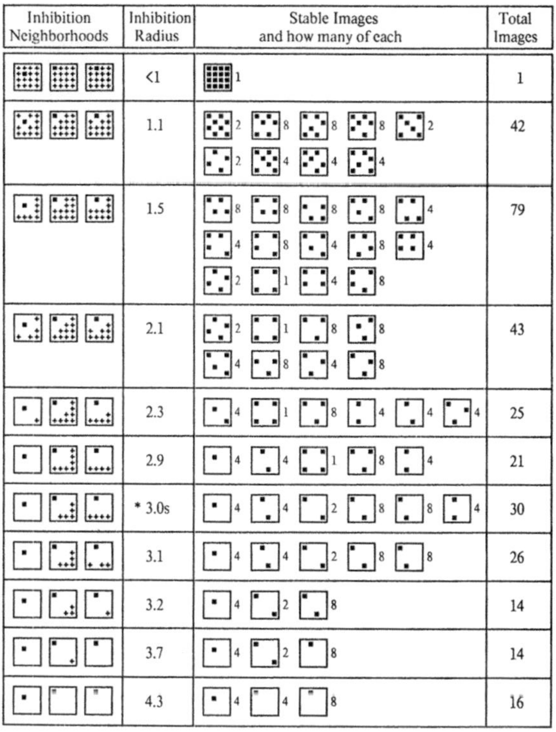

Fig. 1.14 Inhibition patterns and spot patterns for a range of radii of inhibition. The 3.0 s inhibition yields a useful set of 30 stable images with one or two spots each

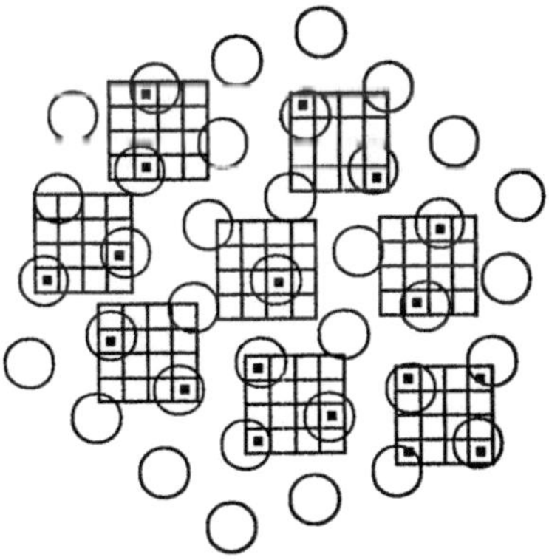

Fig. 1.15 How a 4 × 4-pixel imager might see one, two, three, or four *light dots* when viewing a hexagonal array. For the inhibition pattern we chose, the three- and four-dot versions are not allowed, so only two of the *dots* on opposite edges (and not on adjacent corners) will be seen in those cases

from the detected correlations is shown in Fig. 1.16, to control the output quadrature signals shown in Fig. 1.17.

The clocked logic does not have much state besides the sensor pixels themselves: just one 16-bit old image to be compared with a new image, and a pair of three-bit counters for x and y positions; compare the 4-bit image register and single counter of the one-dimensional version in Fig. 1.8. Only two bits per dimension are taken as out-

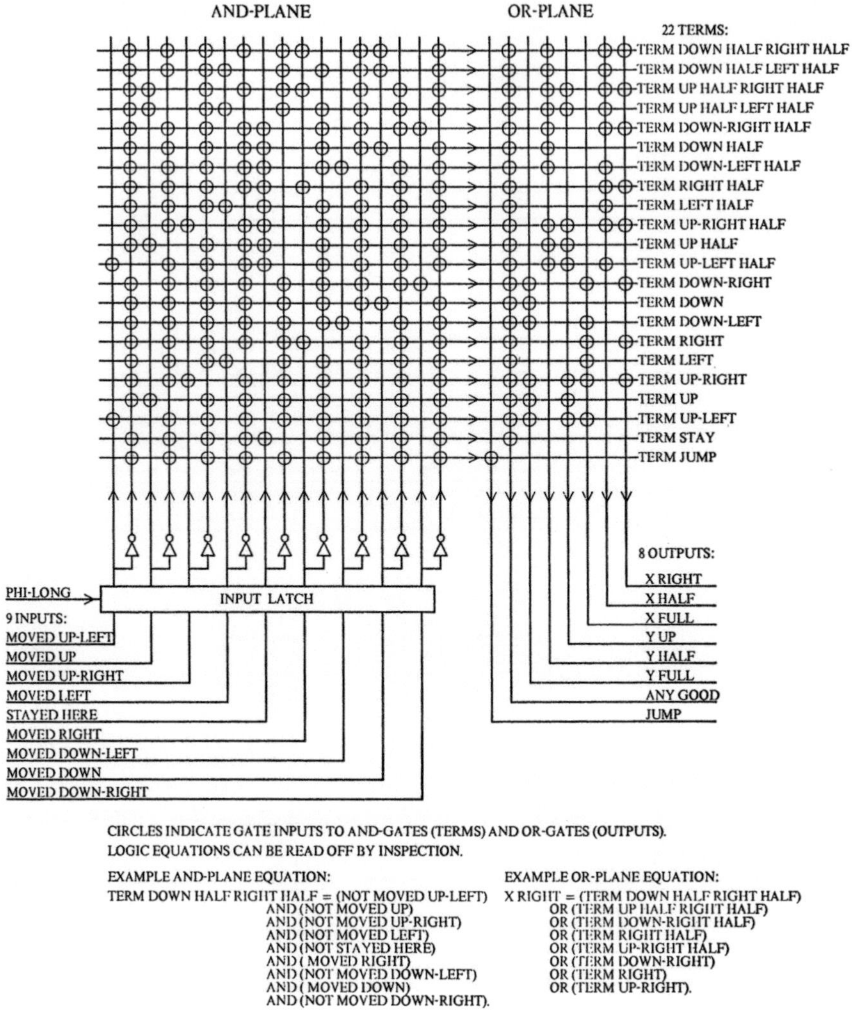

Fig. 1.16 This programmed logic array (PLA) converts the cross-correlation bits to counter-control signals. If an image has no light pixel adjacent to one in the previous frame, the "Jump" output is asserted to signal this exception, and the counters are not moved, by not asserting either "Half" or "Full" as the increment size

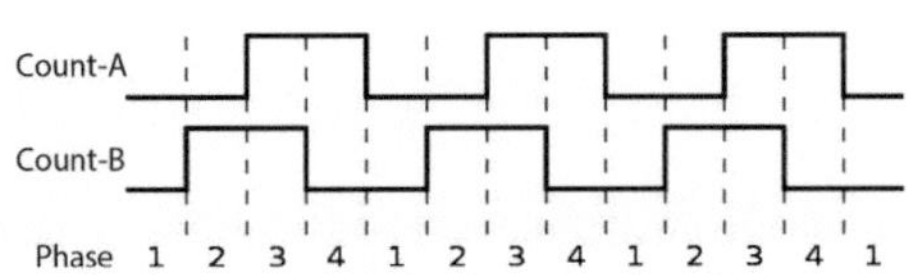

Fig. 1.17 Four-phase quadrature encoding, or 2-bit Gray code, is reported in each dimension. Motion in one direction makes square waves in quadrature (90° out of phase with each other)

put, using a quadrature encoding, also known as a two-bit Gray code. This is the same encoding that ball mice generated by a pair of shaft encoders (optical shaft encoders in some designs). It assures that a device receiving the signals asynchronously will not get an error from two bits switching at not quite the same time.

1.6 Dynamic Logic

The two-phase nonoverlapping-clock pass-transistor-based dynamic logic used in the Mead–Conway nMOS VLSI methodology was almost a good match to the self-timed optical sensor approach. But since the duration of the long phase was not bounded, dynamic nodes set on the short phase could have decayed away, especially due to light falling on the chip, during that time. This potential problem was anticipated and was easily avoided by adding gated positive feedback to those nodes during the long phase, so that all data was held statically during those times. With this simple addition to the usual two-phase latches, and with the short phase being less than a microsecond, the logic was robust enough that no light shielding was needed.

1.7 Testing

I tested the first mouse chip by wiring it into the mouse port of my Xerox Alto computer and projecting patterns onto it. When I got the cursor to move in all directions, I declared success. Unfortunately, more rigorous testing was complicated by the fact that I had forgotten to give the chip any electrical input paths. With my team-mate Martin Haeberli, we soon set about designing the next version, with a more compact pixel array better suited to a short optical path, and with inputs that would allow selectively discharging any set of photodiodes, so that all the logic could be tested on a standard electronic chip tester [26]. The resulting product chip layout is shown in Fig. 1.18, and the cover of the magazine that featured it is shown in Fig. 1.19.

1.8 Going Meta

My manager at the time, Lynn Conway, always had (and ever since has) encouraged me to "go meta" with my ideas, which is why my original optical mouse report included the subtitle "and an Architectural Methodology for Smart Digital Sensors." A condensed version of the report, with the same title, was created to go with my invited opening talk at the 1981 *VLSI Systems and Computation* meeting at CMU [20]. The methodology was basically to combine the Mead–Conway digital design methods, including concepts of self-timed logic, with analog sensors such as

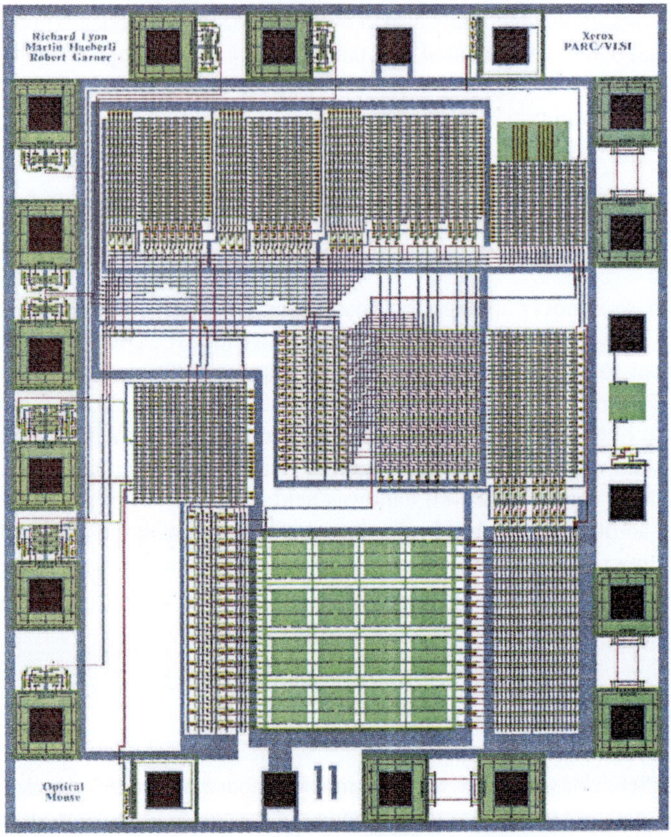

Fig. 1.18 The layout of the second-generation Xerox optical mouse chip, completed by Martin Haeberli and Robert Garner after I left Xerox, incorporated more regular arrays outside the more compact photodiode array, which was a more efficient use of space. This new version also incorporated testability features; a second connection to each photodiode allowed it be discharged electrically, simulating light falling on it

photodiodes, in a way that leads to simple and elegant semi-digital designs that could be prototyped on a by-then-standard MOS fabrication service based on Conway's simplified design rules [25].

The 1981 patent filing (see Fig. 1.20) did not go very meta; it was divided into an imaging array with predetermined stable output states (… each of said cells coupled with several of said neighboring cells in said array to alter the output of said neighboring cells resulting in the recognition of said intermediary pattern as being one of a limited plurality of predetermined such patterns …), and a cursor control device using it.

In 1982, I presented the optical mouse design at the *Physics of Computation* class that Mead, Hopfield, and Feynmann were jointly running at Caltech. This connection led to my joining the Caltech faculty as visiting associate for 13 years, where I helped

Fig. 1.19 The redesigned optical mouse chip with testability features was featured—via Charles Bragg's 1966 painting *Salute*—on the cover of *VLSI Design* magazine in 1982 [26]. The caption reads "There are times when your mouse must be able to see. A single chip may be the solution."

Mead and his students with a wide range of neuromorphic vision and hearing chips. The mouse design influenced the development of some of their silicon retina ideas, such as motion sensing chips [35], and the winner-take-all and the address-event schemes for sparse digitization of analog signals [21, 27], as well as silicon cochlea chips [23, 37]. Researchers elsewhere took the ideas in different directions, such as a 60×60 binary smart imager in CMOS [15].

The small size of the optical, as opposed to mechanical, motion sensor allowed researchers to experiment with other configurations, such as following up the suggestion in my original report that "a pen-like device with a big base that keeps it from falling over might be desirable" [6]; and a 93-pixel analog motion tracker chip developed for the Logitech Marble [2], a trackball version of my suggested "device that watches a golfball-like pattern of dots on a rolling ball."

The optical mouse implements a simple version of what in modern vision systems is called *visual odometry*—essentially, a notion of self tracking by imaging the environment. Gary Bishop credited the inspiration for his 1984 "self-tracker" invention this way [5]: "The inspiration for this research came from Leandra Vicci of the UNC Computer Science Microelectronic Systems Laboratory, who suggested that we could track in three dimensions using something similar to Richard Lyon's

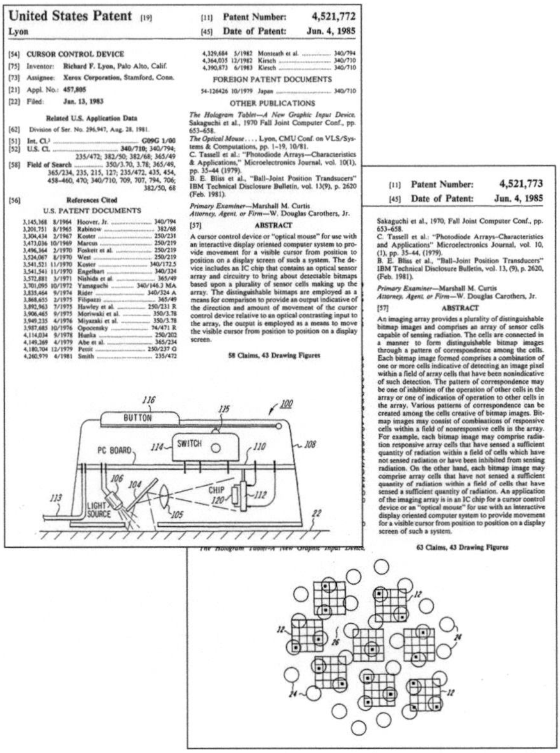

United States Patent [19]
Lyon

[11] Patent Number: 4,521,772
[45] Date of Patent: Jun. 4, 1985

[54] CURSOR CONTROL DEVICE
[75] Inventor: Richard F. Lyon, Palo Alto, Calif.
[73] Assignee: Xerox Corporation, Stamford, Conn.
[21] Appl. No.: 457,805
[22] Filed: Jan. 13, 1983

Related U.S. Application Data
[62] Division of Ser. No. 296,947, Aug. 28, 1981.
[51] Int. Cl.[3] G09G 1/00
[52] U.S. Cl. 340/710; 340/794; 235/472; 382/50; 382/68; 365/49
[58] Field of Search 350/3.70, 3.78; 365/49, 365/234, 235, 215, 127; 235/472, 435, 454, 458–460, 470; 340/710, 709, 707, 794, 706; 382/50, 68

[56] References Cited
U.S. PATENT DOCUMENTS

3,145,368	8/1964	Hoover, Jr.	340/794
3,201,751	8/1965	Rabinow	382/68
3,304,434	2/1967	Koster	250/231
3,473,036	10/1969	Marcus	250/219
3,496,364	2/1970	Foskett et al.	250/219
3,524,067	8/1970	West	250/219
3,541,521	11/1970	Koster	340/172.5
3,541,541	11/1970	Engelbart	340/324
3,572,881	3/1971	Nishida et al.	365/49
3,701,095	10/1972	Yamaguchi	340/146.3 MA
3,835,464	9/1974	Rider	340/324 A
3,868,655	2/1975	Filipazzi	365/49
3,892,963	7/1975	Hawley et al.	250/231 R
3,906,465	9/1975	Moriwaki et al.	350/3.78
3,949,235	4/1976	Miyazaki et al.	350/3.78
3,987,685	10/1976	Opocensky	74/471 R
4,114,034	9/1978	Hunka	250/202
4,149,269	4/1979	Abe et al.	365/234
4,180,704	12/1979	Pettit	250/237 G
4,260,979	4/1981	Smith	235/472
4,329,684	5/1982	Monteath et al.	340/794
4,364,035	12/1982	Kirsch	340/710
4,390,873	6/1983	Kirsch	340/710

FOREIGN PATENT DOCUMENTS
54-126426 10/1979 Japan 340/710

OTHER PUBLICATIONS
The Hologram Tablet—A New Graphic Input Device, Sakaguchi et al., 1970 Fall Joint Computer Conf., pp. 653–658.
The Optical Mouse . . . , Lyon, CMU Conf. on VLS/Systems & Computations, pp. 1–19, 10/81.
C. Tassell et al.: "Photodiode Arrays—Characteristics & Applications," Microelectronics Journal, vol. 10(1), pp. 35–44 (1979).
B. E. Bliss et al., "Ball-Joint Position Trandsucers" IBM Technical Disclosure Bulletin, vol. 13(9), p. 2620 (Feb. 1981).

Primary Examiner—Marshall M. Curtis
Attorney, Agent, or Firm—W. Douglas Carothers, Jr.

[57] ABSTRACT
A cursor control device or "optical mouse" for use with an interactive display oriented computer system to provide movement for a visible cursor from position to position on a display screen of such a system. The device includes an IC chip that contains an optical sensor array and circuitry to bring about detectable bitmaps based upon a plurality of sensor cells making up the array. The distinguishable bitmaps are employed as a means for comparison to provide an output indicative of the direction and amount of movement of the cursor control device relative to an optical contrasting input to the array, the output is employed as a means to move the visible cursor from position to position on a display screen.

58 Claims, 43 Drawing Figures

[11] Patent Number: 4,521,773
[45] Date of Patent: Jun. 4, 1985

Sakaguchi et al., 1970, Fall Joint Computer Conf., pp. 653–658.
C. Tassell et al.: "Photodiode Arrays-Characteristics and Applications" Microelectronics Journal, vol. 10, (1), pp. 35–44, (1979).
B. E. Bliss et al., "Ball-Joint Position Transducers" IBM Technical Disclosure Bulletin, vol. 13, (9), p. 2620, (Feb. 1981).

Primary Examiner—Marshall M. Curtis
Attorney, Agent, or Firm—W. Douglas Carothers, Jr.

[57] ABSTRACT
An imaging array provides a plurality of distinguishable bitmap images and comprises an array of sensor cells capable of sensing radiation. The cells are connected in a manner to form distinguishable bitmap images through a pattern of correspondence among the cells. Each bitmap image formed comprises a combination of one or more cells indicative of detecting an image pixel within a field of array cells that have been nonindicative of such detection. The pattern of correspondence may be one of inhibition of the operation of other cells in the array or one of indication of operation to other cells in the array. Various patterns of correspondence can be created among the cells creative of bitmap images. Bitmap images may consist of combinations of responsive cells within a field of nonresponsive cells in the array. For example, each bitmap image may comprise radiation responsive array cells that have sensed a sufficient quantity of radiation within a field of cells which have not sensed radiation or have been inhibited from sensing radiation. On the other hand, each bitmap image may comprise array cells that have not sensed a sufficient quantity of radiation within a field of cells that have sensed a sufficient quantity of radiation. An application of the imaging array is in an IC chip for a cursor control device or an "optical mouse" for use with an interactive display oriented computer system to provide movement for a visible cursor from position to position on a display screen of such a system.

63 Claims, 43 Drawing Figures

Fig. 1.20 The optical mouse patents—Cursor Control Device and Imaging Array—did not issue until 1985; a lifetime of 17 years after issue means they may have been in force until 2002

Optical Mouse, imaging the room rather than special paper." Modern papers on insect-inspired robot odometry continue to refer to inspiration from my optical mouse [12].

The optical mouse has been described as an inspiration in the books *Vision Chips* [31] and *Smart Cameras* [4] among others. Mostly, though, the Xerox mouse was largely forgotten before the optical mouse was re-invented at Hewlett Packard and released by their spin-out Agilent in 1999 as a high-resolution high-computation imager/correlator for tracking the details of arbitrary surfaces, such as the fibers in paper. They list as one of their 1999 milestones, "Release of Agilent's optical mouse sensor eliminates need for mouse pads, and allows for creation of a more precise and longer lasting computer mouse" [38]. Microsoft used the Agilent chips in their 1999 Intellimouse, and Apple used them in their 2000 Pro Mouse.

1.9 Conclusion

The optical mouse was a successful union of ideas in VLSI design, vision, and neural networks. In hindsight, it was a smart camera and an embedded vision system before those concepts were invented. It was a silicon retina before Carver Mead coined that term, and a Hopfield network before John Hopfield invented that concept, and a self-tracker before Gary Bishop came up with visual odometry. It did this all with only 16 pixels, so it was simple, rather than powerful or general. The chip was at the LSI level of complexity, but was a teaching vehicle and popular example for methods of digital VLSI system design that it embodied.

I enjoyed lecturing on this development at universities all around the world, and I still have my viewgraphs, printed on the world's first color laser printer (Gary Starkweather's "Puffin") in 1981, in case anyone would like to hear a rerun.

Acknowledgments I recall fondly the help of a great many people at PARC during the evolution of the ideas in the optical mouse, but I would like to single out just a few. Carlo Séquin taught me about how silicon detects light, giving me the basis to build on. Dan Ingalls provided ideas about two-dimensional tracking. Chuck Thacker reviewed the first optical mouse chip layout and found two errors that would have killed it. Martin Haeberli volunteered to do the second-generation layout, and took over the effort as I was preparing to leave PARC to lead a speech recognition group at Schlumberger Palo Alto Research. Lynn Conway, Bert Sutherland, and George Pake provided the supportive environment that allowed such ideas to take root.

References

1. Abu-Mostafa YS, St Jacques J (1985) Information capacity of the Hopfield model. IEEE Trans Inf Theory 31(4):461–464
2. Arreguit X, Van Schaik FA, Bauduin FV, Bidiville M, Raeber E (1996) A CMOS motion detector system for pointing devices. IEEE J Solid-State Circuits 31(12):1916–1921
3. Barlow HB (1981) The Ferrier Lecture, 1980: critical limiting factors in the design of the eye and visual cortex. Proc R Soc London Ser B Biol Sci 212(1186):1–34
4. Belbachir AN (2009) Smart cameras. Springer, Berlin
5. Bishop G (1984) Self-Tracker: a smart optical sensor on silicon. PhD thesis, University of North Carolina at Chapel Hill
6. Card SK (1996) The human, the computer, the task, and their interaction: analytic models and use-centered design. In: Steier DM, Mitchell TM (eds) Mind matters: a tribute to Allen Newell. Psychology Press, Hove, pp 259–312
7. Chaney TJ, Molnar CE (1973) Anomalous behavior of synchronizer and arbiter circuits. IEEE Trans Comput 100(4):421–422
8. Chaney TJ, Rosenberger FU (1979) Characterization and scaling of MOS flip flop performance in synchronizer applications. In: Seitz CL (ed) Caltech conference on VLSI. California Institute of Technology, Pasadena, pp 357–374
9. Conway L (1982) The MPC adventures: experiences with the generation of VLSI design and implementation methodologies. Microproc Microprog 10(4):209–228
10. Conway L (2012) Reminiscences of the VLSI revolution: how a series of failures triggered a paradigm shift in digital design. IEEE Solid-State Circuits Mag 4(4):8–31
11. Cook PB, McReynolds JS (1998) Lateral inhibition in the inner retina is important for spatial tuning of ganglion cells. Nat Neurosci 1(8):714–719
12. Dahme H, Millers A, Mallot HA (2010) Insect-inspired odometry by optic flow recorded with optical mouse chips. In: Floreano D, Zufferey J-C, Srinivasan MV, Ellington C (eds) Flying insects and robots. Springer, Berlin, pp 115–126
13. Douglas R, Mahowald M, Carver M (1995) Neuromorphic analogue VLSI. Annu Rev Neurosci 18:255–281
14. Fairbairn DG, Rowson JA (1978) ICARUS: an interactive integrated circuit layout program. In: 15th conference on design automation. IEEE, pp 188–192

15. Garda P, Reichart A, Rodriguez H, Devos F, Zavidovique B (1988) Yet another mesh array smart sensor? In: 9th international conference on pattern recognition. IEEE, pp 863–865
16. Hopfield JJ (1982) Neural networks and physical systems with emergent collective computational abilities. Proc Natl Acad Sci 79(8):2554–2558
17. Hopfield JJ (1984) Neurons with graded response have collective computational properties like those of two-state neurons. Proc Natl Acad Sci 81(10):3088–3092
18. Johnson J, Roberts TL, Verplank W, Smith DC, Irby CH, Beard M, Mackey K (1989) The Xerox Star: a retrospective. Computer 22(9):11–26
19. Knight BW, Toyoda J-I, Dodge FA (1970) A quantitative description of the dynamics of excitation and inhibition in the eye of Limulus. J Gen Physiol 56(4):421–437
20. Kung HT, Sproull B, Steele G (1981) VLSI systems and computations. Springer, Berlin
21. Lazzaro J, Ryckebusch S, Mahowald MA, Mead CA (1989) Winner-take-all networks of O(n) complexity. Neural Inf Process Syst 1:703–711
22. Lyon RF (2010) Machine hearing: an emerging field [exploratory DSP column]. Signal Process Mag IEEE 27(5):131–139
23. Lyon RF, Mead C (1988) An analog electronic cochlea. IEEE Trans Acoust Speech Signal Process 36(7):1119–1134
24. Lyon RF (1981) The optical mouse and an architectural methodology for smart digital sensors. Technical report, Xerox PARC VLSI-81-1
25. Lyon RF (1981) Simplified design rules for VLSI layouts. VLSI Des 2(1):54–59
26. Lyon RF, Haeberli MP (1982) Designing and testing the optical mouse. VLSI Des 3:20–30
27. Mahowald M (1992) VLSI analogs of neuronal visual processing: a synthesis of form and function. PhD thesis, California Institute of Technology
28. Markoff J (1983) In focus: the mouse that rolled. Info World 5(8):26–29
29. Mead C (1989) Analog VLSI and neural systems. Addison-Wesley, Reading
30. Mead C, Conway L (1980) Introduction to VLSI systems. Addison-Wesley, Reading
31. Moini A (2000) Vision chips. Springer, New York
32. Schwartz O, Simoncelli EP (2001) Natural signal statistics and sensory gain control. Nat Neurosci 4(8):819–825
33. Seitz CL (1980) System timing. In: Mead CA, Conway LA (eds) Introduction to VLSI systems., Addison-Wesley, Reading, pp 218–262
34. Shapley RM, Victor JD (1978) The effect of contrast on the transfer properties of cat retinal ganglion cells. J Physiol 285(1):275–298
35. Tanner J, Mead C (1986) An integrated analog optical motion sensor. VLSI Signal Process 2:59
36. von Békésy G (1967) Sensory inhibition. Princeton University Press, Princeton
37. Watts L, Lyon RF, Mead C (1991) A bidirectional analog VLSI cochlear model. In: Sequin C (ed) Advanced research in VLSI. MIT Press, Cambridge, pp 153–163
38. Agilent Technologies web site (2013). Company History Timeline—1999. http://www.agilent.com/about/companyinfo/history/timeline_1999.html

Chapter 2
Consumer Robotics: A Platform for Embedding Computer Vision in Everyday Life

Mario E. Munich, Phil Fong, Jason Meltzer and Ethan Eade

Abstract Consumer robotic devices provide a platform for embedded computer vision algorithms in applications for everyday life. The consumer market is very price-sensitive, so robots must be developed with a single task in mind, aiming to provide the best performance at the lowest cost. Computational resources in consumer robotics are scarce given cost constraints, forcing the design of novel algorithms that elegantly incorporate such constraints. We present a graph-based SLAM approach designed to operate on computationally constrained platforms using monocular vision and odometry. When computation and memory are limited, visual tracking becomes difficult or impossible, and costs for map representation and updating must remain low. Our system constructs a map of structured views using only weak temporal assumptions and performs recognition and relative pose estimation over the set of views. We fuse visual observations and differential measurements in an incrementally optimized graph representation. Using variable elimination and constraint pruning, graph complexity and storage is kept linear in explored space rather than growing over time. We evaluate performance on sequences with ground truth and also compare to a standard graph-SLAM approach.

2.1 Introduction

Over the past decade, computer vision algorithms have transitioned from the lab to the marketplace. Improvements in processors, memory density, and image sensor technology enable the deployment of sophisticated algorithms. The introduction

M.E. Munich (✉) · P. Fong · J. Meltzer
iRobot, Pasadena, CA, USA
e-mail: mmunich@irobot.com

P. Fong
e-mail: pfong@irobot.com

J. Meltzer
e-mail: jmeltzer@irobot.com

E. Eade
Microsoft Research, Redmond, WA, USA
e-mail: ethan@ethaneade.com

B. Kisačanin and M. Gelautz (eds.), *Advances in Embedded Computer Vision*,
Advances in Computer Vision and Pattern Recognition,
DOI 10.1007/978-3-319-09387-1_2

of smartphones and tablets has accelerated the pace of this trend. These mobile devices include powerful processors, ample memory, and high-resolution cameras. Coupled with high-level operating systems such as iOS and Android, these enable the quick development of computer-vision-based applications. One can argue that these devices provide a conduit for the deployment of embedded computer vision in the consumer electronics market. However, these devices are fairly expensive, which allow them to provide the resources computation- and memory-hungry computer vision applications require.

Consumer robotic devices, on the other hand, face severe constraints on the cost of computation. The mass consumer market is very price-sensitive, so the retail cost of the robot is key for the success of the product. The consumer electronics industry standard suggests a retail price for the product that is 3–5 times the cost of parts (bill of materials, or BOM). In other words, for a $300 MSRP robot, the BOM should be between $60 and 100, including all mechanical parts, electrical parts, battery, processor, memory, motors, assembly, packaging, user manuals, and miscellaneous items! These strict cost constraints translate into a reduced availability of computational resources, requiring the development of particularly lean algorithms. Consumer robotics thus serves as an important platform for deploying embedded computer vision applications.

Another interesting factor that distinguishes the smartphone from the robotic use case is autonomy. Unlike in a smartphone app, the vision system in a robot must work reliably with no user assistance, continuously and for long periods of time. There is no opportunity for a user to correct an error or ignore a defect; if the vision system fails, the effectiveness of the overall system is reduced.

Visual localization and mapping is attractive for low-cost robotics applications since cameras are data rich, low power, and inexpensive. The challenge lies in designing an algorithm that can efficiently extract relevant information from this high-rate visual data stream. Despite Moore's Law, low-cost embedded platforms are still constrained by limited processing power, memory, and storage. Many state-of-the-art approaches to visual SLAM rely on interframe tracking, which requires high frame rate processing. Additionally, common constraint graph SLAM methods for agglomerating sensor information often incur computation and storage costs that grow with time rather than with space explored. For a robot operating for extended periods within a limited spatial area—typical of practical applications—this is an undesirable trade-off.

This chapter describes the development of a localization system that can enable systematic navigation of domestic robots in a household environment. The target application is a mobile domestic robot with a price lower than $1000, and ideally below $500. We present an approach to visual localization and mapping designed for a low-cost robotic platform equipped with simple odometry and a single camera. Operating primarily as a recognition engine, the visual measurement subsystem requires only occasional, weak assumptions on processing rate, and intrinsically provides robust loop closing when previously-mapped areas are revisited. Visual measurements and odometry are fused in a graph representation and optimized incrementally. Important novel features of this system include techniques for bounding the

SLAM graph complexity during operation, using variable elimination and constraint pruning with heuristic schedules. These methods keep optimization and storage costs commensurate with explored area rather than with time of exploration while causing minimal loss in mapping and localization accuracy.

An instantiation of the approach is demonstrated on real datasets with planar ground-truth reference. The system operates successfully even at frame rates below 2 Hz. Comparing the results with and without complexity reduction demonstrates that the reduced graph yields similar localization accuracy at a small fraction of the computational cost.

2.2 Related Work

2.2.1 View Recognition for SLAM

View recognition engines have proven attractive components for SLAM systems because they permit robust and flexible loop closing. Instead of making correspondences between individual features or measurements, visual or otherwise, view recognition engines typically match constellations of features or entire images without requiring feature tracking.

Williams et al. [20] rely on tracking for normal EKF SLAM operation, but use view recognition to recover from failure. Several features are matched to the existing map using appearance and structure constraints in order to reinitialize tracking.

The Parallel Tracking and Mapping(PTAM) [10] system also employs view recognition for recovery from tracking failure. Instead of using feature-based methods for identifying candidate views, the system performs image to image correlation using heavily blurred, low-resolution versions of the reference and query images. A crude pose estimate is deduced from the result of the inverse-compositional matching, following which tracking resumes.

Eade and Drummond [4] group subsets of features into local maps during tracking-based SLAM. Correspondences are made between local maps to connect them or to recover from tracking failures. The image-to-map matching first selects a subset of local maps to consider using a bag-of-words ranking, and then performs local matching to determine feature-to-feature correspondences. This two-step process is common to many view recognition systems, often instantiated as a bag-of-words prefilter followed by re-ranking using geometric constraints [17].

The above approaches rely on tracking and use view recognition as an out-of-band method for failure recovery. Our approach instead performs recognition at every time step as the primary source of observations. The system of Karlsson et al. [9] is similar, constructing *landmarks* out of constellations of SIFT [14] features and employing nearest neighbors and a simple Hough transform as the recognition algorithm. The system is further refined by Eade et al. [5] by replacing the particle-filter back end with a graph SLAM back end that is described in further detail in the following sections. The work of Cummins et al. [2] takes a more sophisticated approach to recognition, building a visual vocabulary offline, and approximating the joint probability distribution of visual words with a Chow-Liu tree. Each view's appearance model is updated upon recognition.

Our view recognition front end bears many similarities to the view-based maps of Konolige et al. [12]. That system constructs views from stereo images and performs two-step recognition using first a vocabulary tree and then a geometric matching stage. Views (called *skeleton frames*) are constructed from the output of visual odometry, which requires a frame rate sufficient for tracking. We require only monocular imagery, constructing structured appearance models from two matched views of the same scene. While Konolige et al. use randomized tree signatures for feature matching, we use a simple variant on SIFT features and local and global feature databases.

2.2.2 Graph-Based SLAM

Storing observations and poses in a constraint graph is now a well-explored technique for localization and mapping. The graph formulation provides a straightforward and flexible representation of the underlying Gaussian Markov random field (GMRF) problem that SLAM attempts to solve. The general framework is described in [18], including a description of a graph relaxation procedure identical to batch bundle adjustment in photogrammetry [19]. Relaxation algorithms for SLAM graphs have received much attention, especially with online operation in mind. Olson et al. [16] suggest a stochastic gradient descent method, and Grisetti et al. [7] review that and related methods for incremental graph optimization.

The system of Eade and Drummond [3] forms a graph where each node is a joint distribution over a local map, and the relative nonlinear constraints between nodes are derived from shared features. The graph is relaxed by imposing cycle constraints using preconditioned gradient descent. The network constructed by PTAM is effectively a graph of relative constraints between keyframes, though the optimization, performed asynchronously to the primary tracking task, acts on individual structure elements.

The view-based mapping of Konolige et al. [12] constructs a reduced graph of poses by consolidating consecutive frames tracked by visual odometry into skeleton frames. Then the constraint graph over skeleton frames is incrementally relaxed using the Toro method [8].

While existing graph-based SLAM methods employ incremental graph optimizers to allow online operation, the number of poses in the graph continues to grow with time. One technique suggested for bounding this growth is that the robot be occasionally virtually "kidnapped," disconnecting its current pose in the graph from previous poses and re-inserting it in using only recent observations [8]. This assumes both that the recent observations are sufficiently accurate to allow relocalization, and that the effective uncertainty of these observations is zero. These assumptions are routinely violated in practice, especially in visual systems, where the accuracy and uncertainty of relative pose estimates depends heavily on viewpoint and scene structure.

We instead apply probabilistically sound graph reduction methods that limit the complexity of the graph to a linear factor of the complexity of the explored space. Past poses of the robot that are not used for view recognition can be marginalized out of the estimation, and their incident constraints are collapsed back into the graph. The marginalization procedure, equivalent to the update step of the Kalman filter or the variable elimination step of the GraphSLAM algorithm, is described by Konolige in [11].

Marginalization is used to systematically limit graph complexity in Kretzschmar et al. [13], which employs an approximation rather than exact marginalization. The approximate form is used to bound edge connectivity in the graph. Carlevaris–Bianco and Eustice [1] propose an alternative via generic linear constraint node removal. In contrast, we selectively prune edges incident to nodes of high degree, removing their constraints from the GMRF in a conservative manner. The adaptive application of marginalization and edge removal, discussed in Sect. 2.8, is a significant feature of this system.

2.3 System Overview

The input to the system is a sequence of images from the camera and a sequence of differential motion estimates, derived from wheel odometry measurements or other differential sensors. We refer to these differential measurements collectively as odometry. The system outputs an incrementally updated estimate of the device's current pose (localization) and estimates of a subset of its previous poses during operation (mapping).

Two high-level components constitute the system: the visual recognition front end and the constraint graph SLAM back end (Fig. 2.1). The front-end processes the video stream, yielding a global appearance database, a set of structured local appearance

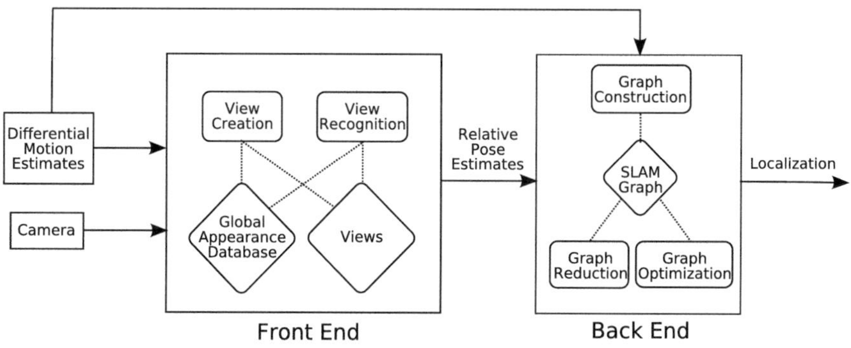

Fig. 2.1 System structure overview

models called *views*, and a sequence of pose estimates relative to these models. The back end fuses the relative pose and differential motion estimates together in a graph representation, incrementally optimizing and distilling it synchronously with updates. The graph nodes include estimates of current and selected previous poses of the robot.

The front end inherently yields 6DoF relative pose estimates and 3D structured views; the back end can be instantiated in 3DoF for planar robot motion or 6DoF in the general case. This chapter shows results for the 3DoF case (Sect. 2.9).

2.4 Viewpoint Invariant Features

The view recognition engine identifies previously constructed appearance models from novel viewpoints based on correspondences between image features. Thus, the image features themselves must have a representation robust to viewpoint and lighting changes. Any efficient feature detector/descriptor combination providing these properties is suitable for this purpose.

We employ Difference-of-Gaussian (DoG) interest points and reduced-dimensionality SIFT [14] descriptors. Our descriptors are computed in a manner similar to 128D SIFT descriptors, but using a 3×3 spatial grid and four angular histogram bins per cell, instead of the 4×4 grid and eight angular bins of the standard configuration. We have determined empirically through recognition tasks that these 36D descriptors perform nearly as well as the higher-dimensional variants, but with reduced memory and computational costs.

The detection and description algorithms can be implemented efficiently. Table 2.1 shows the computational viability of our implementation on different platforms.

2.5 View Creation

The view creation process extracts from the image sequence a set of structured appearance models. These consist of estimated 3D feature locations and associated appearance descriptors. These sets of features are accessible through a database for use by the view recognition process.

Table 2.1 Timings for SIFT feature computation

Task	Core2 (2.4 GHz)	Atom (1.6 GHz)	ARM9 (266 MHz)
Pyramid (ms)	2.0	9.1	42
Detector (ms)	0.6	2.0	8.9
Descriptors (μs/desc)	14	81	219

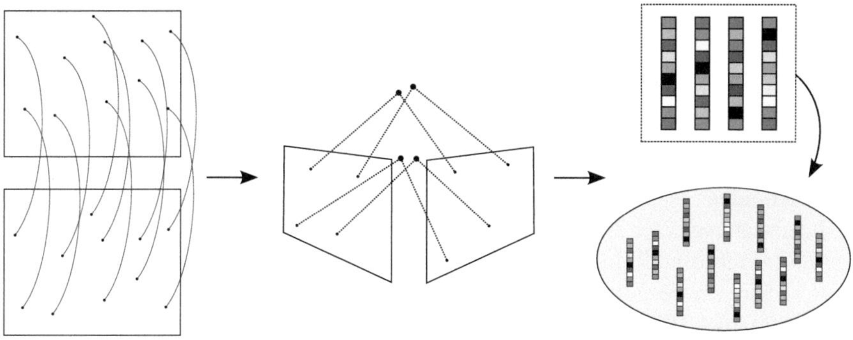

Fig. 2.2 View creation process

View creation proceeds in three steps (see Fig. 2.2):

1. Robust matching: Correspondences are established between features in two or more temporally local images, while enforcing geometric constraints.
2. Structure estimation: From the feature correspondences, three-dimensional point structure is estimated and stored. The (optional) differential motion estimate is used to determine the common scale of the structure.
3. Database management: The appearance model of the view (comprising a set of feature descriptors) is added to a global database for later recognition.

2.5.1 Robust Matching

The interframe matching procedure for view creation first establishes putative correspondences then partitions these correspondences into inliers (correct matches) and outliers (incorrect matches) using geometric constraints.

Putative correspondences can be generated using only the feature descriptors, or by taking advantage of any differential motion estimates supplied by other sensors, such as wheel odometry. In the first case, each feature in the current image is paired with the feature in a recent older image according to distance in the feature descriptor space using a brute-force or approximate nearest neighbors (ANN) method. In the second case, a motion estimate constrains the search for putative correspondences. The nearest feature in descriptor space that also satisfies the corresponding epipolar constraint is taken as a putative correspondence to the older feature.

Given a set of putative correspondences, geometric constraints are applied iteratively to eliminate outliers. If no prior on camera motion is provided, a starting point for the procedure can be computed using RANSAC [6] and the five-point algorithm [15]. This yields an estimate of camera motion (up to scale) and a set of inlier correspondences. When a prior differential motion estimate is available, it is a sufficient starting point for iteration.

The iteration proceeds as follows:

1. An error threshold factor $\tilde{r}$ is chosen as a multiple of the desired final acceptance threshold r.
2. Inliers are selected by finding all putative correspondences whose matches fall within a threshold distance of the epipolar line, whose descriptor distances are low, and whose depth estimates are positive. The epipolar threshold distance for a feature with scale s is given by $\tilde{r} \cdot s$, modeling larger location uncertainty associated with larger-scale features.
3. The motion estimate is refined by nonlinear maximum-likelihood estimation over the current set of inlier correspondences.
4. The threshold factor $\tilde{r}$ is decreased multiplicatively, and the process is repeated from step 2 until $\tilde{r} \approx r$.

We use this approximation to a standard M-estimator scheme (e.g., iterated reweighted least squares with Tukey weighting) in order to reduce the computational cost on embedded platforms.

2.5.2 Structure Estimation

Given feature correspondences between two views, bundle adjustment [19] is performed over the reprojection objective function to yield joint estimates on structure and camera motion. The scale is left unconstrained by the feature correspondences, so the gauge freedom is eliminated by fixing the camera translation to unit magnitude while performing the optimization. The scale is assigned to the view using the differential odometry between the two views used for estimation. Further views can be added to the optimization either at the point of view creation or upon later observation. In this case of upgrading the structure, the camera translation magnitude is constrained only between the first two views, and all six degrees of freedom vary among the others. The previously computed parameter values are used as a starting point in the new, larger optimization.

2.5.3 Database Management

A global appearance database is maintained to aid view recognition. When a new view is created, its appearance model is added to this database.

The global database could take one of many forms, depending on the desired appearance model representation. We describe a simple but effective approach here.

The database contains descriptors for features in all views in a collection of kd-trees for efficient ANN searches. The time required to add new views to the global database is bounded: upon view creation, all descriptors in the view are added to the current kd-tree, which is then rebalanced. If the number of descriptors in the tree exceeds a predetermined constant bound, a new tree is added to the collection and becomes the current tree. ANN searches of the forest are described below in Sect. 2.6.

In addition to the global database update, a local appearance model is also constructed for each view. The local model supports ANN searches over only the descriptors present in the view, and is queried for the second stage of view recognition.

2.6 View Recognition

The view recognition process yields relative pose estimates between single images and existing views. The recognition approach is hierarchical, first performing appearance matching in a global database, and then applying structure constraints at the view-local level.

The input to the view recognition algorithm is a set of viewpoint invariant features extracted from an image, and a global appearance model as described in Sect. 2.5.3. The output is zero, one, or multiple relative pose estimates to existing views.

The recognition method proceeds as follows (see Fig. 2.3)

1. Features in the query image are looked up in the global appearance model database.
2. The results of the database lookup are used to rank potential views by visual similarity, and the m top-ranked views are chosen as candidates (we use $m = 3$ throughout).
3. For each candidate view, correspondences are established between query features and the features in the view.
4. Geometric constraints are applied to these correspondences, using reprojection constraints and the estimated view structure to reject outliers. This yields a rough relative pose estimate.
5. The relative pose and structure estimates are refined using by optimizing over the inlier correspondences and internal correspondences of the view, yielding maximum-likelihood relative pose with covariance.
6. The view's stored structure estimate is optionally updated using the optimization results.

2.6.1 Recognition Candidate Selection

The top k nearest neighbors in the global database for each query feature are determined using ANN search (typically $k = 2$). Then, the putative matches are grouped

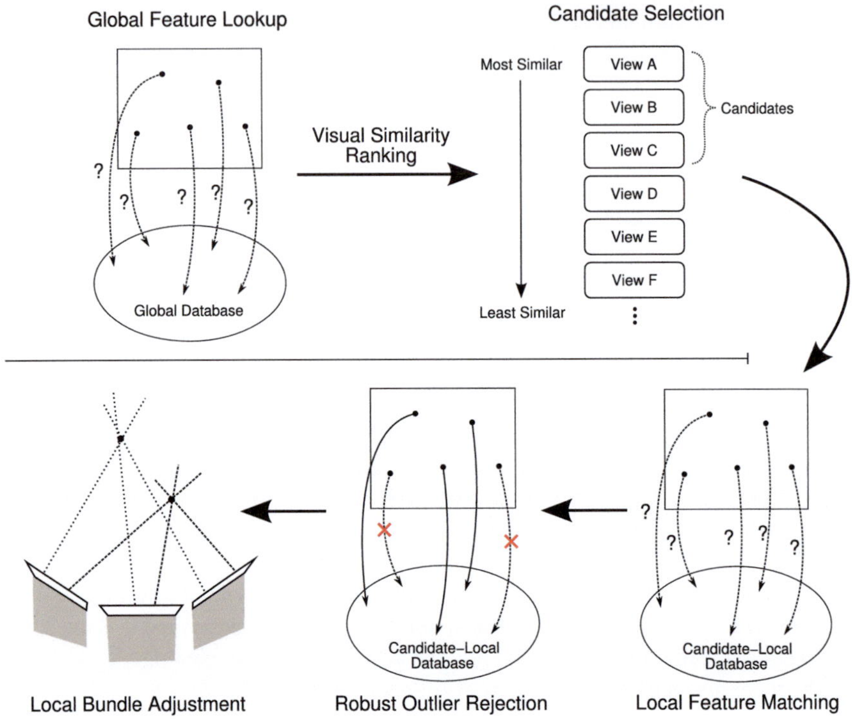

Fig. 2.3 View recognition process

by view. At this point, crude structure constraints can be applied, using a Hough transform or RANSAC to enforce a loose similarity, affine, homography, or reprojection transformation. The views are then ranked by the number of matches satisfying the constraints. The m highest ranked views are kept as candidates.

2.6.2 Robust Matching and Pose Estimation

For each of the m candidate views chosen by the appearance matching stage, the query features are matched to the view's features using the local view appearance model. Each view feature has an associated three-dimensional structure estimate, allowing the three-point pose algorithm [6] to be applied within a standard RANSAC hypothesize-and-test framework. If enough inliers result from this process, they are passed to the pose estimation stage, along with the relative pose estimate given by the three-point algorithm.

The pose estimation stage takes correspondences between query features and view features, and computes the relative camera pose between the query image and the view's base coordinate frame (the first image of the view pair). The relative pose estimate is represented by mean and covariance in the Lie group SE(3) of rigid 6DoF transformations. The covariance is represented by a quadratic form in the tangent space se(3).

The maximum-likelihood estimation is performed using Levenberg–Marquardt iteration. The camera motion between the existing view frames is assumed fixed and known, and the feature structure estimates and relative pose to the novel viewpoint are permitted to vary. The data matrix at the point of convergence is taken as the information matrix (inverse covariance) of the optimum, as per the Cramer–Rao lower bound. The structure parameters are marginalized out of this representation, and the resulting 6×6 matrix is inverted to yield an estimate of the covariance on the relative pose parameters. If the information matrix is singular or poorly conditioned, the pose estimate is under-constrained, and the view recognition is discarded.

2.7 Graph Construction and Optimization

The SLAM back end encodes view observations and robot motion in a graph representation of a Gaussian Markov random field (GMRF). The graph is constructed as the robot moves and processes video frames. The graph is continuously and incrementally optimized to improve the state estimate of view and robot poses.

2.7.1 Graph Representation

The SLAM graph [18] consists of nodes and directed edges between pairs of nodes. Each node represents the pose of the robot at a certain time. Edges encode constraints between nodes, arising from differential motion estimates (odometry), view observations, and combinations thereof. All poses and transformations are parametrized in the Lie group SE(2) (for robot pose in 2D space) or SE(3) (for robot pose in 3D space), and any covariances or information matrices are expressed in the respective tangent spaces.

Each node stores the estimated pose of the robot at a certain time. The pose describes the coordinate transformation from the common global frame to the frame of the robot at the specified time. Nodes are created for every timestep when a view is recognized or created. Nodes corresponding to the robot pose at view coordinate frames are called view nodes and nodes corresponding to the robot pose at any other times are called pose nodes.

Each edge stores a rigid transformation estimate, with covariance, describing a constraint between its source and destination endpoint. The constraint means and covariances are represented in the Lie group and algebra, respectively. Edges that encode only differential motion constraints (from odometry) are called motion edges, and connect temporally consecutive nodes. Edges that encode relative pose estimates from view recognitions are called observation edges. Edges that are formed by combining other edges (described below in Sect. 2.8.2) are called hybrid edges.

2.7.2 Graph Construction

After each image is processed by the front end, the graph representation is updated:

- A new pose node is added for the current pose, and the new node is connected to the preceding pose node by a motion edge, encoding the accumulated differential motion estimate between the two poses.
- If an existing view has been observed, an observation edge is created from the observed view node to the pose node, encoding the observation constraint. When the back end is operating in SE(2), the relative pose estimate (in SE(3)) is first projected into SE(2) before creating the observation edge.
- If a new view has been created, one of the recent pose nodes corresponding to the view is promoted to a view node.

2.7.3 Incremental Optimization

The graph flexibly represents the GMRF corresponding to the SLAM estimation problem. The negative log-likelihood of the parameter estimates (encoded by the nodes) is the sum residuals of the edges. Denote the edge set by $E = \{e_i\}$. For an edge $e \in E$, the source and destination are given by $s(e)$ and $d(e)$ respectively. The edge's constraint mean is denoted by $\mu(e)$ and the covariance by $\Sigma(e)$. Then the negative log-likelihood $-L$ of the graph (up to a constant offset) is given in terms of the residuals v_i by

$$v_i \equiv \mu(e_i) \cdot s(e_i) \cdot d(e_i)^{-1} \tag{2.1}$$

$$-L = \sum_i v_i^T \left(\Sigma(e_i)^{-1} \right) v_i \tag{2.2}$$

When the node pose estimates better satisfy the constraints encoded in the edges, the negative log-likelihood $-L$ is lower. Graph optimization increases the likelihood of the GMRF parameters by minimizing the negative log-likelihood as function of the node parameters.

Because computation time must be bounded and the graph is continually growing and changing, any feasible graph optimization technique must be incremental. Several methods are described in, e.g., [7]. Any general method for incremental nonlinear optimization can be applied successfully to the graph.

We employ spanning tree and blob-based optimizations, which are run for a fixed number of iterations at each time step following the graph update.

2.8 Graph Complexity Reduction

2.8.1 Complexity Growth

The SLAM graph grows every time a view is created or observed. Even when the robot stays within a bounded space, the views there are observed repeatedly, adding pose nodes and edges to the graph and thus increasing the complexity with time. The storage requirements and graph optimization costs grow with the graph complexity, so in order to control these costs, the graph complexity must be bounded.

The view nodes correspond to elements of the front end relative to which pose estimates can be computed. Further, the spatial density of view nodes is bounded by the front end (as existing views will be recognized from nearby viewpoints), so operation within a fixed spatial region implies a bounded number of view nodes. The pose nodes, on the other hand, represent past robot poses that are not directly useful in subsequent operation, except as a data structure for encoding constraints on other nodes. The number of pose nodes grows with the number of observations, instead of with the number of views. The graph complexity can be bounded by removing pose nodes and limiting node connectivity to keep the complexity of the graph linear in the number of views and thus linear in the amount of space explored.

2.8.2 Pose Node Marginalization

The graph represents a GMRF over past poses of the robot, so nodes can be removed in statistically consistent manner by marginalizing out the corresponding pose variables from the GMRF state. The graph directly encodes the Markov property of the system: a node is conditionally independent of all nodes to which it is not directly connected. Thus marginalizing out a node's state involves only the Markov blanket of the node (all of the nodes within one hop in the graph). Further, because the marginal distributions of a Gaussian are also Gaussians, the graph resulting from the removal exactly encodes the appropriate Gaussian distribution over the remaining variables [11].

Removing a node by marginalization induces pairwise constraints between all pairs of nodes connected to the removed node. If a constraint (edge) already exists between such a pair, the new constraint is combined with the existing constraint by multiplication of their Gaussians. A few operations on edges are needed to define the node marginalization procedure:

2.8.2.1 Edge Reversal

An edge e represents an uncertain rigid transformation between its two endpoint nodes, given by a mean and covariance (μ, Σ) in the appropriate Lie group and Lie algebra respectively. The adjoint operator in a Lie group allows elements of the Lie algebra to be moved from the right tangent space of a transformation to the left. Thus, the reversed edge e^{-1}, pointing in the opposite direction in the graph but encoding the same transformation constraint, is given by

$$e^{-1} = \left(\mu^{-1}, \mathrm{Adj}\left[\mu^{-1}\right] \cdot \Sigma \cdot \mathrm{Adj}\left[\mu^{-1}\right]^{T}\right) \tag{2.3}$$

2.8.2.2 Edge Composition

Given an edge $e_0 = (\mu_0, \Sigma_0)$ from node a to node b and an edge $e_1 = (\mu_1, \Sigma_1)$ from node b to node c, the two edges may be composed into one edge from a to c by composing the uncertain transformations, as in a Kalman filter motion update:

$$e_1 \cdot e_0 = \left(\mu_1 \cdot \mu_0, \Sigma_1 + \mathrm{Adj}\left[\mu_1\right] \cdot \Sigma_0 \cdot \mathrm{Adj}\left[\mu_1\right]^{T}\right) \tag{2.4}$$

2.8.2.3 Edge Combination

Given two edges $e_0 = (\mu_0, \Sigma_0)$ and $e_1 = (\mu_1, \Sigma_1)$ connecting the same two nodes in the same direction, their constraints may be combined by multiplying the associated Gaussian distributions together to yield the resulting Gaussian. Because the exponential map from the tangent space to the transformation manifold is nonlinear, the combination procedure for the mean is iterative. The combined covariance Σ_C is computed by summing the information of the two edges:

$$\Sigma_C = \left(\Sigma_0^{-1} + \Sigma_1^{-1}\right)^{-1} \tag{2.5}$$

Let the initial estimate of the combined mean be the first edge's mean:

$$\mu_C^0 = \mu_0 \tag{2.6}$$

Then the combined transformation is updated by taking the information-weighted average between the two transformations and exponentiating the correction into the Lie group:

$$v_j^i = \ln\left(\mu_C^i \cdot \mu_j^{-1}\right), \; j \in \{0, 1\} \tag{2.7}$$

$$\delta_i = \Sigma_C \cdot \left(\Sigma_0^{-1} \cdot v_0^i + \Sigma_1^{-1} \cdot v_1^i\right) \tag{2.8}$$

$$\mu_C^{i+1} = \exp\left(\delta_i\right) \cdot \mu_C^i \tag{2.9}$$

This update is iterated until convergence (usually three or four iterations), yielding the combined edge:

$$e_C = \left(\mu_C^k, \Sigma_C\right) \tag{2.10}$$

Node Removal

Consider a node n_r to be removed by marginalization, with incident edges $E_r = \{e_0, \ldots, e_m\}$. Each pair of such edges (e_i, e_j) is composed into $e_{(i,j)}$ according to the following cases:

$$e_{(i,j)} = \begin{cases} e_i \cdot e_j & s(e_i) = d(e_j) = n_r \\ e_i \cdot e_j^{-1} & s(e_i) = s(e_j) = n_r \\ e_i^{-1} \cdot e_j & d(e_i) = d(e_j) = n_r \\ e_j \cdot e_i & d(e_i) = s(e_j) = n_r \end{cases} \tag{2.11}$$

The resulting composed edge is added to the graph between the two incident nodes that are not n_r. If such an edge already exists, the edges are combined, reversing the composed edge if necessary. Finally, all incident edges E_r are deleted from the graph along with the node n_r. An example is shown in Fig. 2.4.

2.8.3 Edge Pruning

While the node marginalization procedure always decreases the number of graph nodes and attempts to decrease the number of edges, it might fail to bound the degrees of nodes and thus the complexity of the graph. Indeed, marginalizing out all pose nodes results in a completely connected graph over view nodes, with edge cardinality quadratic in the number of views.

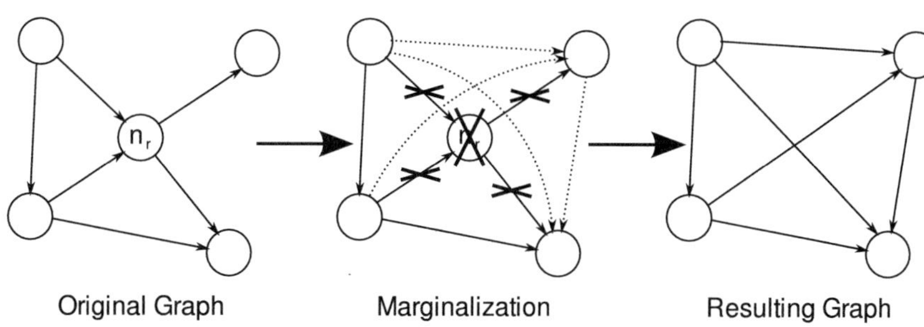

Fig. 2.4 Graph reduction by marginalizing out a node. In this example, the number of edges in the graph is unchanged

To limit the edge complexity of the graph, edges need to be heuristically pruned during operation. Removing an edge from the graph is equivalent to discarding the information represented by the edge, as though the observation or measurement had never been made.

One simple approach to limiting the number of edges is to maintain a priority queue of nodes with degrees exceeding a fixed, predetermined bound. This queue needs to be updated only when edges are added to the graph (measurements or node removals). Edges are removed from each node in the queue until no node degrees exceed the bound.

The heuristic operates as follows: the edges of a high-degree node n are examined one at a time. If the opposite endpoint through edge e is not connected to n through a path that excludes e, with length under a predetermined bound, then e is not eligible for removal, as the graph would be potentially disconnected. The eligible edge with the least residual is deleted. Of the edges incident to n, such an edge is in least disagreement with the current state of the graph, and thus its removal should least affect the graph optimum.

This simple, greedy heuristic does not consider the collective effect of removing multiple edges in series. Nonetheless, our evaluation shows that it performs adequately.

2.9 Evaluation

We use three indoor sequences (SEQ1, SEQ2, SEQ3) to evaluate the performance of the system and the effects of graph complexity reduction. SEQ1 and SEQ2 were collected using an Evolution Robotics Scorpion, and SEQ3 with an iRobot Roomba. In each instance, the robot was equipped with a web camera and wheel odometry. Fiducials placed in the environment were observed by a SICK NAV200 laser range finder mounted on the robot to provide ground truth.

The sequence parameters are described in Table 2.2, and example images are shown in Fig. 2.5. The ground truth trajectories are shown in Fig. 2.6.

Table 2.2 Test sequences

	SEQ1	SEQ2	SEQ3
Environment	Warehouse	Home	Office
Frame rate (Hz)	1.5	1.5	3.0
Timesteps	1,035	1,822	3,896
Extent (m)	24 × 12	20 × 9	19 × 10
Views created	41	103	140

Fig. 2.5 Example images from the SEQ2 (*left*) and SEQ3 (*right*). The reflector beacons are NAV200 fiducials used for ground truth estimation

2.9.1 Metrics

We measure both the accuracy of the incrementally estimated trajectory and of the final view map. The view map is the set of poses of view nodes in the graph at the end of the run, including incremental optimization but without any post-processing.

Comparing the trajectory to the reference reflects localization accuracy during the run. Comparing the map to the appropriate subset of the reference indicates how well the system can be expected to localize in the same environment given subsequent operation. Though the latter metric is more common, and generally shows smaller errors compared to the reference, it does not necessarily reflect how useful the localization is during online operation.

The estimated and ground truth trajectories are compared by first finding the rigid transformation between them that minimizes sum-squared position error, using RANSAC and least squares. The view map corresponds to a subset of the total robot trajectory, so the same method is used to compute the view map error over that subset.

2.9.2 Results

Figure 2.7 shows a portion of the graph computed for SEQ2 with and without reduction. The node and edge density is significantly lower in the latter.

Table 2.3 shows error metrics and graph complexity for full and reduced graphs. In the "Full" columns, the graph is heavily optimized and no nodes or edges are removed. The "Reduced" columns show the same metrics when the number of pose nodes is bounded by the number of views plus ten, and the maximum permitted node degree is eight. The graph complexity is greatly reduced with little or no loss of localization accuracy. As expected, the error of the view map is smaller than that of the causally estimated trajectory consisting of the best estimate at each timestep, as the map has incorporated all the information up to the end of the run.

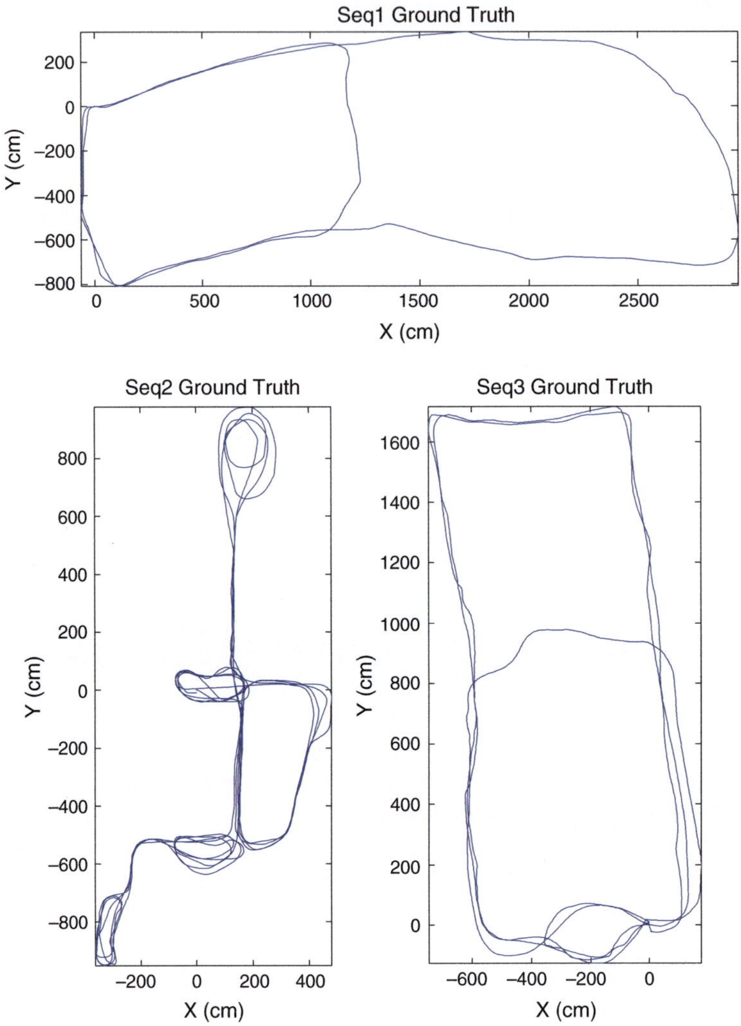

Fig. 2.6 Ground truth trajectories for the test sequences

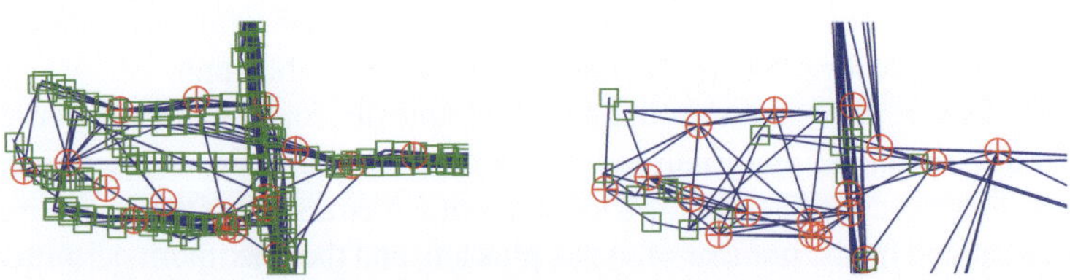

Fig. 2.7 Detail from middle of full and reduced graphs for SEQ2. View nodes are (*red*) *circles*, pose nodes are (*green*) *squares*, and edges are (*blue*) *lines*. Note the reduced density on the *right*

Table 2.3 Metrics for full and reduced complexity graphs

Error (cm)	SEQ1		SEQ2		SEQ3	
Odom. RMS	281		331		469	
Odom. max	773		667		852	
Error (cm)	Full	Reduced	Full	Reduced	Full	Reduced
Traj. RMS	45	44	23	28	59	59
Traj. max	109	105	81	74	138	149
Map RMS	24	18	21	20	43	47
Map max	41	32	47	46	98	103
Number of nodes	709	92	897	216	2,491	290
Number of edges	1,471	155	1,810	414	5,154	501

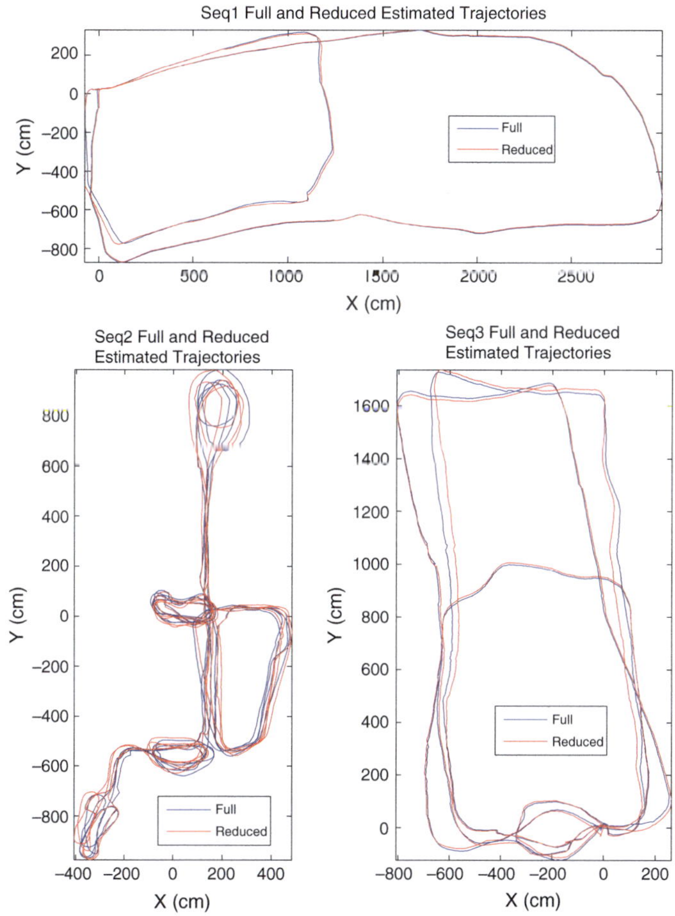

Fig. 2.8 Causally estimated trajectories: graph reduction yields results similar to those computed with full-complexity graphs

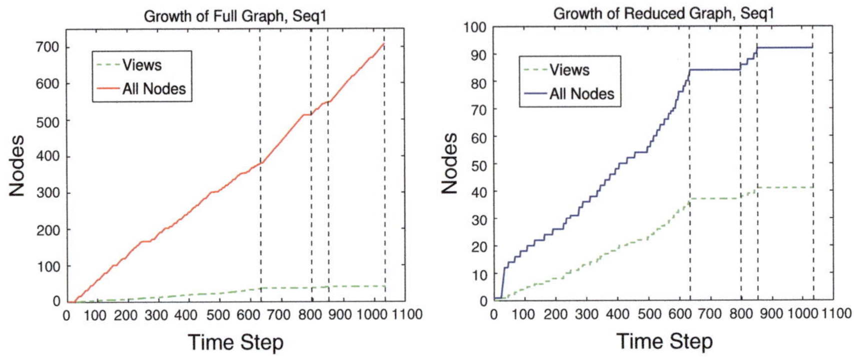

Fig. 2.9 Graph complexity over time for SEQ1, with and without reduction. The two regions bounded by *vertical dotted lines* are periods of revisitation, during which views are reobserved rather than created. The reduced graph complexity remains constant unless new views are created. Note the difference in vertical scale

Figure 2.8 overlays the trajectories computed using the heavily optimized, fully complex graphs with those computed using reduced graphs. The qualitative similarity of the results reflects the quantitative similarity of the errors to ground truth. The deviation between the two traversals of the large loop in SEQ3 occurs because the robot traverses in opposite directions, so views are not reobserved.

Figure 2.9 shows the growth in number of graph nodes over time for SEQ1, with and without reduction. Reduction keeps the complexity linear with number of views rather than time.

2.10 Conclusion

This view-based monocular SLAM system minimizes the computation required for vision-based processing and actively manages the complexity of the SLAM graph to permit operation on constrained computational platforms. Our results show that the complexity reduction methods significantly limit graph node and edge cardinality, while only negligibly affecting localization accuracy. The system uses inexpensive sensors, has low computational requirements, and high reliability, all of which are ideal for low-cost robotic applications.

References

1. Carlevaris-Bianco N, Eustice RM (2013) Long-term simultaneous localization and mapping with generic linear constraint node removal. In: 2013 IEEE/RSJ international conference on intelligent robots and systems (IROS), IEEE, pp 1034–1041

2. Cummins M, Newman P (2008) Accelerated appearance-only SLAM. In: Proceedings of the IEEE international conference on robotics and automation (ICRA'08), Pasadena
3. Eade E, Drummond T (2007) Monocular slam as a graph of coalesced observations. In: Proceedings of the 11th IEEE international conference on computer vision (ICCV'07), Rio de Janeiro, Brazil
4. Eade E, Drummond T (2008) Unified loop closing and recovery for real time monocular slam. In: Proceedings of the British machine vision conference (BMVC'08), Leeds, BMVA, pp 53–62
5. Eade E, Fong P, Munich ME (2010) Monocular graph slam with complexity reduction. In: IEEE/RSJ international conference on intelligent robots and systems (IROS), pp 3017–3024
6. Fischler MA, Bolles RC (1981) Random sample consensus: a paradigm for model fitting with applications to image analysis and automated cartography. Comm ACM 24(6):381–395
7. Grisetti G, Rizzini DL, Stachniss C, Olson E, Burgard W (2008) Online constraint network optimization for efficient maximum likelihood map learning. In: Proceedings of the 2008 IEEE international conference on robotics and automation (ICRA'08), Pasadena, pp 1880–1885
8. Grisetti G, Stachniss C, Burgard W (2009) Nonlinear constraint network optimization for efficient map learning. Trans Intell Transp Sys 10(3):428–439
9. Karlsson N, di Bernardo E, Ostrowski J, Goncalves L, Pirjanian P, Munich ME (2005) The vslam algorithm for robust localization and mapping. In: Proceedings of the 2005 IEEE international conference on robotics and automation (ICRA'05), Barcelona, Spain, pp 24–29
10. Klein G, Murray D (2008) Improving the agility of keyframe-based SLAM. In: Proceedings of the 10th European conference on computer vision (ECCV'08), Marseille, pp 802–815
11. Konolige K (2005) Slam via variable reduction from constraint maps. In: Proceedings of the 2005 IEEE international conference on robotics and automation (ICRA'05), Barcelona, Spain, pp 667–672
12. Konolige K, Bowman J, Chen JD, Mihelich P, Calonder M, Lepetit V, Fua P (2009) View-based maps. In: Proceedings of robotics science and systems, Seattle
13. Kretzschmar H, Grisetti G, Stachniss C (2010) Lifelong map learning for graph-based slam in static environments. Künstliche Intelligenz
14. Lowe D (2004) Distinctive image features from scale-invariant keypoints. Int J Comput Vis 60(2):91–100
15. Nistér D (2004) An efficient solution to the five-point relative pose problem. IEEE Trans Pattern Anal Mach Intell (PAMI) 26(6):756–777
16. Olson E, Leonard J, Teller S (2007) Spatially-adaptive learning rates for online incremental slam. In: Proceedings of robotics science and systems, Atlanta
17. Philbin J, Chum O, Isard M, Sivic J, Zisserman A (2007) Object retrieval with large vocabularies and fast spatial matching. In: Proceedings of the IEEE international conference on computer vision and pattern recognition (CVPR'07), IEEE Computer Society, Minneapolis, pp 1–8
18. Thrun S, Montemerlo M (2006) The graph slam algorithm with applications to large-scale mapping of urban structures. Int J Robot Res 25(5–6):403–429
19. Triggs B, McLauchlan P, Hartley R, Fitzgibbon A (2000) Bundle adjustment—a modern synthesis. In: Triggs B, Zisserman A, Szeliski R (eds) Vision algorithms: theory and practice, of Lecture Notes in Computer Science, vol 1883. Springer, pp 298–372
20. Williams B, Klein G, Reid I (2007) Real-time SLAM relocalisation. In: Proceedings of the 11th IEEE international conference computer vision

Chapter 3
Embedded Vision in Advanced Driver Assistance Systems

Zoran Nikolić

Abstract Throughout history, advances in transportation systems have had large economic and cultural impact. Mobility has changed the way people live and automobiles continue to evolve by becoming smarter and by leveraging cutting-edge technologies. Over the last three decades, we witnessed a tremendous growth of computer vision knowledge through research in academia and industry. More recently, in the last decade, we are finally seeing exciting applications of computer vision. Computer vision plays a fundamental role in the advanced driver assistance systems (ADAS), a field which is of particular interest to the evolution of transportation systems. For example, forward-facing driver assistance functions (such as road sign detection, lane departure warning, and autonomous emergency braking) are heavily relying on information received from a camera. The systems capture video data at high frame rate and process this information in order to warn the driver that the car is moving faster than the posted speed limit or to tell the driver of an unintentional lane drift. The goal of this chapter is to outline key components of ADAS, show how computer vision fits in the system, and describe its contribution to success of ADAS.

3.1 Introduction

Over the course of the twentieth century, automobiles evolved from an expensive toy with a 0.55 kW (less than 1 horsepower) engine and three wire-spoke wheels [1] into, we might say, a basic need of modern life. Today, automobiles dominate passenger travel. The total distance traveled by vehicles in the US increased by 155 % from 1970 to 2010 [2]. In 2013, about 87 million vehicles were produced worldwide, 22 million of those for the Chinese market [3]. The development of the automobile continues to drive economic, environmental, and cultural trends.

Mobility enhances quality of life but this comes at a high price. For example, approximately 1.24 million people died on roads around the globe in 2010 [4]. Even

Z. Nikolić (✉)
Texas Instruments, Inc., Houston, TX, USA
e-mail: nikolicz@ti.com

B. Kisačanin and M. Gelautz (eds.), *Advances in Embedded Computer Vision*,
Advances in Computer Vision and Pattern Recognition,
DOI 10.1007/978-3-319-09387-1_3

though number of fatalities per kilometer driven has fallen by a factor of three since 1980, the growth of transportation still has an unfortunate impact on the modern society in terms of loss of life and property. Half of all road traffic deaths are among pedestrians, cyclists, and motorcyclists. Motor vehicle crashes are ranked number nine among top ten leading causes of death in the world [5] and are the number one cause of death among children between ages 2 and 14 in the US [56].

Thankfully, cars are becoming smarter by leveraging the latest technologies, making driving safer and more enjoyable. Electronic systems promise to make roads nearly accident free. Active safety systems that are engaged prior to an accident (such as antilock braking system, electronic stability system, collision warning/avoidance, or adaptive cruise control) and passive safety systems which are engaged during the accident (such as passenger safety cell, seat belts, air bags, etc.) are helping to achieve this goal.

Advanced driver assistance systems (ADAS) are designed to increase driver situational awareness and safety by providing essential information, automating repetitive or complex tasks, and taking actions to reduce the severity of an accident. Human drivers are fallible: we send text messages while crawling in slow traffic, we forget to check surroundings before changing the lane, or get drowsy while driving at night. By reducing the amount of information to which a driver must react, or even taking over some of the tasks, such as braking or steering, ADAS technology is advancing toward a smart car that eliminates the errors we humans make. According to recent industry reports, ADAS market is one of the fastest growing segments in automotive electronics.

Driver assistance systems are focus of large joint research projects. Car manufacturers and research groups work together to solve the driver assistance challenges, by participating in projects such as CARSENSE (2000–2002) [57], INVENT(2001–2005) [58], and PREVENT(2004–2008) [59].

Embedded vision, along with radar and lidar, is at the forefront of technologies that enable the growth of ADAS. In the next generation of driver assistance systems, they will reduce the incidence of low-impact collisions and allow vehicle autonomy at lower speeds.

In this chapter, we focus primarily on ADAS building blocks based on embedded vision. We first give an overview of ADAS applications, compare different sensor types used in ADAS, and then focus on camera-based systems. In Sect. 3.4, we discuss the main components that make today's vision-based ADAS systems successful.

3.2 Analysis of Key ADAS Sensors

In order to provide support for advanced driver assistance applications, a sensor system must collect timely and relevant information about the environment. Typical sensor types that are used in ADAS are:

- Mono camera sensors. The imaging sensors are covering vision and near-infrared spectrum and have flexible field of view (FOV). Most ADAS functions require imaging sensor dynamic range of at least 115 dB, i.e., more than 19 bits per pixel. Typical frame rate for imaging sensor in driver assistance is 15 or more frames/s.
- Stereo camera pair has the capability of generating scene depth map based on disparity between the views from two cameras. Stereo camera is the most complex and complete sensor for driving assistance.
- Time-of-flight sensors that give accurate depth information by measuring the time it takes for the emitted energy to return to the sensor:
  - Long-range radar with range of 1–200 m and a response time of about 40 ms. Long-range radar is suitable for detection of objects in a highway environment.
  - Short-range radar with working range of 0–80 m. Short-range radars are suitable for near-range detection of vehicles in crowded urban scenarios.
  - Lidar (light detection and scanning) scanner is used in combination with camera for object detection and tracking in functions such as Adaptive Cruise Control, Collision Warning, or Pedestrian Detection).
  - Ultrasound sensors are used for park assist functions (to calculate distances to objects to assist the driver in parking the car).
- Near- and far-infrared sensors are used for night vision.

Camera or Radar?

Camera-based systems have the ability to offer multiple convenience and safety functions, including steering control and automatic emergency breaking, thus offering a cost advantage over radar- or lidar-based systems. Camera-based systems have a maximum range of about 50–100 m (depending on function) and wider field of view compared to long-range radar systems. Imaging technology can categorize type, estimate size of objects, and its wider FOV enables better tracking. Radar is vulnerable to false positives, especially around road curves, due to its inability to recognize object type, therefore in harsh weather conditions, with poor visibility, the radar's might give the driver false sense of security.

Mono cameras also have their limitations. Imaging sensors give 2D perspective of the 3D scene, losing the valuable depth information in the process (depth information offers valuable clues for separating objects from the background). Obtaining 3D information from a single camera is an ill-posed problem which can be solved by a stereo camera pair. In stereo camera systems, depth uncertainty is a quadratic function of distance, while distance is not affecting accuracy of radar and lidar systems. Relative vibrations between the cameras and large temperature swings drive need for online dynamic stereo camera system calibration when vehicle is moving. This online calibration needs to work without test patterns, needs to run in the background while system is operating, and must be guaranteed for the lifetime of the vehicle. Small calibration errors should not have impact on disparity estimation.

Radar offers advantages such as long detection range, resolution, and sensing performance necessary for higher speed systems. Radar can operate off-road and under extreme weather conditions.

Camera and Radar?
Sensor fusion combines the strengths of multiple sensing technologies. Daytime strengths of visible light sensors can be combined with nighttime capabilities of IR sensors. Range information from low angular resolution time-of-flight sensors can be combined with high resolution of imaging sensors to get depth information at higher resolution. When making the high-level safety decisions in automatic emergency breaking systems (AEB), radar or lidar can provide a second source of sensing confirmation.

Combining the results of different sensor types—sensor fusion (i.e., radar, lidar, vision, and ultrasound)—provides a more effective and reliable solution than using one technology in isolation. Sensor fusion can be achieved by either using sequential or parallel configuration. In sequential configuration, radar (or lidar) sensor is used to detect potential candidates in the attention-focusing phase. During the second phase, candidates generate areas of interest in image data for algorithms to verify the target presence. In parallel configuration, inputs from multiple sensors are processed independently and then object data is fused using a decision mechanism [6].

3.3 Camera-Based ADAS Applications

There are multiple imaging sensors around a vehicle, each providing data to one or more ADAS functions. Front-facing imaging sensors provide inputs for lane, traffic sign recognition, forward collision warning, intelligent adaptive front-lighting system, and pedestrian recognition. Rear facing image sensor provides input for parking assistance, object detection, and rear collision warning. Laterally facing imaging sensors provide inputs for surround view systems, blind spot detection, and can be used to replace side mirrors. Imaging sensors inside the vehicle cabin perform occupancy sensing and detect alertness of the driver.

ADAS must operate under all weather and lighting conditions and system should be smart enough to cope with direct sunlight, heavy fog, or snow. In case of sensor occlusion (i.e., mud, sun, etc.) or failure, the system should be auto-disabled and it should warn the driver that it is nonoperational.

Advanced driver assistance systems are spreading across multiple application areas and Fig. 3.1 illustrates main ADAS functions, sensor types, and their typical locations.

The front view camera system is mounted between the rearview mirror and windshield facing forward and typically incorporates camera and lidar. These camera-based sensor platforms now commonly add functionality such as lane keeping assist (LKA) to lane departure warnings (LDW) they supported since their introduction. In addition to LDW/LKA, the front view camera system may include application functions such as forward collision warning/avoidance (FCW), traffic sign recognition (TSR), intelligent adaptive front-lighting system (AFS), and pedestrian detection (PD).

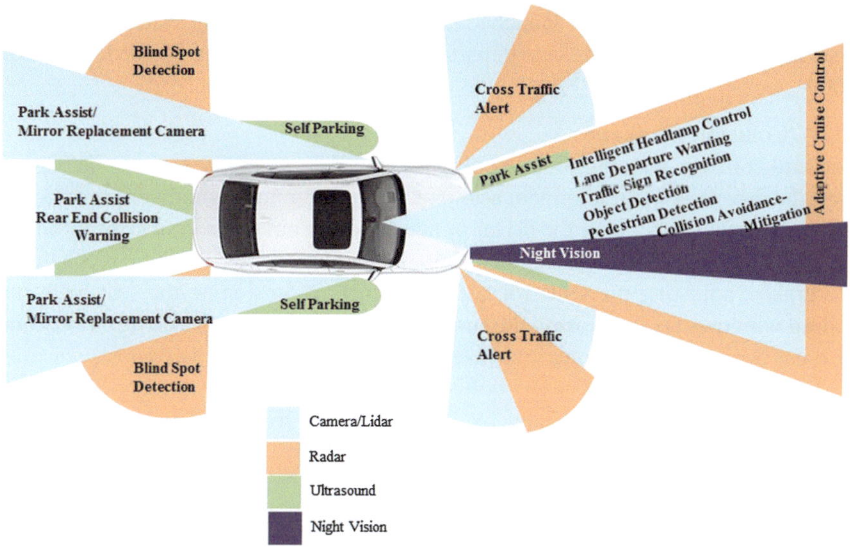

Fig. 3.1 Key application areas for Advanced Driver Assistance (ADAS). Sensor type and position are indicated using different colors

LDW/LKA

According to National Highway Traffic Safety Administration's (NHTSA) data [7], 64.4 % of all single-vehicle accidents in the USA are caused by running off from the road. Among such crashes, 95.1 % of the critical reasons were driver related. Lane keep assist technology is based on input from camera and it can warn the driver when vehicle is about to deviate from its traffic lane. The system can also work in combination with automatic cruise control to help driver steer and keep the vehicle on course.

Typically, lane keep assist has two functions: the lane departure warning (alerts the driver with sound when the car starts to deviate from its lane) and lane keeping assist (helps the car stay on course near the center of the lane by continuously applying a small amount of countersteering force). Vision algorithms can recognize the road lines and structures (yellow lines/white lines, Botts' dots, etc.) and based on vehicle's driving situation, the system can control the electronic power steering (EPS).

The world's first lane departure warning was introduced by Nissan in 2001. Toyota and Honda followed by introducing their lane monitoring systems in 2002 and 2003, respectively. Two years later, Toyota added a lane keep assist to their system. Lexus introduced a stereo camera system with multimode lane keep assist and more sophisticated object recognition processors in 2006. In Europe, Citroen was first to offer lane assist feature in 2005. This system used infrared sensors to monitor lane markings on the road surface, and a vibration mechanism in the seat to alert the driver of deviations. Two years later, Audi offered its lane keep assist feature on Q7. The system was camera based and used the steering wheel vibrations to warn the driver. The same year BMW launched its lane departure warning system on the new 5 series. GM introduced its lane departure warning in 2008 and Mercedes-Benz in 2009.

FCW/Collision Avoidance

Forward collision warning function of the front view camera system can detect and alert the driver about an imminent accident. Once an imminent collision is detected, the systems can either alert the driver or take autonomous braking or steering action (or both), without driver input and even prepare vehicle for the crash by precharging the brakes, adjusting the seats for added support, or tensioning the seat belts and rolling windows up and closing the sunroof. The system typically uses combination of radar and camera and sometime laser to detect imminent collisions.

The first production forward collision warning system was radar-based pre-collision system (PCS) introduced by Toyota in 2003. In order to improve accuracy of the system, Toyota added to the radar a single digital camera sensor in 2004. Two years later, the system was further improved by using a stereo camera pair and a more sensitive radar to detect pedestrians and animals (the system also supported lane keep assist function). Volvo introduced its first collision warning with autobrake in 2007. The system fused information from radar and camera to provide a warning through a Heads-Up Display that visually resembles brake lamps. Later versions of this system were capable of automatically applying the brakes to minimize pedestrian impacts. In 2008, Subaru introduced their forward collision warning system to the Japanese market. Unlike radar-based systems, this system used stereo front view camera. This system also offered adaptive cruise control and lane departure warning functions. The first Audi forward collision warning (pre sense front plus) released to the market in 2010 and 2011 combined information from the front radars with data from a windscreen-mounted front camera to calculate the likelihood of an impact. Ford's collision warning with brake assist was introduced in 2009. The system was relying on a mix of sensors including the front view camera.

TSR

Speed limit and end of speed limit signs are detected by traffic sign recognition function of the front view camera system. Traffic sign function notifies the driver about speed limit by presenting the information on the cluster display.

AFS

The intelligent AFS function of the front view camera system collects illumination data from vehicle surroundings to control distribution of the front lights. A camera detects lights from oncoming traffic and cars ahead and system adjusts the distribution of light from the high beams to mask specific area. This function is also sometimes called Intelligent Headlight Control (IHC).

PD

The pedestrian detection function of the front camera system assists the driver in avoiding pedestrian collision accidents. The assistance can span the range from alerting the driver with a warning signal to taking over control of braking in order to avoid collision with a pedestrian.

In 2013, Mercedes-Benz introduced a stereo front camera system, which in combination with radar offers pedestrian collision warning by autonomous braking, LKA, autonomous driving at low speeds in traffic jams, and an active braking assistance reacting to crossing traffic [55].

Surround View
The surround view system with multiple cameras, mounted at the center of the front grill, under the side mirrors and rearview camera in the back, can be used to check hard-to-view areas by visualizing information about vehicle's surroundings on navigation display. The camera mounted at the center of the front grill provides the driver a better view at intersections with unclear visibility and T-shaped junctions.

Rearview
Entry level rearview/backup camera system supports only park assist function. In addition to park assist, the smart rearview camera supports functions such as rear collision warning and obstacle/object detection.

Blind Spot
Detection of cars in the blind spot can be carried out by using a camera-based system. The system is mounted in the lateral mirrors of a car with the goal to visually detect cars that are located in the blind spot.

In November 2006, Volvo won the safety and technology award from the British "Autocar Magazine" with the driver assistance system for camera-based blind spot monitoring in the exterior mirror. It was one of the first driver assistance systems which automatically recognize moving objects using electronic image processing.

Night Vision
Night vision systems are used to extend the driver's ability to see beyond the vehicle's headlights at night or in bad weather by using information obtained from near- or far-infrared sensors.

Toyota introduced Night View based on near-infrared light in 2002 and 2003. In late 2004, Honda developed an intelligent night vision system, which highlights pedestrians in front of the vehicle by alerting the driver with an audible chime and visually displaying them via Heads-Up Display. In 2008, Toyota added a night view pedestrian detection feature which highlights pedestrians and presents them to the driver on a display. BMW and Mercedes-Benz introduced to the market their first night vision systems that detect and highlight pedestrians in 2008 and 2009, respectively. Volvo introduced a collision mitigation system for pedestrians based on monocular vision and radar in 2010.

Driver Monitoring
Imaging sensors mounted inside the passenger cabin are used to gather data such as driver movements, eyeblink pattern, and respiration. This data can be combined with information from LDW/LKA system measuring the number and level of the steering corrections the driver uses to keep the car in its lane. By combining this data, the system can assess driver state and assist with tasks such as steering or maintaining the following distance and alert the drivers if they are not paying close attention to the road.

In the 2007 model year, Toyota unveiled the first driver monitoring system in the world on the Lexus LS. The system monitors the driver and if driver's head turns away from the road and a frontal obstacle is detected, the system will warn the driver by sound and, if necessary, tighten the safety belts and precharge the brakes. Driver monitoring system released in 2008 added the ability to detect the driver's level of alertness by monitoring the driver's eyes. The system was designed to function even in challenging situations if the driver is wearing sunglasses or at night.

Emerging ADAS Functions

Emerging applications such as mirror replacement camera bring several advantages over conventional mirrors. The advantages include vehicle weight reduction resulting in lower fuel consumption and CO_2 emissions, greater freedom in car design, savings on mirror adjustment switches and motors, and removal of the blind spot. The camera monitor systems (CMS) also open potential path for inclusion of embedded vision analytics features. Standardization of CMS is ongoing under ISO16505 with participation of all European OEMs.

3.3.1 Front View Camera Systems

At the simplest level, front view camera system offers intelligent AFS. The intelligent AFS can adjust the vehicle headlights according to ambient light level or it can detect presence of oncoming vehicles and turn the vehicle's main beams on and off appropriately at night.

At the next level of processor performance, the front view camera system can also detect road lanes and provide functions such as lane departure warning or lane keep assist. This is typically mono camera system shown in left panel of Fig. 3.2. The embedded processor (the number cruncher) receives high dynamic range video input from a megapixel imaging sensor at 30 frames per second.

The system relies on vehicle CAN bus to receive information such as vehicle speed, steering wheel angle, yaw rate, etc., and to send output which can be either warning to the driver or control command to steering/braking subsystems. The processor connects to the vehicle CAN bus via the external microcontroller (MCU). The MCU in the system typically conforms to high level of functional safety.

Further increase in the processor compute power enables functions such as pedestrian detection, FCW, and TSR. Strong interest in TSR in Europe is driven by difficulty for drivers to keep track of the actual speed limit in effect—as some European countries adopted variable speed limits that change at various time of the day or night in order to reduce traffic noise or improve safety at busy intersections.

Vision-based object detection and classification is a key problem in driver assistance. Functions such as detection and classification of objects (i.e., cars, motorcycles, and trucks) and pedestrians require substantial compute power. Adding second imaging sensor to the front camera system improves detection reliability since dense stereo can provide additional cues for pedestrian recognition. The depth information

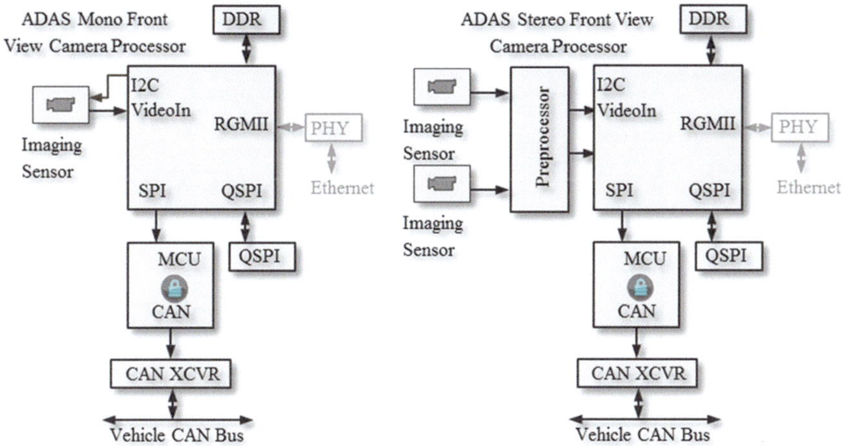

Fig. 3.2 *Left panel* Mono front view camera system; *Right panel* Stereo front camera system. At a higher cost, stereo system is capable to detect objects more reliably. Preprocessing stages (image rectification and disparity calculation) in stereo camera system are typically done in an FPGA or ASIC

makes stereo camera system more accurate and robust than a mono camera system. Typical block diagram of a front view stereo camera system is shown in right panel of Fig. 3.2.

In today's front camera stereo vision systems preprocessing (such as rectification and disparity calculation) is typically hardwired and performed on an ASIC or FPGA before moving data to the processor.

Although stereo front camera system comes at additional cost (increases overall complexity of the system), the two imaging sensors provide means to calculate scene depth which is crucial for reliable object detection.

System size reduction drives a constant demand for higher system integration maximizing number of functions running on a single processor. This drives the need for more compute performance. On the other hand, compute performance increase must come without compromising overall system cost. The system needs to be packaged in a miniature enclosure and must deliver maximum compute performance, while dissipating minimum heat in order to operate at the extreme temperatures of severe desert heat or Arctic freezing cold. The opposing requirements create a very challenging environment.

3.3.2 Rearview Camera Systems

Passive backup video cameras are gaining popularity in the USA, especially on large vehicles such as minivans, pick-up trucks, and SUVs. The rearview camera is designed to help the driver avoid a backup collision while reversing the vehicle.

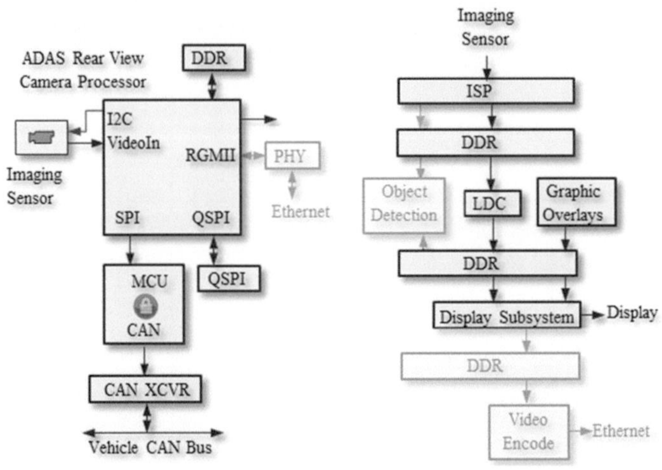

Fig. 3.3 *Left panel* Rearview camera; *Right panel* Smart rearview camera data flow. Optional functions are shown in *light shade of gray*

The imaging sensor is typically pointed at a downward angle and has 190° field of view which allows the camera to see potential obstacles from one rear corner to the other. Entry level rearview camera provides only visual feedback to the driver. In a 'smart' rearview camera, an image sensor provides incoming video frames to a processor to analyze the video content for people and object detection.

Block diagram of rearview camera is shown in left panel of Fig. 3.3.

The system is sending video output (NTSC, digital via LVDS, or compressed video via Ethernet) to be displayed to the driver along with potential obstacle warning. Typical processing stages in the rearview camera system are shown in right panel of Fig. 3.3. In case of imaging sensor with raw output, the video frame needs to be converted to YUV format before the lens distortion correcting (LDC) step. The Image Signal Processor (ISP) processing pipe on the entry level rearview system is tuned to maximize viewing quality when converting the raw input into a standard video format to be displayed to the driver (viewing optimized processing pipe).

There is a constant demand for size reduction of the rearview camera system. The miniaturization trend creates even more challenging thermal environment compared to the front camera system.

3.3.3 Surround View Camera Systems

Surround view systems (SVS) present to the driver—a real-time 360° view around the vehicle, as well as park assist and bird's-eye view. The system operates with minimum glass-to-glass latency and allows the driver to be fully aware of vehicle's surroundings. For example, the system could allow a driver to see a toy that has been left behind a parked car or it can show how close the vehicle is getting to other vehicles when trying to park in a tight spot. In fully automated systems, the vehicle is able to use this information to actually park itself. The surround view system cameras typically have 190° field of view and stream video to the central processor either as analog NTSC, digital uncompressed via Low Voltage Differential Signaling (LVDS/FPD-Link), or compressed (MJPEG or H.264 format) via Ethernet (using Ethernet AVB protocol [8]). The camera streams can then be stitched together to form a cohesive and seamless view around the outside of the car. Outputs from the surround vision system are sent to a console at VGA or higher resolution. This display makes it easy for the driver to recognize and react to any hazards surrounding the car. Additionally, 3D graphic rendering could be used for highly realistic surround views. A high-level block diagram LVDS/FPD-Link-based surround view system is shown in Fig. 3.4.

In this example, four satellite cameras are sending video over LVDS link to the central processor. The surround view central processor is synchronizing the satellite cameras via back channel LVDS communication. Simplified data flow for surround view central processor is shown in right panel of Fig. 3.4. Prior to frame photometric matching and stitching, video captured from the satellite cameras is corrected for lens distortion. Optionally, the system can use incoming video to check for objects around the vehicle and to give cross traffic alerts to the driver.

By connecting the camera system directly to the central processor via LVDS link (or though analog connection), the video streams cannot be exploited by other systems in the vehicle. To address this challenge, it is possible to use an in-vehicle Ethernet-based network architecture. In this case, each system connected to the network is capable of receiving data from any camera distributing compressed and packetized bit stream across the network.

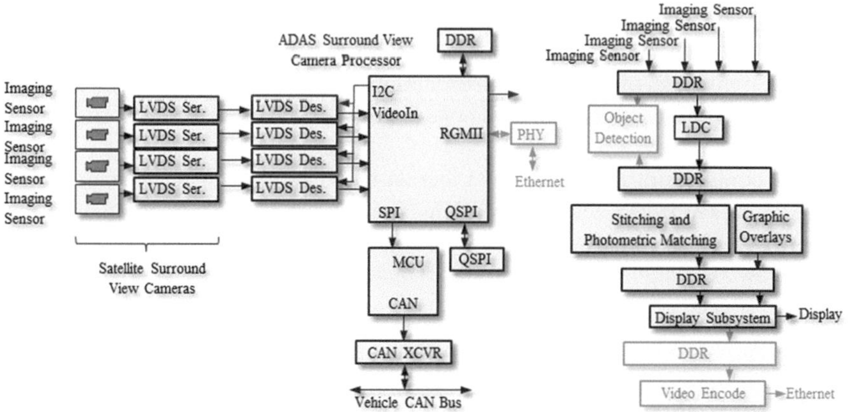

Fig. 3.4 *Left panel* Block diagram of LVDS-based surround view system; *Right panel* Simplified data flow in LVDS-based surround view system. Optional processing steps are presented in *light shade of gray*

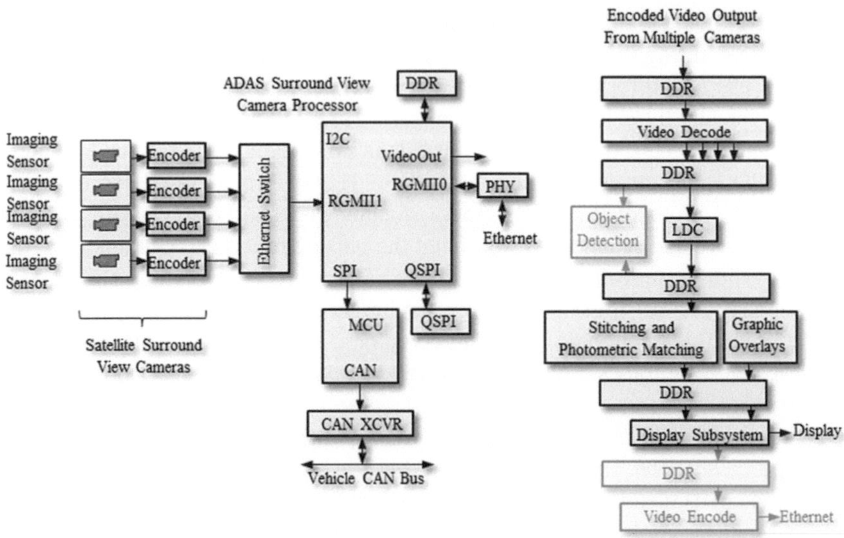

Fig. 3.5 *Left panel* Block diagram of Ethernet-based surround view system; *Right panel* Simplified data flow in Ethernet-based surround view system. Optional processing steps are shown in *light shade of gray*

Ethernet-based version of surround view system is presented in the left panel of Fig. 3.5. The satellite cameras, if needed, convert imaging sensor output from raw format to YUV, and then compress the video frames by either using MJPEG or H.264 before sending them via Ethernet to the central surround view processor. In this case, Ethernet AVB protocol is used for synchronization of satellite cameras and to minimize overall system latency. The compressed video streams from the satellite camera are decoded on the central ECU.

Simplified data flow for the Ethernet-based surround view central processor is shown on right panel of Fig. 3.5. With exception of the very first step (video decode), the data flow looks very similar to the one from LVDS-based surround view central processor.

Video compression artifacts in the Ethernet-based system might influence performance of the embedded vision algorithms. Some work is being done on assessing impact of the video compression on night vision pedestrian detection [9], automotive optical flow algorithms [10], and on stereo matching [11].

3.4 Key Components of Vision-Based ADAS

Powerful, energy-efficient systems-on-chip (SOC), along with low-cost wide dynamic range imaging sensors, enabled the spread of embedded vision in ADAS. Vision-based driver assistance systems require a variety of processors and image sensors operating at different resolutions, frame rates, under different lighting conditions, and with different optics. Embedded vision algorithms are the "brains" of ADAS along with components such as software framework, real-time operating system, and tools.

The development of advanced driver assistance system starts with a definition of the requirements outlining functions and operational constraints. Hazard and risk analysis is then performed in order to determine the system safety requirements.

These key components of the vision-based driver assistance systems are discussed in this section.

3.4.1 Functional Safety

Advanced driver assistance systems can take over elements of driving such as steering or braking where undetected dangerous failure can be catastrophic. When designing a vision system for ADAS, how can we provide the evidence that risks have been minimized? Functional safety has immense implications on all components in ADAS and safety must be embedded in the culture of every organization and the supply chain. For example, offset error of just one pixel when calculating disparity could generate a wrong assessment of distance between the car and a pedestrian, resulting in a disaster.

The development of ADAS systems is governed by international safety standard for road vehicles ISO 26262. Implementing ISO 26262 allows leveraging a common standard to measure how safe a system will be in service. The ISO 26262 standard provides regulations and recommendations throughout the product development process from conceptual development through decommissioning. It details how to assign an acceptable risk level to a system or component and document the overall testing process. ISO 26262 also contains detailed guidance on software tool qualification. The objective of tool qualification is to provide evidence that a software tool is suitable for use in the development of safety-related software according to the standard.

In order to classify risk level and to quantify the degree of rigor that should be applied in development, implementation, and verification, the ISO 26262 defines Automotive Safety Integrity Levels (ASIL). There are four ASIL levels identified by the standard: A, B, C, and D. ASIL A dictates the lowest integrity requirements on the product while ASIL D dictates the highest safety requirements. The ASIL level is established by performing a risk analysis of a potential hazard by looking at severity, exposure, and controllability of the vehicle operating scenario.

ASILs can be decomposed over a system and high ASILs can be met by multiple redundant components working together, each with lower ASIL.

3.4.2 Imaging Sensors

Driving force behind the perfection of CMOS-based imagers were high volume and relatively short product life cycle applications such as mobile telephones, tablets, and PCs. The technical specifications required by automotive suppliers for imaging sensors targeted toward ADAS market are different and very application specific. High dynamic range and low light performance, wide operating temperature range, fast motion, support for functional safety, and device cost are five most important parameters for imaging sensors in ADAS.

The requirements for an automotive imaging sensor are challenging as device needs to produce reliable image output under rapidly changing illumination level conditions at extreme temperatures.

The human eye has a wide dynamic range of about 200 dB. The eye has three mechanisms to achieve such a wide dynamic range: two types of photoreceptor cells (rods and cones) with different photosensitivities, logarithmic photoreceptor response, and shift of the response curve according to the ambient light level. The front camera system must exhibit extremely high optical dynamic range to capture scene details and detect objects in very bright and very dark parts of frame ($>$115 dB for front view camera applications). To achieve Wide Dynamic Range (WDR), automotive imaging sensor suppliers typically use different techniques [12, 13] such as: skimming WDR, staggered multicapture WDR, down-sampling WDR, split pixel WDR, and log sensors.

Although imaging sensors with global shutter offer elimination of motion artifacts through simultaneous capture of the entire frame, this advantage comes at the expense of increased pixel noise and reduced light sensitivity. Today majority of automotive imaging sensors use a rolling shutter and algorithms are designed to deal with motion artifacts.

Unlike the human eye, all imaging sensors are monochromatic. To obtain the color information, a color mosaic filter is placed over the sensor pixels, which typically cuts spatial resolution of a color sensor in half compared to grayscale. As they offer nearly double the spatial resolution of a color sensor, grayscale sensors are much more sensitive to variations in brightness.

Development life cycle timeline of ADAS sets pace for automotive imaging sensor road maps. Typically automotive imager resolution increases every three to four years. Downside of frame resolution increase is lower sensitivity to light due to reduction of pixel size. To combat reduced pixel light sensitivity imaging sensor suppliers are introducing ‘clear pixels’ without color filter. In addition to monochrome and Bayer color pattern, the imaging sensors in ADAS support different arrangements of color filters, such as RCBC (Red-Clear-Blue-Clear), RGBC (Red-Green-Blue-Clear), RGBIr (Red-Green-Blue-InfraRed), and RCCC (Red-Clear). Typically a specialized ISP is required to convert this raw output from an imaging sensor to a format that can be used by embedded vision algorithms. Low-resolution imaging sensors typically integrate the ISP functionality on the die.

Crossing image resolution boundary beyond 1Mpix has processing and connectivity implications on architecture of the embedded processor in ADAS. At these resolutions, size of the ISP logic starts to dominate which is pushing the ISP functions off the sensor die to either embedded processor or to a separate ISP companion device. Secondly, the increase of resolution and frame rate drives demand for a more effective hardware interface offering higher data bandwidth between the imaging sensor and the embedded processor. The MIPI CSI2 interface is emerging as a solution to data bandwidth and pin count challenges of the parallel camera interface used in all legacy driver assistance systems.

3.4.3 Embedded Processors

Constant demand for higher resolution, higher frame rate, algorithm robustness, and lower processing latency is driving an exponential increase in processing and memory bandwidth requirements. Embedded processor for ADAS needs to deliver high performance, while dissipating minimum amount of heat and at the same time must meet strict low-cost requirements.

A compromising solution satisfying the conflicting requirements lays somewhere between two extreme architectures: dedicated hardwired accelerators on one end and general purpose CPUs on the other. The hardwired acceleration offers high performance at low cost but gives low flexibility. Programmability of general purpose CPUs gives them high flexibility, while impacting their performance or their energy efficiency.

In order to meet the challenging compute targets while dissipating minimum power, ADAS architects have to embrace the power of heterogeneous computing, where each of the heterogeneous elements has a unique strength allowing it to excel on specific types of processing. A flexible architecture is required to cover many functions and to maximize reuse across different product lines.

Most, if not all vision algorithms start off with processing characterized by repetitive operations at pixel level with high computational requirements and memory bandwidth (low-level processing). Typical examples of low-level vision processing functions are image filtering, gradient calculation, edge detection, corner detection, image pyramids, etc. Low-level processing is typically best served by applying single instruction on multiple data (SIMD). Next processing stage has focus on certain objects or regions of interest that meet particular classification criteria (mid-level processing). Typical examples of mid-level vision processing functions are integral image, feature calculation, classification, optical flow, Hough transform, etc. Mid-level vision is typically best served by using some combination of SIMD and multiple instructions on multiple data (MIMD). High-level processing is typically responsible for final decision-making and tracking and takes input from previous processing stages. High-level vision includes algorithms with high variability in processing and data accesses characterized by highly conditional processing [14].

Antagonistic requirements to increase compute performance while keeping power dissipation at same (or even lower) level can be met by off-loading some of low- and mid-level vision processing to a hardware accelerator. They can be broadly divided in two groups: hardwired/fixed and programmable.

Hardwired Hardware Accelerators—Selection of processing primitives to accelerate in fixed hardware acceleration is not a trivial task as the industry lacks standards for embedded vision processing algorithms. To preserve flexibility across different systems, the best candidates for fixed hardware acceleration are low- and mid-level processing kernels. Some examples of fixed hardware accelerators for vision include: Pipelined Vision Processor (PVP) on Analog Devices Processors [15], image processing accelerators on Toshiba Visconti 3 (affine, filter, histogram, histogram of gradients, and matching) [16] or PW and CE engines on MobilEye EyeQ2 processor [17].

Programmable Hardware Accelerators—Programmable hardware accelerators give more flexibility than fixed hardware acceleration. To address challenges of low- and mid-level vision processing, the most deeply embedded vision applications have used proprietary programmable hardware accelerator architectures with a strong DSP pedigree, such as the NEC IMAPCAR [18], Image processor IMP2-X2 on Renesas SH7766 device [19, 20], VMP2 on Mobileye EyeQ2 [17], Media Processor Engine (MPE) on Toshiba Visconti-3 [16], GPU [21], Cognivue Apex [22], and Texas Instruments EVE [14, 60] architectures, augmented by FPGAs for blocks with extreme compute requirements.

General Purpose Programmable Processors—General purpose CPU such as ARM Cortex A8, A9, A15, or A53 processors and DSP architectures are best fit for high-level vision processing. The internal processor architecture, number and precision of computational units, cache architecture, number and size of the internal and external data paths all play an instrumental role in how fast the task will be carried out [23]. Hardware support for functional safety helps to relieve the embedded processor from running periodic system and memory checks leaving more programmable resources for analytics. Large internal memory helps reduce system latencies and lower power dissipation by minimizing number of accesses to the external double data rate (DDR) memory.

While each architecture has its own strengths and weaknesses, TDA2x SOC is the only one in the industry that offers automotive vision developers both a state-of-the-art DSP along with multiple instances of a fully programmable vision accelerator an unparalleled level of programmable vision analytics performance.

TDA2x SOC ADAS processor architecture is shown in Fig. 3.6:

The TDA2x SoC [24] incorporates a scalable architecture that includes a mix of TI's fixed and floating-point TMS320C66x digital signal processor (DSP) generation cores, Vision AccelerationPac (EVE), ARM Cortex-A15 and dual-Cortex-M4 processors. The integration of a video accelerator for decoding multiple compressed videos treams received over an Ethernet AVB network, along with the graphics accelerators (SGX544) for rendering virtual views, and enables a 3D viewing experience for surround view applications.

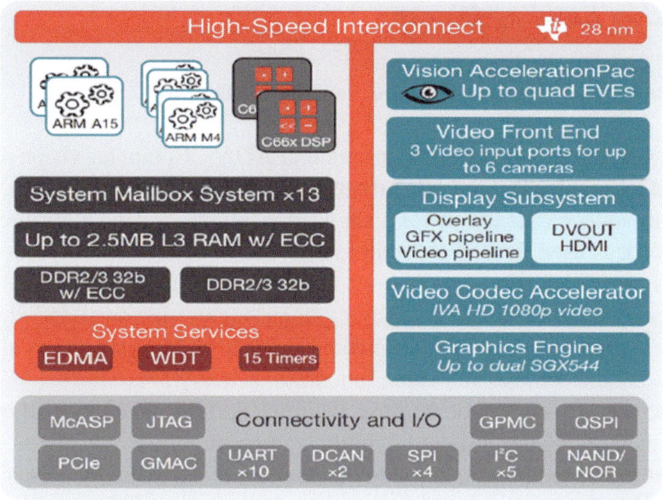

Fig. 3.6 SOC ADAS heterogeneous architecture

The dual core A15's on TDA2x run at 750 MHz with an out-of-order superscalar pipeline with a tightly coupled low-latency level-2 cache with additional improvements in floating point and NEON™. The dual core Cortex M4, is an efficient controller engine for streaming image capture. TI's IVA-HD core is an imaging and video codec accelerator that runs at 532 MHz to enable full HD video encode and decode. Even with all of this compute power, vision analytics is still critically dependent on the TMS320C66x DSP for high-level vision and Vision AcceleratorPAC EVE for low- and mid-level vision to meet the challenging requirements.

The Vision AccelerationPac (EVE) is an accelerator purposely built for computer vision, fully programmable in a high-level language environment, which delivers more than eight times improvement in compute performance for advanced vision analytics than existing ADAS systems at same power levels. The Vision AccelerationPac for this family of products includes multiple embedded vision engines (EVEs) offloading the vision analytics functionality from the application processor while also reducing the power footprint.

Today's SOC architectures enable further efficiencies by integrating all of the peripherals necessary for a complete video/image processing system within a single chip. Given the lack of interoperability specification for lidar, laser, radar, and video data in the car network and that today the industry is using multiple data communication standards (i.e., camera, display, Ethernet AVB, LVDS, CAN, etc.) the SOC must support a swarm of interfaces to ensure adoption across a broad spectrum of possible use cases.

3.4.4 Vision Building Blocks

3.4.4.1 Common Preprocessing and Feature Detection

Computer vision has entered the mainstream of ADAS. Computer vision algorithms detect road lanes, objects, and pedestrians, anticipate and augment driver's actions. There are no industry standards for embedded vision processing algorithms (unlike for video codecs used for video compression) and if we ask ten different people to develop a forward collision warning, we will end up with ten different solutions.

To properly capture images of moving objects, exposure time and shutter type are critical. Concurrent algorithms/functions running in the system typically require different exposure settings and some functions such as TSR require more than one exposure setting. To accommodate these requirements typical ADAS imaging sensors have high dynamic range and output multiple exposures.

Some common preprocessing steps in the driver assistance systems based on the embedded vision are: custom image signal processing (ISP); various filtering, creation of image pyramids; integral image; and feature extraction. The ISP block is typically taking a raw high dynamic range input from an imaging sensor and converting to a format used by the algorithms.

Surround view and rearview systems rely on cameras with wide field of view at a cost of large distortion. Lens distortion correction is typically one of the first processing steps in these systems. Depending on situation, the software can change viewing angle (i.e., render top view image) before displaying video to the driver. The most efficient way to handle this homographic transform is via look-up table.

Surround view systems combine inputs from multiple satellite cameras positioned around car in one 360-degree image (Figs. 3.1, 3.4, and 3.5). In computer vision, extensive work has been done in the field of image stitching and photogrammetric matching. During image registration features (using feature descriptors such as SIFT, ORB, SURF [54] etc.) are extracted from each view, and matched to features in the other overlapping views. Random sampling consensus (RANSAC) of matched features is used in order to remove any mismatched points and to estimate the homography between overlapping views.

Key components of lane detection are: extraction of road markings; road modeling; post processing; and position tracking. Edge-based techniques for road marking extraction give good results on solid and segmented lines, but they typically fail in situations which contain many nonessential lines. Different approaches have been proposed to overcome this limitation [25]. To improve estimates, it is necessary to include a priori knowledge of the road in the postprocessing steps. The most common tracking technique used in lane-position-detection systems is Kalman filtering. A survey of vision-based lane detection can be found in [25].

In some systems, color is required for traffic sign recognition algorithms, while in most cases vision-based ADAS functions rely purely on monochrome imaging sensors as they offer higher light sensitivity compared to color sensors. Traffic sign recognition is a classic example of rigid object detection although road signs differ from country to country across shape, color, text font, and language. For detection of circular road signs Zelinski Transform [26] gives good results, while an effective way to capture general traffic shape information is histogram of gradients (HOG) [27].

3.4.4.2 Estimating Depth and Motion and Pedestrian Detection

Pedestrians are the most vulnerable participants in traffic and vision-based recognition of pedestrians is a key problem of smart vehicles. Pedestrian detection requires a variety of features (i.e., Haar wavelets, HOG, CoHOG, LRF, etc.) and classification methods (i.e., Adaboost, SVM). A number of related surveys exist on pedestrian detection [6, 28–30, 39, 40].

In most cases, precise and robust estimation of depth and motion is a key element for pedestrian detection and obstacle avoidance functions in automotive driver assistance [31]. In order to maximize knowledge about the scene ahead, every sensor pixel should be utilized. By calculating position and motion of every frame pixel, the front view camera system can anticipate more accurately pedestrian behavior. Therefore, it is very beneficial to obtain dense disparity and dense optical flow. On the other hand, optical flow and stereo vision are extremely challenging algorithms for embedded environment due to their compute and bandwidth requirements.

The perception of motion is instrumental for ADAS. The optical flow algorithm is a key building block for ADAS functions such as estimation of vehicle egomotion, obstacle/pedestrian detection, detection of cars in the blind spot and structure from motion. Optical flow used in advanced driver assistance environment must cope with weakly textured areas, large displacements, and constant change of illumination conditions caused by either scene change or unanticipated and unknown adjustments of camera parameters such as exposure time.

Most variation-based optical flow algorithms use the brightness constancy constraint between successive frames, which is often violated in real-world scenes while driving. Second serious limitation of typical optical flow methods suggested in literature is that they can only cope with small displacements, while typical real-world scenes exhibit large motion vectors especially in curves or areas near the vehicle. A quantitatively different approach was suggested in [32], where the Census Transform was used to represent small image patches and the primitives were matched using a table based indexing scheme. Another approach to improve robustness to change in brightness is to replace the simple gray value illumination constancy constraint from classical optical flow approaches by Hamming distances between different census signatures [33]. To overcome large displacement challenge, integration of rich descriptors into the variational optical flow setting is suggested in [34]. Use of Rudin-Osher-Fatemi (ROF) denoising scheme [35] to achieve resistance to illumination change is proposed by several authors [36]. While the method improves resistance to illumination change it is computationally intensive and struggles with large displacements even when a pyramid scheme is used. A different approach which explicitly models the varying illumination by adding an additional scalar function is proposed in [37]. The function is estimated in a joint optimization of the optical flow field and since this function must be smooth on image domain, the method requires number of iterations which is computationally expensive and might not be friendly for a real-time implementation.

Including additional information into a variational scheme can improve optical flow results. In stereo camera systems information such as depth and vehicle ego-motion can be used in variational approach to regularize the optical flow estimate [38].

Obstacle detection involving stereovision typically uses different approaches and various simplifications of the classic problem in order to achieve real-time performance [30]. There are two main algorithm approaches depending on the domain where calculation is performed: 3D space based and disparity based. Disparity based algorithms are more popular as they operate directly on output from stereo reconstruction—on disparity map. Due to limitation in resolution of the imaging sensors and the stereo camera baseline constraints precise subpixel interpolation is required in stereo based driver assistance camera systems.

Most of conventional stereo engines use local correlation methods that search for pixel matches between two rectified views by comparing small patches along the epipolar line [41]. Contrasting approach are global methods which exploit the fact that the scene consist of smooth structures with very little discontinuities and formulate the stereo problem in terms of energy function. The energy function typically includes data and smoothness terms and is then subject of optimization such as graph-cuts, belief propagation or semi-global matching (SGM) [42]. The global methods perform global disparity optimization, so chance of gross errors which would cause unnecessary emergency breaking scenarios is minimized compared to local correlation-based approaches which estimate disparity based on a small local neighborhood.

SGM method calculates optimum disparity map by using dynamic programming on multiple one-dimensional paths crossing each pixel [42]. The global stereo method requires substantial compute and memory bandwidth resources. First real-time implementation of SGM was published on FPGA in 2009 [43]. To obtain real-time SGM performance on the CPU the key design choices are: parallelization of the most time-consuming blocks, image subsampling, and result reuse for full resolution computation [44].

In some systems, the depth map is first segmented and then detected objects are tracked over time and their velocity is estimated. In these systems, performance of the detection heavily depends on the correctness of the segmentation. The segmentation step might merge moving object to a nearby stationary object and fail to detect a pedestrian or cyclist moving in front of parked minivan. A solution to this challenging problem was proposed in [45]. The basic idea for detection is to use not only the depth map but also to include 3D motion field information. The 3D motion field information is calculated by tracking points with known depth over multiple consecutive frames.

3.4.5 Software

All processes and components used to build ADAS must be safe, secure, and reliable, including software development process, software itself, tools, and operating system.

Development of safety-related electronics products such as ADAS not only requires SPICE (ISO/IEC 15504) compliant process but also needs to fulfill process development requirements specified by ISO 26262 functional safety standard [50].

In order to facilitate code safety, reliability, and portability in the context of embedded systems, Motor Industry Software Reliability Association (MISRA) formulated a software development standard for C programming language. Published in March 2013, the latest version of MISRA standard (MISRA-C:2012) includes a number of improvements that can reduce the cost and complexity of compliance, while aiding consistent, safe use of C in critical systems. There is also a set of guidelines for MISRA C++.

To meet low-latency processing time requirements and minimize any delays caused by operating system, ADAS typically use real time operating systems (RTOS). The RTOS in ADAS is not just responsible for memory partitioning, context switching, task scheduling, event handling, and locking mechanisms, but also for controlling the entire program flow, including safety mechanisms. For these reasons, the kernel requirements, design, implementation, and tests must include functional safety as one of key components along with minimal interrupt latency and minimal thread switching latency.

Ideally, RTOS for ADAS should be developed for seamless integration into AUTOSAR environment. Some of RTOS that are certified for highest ISO 26262 ASIL D tool qualification level D are: Green Hills Integrity, ElectroBit Tresos AutoCore OS, and Microsar OS SafeContext from Vector.

3.4.6 Development Flow

The ADAS algorithm development usually starts on a PC or workstation which offers 'unlimited' compute performance, memory, and memory bandwidth. Algorithm optimization is a critical component of the cost reduction effort because optimized code can achieve real-time operation on less expensive embedded processors. In order to map the algorithms to an embedded platform with very restricted resources an embedded vision system typically requires optimization on three levels that are not always orthogonal to each other [23, 46–49]: algorithmic, software, and system level optimization.

A typical vision application can run ten or more times faster when critical algorithms are called from a highly optimized library than if they are implemented without much regard for the internal processor architecture. Use of computer vision libraries such as OpenCV could be suitable in most cases as a proof of concept but in the end, optimization for the target processor architecture will significantly improve the system performance.

The algorithm development represents only a small fraction in ADAS design cycle as the major challenge in the development of these systems is to take into account the variety of traffic scenarios. Extensive test and validation is an enormous undertaking and the most challenging aspect of ADAS development, especially when it comes to the vision systems. In an effort to test all scenarios and to achieve 100 % accuracy and zero false positives, under all possible conditions, thousands of hours of video clips must be gathered and run in regression test database. As the test databases would not be able to cover all test cases, suppliers spend years of testing and validating systems and performing real-world field trials.

3.5 Conclusion

We have come a long way since first demonstration of an autonomous car at New York World's Fair in 1939. New kinds of sensors and state-of-the-art embedded processors, with sufficient compute power to support rapid growth of computer vision, are factors catalyzing growth of camera-based advanced drivers systems.

Regulation will further drive the proliferation of multifunction cameras to the most cost-sensitive segment of the automotive market, which is also the most crash vulnerable segment. The propagation is led by New Car Assessment Program (NCAP) changes in Europe, but introduction of cameras in the mainstream vehicles is expected to become noticeable in the USA too, driven by the National Highway Transportation Safety Administration (NHTSA), the National Transportation Safety Board (NTSB), and the Insurance Institute for Highway Safety (IIHS).

In order to reduce the number of backover injuries and deaths and to improve visibility when a car is backing out of a driveway or parking space, NHTSA issued a rule which mandates use of rear view cameras in all new vehicles in the US starting from May 2018. The regulation, depending on final performance requirements, might stimulate spread of passive or active rearview camera systems.

Projects such as Prometheus, ARGO [51], and DARPA Urban Challenge, were instrumental in helping Google's driverless vehicle come to life. Today, many major automotive manufacturers including Mercedes-Benz, BMW, Audi, Volkswagen, Ford, GM, and Toyota are testing driverless cars.

Eventually, we might see a circuit fail and that one defect in one billion could cause a fatal crash. Who is responsible when things go wrong? How should the cars with such systems be tested? The number of electronic components networked together in vehicles together with communication systems between cars, creates opportunities that could potentially be exploited by a malicious attacker. Cyber security is a concern and several researchers have shown possible ways to compromise security of automobiles and hijack functions such as steering or braking by exploiting a broad range of attack vectors, including CD players, Bluetooth, and cellular radio [52, 53].

There are many challenges and obstacles on the path toward autonomous cars, but we expect that they are solvable. Consumer acceptance and demand will drive us on our way to autonomous vehicle and embedded vision will keep us safe on this journey.

References

1. Stiller C (2011) The automobile becomes 125 years old. IEEE intelligent transportation systems magazine, Spring
2. Sivak M (2013) Effects of vehicle fuel economy, distance traveled, and vehicle load on the amount of fuel used for personal transportation in the U.S.: 1970–2010, University of Michigan, Transportation Research Institute, UMTRI-2013-10; February 2013
3. http://www.oica.net/category/production-statistics/
4. http://www.who.int/gho/road_safety/mortality/traffic_deaths_number/en/
5. http://www.who.int/mediacentre/factsheets/fs310/en/
6. Gandhi T, Trivedi MM (2007) Pedestrian protection systems: issues, survey, and challenges. IEEE Trans Intell Transp Syst 8(3):549–562
7. Run-Off-Road Crashes: An on-scene perspective, DOT HS 811 500, NHTSA 2011
8. Alderisi G, Iannizzotto G, Bello LL (2012) Towards IEEE 802.1 ethernet AVB for advanced driver assistance systems: a preliminary assessment. In: IEEE 17th conference on emerging technologies and factory automation (ETFA), Krakow
9. Rahmani M, Kloess H, Hintermaier W, Steinbach E (2008) Real time video compression for driver assistance camera systems, ISVCS 2008 22–24 July, Dublin, Ireland
10. Foster J, Jiang X, Terzis A, Rothermel A (2011) The effect of image compression on automotive optical flow algorithms. In: 14th ITG conference on electronic media technology (CEMT), Dortmund
11. Foster J, Jiang X, Terzis A, Rothermel A (2012) Evaluation of compression algorithms for automotive stereo matching. In: 2012 intelligent vehicles symposium, Alcala de Henares, Spain
12. Solhusvik J, Kuang J, Lin Z, Manabe S, Lyu J, Rhodes H (2013) A comparison of high dynamic range CIS technologies for automotive applications. In: 2013 international image sensor workshop, Snowbird Resort, Utah, 12–16 June
13. Ohta J (2008) Smart image sensors and applications. CRC Press, Boca Raton
14. Sankaran J, Nikolić Z (2014) TDA2x, an SOC optimized for advanced driver assistance systems. In: ICASP
15. ADSP-BF606/ADSP-BF607/ADSP-BF608/ADSP-BF609 Technical Data
16. Toshiba TMPV7528XBG Press Release, Dusseldorf, Germany, March 2013
17. http://www.mobileye.com/technology/processing-platforms/eyeq2/
18. Kyo S, Okazaki S, Koga T, Hidano F (2008) A 100GOPS in-vehicle vision processor for pre-crash safety system based on a ring connected 128 4-Way VLIW processing elements. In: IEEE symposium on VLSI circuits, Honolulu
19. Hamasaki H, Hoshi Y, Nakamura A, Yamamoto A (2010) SOC for car navigation system with a 55.3GOPS image recognition engine. In: 15th Asia and South Pacific design automation conference (ASP-DAC), Taipei
20. http://am.renesas.com/applications/automotive/adas/surround/sh7766/index.jsp
21. http://www.nvidia.com/object/tegra-k1.html
22. http://www.cognivue.com/technology.php
23. Kisačanin B, Nikolić Z (2010) Algorithmic and software techniques for embedded vision on programmable processors. Signal Process Image Commun 25:352–362
24. TDA2x SOC: www.ti.com/pro-ap-tda2x-b-lp
25. McCall JC, Trivedi MM (2006) Video-based lane estimation and tracking for driver assistance: survey, system and evaluation. IEEE Trans Intell Transp Syst 7(1):20–37

26. Loy G, Zelinsky A (2003) A fast radial symmetry transform for detecting points of interest. IEEE Trans Pattern Anal Mach Intell 25(8):959–973
27. Mathias M, Timofte R, Benenson R, Gool LV (2013) Traffic sign recognition—how far are we from the solution. In: Proceedings of IEEE international joint conference on neural networks (IJCNN 2013), Dallas, August 2013
28. Dollar P, Wojek C, Schiele B, Perona P (2009) Pedestrian detection: a benchmark. In: CVPR, Miami, Florida
29. Enzweiler M, Gavrila DM (2009) Monocular pedestrian detection: survey and experiments. IEEE Trans Pattern Anal Mach Intell 31(12):2179–2195
30. Geronimo D, Lopez AM, Sappa AD, Graf T (2010) Survey of pedestrian detection for advanced driver assistance systems. IEEE Trans Pattern Anal Mach Intell 32(7):1239–1258
31. Keller C, Dang T, Joos A, Rabe C, Fritz H, Gavrila DM (2011) Active pedestrian safety by automatic braking and evasive steering. IEEE Trans Intell Transp Syst 12(4):1292–1304
32. Stein F (2004) Efficient computation of optical flow using the census transform. In: DAGM-symposium
33. Müller T, Rabe C, Rannacher J, Franke U, Mester R (2011) Illumination robust dense optical flow using census signatures. In: Proceedings of the 33th DAGM symposium, September 2011
34. Brox T, Malik J (2011) Large displacement optical flow: descriptor matching in variational motion estimation. IEEE Trans Pattern Anal Mach Intell 33(3):500–513
35. Rudin LI, Osher S, Fatemi E (1992) Nonlinear total variation based noise removal algorithms. Phys D 60:259–268
36. Wedel A, Pock T, Zach C, Bischof H, Cremers D (2009) Statistical and geometrical approaches to visual motion analysis, chap, an improved algorithm for TV-L1 optical flow. Springer,Berlin, pp 23–45
37. Chambolle A (2004) An algorithm for total variation minimization and applications. Math Imaging Vis 20(1):89–97
38. Muller T, Rannacher J, Rabe C, Franke U (2011) Feature- and depth-supported modified total variation optical flow for 3D motion field estimation in real scenes. In: IEEE conference on computer vision and pattern recognition (CVPR)
39. Keller C, Enzweiler M, Rohrbach M, Llorca D-F, Schnörr C, Gavrila DM (2011) The benefits of dense stereo for pedestrian detection. IEEE Trans Intell Transp Syst 12(4):1096–1106
40. Shashua A, Gdalyahu Y, Hayun G (2004) Pedestrian detection for driving assistance systems: single-frame classification and system level performance. In: Proceeding of IEEE intelligence vehicle symposium
41. Woodfill JI et al (2006) The TYZX deepsea g2 vision system, a taskable, embedded stereo camera. In: Embedded computer vision, workshop, pp 126–132
42. Hirschmueller H (2005) Accurate and efficient stereo processing by semi-global matching and mutual information. In: Proceedings of international conference on computer vision and pattern recognition 05, vol 2, pp 807–814. San Diego, June 2005
43. Gehrig S, Eberli F, Meyer T (2009) A real time low power stereo vision engine using semiglobal matching. In: ICVS, pp 134–143
44. Gehrig SK, Rabe C (2010) Real-time semi-global matching on the CPU. In: Proceedings of the IEEE computer vision and pattern recognition workshops, San Francisco, pp 85–92, June 2010
45. Franke U, Rabe C, Badino H, Gehrig S (2005) 6D-Vision—fusion of motion and stereo for robust environment perception. In: DAGM symposium 2005, Vienna, pp 216–223
46. Kisa čanin B, Dedeoglu G, Moore D, Sharma V, Nikolić Z (2009) DSP software libraries for automotive vision applications. In: Proceedings of the 2009 DSP for in-vehicle systems and safety workshop
47. Kisačanin B (2008) Integral image optimizations for embedded vision applications. In: Proceedings of the 2008 southwest symposium on image analysis and interpretation
48. Nikolić Z (2008) Implementation considerations for automotive vision systems on a fixed point DSP. In: Kisačanin B, Bhattacharyya SS, Chai S (eds) Embedded computer vision. Springer, London

49. Kisačanin B, Schonfeld D (1994) A fast thresholded linear convolution representation of morphological operations. IEEE Trans Image Process 3:455–457
50. Petry E (2010) How to upgrade SPICE-compliant process for functional safety. In: 10th international SPICE conference, Pisa, Italy, 18th to 20th May
51. Broggi A, Bertozzi M, Fascioli A, Conte G (1999) Automatic vehicle guidance: the experience of the argo vehicle. World Scientific, Singapore. ISBN 981-02-3720-0
52. Checkoway S, McCoy D, Kantor B, Anderson D, Shacham H, Savage S, Koscher K, Czeskis A, Roesner F, Kohno T (2011) Comprehensive experimental analyses of automotive attack surfaces, USENIX Security, 10–12 August
53. Raya M, Hubaux JP (2007) Securing vehicular ad hoc networks. J Comput Secur 15:39–68 (IOS Press)
54. Rublee E, Rabaud V, Konolige K, Bradsky G (2011) ORB: an efficient alternative to SIFT or SURF. In: International conference on vision, Barcelona
55. https://www.youtube.com/watch?v=mEpPww4AXMI
56. http://www-nrd.nhtsa.dot.gov/Pubs/810803.PDF
57. CARSENSE, IST 1999–12224, Sensing of car environment at low speed driving, final report, deliverable D25, report version F, 2002
58. http://invent-online.de/en/driver_assistance.html
59. http://www.ertico.com/prevent
60. Sankaran Jagadeesh, Hung Ching-Yu, Kisacanin Branislav (2014) Eve: a flexible SIMD coprocessor for embedded vision applications. J Sign Process Syst 75:95–107

Part II
State of the Art

Chapter 4
Computer Vision for Micro Air Vehicles

Roland Brockers, Martin Humenberger, Yoshi Kuwata, Larry Matthies and Stephan Weiss

Abstract Autonomous operation of small UAVs in cluttered environments requires three important foundations: fast and accurate knowledge about position in the world for control; obstacle detection and avoidance for safe flight; and all of this has to be executed in real-time onboard the vehicle. This is a challenge for micro air vehicles, since their limited payload demands small, lightweight, and low-power sensors and processing units, favoring vision-based solutions that run on small embedded computers equipped with smart phone-based processors. In the following chapter, we present the JPL autonomous navigation framework for micro air vehicles to address these challenges. Our approach enables power-up-and-go deployment in highly cluttered environments without GPS, using information from an IMU and a single downward-looking camera for pose estimation, and a forward looking stereo camera system for disparity-based obstacle detection and avoidance. As an example of a high-level navigation task that builds on these autonomous capabilities, we introduce our approach for autonomous landing on elevated flat surfaces, such as rooftops, using only monocular vision inputs from the downward-looking camera.

4.1 Introduction

Miniature rotorcrafts are an ideal platform for exploration and reconnaissance missions, since they can operate in highly cluttered environmentsforest, close to the ground) or confined spaces (indoors, collapsed buildings, caves) and allow with

R. Brockers (✉) · Y. Kuwata · L. Matthies · S. Weiss
Jet Propulsion Laboratory, California Institute of Technology, Pasadena, USA
e-mail: roland.brockers@jpl.nasa.gov

Y. Kuwata
e-mail: kuwata@alumni.mit.edu

L. Matthies
e-mail: lhm@jpl.nasa.gov

S. Weiss
e-mail: stephan.weiss@ieee.org

M. Humenberger
AIT Austrian Institute of Technology, Vienna, Austria
e-mail: martin.humenberger@ait.ac.at

B. Kisačanin and M. Gelautz (eds.), *Advances in Embedded Computer Vision*,
Advances in Computer Vision and Pattern Recognition,
DOI 10.1007/978-3-319-09387-1_4

their hovering ability to position a sensor payload in 3D space only constrained by the mission profile. However, in order to be deployable, a human–machine interface which allows an operator to easily control such a platform is key. The ingredient that most facilitates operation is autonomy, since autonomous vehicles can execute high-level commands without any further human interaction.

Thus, it requires the vehicle to know its position within the environment, and to have a capability to avoid collisions in flight and during takeoff and landing. All processes enabling such autonomy have to be implemented onboard, without requiring any external sensor input.

Miniature rotorcrafts (e.g., quadrotors) offer very high maneuverability and agility but require high rate of control because of their natural instability. Subsequently, sensor signals and images used for accurate pose estimation and for control input need to be processed fast. Since the platform has to be self-contained and payload capacities on micro air vehicles (MAVs) are in general very limited, only light-weight and low-power sensors and processing units can be used on-board the vehicle. This favors vision-based solutions that use small light-weight cameras and microelectromechanical systems (MEMS) inertial sensors. As recent developments in multicore smartphone processors are driven by the same size, weight, and power (SWaP) constraints, MAVs can directly benefit from new products that provide more computational resources at lower power budgets and low weight. This enables miniaturization of aerial platforms that are able to perform navigation tasks fully autonomously. In the subsequent sections, we introduce our autonomous navigation framework with focus on pose estimation, collision avoidance, and an example for a high-level navigation task that builds on these lower level functions: autonomous landing.

Viable solution for GPS-independent pose estimation from visual and inertial sensor inputs have been proposed in the literature [29, 41]. However, a major algorithmic challenge is to process sensor information at high rate to provide vehicle control and high-level tasks with real-time information about position and vehicle states.

In Sect. 4.2, we approach the issue of processing the vast camera information in real-time, rendering the camera a 6 degrees of freedom (DoF) pose sensor or a 3DOF velocity sensor. We discuss two methods representing two flavors of vision-based MAV state estimation. The first is a *map-based* approach using feature matches over long periods. The second is a *map free* and thus inherently fail-safe approach without using any kind of feature history. We will discuss that the first approach is more suitable for local drift-free navigation, while the latter is useful as a fall-back to keep the MAV airborne if a map corruption occurs. We will show that such an approach can quickly stabilize a thrown MAV and keep it at a constant heading and distance to the scene even though only two consecutive images and no feature history are used.

Once pose estimation is available, higher level autonomous navigation tasks which leverage and require this information can be executed. Examples for such tasks are: obstacle avoidance, autonomous landing, ingress, surveillance, exploration, and other.

In order to maneuver safely in highly cluttered environments and at low altitude, a MAV needs the ability to detect and avoid obstacles in its flight path autonomously.

Sophisticated solutions using active sensors (lidar, radar, etc.) exist for large aircraft, but they are in general unsuitable for small platforms with limited power, payload, and computational resources. To cope with these limitations, we developed a novel stereo vision-based obstacle avoidance approach, that is especially suited for onboard implementation on small aerial vehicles. Our approach is inspired by bird vision [36], using a forward-looking stereo camera system to provide depth information in the direction of flight, that can be expanded by range estimates from peripheral monocular optical flow. In Sect. 4.3, we explain our stereo vision-based obstacle avoidance system, that is designed for fast execution with small memory footprint by using: (1) a polar-perspective world representation in disparity space; (2) configuration space (C-space) expansion in image space; and implements (3) collision checking as a z-buffer like operation in disparity space. For motion planning, we use a closed-loop RRT approach that incorporates a vehicle model to plan local avoidance maneuvers in full 3D, which we believe to be scalable for flights at higher speeds.

As an example for a high-level navigation task, we explain autonomous landing with our MAV platform in Sect. 4.4. Autonomous landing is especially important not only for safety reasons, but also for mission endurance. Small rotorcrafts inherently suffer from overall short mission endurance, since payload restrictions do not allow carrying large batteries. For surveillance or exploration tasks, endurance can be greatly improved by not requiring the platform to be airborne at all time. Instead, such tasks may even favor a steady quiet observer at a strategic location (e.g., high vantage points like rooftops or on top of telephone poles)—still with the ability to move if required—which also could include recharging while in sleep mode (e.g., from solar cells).

4.1.1 Embedded Hardware Platforms

To evaluate the performance of our algorithms on an embedded system, we tested our framework with two different MAV platforms: an Asctec Pelican quadrotor equipped with an Asctec Mastermind flight computer (Core2Duo, 2×1.86 GHz CPU [4]) (total weight: ~1.3 kg), and an Asctec Hummingbird quadrotor equipped with either an Odroid-X2 or a modified Odroid-U2 flight computer (total weight: ~500 g; Fig. 4.1).

Both Asctec MAV platforms share the same low-level autopilot boards that include a MEMS IMU, and were equipped with a downward-looking Matrix Vision camera (mvBlueFOX-MLC200wG, CMOS, 752×480, grayscale, global shutter, up to 90 fps, 18.3 g with 100 FOV lens) that is connected to the flight computer.

The Odroid board (manufactured by Hardkernel [21]) is based on the Samsung Exynos 4412 system-on-a-chip (SoC)—a quadcore microcontroller for mobile applications that provides four ARM-cortex A9 for parallel computation, while only consuming 2.2 W (CPU only). For our implementation, we removed all non-necessary hardware components from the U2 in order to save weight, which included various connectors and the original heat sink. The final weight of the U2 flight computer was 12 g including the SD card which hosts the operation system.

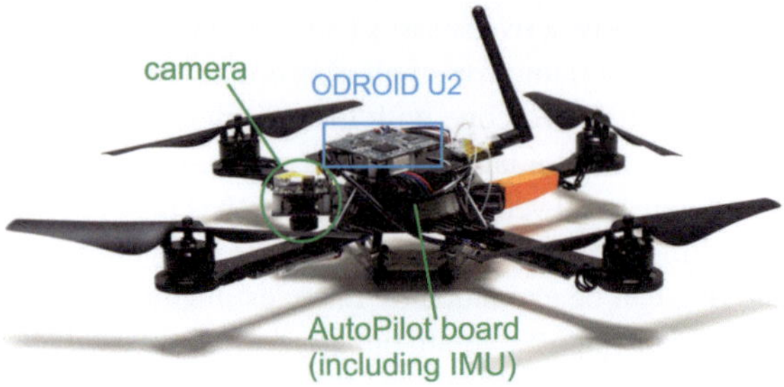

Fig. 4.1 Asctec Hummingbird with Odroid-U2 flight computer mounted on *top*

4.2 Pose Estimation

We start with explaining our pose estimation framework that is running onboard our quadrotors only using inputs from a camera and an IMU. We first present the related work followed by the detailed description of our two approaches and conclude with experimental results using the embedded hardware.

4.2.1 Related Work

Autonomous flights in unknown environments exclude the use of motion capture systems for MAV pose estimation as done for example in [39]. Furthermore, using GPS is not always reliable due to effects such as shadowing or multipath propagation in city-like environments. Therefore, commonly used sensors for GPS-independent MAV state estimation are stereo [38] and monocular cameras [63] as well as laser scanners [57]. Since heavy sensors cannot be used on low SWaP platforms and additional payload directly reduces endurance, monocular visual-inertial state estimators might be the most viable choice for MAVs.

Processing the vast information of the camera is a computationally complex task and cannot be processed at high rate. Multicopter MAVs require fast and precise control (and thus state estimates) at all times because the systems are inherently unstable. Hence, we propose to fuse the visual information with high-rate inertial cues from an IMU. We can categorize such a fusion into *loosely-coupled* and *tightly-coupled*. The loosely-coupled philosophy treats the inertial and visual units as two separate modules running at different rates and exchanging information, while the tightly-coupled paradigm combines both sources of information into a single, optimal filter. In general, loosely-coupled approaches are much less computationally expensive, since they use the low-dimensional processed visual information as measurement rather than every single feature. For this reason, we discuss a loosely-coupled Extended Kalman Filter (EKF) approach in this work. Among the loosely-coupled approaches are the works of [2, 3, 15, 19, 42, 51, 67], while among the tightly-coupled ones are those of [8, 13, 24, 27–29, 33, 34, 47, 58].

A filter-based approach not only allows to estimate the pose of the vehicle for control but also can estimate calibration parameters such as IMU biases, camera-IMU extrinsics, and visual drifts. Such *self-calibration* is crucial for long-term missions and renders the system *power-up-and-go* without the need of pre-mission calibration procedures. With a *map-free* inherently fail-safe vision module as we discuss below, it is further possible to eliminate the visual initialization procedure and failure modes. This literally renders the MAV *throw-and-go* as the MAV can be powered on and immediately be thrown in the air to deploy it.

4.2.2 Visual-Inertial State Estimation Approaches

A camera can be used in various ways to compute its pose in 3D space. We will discuss two approaches which can be classified into two main categories which we call *map-based* and *map free*. The first is a key frame-based visual odometry approach using a local map to estimate the arbitrarily scaled 6DoF of the camera. The second approach does not use temporal information or features (i.e., a local map) but only uses the current optical flow measurement to estimate the 3DoF arbitrarily scaled camera velocity vector, 3DoF attitude of the MAV, and distance to the current scene.

4.2.2.1 Map-Based Approach

The first approach is described in detail in [63, 67] which shows that, fusing with an IMU, we can navigate a MAV in large environments and high altitude with visual and inertial cues only. Because of robustness, real-time performance, and position accuracy, the keyframe based solution proposed in [31] was selected and tailored to run on our embedded architecture. Our implementation uses a downward-looking camera and executes a sliding-window, vision-based self localization and mapping (VSLAM) feature tracking approach to extract pose estimates from visual inputs, maintaining constant computational complexity. This method is viable for large outdoor environments and long missions—only limited by the battery lifetime and not by processing power nor memory. We show how the proposed algorithm in [63] can be implemented on a 12 g, 5 W processing unit while still running at 50 Hz. This renders even a very light-weight MAV truly power-on-and-go.

The 6DOF pose of the VSLAM algorithm is fused with the inertial measurements of an IMU using an Extended Kalman Filter (EKF). More details are given in [63, 67]. An EKF framework consists of a prediction and an update step. The computational load required by these two steps is distributed among the different units of the MAV as described in [64]. The state of the filter is composed of the position $p_{\mathrm{w}}^{\mathrm{i}}$, the attitude quaternion $q_{\mathrm{w}}^{\mathrm{i}}$, and the velocity $v_{\mathrm{w}}^{\mathrm{i}}$of the IMU in the world frame. The gyroscope and accelerometer biases b_{ω} and b_{a} as well as the missing-scale factor λ are also included in the state vector. For completeness, the extrinsic calibration parameters describing the relative rotation $q_{\mathrm{i}}^{\mathrm{s}}$ and position $p_{\mathrm{i}}^{\mathrm{s}}$ between the IMU and the camera frames were also added. This yields a 24-element state vector X:

$$X = \{p_{\mathrm{w}}^{\mathrm{i}^{\mathrm{T}}} v_{\mathrm{w}}^{\mathrm{i}^{\mathrm{T}}} q_{\mathrm{w}}^{\mathrm{i}^{\mathrm{T}}} b_{\omega}^{\mathrm{T}} b_{\mathrm{a}}^{\mathrm{T}} \lambda\ p_{\mathrm{i}}^{\mathrm{s}}\ q_{\mathrm{i}}^{\mathrm{s}}\}. \tag{4.1}$$

Details about the EKF prediction and update equations can be found in [63]. A nonlinear observability analysis [62] reveals that all state variables are observable, including the intersensor calibration parameters $p_{\mathrm{i}}^{\mathrm{s}}$ and $q_{\mathrm{i}}^{\mathrm{s}}$. Note that the VSLAM pose estimates are prone to drift in position, attitude, and scale with respect to the world-fixed reference frame. Since these quantities become observable when fusing with an IMU (notably roll, pitch, and scale), gravity-aligned metric navigation becomes possible even in long-term missions. This is true as long as the robot excites the IMU accelerometer and gyroscopes sufficiently as discussed in [29]. Additionally, since the gravity vector measured by the IMU is always vertically aligned during hovering, the MAV will not crash due to gravity misalignment—even during long-term operations.

4.2.2.2 Map-Free Approach

The map-based approach described above is locally drift free. However, it requires to redetect the same features over several camera frames. This is prone to failure and mismatches, and can lead to corrupting the local map which in turn can lead to a crash of the MAV because of a wrong state estimate based on the corrupted map.

In [65, 66], we present an approach which only uses two consecutive camera images and inertial cues for MAV navigation. This inertial-optical flow (IOF)-based approach does not use any kind of history that can be corrupted and does not require to find the same features in later frames. In [66], we show that we still can estimate the metric velocity of the MAV, its metric distance to the scene, and its full attitude (roll, pitch, yaw) drift free while maintaining a self-calibrating system. That is, in addition to the states used for control, we can estimate the IMU biases and the camera-IMU extrinsics, and do not need specific calibration steps prior to launch. In fact, in this work, we show that this state estimation is robust and fast enough such that the MAV can be deployed by simply tossing it into the air rendering it a *throw-and-go* system. The state vector

$$\chi = \{p_{\mathrm{w}}^{\mathrm{i}} v_{\mathrm{w}}^{\mathrm{i}}\ q_{\mathrm{w}}^{\mathrm{i}}\ b_{\omega}\ b_{\mathrm{a}}\ \Lambda\ p_{\mathrm{i}}^{\mathrm{c}}\ q_{\mathrm{i}}^{\mathrm{c}}\ \alpha\} \tag{4.2}$$

contains the IMU-centered MAV position $p_{\mathrm{w}}^{\mathrm{i}}$, velocity $v_{\mathrm{w}}^{\mathrm{i}}$ and attitude $q_{\mathrm{w}}^{\mathrm{i}}$ with respect to the world frame. It also contains the IMU biases on gyroscopes b_{ω} and accelerometers b_{a}, the common visual scale factor Λ and the 6D transformation between the IMU and the camera in translation $p_{\mathrm{i}}^{\mathrm{c}}$ and rotation $q_{\mathrm{i}}^{\mathrm{c}}$. The system can additionally estimate the inclination α of the scene plane it currently observes (see Fig. 4.2).

A nonlinear observability analysis reveals that all states are observable except two dimensions in position. This is expected since optical flow and inertial measurements

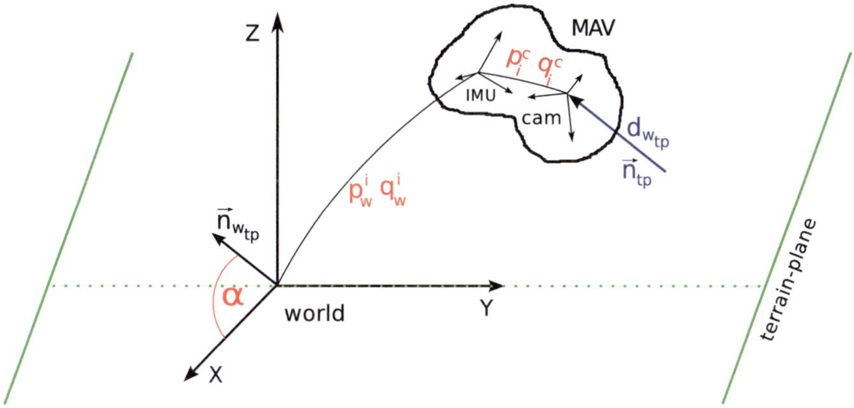

Fig. 4.2 Frame setup and state definition for the EKF framework. Without loss of generality, we can lock the gravity-aligned world y-axis along the terrain plane. The terrain plane normal vector can then be described as $n_{w_{tp}} = [\cos(\alpha)\ 0\ \sin(\alpha)]^T$ in the world frame. The *red* values are states estimated in the EKF framework, whereas the *blue* values are the scaled visual measurements normalized with our proposed approach aid of the terrain plane

only allow to estimate the distance to the scene. If this scene is inclined with respect to gravity, the system additionally can estimate the vehicle's heading with respect to the scene. Motion in parallel to the scene plane, however, is unobservable. We could overcome this issue and implement position hold by a place recognition or feature-tracking method. However, this would include a feature history and would defeat the purpose of a fail-safe algorithm.

Without having any type of history, an erroneous measurement will get rejected in the EKF update but would not corrupt a map, i.e., the next measurement will be independent of the previous one which is in line with the EKF assumptions. Such an inherently fail-safe approach allows the MAV to move very quickly and in an agile way since erroneous measurements get rejected and simply the next good measurement is taken into the filter process.

4.2.3 Embedded Implementation

While the previous sections described our algorithms, this section focuses on their implementation, parameter selection, and design choices on the embedded computing architecture on a MAV. To evaluate performance differences and the influence of weight reduction, we implemented our algorithms on the two different MAV platforms mentioned in Sect. 4.1.1, an Asctec Pelican quadrotor equipped with an Asctec Mastermind flight computer and an Asctec Hummingbird quadrotor equipped with an Odroid-U2 flight computer (Table 4.1). This renders even a very lightweight MAV truly throw-and-go.

Table 4.1 SWaP performance of tested computing platforms

Platform	Size (footprint) (mm)	Weight (g)	Power consumption (W)	Cores	Vision front-end frame rate (Hz)	CPU load (%)	Workload (%)
Asctec mastermind	144 × 135	300	30	2	30	59	30
Odroid-X2 dev. board (4412) including heat sink	90 × 94	122	8	4	30	125	31
Odroid-U2 (4412) stripped down version	48 × 52	12	5	4	30	125	31

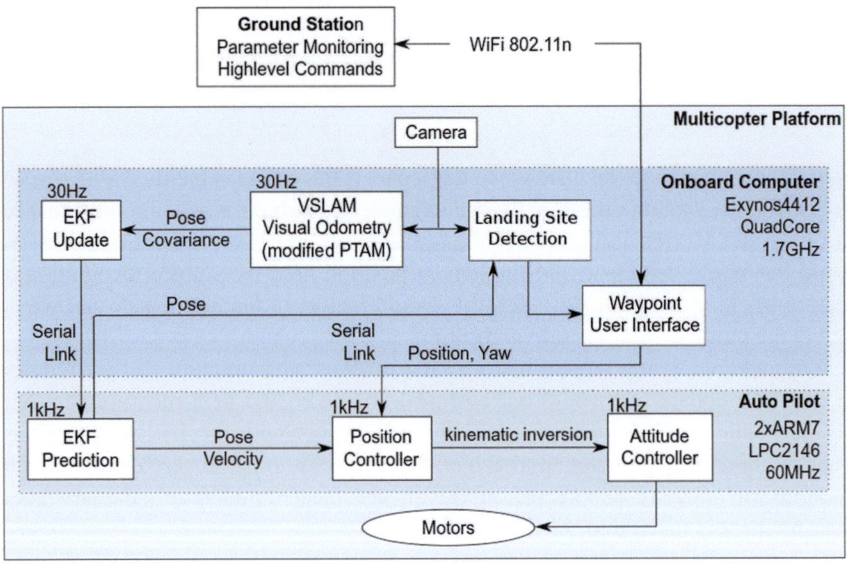

Fig. 4.3 System overview of the vision-aided pose estimation frame work

4.2.3.1 Map-Based Approach

Figure 4.3 gives an overview of the distributed implementation of our approach on the vehicle. All computational-expensive components are executed on the high-level flight computer, which includes VSLAM and pose filter update (EKF-update) as well as landing site detection. The EKF-update is passed down to the prediction loop that is executed on the autopilot board for efficiency reasons: the prediction loop, which includes IMU integration, and the position controller that uses the estimated pose to control the vehicle, both run at 1 kHz on a dedicated ARM7 microcontroller.

We ported the initial estimator implementation from the Asctec Mastermind to the U2 by using system specific changes in order to speed up the execution on the SoC. We used a highly ARM-customized Ubuntu version as operating system and Robot Operating System (ROS) [49] for interprocess communication. Our VSLAM implementation primarily consist of a *tracking* and a *mapping* part which we enforce to be executed on separate cores. *Tracking* is the most critical part, since it yields instantaneous pose measurements which are used to generate filter updates. Therefore, running this part on a dedicated core ensures uninterrupted pose handling at all time. *Mapping* is responsible for pose refinement and windowed bundle adjustment, and is thus less time critical. Note that the adjustments are refinements and we do not use global loop closure techniques. This avoids large and abrupt pose changes. Since the mapping task runs at a lower frequency and is less time critical, it shares its dedicated core with other system tasks. After optimization, the vision front end produced visual pose estimates at a stable 50 Hz rate.

4.2.3.2 Map-Free Approach

Our inertial-optical flow (IOF)-based approach is designed to keep the MAV airborne at all times in a fail-safe manner. Thus, it has to have low-computational cost requiring low system resources and it has to be fail safe.

We implement IOF on our 12 g Odroid U2 platform and use similar NEON optimization instructions than for the above explained map-based approach. We use the same (FAST) feature extraction method but simplified the matching process by not warping patches. Since we only use two consecutive images at high frame rate, the distortion is small and warping is not required.

Computing the normalized camera velocity vector requires normalizing all optical flow vectors with their scene depth. As detailed in [65], this normalization uses a computational complex SVD per feature i including the optical flow $\dot{\mathbf{x}}_i(t)$, the feature direction vector $\mathbf{x}_i(t)$, and the camera velocity direction vector $\mathbf{v}(t)$. The unknowns are the feature scale factor and scale factor change $\dot{\lambda}_i(t)$, $\lambda_i(t)$ and velocity normalization factor η:

$$\dot{\lambda}_i(t)\mathbf{x}_i(t) + \lambda_i(t)\dot{\mathbf{x}}_i(t) = \eta\mathbf{v}(t). \tag{4.3}$$

which can be stacked to a feature×features matrix M containing optical flow and velocity vector measurements ($\mathbf{x}_i(t)$, $\dot{\mathbf{x}}_i(t)$, $\mathbf{v}(t)$) and λ is the solution vector containing a scale factor per feature ($\dot{\lambda}_i(t)$, $\lambda_i(t)$) and a scale factor η for the velocity vector. λ is a solution up to an arbitrary global scale (which will be estimated in the EKF using the IMU). Thus without loss of generality, we can set $\eta = 1$ and use the block sparsity of M to efficiently compute the SVD in a block-wise parallel fashion on the Odroid-U2. The optimized code runs at 50 Hz with an image resolution of 572×480 (WVGA) on the Odroid-U2 using only about 20 % of the overall computation capacity of system.

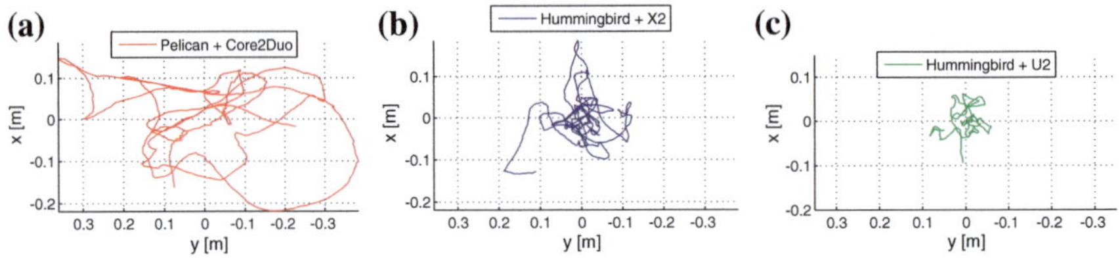

Fig. 4.4 Hover performance of the Pelican with Mastermind (**a**), the Hummingbird with a heavier Odroid-X2 evaluation board (**b**), the Hummingbird with modified U2 (**c**)

4.2.4 Experimental Evaluation: Map Based

To evaluate the influence of the reduced weight on the control stability of the platform, we executed a position hold maneuver with all three vehicle/flight computer configurations, where the MAV was controlled only with position estimates from our pose estimation software (the vision front end was again executed at a frame rate of 30 Hz).

Neglecting the influence of different flight performances of the two quadrotor systems, the reduced gross weight resulted in significantly better control performance: the hovering ellipse was reduced from ±35 cm for the heavy Asctec Pelican with Mastermind (RMS(x y z) = [8.3 cm 15.8 cm 1.5 cm]) to about ±15 cm for the Hummingbird with the X2 (RMS(x y z) = [5.4 cm 5.7 cm 1 cm]) and to ±7 cm for the Hummingbird with the final stripped down version of the U2 (RMS(x y z) = [2.9 cm 3.0 cm 0.8 cm]) (Fig. 4.4). Extensive tests in different environments were done in [63].

4.2.5 Experimental Evaluation: Map Free

We showed in [66] that we can control the MAV with IOF drift free in metric velocity, full attitude, and metric scene distance. Being able to keep the MAV constant in heading and scene distance is crucial for automatic initialization of more powerful algorithms (e.g., VSLAM) to control the vehicle in full 6DoF pose. Our IOF approach is sufficiently robust to estimate the vehicle pose even in drastic motion as it occurs when tossing the MAV in the air.

We start our IOF-based state estimation at $t = 38$ s and toss it at $t = 42$. The 4 s of "initialization" are sufficient to stabilize the MAV after the throw. After about 1 s the vehicle stabilizes already in attitude and in velocity. The convergence of the scene depth requires about 6 s longer. This is due to the wrong initialization of the metric scale factor which generally converges slower than the other states in the system.

Once all states are converged and the vehicle fully stabilized (after about 7 s in the test in Fig. 4.5), we have time to initialize a full VSLAM system as shown in [65].

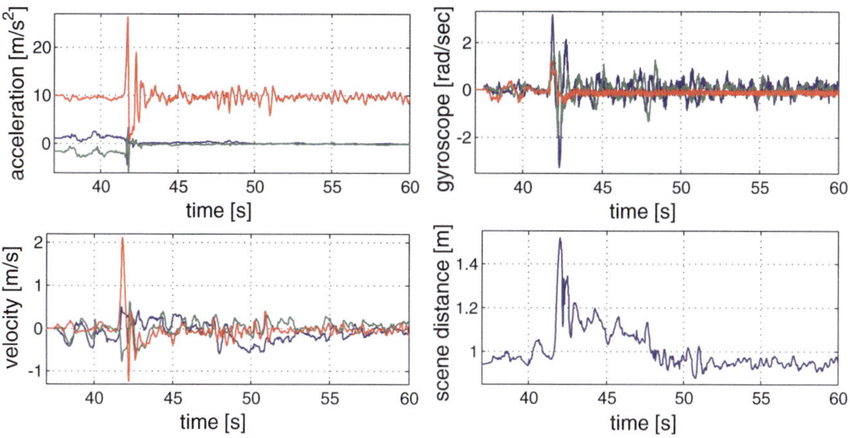

Fig. 4.5 Acceleration and velocity in *x* (*blue*), *y* (*green*) and *z* (*red*) when throwing the MAV in the air. At the throw, the MAV experiences an acceleration of $16.5\,\text{m/s}^2$ (*top left*). The angular velocities when throwing the MAV rise to 190 °/s (*top right*). And the velocity rises up to 2.3 m/s (*bottom left*). The scene depth is estimated correctly at all times (*bottom right*) and that the MAV can maintain it drift free after convergence. This allows good initialization of a subsequent, more powerful VSLAM algorithm

4.3 Obstacle Detection and Avoidance

The ability to sense obstacles and avoid collisions autonomously is a critical safety component for MAVs flying in cluttered environment and at low altitude (Fig. 4.6). Driven by payload and processing constraints and the requirement to accurately detect every obstacle within collision range, new algorithms have to be developed that reflect the limited capabilities of such small platforms. In the following section, we present our obstacle avoidance subsystem that uses stereovision for range perception, and a polar-perspective, inverse-range world representation (disparity space) for collision checking. The perception system is used by a closed-loop RRT motion planner, to navigate around detected obstacles, incorporating vehicle dynamics.

4.3.1 Related Work

Significant progress has been made recently on deliberative obstacle avoidance using active optical range sensors, such as single-axis scanning lidar and RGB-D structured light [5, 56]. The lack of a second axis for scanning lidar is a significant limitation and structured light sensors are ineffective in sunlight. Very compact, electronically beam-steered radar with large maximum range is under development for this application, but again has a single-axis scan [52]. Optical flow can cover a wide field of view and has been used for reactive obstacle avoidance [14, 25]; however, this

Fig. 4.6 Asctec Pelican quadrotor flying through forest

only provides information when the aircraft is moving, and poor estimation of time to collision near the focus of expansion limits the ability to perceive obstacles in the direction of motion. Stereo vision can provide 3D perception around the focus of expansion whether the aircraft is moving or not, but so far with relatively short look-ahead distance [18]. Stereo and optical flow have been used together in purely reactive obstacle avoidance based on sparse perception with point features [23].

The most common obstacle representations for MAV are image space data products that serve reactive obstacle avoidance [14, 25, 50] and Cartesian voxel data structures that serve deliberative planning [5, 18, 56]. Reactive obstacle avoidance with image space data structures use very little memory and computation, but have limited ability to reason about 3D structure and vehicle dynamics. Cartesian voxel data structures enable much greater 3D reasoning, have mature temporal fusion algorithms for error reduction, and have been used to plan high speed, aggressive maneuvers [48]; however, they use much more memory and computing time. Uniform voxel sizes are also problematic for representing both very near and very far objects, which can lead to more complex, multiresolution data structures. Polar representations parameterized by azimuth and range have been used in a few efforts because they naturally capture range-dependent variations in angular and range resolution [7, 68]; however, these efforts were only tested in simulation and [68] only represented sparse, discrete obstacles. Some stereo vision-based navigation systems for ground vehicles have had characteristics that are interesting for MAVs. A simple version of collision testing and path planning with the stereo disparity image was done in [44]. A 2D polar grid-based representation in the ground plane was used in [6], where the radial axis was parameterized as inverse range; this matched the angular and range resolution characteristics of stereo and gave a compact representation of all space from a minimum range to infinity. This was used to represent and reason about distant obstacles, while a 2D Cartesian map was used for nearby obstacles. Inverse range is equivalent to nearness fields that have been used for reactive MAV obstacle avoidance with optical flow [25].

Reactive obstacle avoidance controllers have been based on image space nearness fields computed from optical flow [25] and trained from human behavior via imitation learning [50]. Recent deliberative planners have used techniques including anytime, incremental A* for nonsymmetric vehicles moving slowly in cluttered spaces [35] and RRT* with path optimization [48] and lattice search with precomputed motion primitives [45] for fast, aggressive maneuvers.

4.3.2 Vision-Based Autonomous Navigation System

Traditional deliberative motion planning approaches usually implement a 3D grid-based world representation to expand trajectories and check for collisions [5, 18, 56], and more or less assume that a planned trajectory would be accurately followed by a relatively slow moving vehicle. Applying such an approach to a micro air vehicle generates several issues. Computational resources usually do not permit processing large 3D grid representations in reasonable time, and the agility of the system requires a complex planning approach which incorporates additional vehicle states to reflect fast vehicle dynamics. In our approach, we introduce two key features to mitigate these issues. To reduce complexity of path verification, our system uses an image-based world representation generated from stereo vision with a fixed memory footprint, and to allow planning in a low dimensional planning space, trajectories are planned over closed-loop vehicle dynamics.

Figure 4.7 gives an overview of our system architecture. 3D perception follows a stereo vision pipeline. When images are acquired with a forward-looking stereo camera head, a stereo disparity map is calculated with a real-time stereo algorithm, and then expanded into configuration space (C-space), which is used for collision checking. Stereo, C space expansion, and collision checking all take place within an image-based representation: 3D world points are characterized by their polar-perspective image coordinates in the frame of the reference camera and an assigned stereo disparity value (disparity space). The resulting 2.5D inverse-depth representation is very well suited for fast obstacle avoidance: close range where accurate object

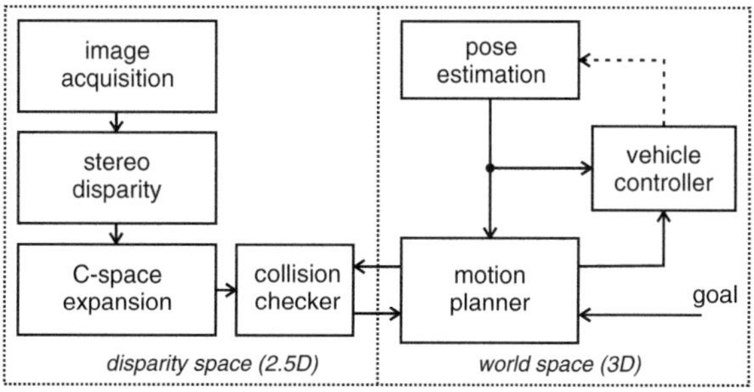

Fig. 4.7 Autonomous navigation system architecture

reconstruction is essential, is resolved with the highest accuracy, whereas accuracy for far distances decreases. At the same time, the polar-perspective character of an image-based representation significantly reduces the memory foot print of a world representation, making this method suitable for small hardware platforms.

The vehicle navigation system follows a standard control loop scheme: the motion planner module plans 3D vehicle trajectories in world space based on vehicle pose and a predefined goal input, and issues control commands to a vehicle controller, which maneuvers the vehicle. For collision checking, 3D trajectory segments are projected into disparity space and verified using the C-space map.

In our simulated experiments, we use simulated vehicle positions as pose estimation inputs. Our onboard implementation uses a vision-aided pose estimation approach [65] to provide pose. As any pose estimation framework on a real system will incorporate pose errors, we evaluate the robustness of our planning approach in Sect. 4.3.7.

In the following, we describe the individual parts of the approach in more detail.

4.3.3 Image-Based Collision Checking

For efficiency reasons, collision checking is performed directly in disparity space. When a new disparity image is obtained from stereo, C-space expansion is applied in the disparity domain, allowing to treat the MAV as a single point in space for planning purposes. During motion planning, small trajectory segments are verified by projecting them into disparity space and comparing the reconstructed disparity values along the segment with the corresponding C-space disparity values to detect collisions.

4.3.3.1 C-Space Expansion

C-space expansion is implemented as an image processing function (Fig. 4.8). To illustrate this operation, we first project a pixel of the stereo disparity map $p(u, v, d)$ into world coordinates using the stereo base b_s and the focal length f (in pixels), assuming rectified images and a disparity map that corresponds to the left camera view:

$$z_{\mathrm{w}} = -f b_{\mathrm{s}}/d \tag{4.4}$$

$$P(x_{\mathrm{w}}, y_{\mathrm{w}}, z_{\mathrm{w}}) = [u z_{\mathrm{w}}/f, v z_{\mathrm{w}}/f, z_{\mathrm{w}}]^T \tag{4.5}$$

Considering an expansion sphere S around $P(x_{\mathrm{w}}, y_{\mathrm{w}}, z_{\mathrm{w}})$ with the expansion radius r_{v}, we calculate the position of the rectangle that perfectly hides the sphere from the viewpoint of the camera (Fig. 4.9) and assign to it a disparity value that corresponds to the distance to the point on S that is closest to the camera origin.

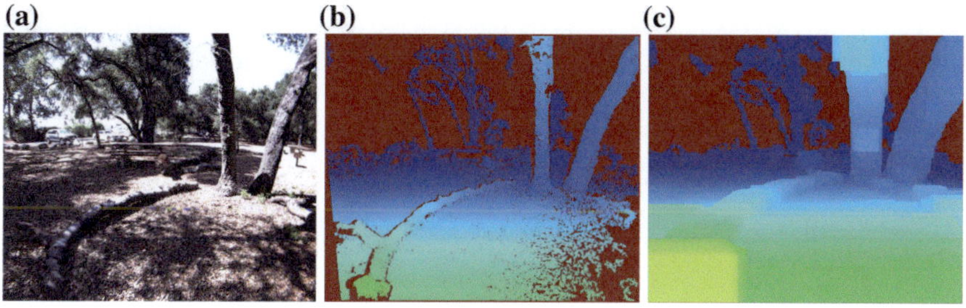

Fig. 4.8 C-space expansion in disparity space: original left view image (**a**), stereo disparity map (**b**), C-space expanded disparity map (**c**), pixels with warmer colors are located closer to the observer

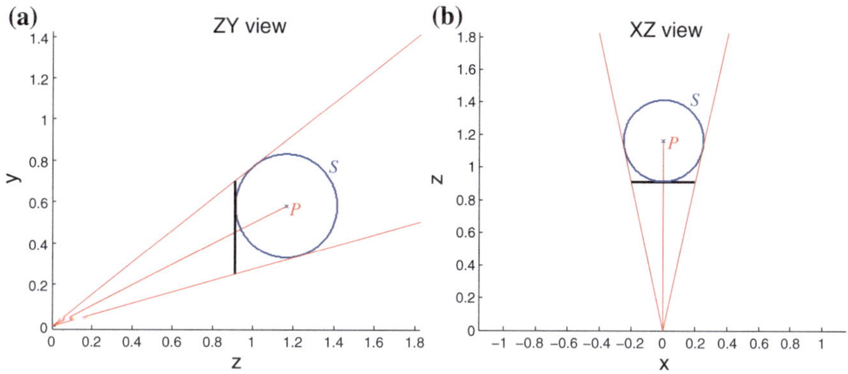

Fig. 4.9 C-space expansion example: The expansion *square* covers the expansion *sphere* from the camera view point (0, 0, 0) completely—its disparity is constant. **a** side view in ZY plane, **b** top down view in XZ plane

Technically, this expansion operation increases the expansion volume around a world point, since the correct projection of a sphere into the image is a circle, but this method has the advantage that the operation now is separable into two 1D operations—a horizontal expansion along image scan lines and a vertical expansion along image columns—reducing computational cost significantly.

The horizontal and vertical expansion limits depend on the viewing angle of each pixel and the expansion radius r_v. The horizontal viewing angle α to a point P in world coordinates is defined as

$$\alpha = \tan^{-1}(z_w/x_w) \tag{4.6}$$

and the horizontal angular field of view γ of the expansion sphere S around P is defined by the distance of P from the camera origin and the expansion radius r_v

$$\gamma = 2\alpha_1 = 2\sin^{-1}\left(r_v/\sqrt{z_w^2 + x_w^2}\right) \tag{4.7}$$

Projecting the two rays r_1 and r_2 along the viewing angles $\alpha + \alpha_1$ and $\alpha - \alpha_1$ back into the image defines the horizontal extension of the expansion sphere in the image

$$\begin{aligned} r_1 &= [r_{1_x}, r_{1_y}, r_{1_z}] = [z_w/\tan(\alpha + \alpha_1), y_w, z_w] \\ u_1 &= f r_{1_x}/r_{1_z} \end{aligned} \tag{4.8}$$

$$\begin{aligned} r_2 &= [r_{2_x}, r_{2_y}, r_{2_z}] = [z_w/\tan(\alpha - \alpha_1), y_w, z_w] \\ u_2 &= f r_{2_x}/r_{2_z} \end{aligned} \tag{4.9}$$

The vertical extension can be calculated similarly:

$$\beta = \tan^{-1}(z_w/y_w) \tag{4.10}$$

$$\beta_1 = \sin^{-1}\left(r_v/\sqrt{z_w^2 + y_w^2}\right) \tag{4.11}$$

$$\begin{aligned} r_3 &= [r_{3_x}, r_{3_y}, r_{3_z}] = [x_w, z_w/\tan(\beta + \beta_1), z_w] \\ v_1 &= f r_{3_y}/r_{3_z} \end{aligned} \tag{4.12}$$

$$\begin{aligned} r_4 &= [r_{4_x}, r_{4_y}, r_{4_z}) = (x_w, z_w/\tan(\beta - \beta_1), z_w] \\ v_2 &= f r_{4_y}/r_{4_z} \end{aligned} \tag{4.13}$$

To determine the new disparity of the rectangular defined by the image coordinates u_1, u_2, v_1 and v_2 the expansion radius r_v is subtracted from the z-component of P and transformed into a disparity value:

$$z_{new} = z_w - r_v \tag{4.14}$$

$$d_{new} = -f b_s/z_{new} \tag{4.15}$$

To calculate the full C-space map, (4.6)–(4.15) are applied to every pixel in the stereo disparity image. Each (u, v, d) triplet defines a rectangular image region (u_1, v_1, u_2, v_2) with a constant disparity d_{new}, that is written into an output map. Individual pixels are only updated if the new disparity is larger than the previous disparity value that was generated by a different (u, v, d) triplet.

4.3.3.2 Implementation Aspects

Equations (4.6)–(4.15) can be precalculated over the disparity space volume. Since the calculation of u_1 and u_2 in (4.6)–(4.9) is independent of the y coordinate it suffice to precalculate a look-up table to store the values of u_1 and u_2 for each defined (x, d) combination. Similarly, a look-up table for v_1 and v_2 is calculated for each (y, d) combination, and finally, the values for d_{new} can be precalculated for all valid disparities. Because of this separability, the C-space expansion can be implemented very efficiently. In a first step, an intermediate disparity image is generated by horizontally expanding all disparity values from the stereo disparity map using the u_1/u_2 look-up table. In a second step, each pixel in the intermediate disparity image is expanded vertically using the v_1/v_2 look-up table and the expansion column is stored with a new disparity value from the d_{new} look-up table in the final C-space disparity map.

4.3.4 Collision Checking in Disparity Space

The queries from the motion planner come as a sequence of short linear 3D trajectory segments. The collision checker module takes each segment that is defined through its start and end point, projects it into the current C-space disparity map D_{cm}, and checks all pixels that are located on the straight line between the projected start and end point for collision. Collision checking itself depends on the reconstructed disparity value $d(p_{\text{s}})$ of a point p_{s} on the segment and the actual disparity of the underlying pixel p_{cm} in the C-space map. If the disparity of p_{s} is larger than the disparity of p_{cm}, the pixel is classified as *safe*. If the disparity of p_{s} is smaller than p_{cm} the point on the trajectory is located behind an obstacle, and it is classified depending on the disparity difference

$$\begin{aligned} d(p_{\text{s}}) > d(p_{\text{cm}}) &: \text{SAFE} \\ d(p_{\text{s}}) < d(p_{\text{cm}}) \wedge d(p_{\text{s}}) - d(p_{\text{cm}}) < k &: \text{COLLISION} \\ d(p_{\text{s}}) < d(p_{\text{cm}}) \wedge d(p_{\text{s}}) - d(p_{\text{cm}}) \geq k &: \text{OCCLUDED} \\ p_{\text{s}} \notin D_{\text{cm}} &: \text{OUTSIDE} \\ d(p_{\text{cm}}) = \textit{invalid} &: \text{NO\_DATA} \end{aligned} \tag{4.16}$$

If the difference is smaller than a threshold, a collision occurred. If it is larger, the trajectory point is labeled as *occluded* as shown in Fig. 4.10. If the C-space map contains no valid disparity data at a checked pixel location p_{cm}, the trajectory segment is labeled as *no_data*—which can be caused, e.g., by a nontextured surface when applying a real-time stereo approach.

How the planner uses these different trajectory classifications is explained in the following section.

4.3.5 Motion Planning over Closed-Loop Dynamics

Motion planning of aerial vehicles has several challenges. First, the state space is high dimensional—6DOF position and orientation, and their time derivatives (velocity/angular velocity, etc.), resulting in at least 12 states. Second, the system is very agile and consequently has poor stability, and naively propagating the open-loop vehi-

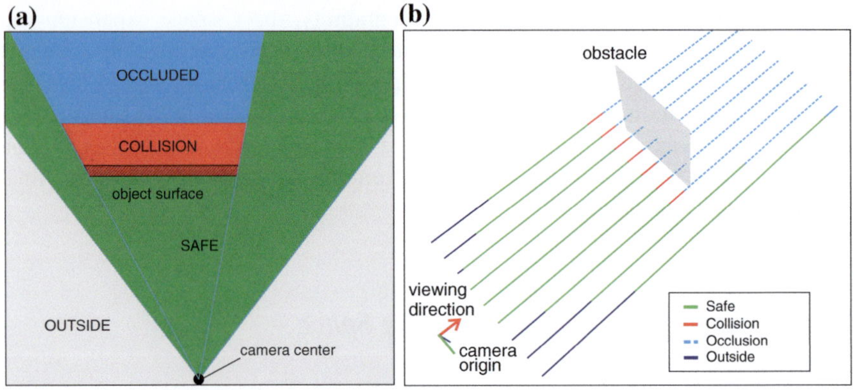

Fig. 4.10 Collision checking logic: **a** trajectory segments inside the viewing volume of the camera are classified as: SAFE if unobstructed (*green*), COLLISION if directly behind an object surface (*red*), and OCCLUDED if behind on object; **b** test trajectories in a simulation: collision checking result for a set of nine *horizontal* trajectories

cle dynamics quickly results in undesirable trajectories. Third, the dynamics become highly nonlinear especially when performing aggressive maneuvers. To address these challenges, we deploy a motion planning approach that incorporates vehicle dynamics by forward-simulating vehicle responses to waypoint control inputs, which effectively reduces the planning space to only 3D.

We extended an approach that was previously used for autonomous urban driving [31] to 6DOF motion with agile vehicle dynamics.

Our planner deploys a closed-loop RRT approach (CL-RRT) to grow a tree of waypoint inputs that are used in a feedback loop to estimate flight trajectories using a low-level controller and the quadrotor model described by How et al. [22]. The low-level controller consists of two layers: a linear *feedback controller* and a *waypoint tracker*. The *waypoint tracker* keeps track of which waypoint to visit next, and when to switch to the next waypoint segment (Fig. 4.11). It also computes the reference position/velocity and the position/velocity tracking errors. Given these tracking errors, the *feedback controller* computes the vehicle inputs $u_{\text{collective}}$, u_{roll}, u_{pitch}, and u_{yaw} to maneuver the vehicle along the trajectory using regular PID controllers for each channel.

The output of the control loop are the predicted vehicle states which define trajectory segments that are used for collision checking. Note, that the planner simultaneously grows a tree of controller inputs (straight lines connecting the controller input of a selected node to a sample, which forms an input to the forward simulation) and a tree of collision-free dynamically feasible trajectories (output of the forward simulation) as illustrated in Fig. 4.12.

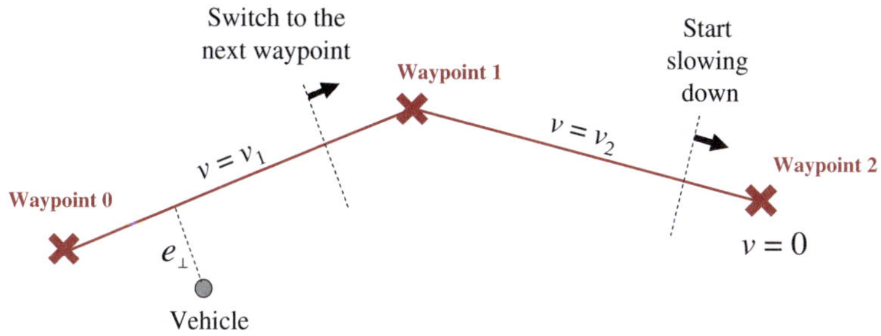

Fig. 4.11 Waypoint tracking logic. A cross-track controller minimizes the cross-track tracking error $e_\perp$, while an along-track controller maintains a commanded velocity along the lines that connect waypoints. The tracker switches waypoints when the along-track distance to the next waypoint becomes smaller than a threshold. Waypoints are marked with $\times$

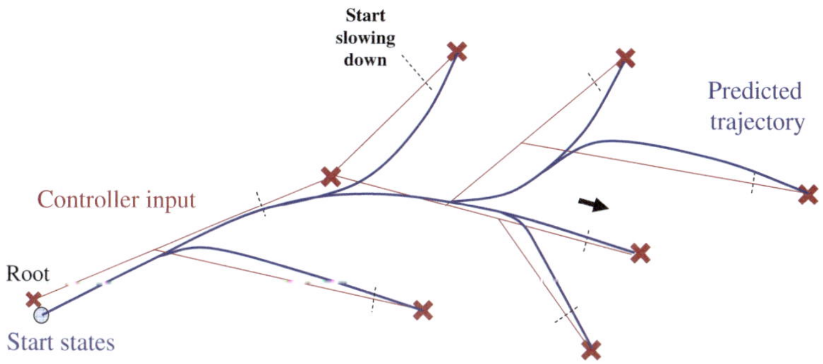

Fig. 4.12 RRT with closed-loop dynamics. The *red lines* represent the input to the controller, which are constructed by connecting a sample (marked with $\times$) to the tree. The *blue lines* represent the predicted vehicle trajectory, which is computed by the forward simulation

The main steps of the RRT algorithm are

1. Randomly sample the 3D world space.
2. Select a node in the tree.
3. Form a controller input from the selected node to the sample.
4. Forward simulate the closed-loop dynamics from the selected node, using the controller input generated in step 3, and obtain a dynamically feasible trajectory.
5. Check if the predicted trajectory collides with or is occluded by obstacles (Sect. 4.3.3). If there is a collision, or the occlusion is in a close range, discard the sample and go to step 1.
6. Add a sample and associated propagated trajectory to the tree. Also generate intermediate nodes on the trajectory, so that it can branch off to another trajectory for future samples.

4.3.6 Motion Planning Strategies

When the low-level controller executes the planned waypoints, different real-world considerations require specific execution strategies.

First, our planner is designed to maintain a safety invariance while the vehicle is flying [54] by adapting vehicle velocities such that the vehicle can come to a hover from the current state without collision. Note, that hovering is an invariant state of the quadrotor—once the vehicle is in a hover state, it can theoretically remain in hover without collision indefinitely in a static environment. Second, paths planned a certain distance behind a perceived obstacle are considered as feasible, which allows to plan into potentially free space behind obstacles. The maintained safety invariance ensures an early replanning should this space not be free. Space with no available data is treated similarly, since we expect that obstacles will have enough surface texture to be captured in the collision checking process.

Third, the predicted trajectory and the actual trajectory flown are generally close [32]. To account for nonzero prediction errors and changes in the environments, the planner repropagates the latest states and changes the trajectory accordingly to ensure collision-free flight from the current position.

Last, if the collision checker rejects a trajectory because it ends in occluded space or outside the field of view, we retain the feasible portion of such a trajectory in the tree, so that RRT can quickly connect future samples and grow trees from it.

4.3.7 Experimental Results

To evaluate our approach, we implemented our navigation algorithm both in a simulation environment (Fig. 4.13) and on a Asctec Pelican quadrotor system (Fig. 4.6). The simulation environment mimics a quadrotor within a virtual 3D world that is composed of cuboids.

At the beginning of a simulated flight, the quadrotor is placed at a starting position above the ground and the planner is executed a few seconds ahead of the controller to allow the construction of an initial tree of decent size. Figure 4.13 gives an example of such a step, where the stationary vehicle has planned trajectories toward the goal at the top of the scene. When the controller is started, the vehicle begins to execute the planned trajectory, replanning simultaneously during flight. As the position of the vehicle changes, new parts of the scene come into view, and trajectories are updated accordingly, until the goal is reached. To verify the robustness of our approach, we repeatedly executed a simulated flight for several example scenes. One standard scenario for performance evaluation of planning stability is the flight through a vertical opening in a wall (Figs. 4.14 and 4.15), which we use to measure the influence of a corrupted pose on the planning approach. In a Monte Carlo simulation, we commanded the vehicle to pass the vertical opening with noise added to the pose estimate and recorded the flown flight paths for 100 flights for each experiment.

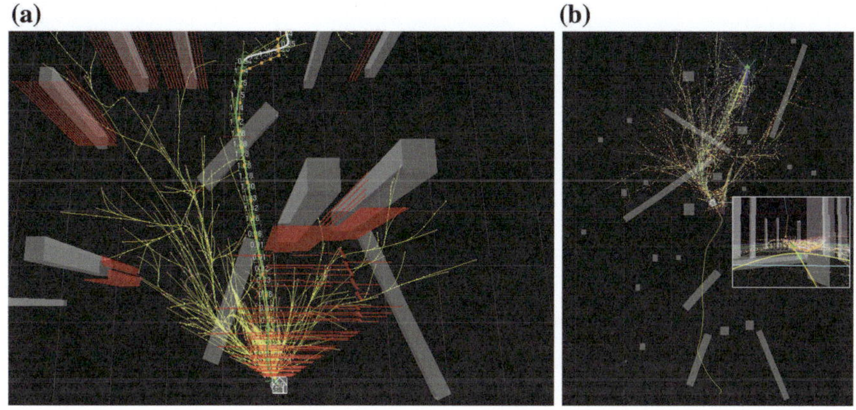

Fig. 4.13 Simulated flight through virtual forest: **a** Initial flight trajectory from the vehicle position at the *bottom* toward the goal at the *top* with overlaid 3D C-space point positions (*red*); the *horizontal red lines* in front of the vehicle correspond to C-space points above the ground; **b** *top-down* view during traverse with overlaid current view of the vehicle

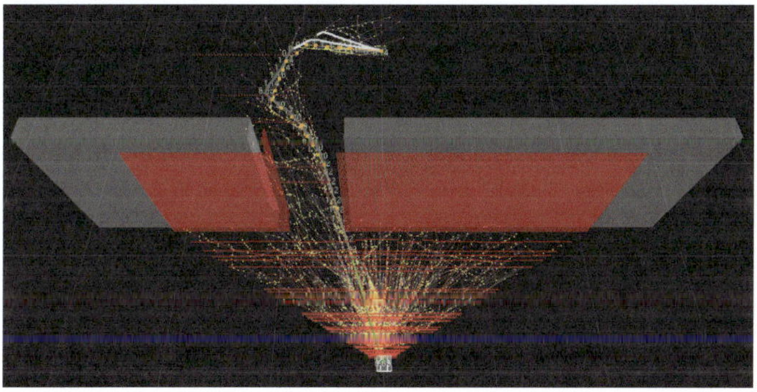

Fig. 4.14 Flying through a door opening with added pose noise: Scene view from the starting position with overlaid C-space point cloud (*red*)

With no pose noise added, the vehicle was able to fly safely through the opening on each run (Fig. 4.15a). Figure 4.15b illustrates the same flight experiment, where limited white noise ($\eta \in [-15\,\text{cm}, 15\,\text{cm}]$) was added to the position of the collision sensor (stereo camera system) prior to each planning cycle. When treating the pose of the collision sensor (with noise overlay) as true vehicle pose, all node positions on the RRT-tree become erroneous, simulating the effect of a noisy pose estimate on the planning process. In this case, collision checking invalidates additional tree branches, due to the added noise, forcing the vehicle to re-plan a valid trajectory when needed. As shown in Fig. 4.15b, additive noise affects the planning result only marginally. The vehicle was able to execute all runs properly and pass the opening at all times, since the added noise had zero mean (no drift).

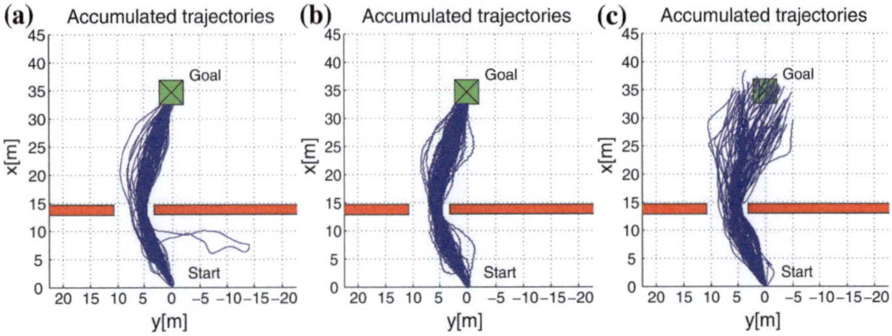

Fig. 4.15 Door experiment: *top-down* view of Monte Carlo simulation with 100 runs with **a** no pose noise, **b** additive white noise in x and y ($\leq$15 cm), **c** random walk bias in x and y (13.4 cm/s, random direction for each run)

This changed when a drifting pose estimate was simulated as shown in Fig. 4.15c. To simulate a random walk bias on the position estimates, a fixed position offset of 1.3 cm (a 10 % drift when operating at maximum speed of 1.3 m/s with a 100 Hz simulation rate) in a random direction within the x/y plane was defined at the beginning of each run, and added as a pose offset prior to each planning step. In this experiment, the vehicle kept a stable orientation to maintain correct heading, which we assume closely related to real flight experiments, since roll and pitch would be stabilized around a drift-free gravity vector and yaw can be assumed to be measured locally drift free by an onboard magnetometer or a vision-aided pose estimation approach. Since all world point coordinates drift with the amount of bias on pose, the goal cannot be reached and serves as a desired flight direction indicator.

The vehicle was able to pass the obstacle without a collision in 96 % of all cases. Collisions only occurred when the vehicle was already within the opening and drifting sideways, so that the camera could not see the closing in obstruction.

Figure 4.16 illustrates the performance of our navigation system in a real-world scenario. We implemented our algorithm onboard an Asctec Pelican quadrotor which was equipped with an Intel Core2Duo, 1.86 GHz processor and conducted flight experiments in a test forest (Fig. 4.6).

Our system setup used the sensor fusion approach from [63] for pose estimation. It fuses IMU and position updates from a visual SLAM algorithm (Parallel Tracking and Mapping (PTAM) [30]) that uses images from a downward-looking camera (752 $\times$ 480, grayscale, 100 FOV).

To generate stereo disparity maps, we mounted a stereo camera system [20] on top of the quadrotor that included an embedded OMAP3730 to off-load the calculation of real-time disparity maps (376 $\times$ 240, 25 Hz, 12 cm baseline, 110 FOV) from the main processor, which only performed postprocessing of disparity maps within the stereo vision pipeline.

In this setup, the pose estimation framework used 59 % of the total resource (camera and PTAM (30 Hz) 48 %, pose filter (30 Hz) 11 %), stereo postprocessing

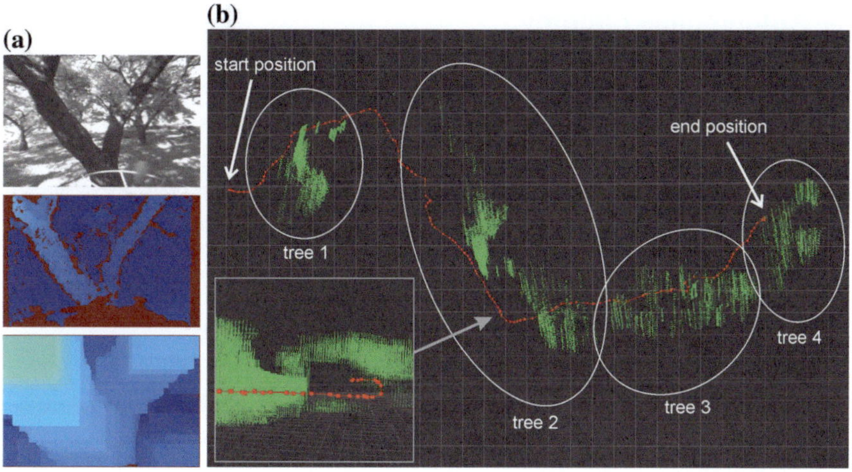

Fig. 4.16 Flying under tree canopy: **a** *top* to *bottom*: left rectified stereo camera view; disparity map; C-space map with expansion size of 60 cm; **b** *top–down* view of flown trajectory (*red*) with overlaid accumulated C-space point clouds (*green*) that are generated from subsampled C-space disparity maps; only points are shown that are more than 2.5 m above the ground and not farther away from the vehicle than 2 m. The *inset* shows a view from behind the vehicle in an upright view, illustrating flight below a tree branch

used 9 %, and motion planning used 65 % (RRT planner 60 %, trajectory server 5 %), generating motion plans at 2 Hz. On average, 6.51 % of the time used by the RRT planner was spent on C-space expansion, and 8.19 % on collision checking, which demonstrates the effectiveness of our approach. Additionally, C-space expansion and collision checking required less than 1.5 MB of memory for processing 376 × 240 disparity images from the stereo system. In total, the navigation frame work used 133 % of the available 200 % processing power of our two core CPU.

Figure 4.16a gives an example of the viewing volume that is used for motion planning when approaching a tree. Figure 4.16b illustrates the flight trajectory of a representative experiment in a top-down view. The vehicle started at the left of the image and was commanded to fly to the right, avoiding four different trees on its traverse.

At the beginning of each experiments, we started generating motion plans at an altitude of 4 m and restricted the planning volume to sample 3D points between 2 and 5 m altitude. The vehicle was able to avoid obstacles autonomously and plan its motion around tree branches. This included a portion of the trajectory where the vehicle flew correctly below an overhead branch (tree 2, Fig. 4.16b).

4.4 Autonomous Landing

In this section, we introduce autonomous landing as a high-level navigation application. Even if autonomous landing is a specific task, its single parts can easily be adapted to a series of different applications. Our approach comprises two research topics, dense monocular 3D reconstruction and visual surface analysis. First, we will describe the related work, then introduce our landing algorithm, followed by the embedded implementation, and concluded with experimental results.

4.4.1 Related Work

Most prior work on autonomous landing of unmanned aerial vehicles addresses landing on terrain, instead of finding elevated perches like rooftops. Due to the severe constraints on size, weight, and power (SWaP) for especially micro aerial vehicles, applicable methods must use much lighter, lower performance sensing and computing resources than available on larger scale systems [53]. Approaches amenable to these SWaP constraints frequently employ monocular [10, 26, 40, 60] and binocular stereo [37, 61] camera systems to map and analyze terrain. Most approaches perform some form of 3D terrain reconstruction, then assess planarity and slope of appropriately-sized terrain patches. Binocular stereo vision approaches are, due to the fixed intercamera geometry, algorithmically simpler, but are limited by the fixed interocular baseline and also heavier due to the additional camera. Three monocular approaches are particularly relevant here. The first tracks point features to estimate homographies from image pairs for predominantly planar terrain, then analyzes correlation coefficients for dense matches to segment in-plane and out-of-plane pixels [10]. The second uses a recursive filter at each pixel, image matching via gradient descent with intensity derivatives, and a plane plus parallax formulation of structure from motion to estimate dense elevation maps from image sequences [60]. Both of these address finding landing sites on the ground. The third uses multiplanar homography alignment with tracked features to segment a planar ground-level surface from an elevated, planar landing site [11].

In the last couple of years, significant progress has been made in dense monocular 3D reconstruction as well. Recently published approaches use Bayesian and variational estimation models with known camera motion [43, 46, 59]. All of them use powerful processing hardware, such as GPUs, to achieve real-time capability. An overview about earlier work can be found in [55].

4.4.2 Algorithm Description

Our approach can find flat landing platforms everywhere in the 3D model and is not limited to dominant planes. The presented algorithm consists of three parts, whereas the whole approach is designed to achieve reasonable short and constant processing time even on limited computing hardware. First, we use a dense motion stereo method to determine a 3D model of the scene beneath the MAV. We present a frame list approach with variable baseline which enables arbitrarily selection of depth accuracy of the 3D model as long as the motion between an image pair could be found correctly. The scale can be determined from any metric pose estimator or altitude sensor. Here, we use the pose estimator presented in Sect. 4.2. Second, we analyze the 3D model in order to find potential landing candidates. Most of the mentioned work uses the dimensions of the MAV, the size, the planarity, and slope of the landing spot as main criterion of landability. We reduce all these criterions to simple steps which enable efficient onboard implementation. Third, we pick the most promising candidate and approach it, e.g., with a two-waypoint trajectory. Figure 4.17 illustrates the processing pipeline of our autonomous landing approach. Besides experiments where we actually land autonomously in a controlled environment, we present more detailed analysis about the system performance with hand-labeled ground truth data.

4.4.2.1 3D Reconstruction

Dense motion stereo is based on the same principle as conventional stereo, with the difference that the two views of the captured scene are generated by a single moving camera instead of a rigid stereo bar. The extrinsic parameters (rotation R and translation t between the two camera positions) have to be determined for each image pair individually. Translation can be estimated up to scale using visual information only. We assume the intrinsic parameters do not change and calibrate them in advance. We use a CAHVORE camera model [17] to model lens effects and to generate linearized camera models that describe the perspective projection.

For selection of a proper image pair, we maintain a frame list of the last n images. Each element of the frame list consists of camera image, camera pose in the world frame, extracted features (STAR [1], MSURF [9]), and a feature track list to record how often each feature has been found in the frame list. Given this data, we can select image pairs using two criteria. First, since depth accuracy is a function of the stereo baseline, we look for images that are an appropriate distance apart to achieve enough depth accuracy (at ground level) at the current altitude of the MAV. Second, we chose the image which exceeds a minimum number of successive feature matches with the current image. As soon as an image pair is found, we estimate R and t between the images with a multiplanar homography alignment approach [12]. Since we can estimate translation only up to scale from pure visual information (without some metric context), the translation vector is then scaled with the real-world baseline from the visual-inertial state estimator described in Sect. 4.2. Having R and t, stereo rectification can be applied. The quality of the motion estimation strongly depends on the accuracy of the feature locations and, thus, is scene dependent. To discard poor motion estimates in order to prevent wrong 3D reconstruction, we calculate the average 3D reprojection error of the feature pairs and accept only image pairs with an error in subpixel range. Finally, we use a real-time sum of absolute difference stereo matching algorithm to estimate a disparity map from which we generate a 3D point cloud to model the captured scene beneath the MAV.

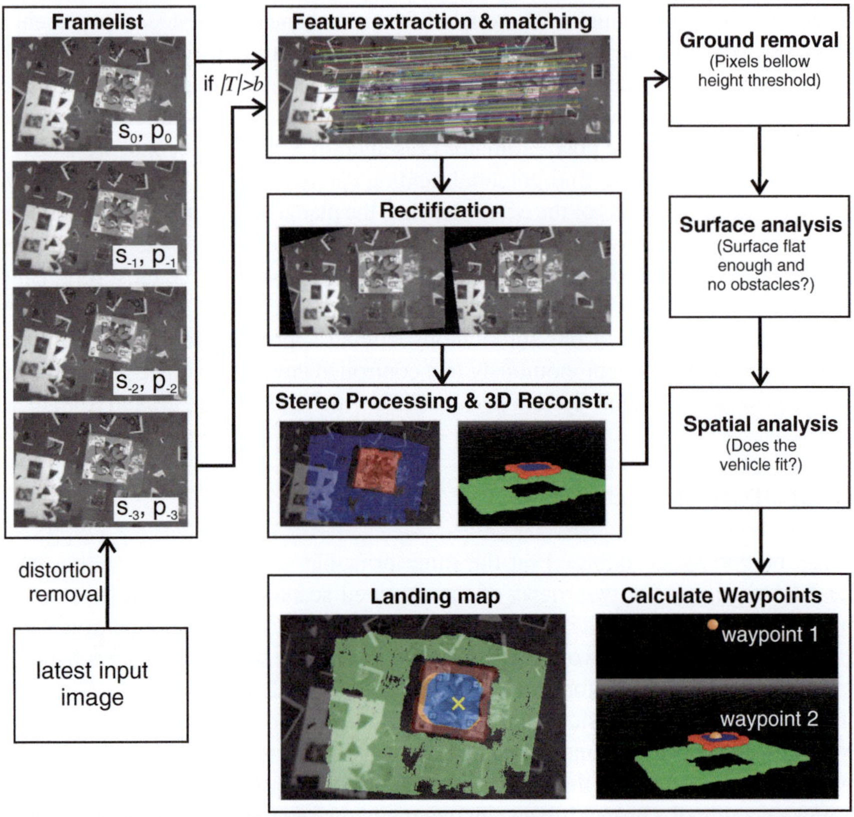

Fig. 4.17 Autonomous landing overview: New input images are stored in a frame list, together with detected features, and camera poses. For selected image pairs, camera motion is estimated, and the 3D model is determined. The result of the landing site detection is a landing map which labels all pixels as: *green* (ground level), *red* (on rooftop but unsafe), *orange* (insufficient space), or *blue* (safe landing area). The location with the highest confidence is labeled by ×

4.4.2.2 Landing Site Detection

After 3D reconstruction, the next step is to find potential landing candidates. We define the following requirements for a suitable landing site: (a) A landing site has to be planar, close to parallel to the ground plane, and free of obstacles and hazards, (b) it has to be large enough to fit the MAV, and (c) it has to provide enough free space around it for a safe approach.

To fulfill these requirements, we developed an efficient multistep algorithm which uses the determined range data to reduce the problem to a basic probabilistic model. Since our application is targeted to land on elevated surfaces for surveillance, we first remove all candidates close to the ground level. Then we calculate the standard deviation of the disparity map because the variance of the disparity map along the gravity vector, after projection into world frame, corresponds to the planarity of the landing surface. The smaller the standard deviation in the disparity map, the more planar the corresponding area and, thus, the higher the landing site confidence (normalized standard deviation). Standard deviation is calculated in an adaptive neighborhood

$$n(d, h) = \frac{r z_{acc} f}{h^2} d \tag{4.17}$$

which depends on the disparity values d and the MAV's altitude h. The size of the MAV (r is the radius), the focal length f, and the target depth accuracy z_{acc} are constant. The target depth accuracy is the first derivative of z (here h) in respect to the disparity. The needed space for the MAV is its size divided by the lateral resolution. These two equations combined result in Eq. 4.17. In fact, we make sure that the window size (in pixels) for the standard deviation corresponds to the size (in meters) the MAV needs to land. The result of the algorithm is a landing map which labels all pixels (i.e., landing sites) as whether or not they are safe to land. A confidence map assigns each landing candidate a quality value which can further be used to pick the final landing target.

4.4.3 Embedded Implementation

We initially implemented our landing framework on a standard PC and then ported the software to the processing board (see Sect. 4.1.1). First, we applied thorough software optimization techniques to make sure that no redundant calculations are done and all data structures can be accessed fast. Additional software optimization steps were including NEON and ARM specific instruction sets. We also reduced of image resolution to 376 × 240 which increased the processing speed significantly, while still maintaining sufficient resolution. The decreased depth and lateral resolution, which come along with the smaller image resolution, are not an issue: For depth, our approach compensates this by automatically choosing a larger baseline and the lateral resolution turned out to still be high enough, even for a flight altitude of above 10 m. When running the landing site detection algorithm in parallel with our pose estimation frame work on the Hummingbird/U2, we achieved a frame rate of 1 Hz for landing map updates. Our experiments showed that this frame rate is reasonable for fully autonomous landing site detection.

4.4.4 Experimental Evaluation

To evaluate proper system performance, we ran three indoor experiments and one outdoor experiment. All indoor experiments were conducted with the Asctec Hummingbird carrying the modified U2 flight computer and all outdoor experiments were

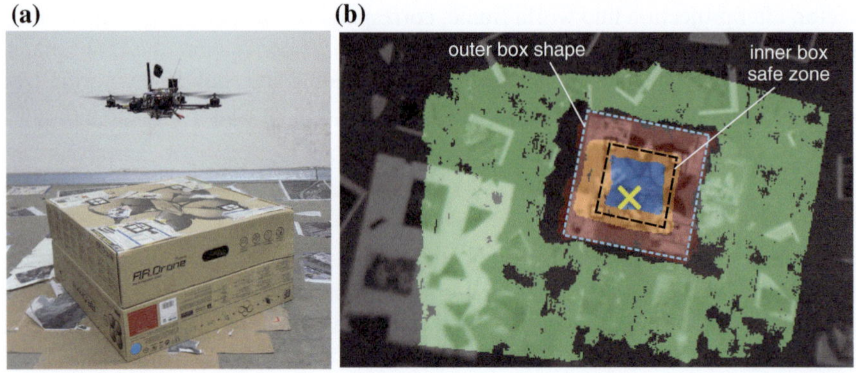

Fig. 4.18 First indoor experiment: **a** *Box* as surrogate rooftop; **b** hand-labeled landing map, *outer box* shape is the edge of the box surface, *inner box* safety zone is the box surface without the 13 cm border region

conducted with the Asctec Pelican carrying the Asctec Mastermind flight computer. Even if the whole processing pipeline runs onboard, for the presented experiments, we recorded the data and processed it offline.

4.4.4.1 Indoor Evaluation

The first indoor experiment was designed to generate quantitative error metrics from hand-labeled ground truth data. We fly our quadrotor system at three different altitudes over a box ($57 \times 57 \times 27\,\text{cm}^3$, Fig. 4.18) to simulate a rooftop landing scenario. In all experiments, the vehicle radius was set to 13 cm to allow for a sufficiently-sized valid landing area in the middle of the box, and the arbitrary ground-level cut off threshold was set to 20 cm. For ground truth, the true landing area in the middle of the box surface was marked by corner marks that were located at 13 cm distance from the box edges, and these were manually identified in the input images (see Fig. 4.18b). The first three rows of Table 4.2 give an overview of the evaluation results. Altitude, baseline, and feature reprojection error during image alignment correspond to the average value for each experiment. For this evaluation, we only considered frames where the box surface was completely visible in the disparity image to avoid border effects, and were valid stereo results could be calculated (enough baseline and more than 40 feature matches for image alignment) ("frames visible"). Within these frames, we defined a successful detection ("frames successful") as frames where at least one valid landing location was detected on the box and no landing location was detected falsely on the ground. For these successful frames, we also calculated false positives (FP) rates (pixels that were classified as valid landing area that are located in the border area), false negatives (FN) rates (not as landing area classified pixels that were located in the correct center area of the box). Note that we only consider pixels with valid disparity values in this metric.

Table 4.2 Evaluation of landing site detection

Altitude (m)	Baseline (m)	Reprojection error (pixel)	Number of frames			FP (%)	FN (%)
			Visible	Successful			
1.47	0.39	0.21	116	106	91.4 %	0.028	39.34
2.19	0.86	0.20	63	62	98.4 %	0.046	43.57
3.34	2.00	0.18	67	63	94.0 %	0.0026	53.14
6.51	1.16	0.28	337	325	96.3 %		
10.15	2.28	0.22	480	433	90.2 %		

Row 1–3 Indoor experiment at three different altitudes (r = 13 cm, depth accuracy at ground level = 3 cm), *Row 4–5* outdoor experiment (depth accuracy at ground level = 20 cm)

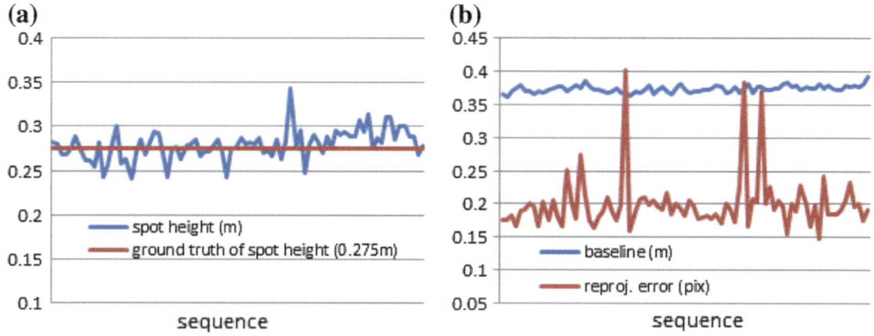

Fig. 4.19 Second indoor experiment: **a** box height calculation for valid landing point with highest confidence. **b** Feature reprojection error of feature matches and estimated baseline (depth accuracy 3 cm)

Our approach is able to robustly detect the landing zone with a success rate of more than 90 % in all experiments and a false positive rate below 0.05 %. The false positive (FP) and false negative (FN) rates are largely defined by the quality of the disparity input. Border-fattening effects (caused by our correlation-based stereo matching) usually increase the FP rate, whereas missing disparity pixels on top of the target increase the FN rates, since we treat missing data as unsafe. To mitigate these two effects, we introduced two thresholds to maximize safety: (1) at disparity edges, we disable all pixels that are located within half a correlation window size to the edge, and (2) we use a percentage threshold which defines the minimum number of pixels with valid disparity around a landing site (98 % in our experiments).

In the second experiment, in order to verify the accuracy of our 3D reconstruction, we plotted the height of the landing point with the highest confidence for one of the sequences (Fig. 4.19). The error follows the expected depth accuracy of 3 cm (min. depth acc.) within the true box height of 27.5 cm. The low average feature reprojection error confirms valid motion estimation results.

The third indoor landing experiment consisted of landing site detection and target approach. In this indoor experiment, the landing target also consisted of a cardboard box to simulate an elevated landing surface. We commanded the quadrotor to fly

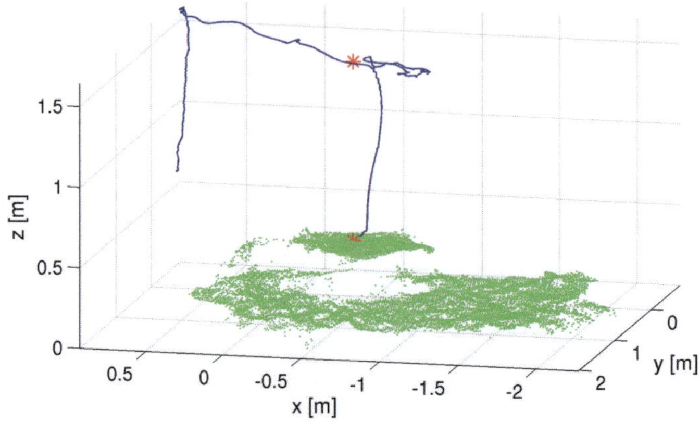

Fig. 4.20 Third indoor experiment: The MAV is commanded to take off autonomously and rise up to 1.5 m. Then we continuously set waypoints to explore the environment (the *solid line* follows the flight trajectory). Once a valid landing spot is detected, the two approach waypoints are generated (*stars*) which are used by the MAV for the landing maneuver. Note that each waypoint includes a tolerance radius (the trajectory does not hit the *red star* at 1.5 m altitude exactly). We reduced this tolerance for the actual landing spot on the surface to enable high-precision landing

over the landing zone by defining manual waypoints, which were approached by the vehicle autonomously while executing the landing site detection algorithm to analyze the area beneath the MAV. As soon as an appropriate landing spot was detected, the two approach waypoints were submitted and executed by the vehicle (Fig. 4.18a).

Figure 4.20 depicts the 3D point cloud of the reconstructed box and ground surface together with the flight trajectory and the issued approach waypoints. The vehicle took off to the left of the illustrated scene and landed correctly on top of the box. Example scene views, together with a resulting landing map are illustrated in Fig. 4.17. All pixels in the middle of the box have been labeled correctly as safe to land (blue), whereas pixels close to the edges of the box are detected as either unsafe (red) or provide not enough space to land on (orange).

4.4.4.2 Outdoor Evaluation

For the outdoor experiments, we conducted overflights over a one story building (Fig. 4.21) and recorded image sequences from the downward-looking camera together with pose data for offline analysis. A quantitative evaluation for two different overflights is given in Table 4.2 row 3–4. The average altitude of the first flight was 6.5 m which lead to an average required baseline of 1.16 m. The second overflight was at a higher altitude of approximately 10.15 m requiring a slightly higher minimum baseline of 2.28 m on average. From all frames, were at least a part of the safe landing zone on top of the building was visible in the disparity images, we could successfully identify a valid landing target in over 90 % for both flights.

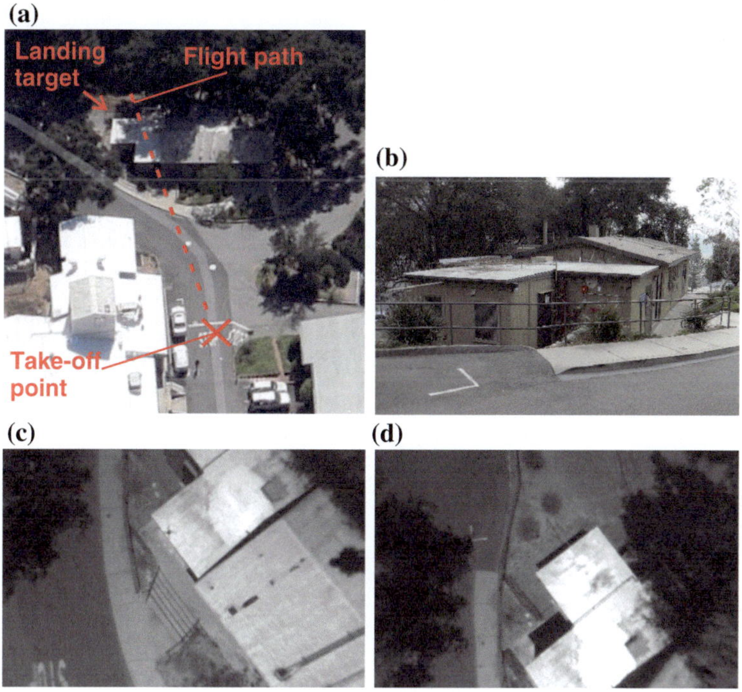

Fig. 4.21 Outdoor experiment environment and data set images. **a** Aerial view of the flight area and target building; **b** the flat area on the roof is the landing target; **c** raw input image with good texture on roof; **d** image with saturation area which leads to missing stereo data

4.5 Conclusion and Future Work

Vision-based navigation algorithms have the potential to become an enabling technology for micro air vehicle autonomy. With the advent of small, low-power processing units and miniature camera modules from the cell-phone sector, low SWaP computing for vision applications is ready to be deployed, enabling fully autonomous navigation of very small platforms for the first time. In this chapter, we presented three different fundamental building blocks for platform autonomy: vision-based pose estimation, onboard obstacle avoidance, and autonomous landing. Fast pose estimation that is independent of external sensor inputs is the basis for safe MAV operations. Our approach fuses accurate map-based localization with a fast map-free approach to estimate vehicle velocities in emergency situations when a map-based approach might fail.

Obstacle avoidance is a key capability for flights in highly cluttered environment or close to the ground. We use frontal stereo vision approach which provides a polar-perspective, inverse-range world representation for obstacle detection and collision checking with low computational complexity, and deploy a closed-loop motion planning approach that plans collision-free trajectories while accounting for vehicle dynamics.

Our autonomous landing approach finds elevated landing surfaces by executing a dense structure from motion approach, and searching for safe landing zones in the reconstructed terrain.

We implemented all three algorithms on our quadrotor platforms and demonstrated autonomous flights using only onboard resources.

In the future, we plan to further integrate our embedded platform components towards ultimately having a fully capable avionics package (flight computer, camera, and IMU) under 15 g. This will enable fully autonomous control of ultra-small quadrotor systems (as, e.g., the 15 cm, 25 g Bitcraze miniature quadrotor system [16]) that can be operated in highly cluttered environment or confined spaces, indoor and outdoor.

Acknowledgments This work was carried out at the Jet Propulsion Laboratory, California Institute of Technology, under a contract with the National Aeronautics and Space Administration.

References

1. Agrawal M, Konolige K, Blas MR (2008) Censure: center surround extremas for realtime feature detection and matching. Computer vision ECCV 2008. Lecture Notes in Computer Science, vol 5305. Springer, Berlin, pp 102–115
2. Armesto L, Tornero J, Vincze M (2007) Fast ego-motion estimation with multi-rate fusion of inertial and vision. Int J Robot Res 26(6):577–589
3. Armesto L, Chroust S, Vincze M, Tornero J (2004) Multi-rate fusion with vision and inertial sensors. In: Proceedings of the IEEE international conference on robotics and automation, New Orleans, US
4. Ascending Technologies GmbH. http://www.asctec.de/uav-applications/research/products/asctec-mastermind/
5. Bachrach A, Prentice S, He R, Henry P, Huang AS, Krainin M, Maturana D, Fox D, Roy N (2012) Estimation, planning and mapping for autonomous flight using an RGB-D camera in GPS-denied environments. Int J Robot Res 31(11):1320–1343
6. Bajracharya M, Howard A, Matthies L, Tang B, Turmon M (2009) Autonomous off-road navigation with end-to-end learning for the LAGR program. Field Robot 26(1):3–25
7. Bakolas E, Tsiotras P (2008) Multiresolution path planning via sector decompositions compatible to on-board sensor data. In: AIAA guidance, navigation, and control conference
8. Baldwin G, Mahony R, Trumpf J (2009) A nonlinear observer for 6 DOF pose estimation from inertial and bearing measurements. In: Proceedings of the IEEE international conference on robotics and automation, Kobe
9. Bay H, Ess A, Tuytelaars T, Van Gool L (2008) Speeded-up robust features (surf). Comput Vis Image Underst 110(3):346–359
10. Bosch S, Lacroix S, Caballero F (2006) Autonomous detection of safe landing areas for an uav from monocular images. In: Proceedings of the IEEE/RSJ international conference on intelligent robots and systems, pp 5522–5527
11. Brockers R, Susca S, Zhu D, Matthies L (2012) Fully self-contained vision-aided navigation and landing of a micro air vehicle independent from external sensor inputs. In: Proceedings of the SPIE, 8387:83870Q-1–83870Q-10

12. Cheng Y (2010) Real-time surface slope estimation by homography alignment for spacecraft safe landing. In: Proceedings of the IEEE international conference on robotics and automation, pp 2280–2286
13. Chroust SG, Vincze M (2004) Fusion of vision and inertial data for motion and structure estimation. J Robot Syst 21(2):73–83
14. Conroy J, Gremillion G, Ranganathan B, Humbert J (2009) Implementation of wide-field integration of optic flow for autonomous quadrotor navigation. Auton Robot 27(3):189–198
15. Corke P (2004) An inertial and visual sensing system for a small autonomous helicopter. Int J Robot Syst 21(2):43–51
16. Crazyflie Micro Quadrotor. http://www.bitcraze.se/crazyflie/
17. Di K, Li R (2004) CAHVOR camera model and its photogrammetric conversion for planetary applications. J Geophys Res 109:E04004
18. Fraundorfer F, Heng L, Honegger, D, Lee GH, Meier L, Tanskanen P, Pollefeys M (2012) Vision-based autonomous mapping and exploration using a quadrotor MAV. In: IROS, pp 4557–4564
19. Gemeiner P, Einramhof P, Vincze M (2007) Simultaneous motion and structure estimation by fusion of inertial and vision data. Int J Robot Res 26(6):591–605
20. Goldberg SB, Matthies L (2011) Stereo and IMU assisted visual odometry on an OMAP3530 for small robots. In: 2011 IEEE computer society conference on computer vision and pattern recognition workshops (CVPRW), pp 169–176
21. Hardkernel. http://www.hardkernel.com
22. How JP, Bethke B, Frank A, Dale D, Vian J (2008) Real-time indoor autonomous vehicle test environment. IEEE Control Syst Mag 28(2):51–64
23. Hrabar S, Sukhatme GS, Corke P, Usher K, Roberts J (2005) Combined optic-flow and stereo-based navigation of urban canyons for a uav. In: IROS
24. Huster A, Frew EW, Rock SM (2002) Relative position estimation for AUVs by fusing bearing and inertial rate sensor measurements. In: Proceedings of the oceans conference, vol 3. MTS/IEEE, Biloxi, pp 1857–1864
25. Hyslop AM, Humbert JS (2010) Autonomous navigation in three-dimensional urban environments using wide-field integration of optic flow. Guid Control Dyn 33(1):147
26. Johnson A, Montgomery J, Matthies L (2005) Vision guided landing of an autonomous helicopter in hazardous terrain. In: Proceedings of the IEEE international conference on robotics and automation, pp 3966–3971
27. Jones E (2009) Large scale visual navigation and community map building. PhD thesis, University of California at Los Angeles
28. Jones E, Soatto S (2010) Visual-inertial navigation, mapping and localization: a scalable real-time causal approach. Int J Robot Res 30:407–430
29. Kelly J, Sukhatme GS (2011) Visual-inertial sensor fusion: localization, mapping and sensor-to-sensor self-calibration. Int J Robot Res (IJRR) 30(1):56–79
30. Klein G, Murray D (2007) Parallel tracking and mapping for small AR workspaces. In: Proceedings of the 2007 6th IEEE and ACM international symposium on mixed and augmented reality, ISMAR'07. IEEE Computer Society, p 110
31. Kuwata Y, Teo J, Fiore G, Karaman S, Frazzoli E, How JP (2009) Real-time motion planning with applications to autonomous urban driving. Trans Control Syst Tech 17(5):1105–1118
32. Luders B, Karaman S, Frazzoli E, How J (2010) Bounds on tracking error using closed-loop rapidly-exploring random trees. In: American control conference, Baltimore, MD, pp 5406–5412
33. Lupton T, Sukkarieh S (2008) Removing scale biases and ambiguity from 6DoF monocular SLAM using inertial. In: International conference on robotics and automation, Pasadena, California
34. Lupton T, Sukkarieh S (2009) Efficient integration of inertial observations into visual SLAM without initialization. In: IEEE/RSJ international conference on intelligent robots and systems, St. Louis

35. MacAllister B, Butzke J, Kushleyev A, Pandey H, Likhachev M (2013) Path planning for non-circular micro aerial vehicles in constrained environments. In: ICRA, pp 3918–3925
36. Martin GR (2009) What is binocular vision for? a birds eye view. J Vis 9(11):245–267
37. Meingast M, Geyer C, Sastry S (2004) Vision based terrain recovery for landing unmanned aerial vehicles. In: Proceedings of the IEEE conference on decision and control, vol 2. pp 1670–1675
38. Mei C, Sibley G, Cummins M, Newman P, Reid I (2009) A constant time efficient stereo SLAM system. In: Proceedings of the British machine vision conference (BMVC)
39. Mellinger D, Kumar V (2011) Minimum snap trajectory generation and control for quadrotors. In: Proceedings of the IEEE international conference on robotics and automation (ICRA)
40. Montgomery J, Johnson A, Roumeliotis S, Matthies L (2006) The jet propulsion laboratory autonomous helicopter testbed: a platform for planetary exploration technology research and development. J Field Robot 23(3–4):245–267
41. Mourikis AI, Roumeliotis SI (2007) A multi-state constraint Kalman filter for vision-aided inertial navigation. In: Proceedings of the IEEE international conference on robotics and automation (ICRA)
42. Mourikis AI, Trawny N, Roumeliotis SI, Johnson AE, Ansar A, Matthies L (2009) Vision-aided inertial navigation for spacecraft entry, descent, and landing. IEEE Trans Robot 25(2):264–280
43. Newcombe RA, Lovegrove JS, Davison AJ (2011) Dtam: dense tracking and mapping in real-time. In: IEEE international conference on computer vision (ICCV), pp 2320–2327
44. Otte MW, Richardson SG, Mulligan J, Grudic G (2009) Path planning in image space for autonomous robot navigation in unstructured outdoor environments. Field Robot 26(2):212–240
45. Pivtoraiko M, Mellinger D, Kumar V (2013) Incremental micro-UAV motion replanning for exploring unknown environments. In: ICRA
46. Pizzoli M, Forster C, Scaramuzza D (2014) Remode: probabilistic, monocular dense reconstruction in real time. In: Proceedings of the IEEE international conference on robotics and automation
47. Qian G, Chellappa R, Zheng Q (2002) Bayesian structure from motion using inertial information. In: International conference on image processing, Rochester, New York
48. Richter C, Bry A, Roy N (2013) Polynomial trajectory planning for quadrotor flight. In: RSS workshop on resource-efficient integration of perception, control and navigation
49. Robot Operating System, (ROS). http://www.ros.org
50. Ross S, Melik-Barkhudarov N, Shankar KS, Wendel A, Dey D, Bagnell JA, Hebert M (2013) Learning monocular reactive uav control in cluttered natural environments. In: ICRA, pp 1757–1764
51. Roumeliotis SI, Johnson AE, Montgomery JF (2002) Augmenting inertial navigation with image-based motion estimation. In: Proceedings of The IEEE international conference on robotics and automation, Washington, pp 4326–4333
52. Sarabandi K, Vahidpour M, Moallem M, East J (2011) Compact beam scanning 240 GHz radar for navigation and collision avoidance. In: SPIE, vol 8031
53. Scherer S, Chamberlain L, Singh S (2012) Autonomous landing at unprepared sites by a full-scale helicopter. Robot Auton Syst 60(12):1545–1562
54. Schouwenaars T, De Moor B, Feron E, How J (2001) Mixed Integer Programming for Multi-Vehicle Path Planning. In: Proceedings of the European control conference, Porto, Portugal
55. Seitz SM, Curless B, Diebel J, Scharstein D, Szeliski R (2006) A comparison and evaluation of multi-view stereo reconstruction algorithms. In: IEEE computer society conference on computer vision and pattern recognition, 2006, pp 519–528
56. Shen S, Michael N, Kumar V (2011) 3d indoor exploration with a computationally constrained mav. In: Robotics science and systems
57. Shen S, Michael N, Kumar V (2011) Autonomous multi-floor indoor navigation with a computationally constrained MAV. In: Proceedings of the IEEE international conference on robotics and automation

58. Strelow D, Singh S (2003) Online motion estimation from image and inertial measurements. In: Workshop on integration of vision and inertial sensors (INERVIS), Coimbra, Portugal
59. Stühmer J, Gumhold S, Cremers D (2010) Real-time dense geometry from a handheld camera. In: Proceedings of the 32nd DAGM conference on pattern recognition, pp 11–20
60. Templeton T, Shim DH, Geyer C, Sastry SS (2007) Autonomous vision-based landing and terrain mapping using an MPC-controlled unmanned rotorcraft. In: Proceedings of the IEEE international conference on robotics and automation, pp 1349–1356
61. Theodore C, Rowley D, Hubbard D, Ansar A, Matthies L, Goldberg S, Whalley M (2006) Flight trials of a rotorcraft unmanned aerial vehicle landing autonomously at unprepared sites. In: Forum of the American helicopter society, Phoenix
62. Weiss S (2012) Vision based navigation for micro helicopters. PhD thesis, ETH Zurich, March 2012
63. Weiss S, Achtelik MW, Lynen S, Achtelik MC, Kneip L, Chli M, Siegwart R (2013) Monocular vision for long-term micro aerial vehicle state estimation: a compendium. Field Robot 30(5):803–831
64. Weiss S, Achtelik MW, Chli M, Siegwart R (2012) Versatile distributed pose estimation and sensor self-calibration for an autonomous MAV. In: IEEE International conference on robotics and automation (ICRA)
65. Weiss S, Achtelik MW, Lynen S, Chli M, Siegwart R (2012) Real-time onboard visual-inertial state estimation and self-calibration of MAVs in unknown environments. In: IEEE International conference on robotics and automation (ICRA)
66. Weiss S, Brockers R, Matthies L (2013) 4dof drift free navigation using inertial cues and optical flow. In: IEEE/RSJ International conference on intelligent robots and systems (IROS), pp 4180–4186
67. Weiss S, Siegwart R (2011) Real-time metric state estimation for modular vision-inertial systems. In: Proceedings of the IEEE International conference on robotics and automation (ICRA)
68. Yu H, Beard RW (2013) A vision-based collision avoidance technique for miniature air vehicles using local-level frame mapping and path planning. Auton Robots 34(1–2):93–109

Chapter 5
Stereo Vision Algorithms Suited to Constrained FPGA Cameras

Stefano Mattoccia

Abstract The advent of cheap RGBD active 3D sensors, such as those based on structured light (e.g., the Microsoft Kinect) or those based on time-of-flight technology, has significantly increased the interest in computer vision applications based on depth data that, in most cases, enables higher robustness compared to solutions based on traditional 2D images. Unfortunately, active techniques are quite noisy or even completely useless in outdoor environments (in particular under sunlight). An effective and well-known technique to infer depth suited to indoor and outdoor environments is passive stereo vision. Nevertheless, despite the frequent deployment of this technology in many research projects since the 1960s, stereo vision is often perceived, especially in consumer applications, as an expensive technology due to its high demanding computation requirements. In this paper, we will review a subset of state-of-the-art stereo vision algorithms that have the potential to fit with a basic computing architecture made of a low-cost field-programmable gate arrays (FPGAs), without additional external devices (e.g., FIFOs, DDR memories, etc.) excluding a USB or GigaEthernet communication controller. Compared to more complex designs based on expensive FPGAs coupled with additional external memory devices, clear advantages of the outlined simplified computing architecture are the reduced design and manufacturing costs as well as the reduced power consumption. Another significant advantage consists in better code portability as well as in improved robustness with respect to obsolescence of electronic devices being almost the whole design self-contained into the FPGA logic. On the other hand, mapping stereo vision algorithms into a similar low-power, low-cost architecture poses a very challenging task and only a subset of existing algorithms appropriately modified are suited to this constrained computing platform. Nevertheless, we believe that devices based on such a proposed simplified computing architecture would make RGBD sensors based on stereo vision suitable to a wider class of application scenarios not yet fully addressed by this technology.

S. Mattoccia (✉)
Department of Computer Science and Engineering, University of Bologna, Bologna, Italy
e-mail: stefano.mattoccia@unibo.it

B. Kisačanin and M. Gelautz (eds.), *Advances in Embedded Computer Vision*,
Advances in Computer Vision and Pattern Recognition,
DOI 10.1007/978-3-319-09387-1_5

5.1 Introduction

In recent years, with the widespread diffusion of 3D sensors, there has been increasing interest in consumer and research applications based on dense range data. Some of these sensors provide a depth map and an RGB (or monochrome) image of the sensed scene and, for this reason, they are often referred to as RGBD (RGB plus Depth) sensors. A well-known and representative example of such devices is the Microsoft Kinect, a cheap and accurate RGBD sensor based on structured light technology. Since its presentation in 2010, it has been deployed in many scientific and consumer applications. This technology, developed by Prime Sense, relies on a standard color camera, an infrared projector, and an infrared camera. The projected pattern is sensed by the infrared camera and analyzed according to a patented technology in order to infer depth. The Kinect enables the user to obtain accurate depth maps and images at VGA resolution in indoor environments. Another interesting technology that in recent years gained popularity is *Time of Flight* (ToF). In this case, the sensor emits a modulated light and, by measuring the time required to receive the bounced light, it infers depth. In most cases, this technology also provides a monochrome image of the sensed scene and hence belongs to the class of RGBD sensors. However, compared to the Kinect technology, ToF currently provides depth maps and images at a reduced resolution compared to structured light sensors as well as to stereo vision based sensors. Nevertheless, Microsoft recently presented for its new gaming console an evolution of the original Kinect based on time-of-flight technology enabling increased resolution compared to other time-of-flight sensors currently available. Active technologies have specific strengths and limitations [25]; however, they are ill-suited to environments flooded with sunlight (the Kinect in particular becomes useless in these circumstances). On the other hand, it is worth observing that, in stereo vision technology, depth and image resolutions are only constrained by the computational requirements of the stereo matching algorithm. For these reasons, especially for the limitations concerned with ToF sensors, there have been attempts to improve resolution and effectiveness of active sensors by means of sensor fusion techniques (e.g., [6]). These approaches combine the depth maps provided by active sensors with registered images and depth maps provided by high-resolution stereo vision systems.

Stereo vision is a well-known technology for inferring depth and, excluding projection-based approaches, it is a passive technology based on standard imaging sensors. Stereo vision systems infer dense depth maps by identifying corresponding projections of the same 3D point sensed by two or more cameras in different positions. This challenging task, often referred to as the *correspondence problem*, can be tackled with many algorithms (the Middlebury stereo evaluation website [28] provides a quite updated list and evaluation of stereo vision algorithms) and consequently produces different outcomes in terms of accuracy and computational requirements. This means that, in stereo vision, the algorithm aimed at tackling the correspondence problem plays a major role in the overall technology and, in recent years, there has been a dramatic improvement in this area. Another important factor that has made stereo vision more suitable to a wider range of applications has been the recent availability of low-cost powerful computing platforms such as FPGAs, GPUs, and CPUs with DPS capabilities. Of course, stereo vision technology intrinsically provides RGB or monochrome images, and thus belongs to the class of RGBD sensors. Compared to active technologies such as structured light or ToF, stereo vision may provide unreliable results in regions where the correspondence problem becomes ambiguous (e.g., in poorly textured regions or in presence of repetitive patterns along image scanlines). However, compared to active technologies, it is well suited to both indoor and outdoor environments, as well as to close-range and long-range depth measurements by simply changing the relative position of the digital imaging sensors and/or their optics. Finally, being a passive technology, multiple stereo vision sensors sensing the same area do not interfere with each other enabling multicamera setups. Nevertheless, despite these positive aspects and a widespread deployment in many research applications in the last few decades, stereo vision is often perceived as a bulky and expensive technology not suited to mainstream or consumer applications. In this paper, we will try to address this concern by outlining a simple and cheap computing architecture mainly based on low-cost FPGAs. We will also review a subset of state-of-the-art stereo matching algorithms that have the potential to entirely fit within this constrained architecture without other external device (e.g., FIFOs, DDR memories, etc.), with the exception of a high-speed communication controller. In some cases, the constraints imposed by such simplified computing architecture require modifications to the original algorithms that will be discussed in the remainder of this chapter. The topic addressed in this paper is related to an ongoing research activity aimed at developing a cheap, accurate, self-powered RGBD sensor based on stereo vision technology, deploying as a computing platform only the reconfigurable logic available in standard low-cost FPGAs. This choice has several advantages and also some limitations that will be discussed in the remainder of this chapter.

Figure 5.1 reports preliminary experimental results, computed on a frame of the KITTI dataset [10], concerned with three algorithms discussed in this chapter and implemented on the constrained computing architecture. Additional and updated results can be found here.[1]

5.2 Related Work

Dense stereo vision has been a widely researched topic for decades [31] and, due to its highly demanding computational requirements, many different computing platforms (e.g., CPUs, GPUs, DSPs, FPGAs, ASICs, etc.) have been deployed to obtain depth maps (hopefully) in real time. However, some of these computing architectures, such as those based on standard CPUs or GPUs, are currently ill-suited to

[1] Videos and applications of the 3D camera are available at this links:
http://www.youtube.com/channel/UChkayQwiHJuf3nqMikhxAlw
http://www.vision.deis.unibo.it/smatt.

Fig. 5.1 Preliminary experimental results for three algorithms implemented in the target computing architecture. Disparity maps are concerned with frame ♯66 of the KITTI dataset [10], using a simple x-Sobel filter as prefiltering step. From *top* to *bottom* rectified reference image, disparity map computed by the FW implementation, disparity map computed by a modified version of the [5] algorithm using two paths, and disparity maps computed by a modified version of the SGM [13] algorithm using four paths. Additional experimental results are available at this link: http://www.youtube.com/channel/UChkayQwiHJuf3nqMikhxAlw

consumer/embedded applications due to their high power requirements, cost, and size. Computing architectures, such as those based on high-end FPGAs, are often too expensive as well, while solutions based on custom *application specific integrated circuits* (ASICs), despite the limitations regarding their reconfigurability and *time to market* compared to FPGAs, represent a less expensive solution in large volumes. Finally, we point out that interesting low-power, low-cost, reconfigurable architectures for real-time dense stereo vision are represented by embedded CPUs coupled with integrated DSPs, such as the OMAP platform [11], extensively used for stereo vision. A recent and detailed review of stereo vision algorithms for different computing architectures can be found in [33]. In this chapter, we will consider a simple computing architecture based entirely on low-cost FPGAs that, in our opinion, represent an optimal solution to design compact, low-cost, low-power 3D sensors based on stereo vision.

5.2.1 Field-Programmable Gate Arrays

FPGAs can be configured, and in most cases reconfigured many times, by means of hardware description languages (HDLs) such as VHDL or Verilog. The internal structure of an FPGA consists of a large amount of *logic cells*, each containing a small amount of elementary logic blocks (e.g., Flip-Flops, multiplexers, and lookup tables). Distributed into the FPGA, there are also small multiport memories, often referred to as *block RAM*, with fast access time. Moreover, modern low-cost FPGAs often integrate configurable DSPs for efficient arithmetic operations, clock managers, and high-speed transceivers. All these components can be configured by programmers/designers according to their specific requirements by means of HDLs. For instance, considering a Xilinx Spartan 6 Model 45 FPGA, we can find roughly 44,000 logic cells, 116 dual-port block RAMs (18 Kb each), 58 DSPs, 4 clock managers, and 358 configurable I/O pins. It is worth noting that the reconfigurable logic of an FPGA can be configured/programmed with HDLs at a higher level of abstraction using a *behavioral* programming methodology. However, mapping computer vision algorithms on the reconfigurable logic with HDLs is not as simple as mapping the same algorithms on CPUs with traditional high-level programming languages. Nevertheless, recent years have seen the appearance of effective high-level synthesis (HLS) tools that enable the automatic conversion of code written in a standard programming language, such as C/C++ or Matlab, into HDLs. Despite these facts, being the hardware resources of the reconfigurable logic highly constrained, a clear understanding of the overall FPGA architecture and of the available resources is crucial for writing optimized code with HDLs as well as with HLS tools. The key advantage, compared to most other computing architectures, is that FPGAs, thanks to their complete reconfigurability, can be programmed to massively exploit parallelism and tailored to specific application requirements enabling one to obtain the optimal performance/Watt.

5.2.2 Stereo Vision

Stereo vision [31] is a technique aimed at inferring dense or sparse depth maps from two or more views of the same scene observed by two or more cameras. Although increasing the number of cameras has the potential to improve accuracy and reliability, the binocular setup (i.e., deploying two imaging sensors) is frequently deployed in practice. Due to the many applications that can take advantage of dense depth data, this topic has received a constant research interest in the last decades, and significant algorithmic improvements have been proposed [15, 31]. However, most dense stereo vision algorithms are computationally demanding, and parallel computing architectures are in most cases mandatory if one is to obtain dense depth measurements in real time. Not surprisingly, for this reason, FPGAs have attracted the interest of many researchers working in this field [33].

5.3 Overview of the Constrained Computing Architecture

Our target computing architecture is aimed at minimizing cost, power consumption, and at enabling better portability with respect to future evolutions of the FPGA core that, in our case, currently relies on the Xilinx Spartan 6 family. The design strategy adopted here would easily enable the porting of algorithms to FPGA devices provided by different manufacturer to high-end devices manufactured by Xilinx, such as devices belonging to the high-end Virtex class as well as to new computing architecture made of multicore and programmable logic such as those recently proposed by Altera or Xilinx (e.g., the Zynq platform for Xilinx). In particular, these latter *hybrid* architectures, made of ARM cores tightly coupled with powerful reconfigurable logic, would perfectly match our strategy enabling the design of self-contained smart cameras with a very simplified and almost standard hardware design.

A brief overview of our current computing architecture is depicted in Fig. 5.2. It is based on a single FPGA and aims to obtain dense depth maps at more than 30+ fps processing WVGA (752×480) stereo pairs sensed by monochrome or color sensors. These specific imaging sensors, manufactured by Aptina (specifically the MT9V034 model adopted for our evaluation), provide some interesting features well suited to smart cameras for computer vision applications. In fact, these imaging sensors have global shutter capability, are available in monochrome or color (based on the Bayer pattern) format, have a maximum frame rate of 60 fps, provide an optional LVDS data communication between sensors and the device (the FPGA in our case) that manages the video streams and also enable simultaneous acquisition by means of hardware synchronization. Nevertheless, it is worth pointing out that our design is not constrained to this specific imaging sensor and other devices could be used in place with minimal modifications to the overall design. Observing Fig. 5.2, we can notice that the two synchronized color or monochrome imaging sensors are connected, through two *low-voltage differential signaling* (LVDS) channels for clocks and data, to the FPGA. This choice, plus the additional LVDS link between the two imaging sensors, enables us to put the sensors and the computing platform in arbitrary positions, even at distances of meters, in order to deal with different setups according to different application requirements. For instance, in gesture recognition applications, the baseline is typically very small (few centimeters), while for systems aimed at autonomous navigation, the baseline can be significantly larger (50 cm or more). Both cases would be easily handled by the depicted solution. Despite this important fact, other crucial design goals in our project were minimal power require-

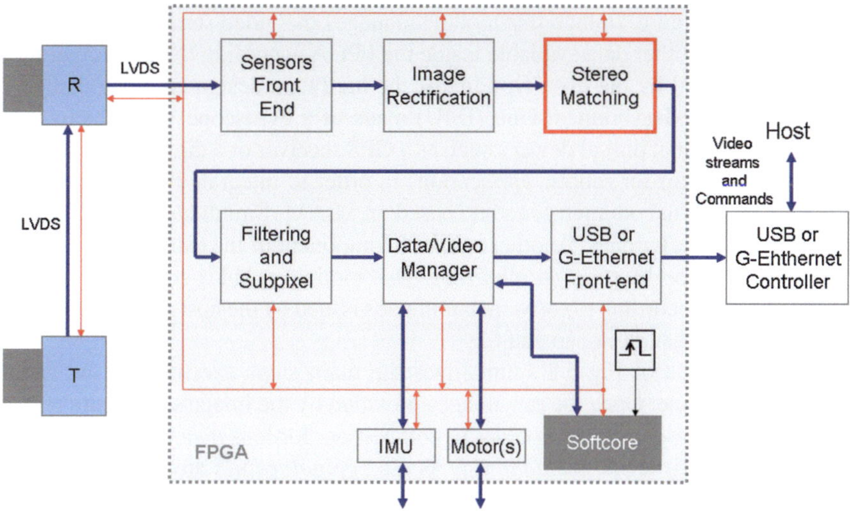

Fig. 5.2 Basic architecture of the target computing platform. The overall design contains the imaging sensors (e.g., at WVGA resolution), a low-cost FPGA (e.g., a Spartan 6 Model 45 or better), and an external high-speed communications controller (e.g., USB 2.0 or 3.0, GigaEthernet). The overall processing pipeline, including the FIFO aimed at handling transfers to/from the high-speed communications controller and a softcore that supervises the whole system, is synthesized into the reconfigurable logic of the FPGA

ment, compactness, and reduced bill of materials. Concerning power requirements, the overall design has a power consumption of about 2.0 W supplied by a standard USB 2.0 data connector. The overall size of the computing platform depicted in Fig. 5.2, excluding the imaging sensors modules, has an area smaller than a credit card. Finally, the bill of materials can be summarized by considering a small amount of inexpensive hardware devices. Namely, it results in the FPGA, the imaging sensors and the external USB or GigaEthernet controller plus some standard electronic components such as clocks and passive devices. According to this overview, it is clear that the considered computing platform is not equipped with any external memory device such as a SRAM or a DDR. This choice simplifies the overall design (enabling power, area, and costs reduction) but, on the other hand, enforces strong constraints to the processing capabilities of such a processing platform that will be thoroughly discussed in the remainder of this chapter.

Observing Fig. 5.2, we can also notice that our design contains a *softcore* synthesized into the FPGA logic; this is a small RISC processor mainly aimed at handling communications with the host computer in order to change camera parameters, such as the frame rate or other features of the imaging sensors, by means of standard serial communication protocols (e.g., I2C). The softcore, by means of software commands issued by the host, also allows us to select, among those available within the processing pipeline, the video streams actually required by the user. For video stream configuration, the softcore is tightly coupled with the Data/Video manager unit as depicted in the figure. In fact, this module manages the video streams processed by the pipeline and other data available inside the FPGA according to the configuration commands issued by the host. Optionally, the hardware design could be equipped with an Inertial Measurement Unit (IMU) made of a gyroscope, an accelerometer and other additional digital devices such as a GPS receiver or a digital compass. The IMU can be useful for robotic applications in order to integrate the measurements provided by a visual odometry module based on SLAM (Simultaneous Localization And Mapping) techniques. Another optional component of the camera, managed by the softcore, is the Motor controller unit. This module enables control of multiple stepper motors according to software commands issued by the host and can be useful, for instance, for handling pan and tilt.

The upper side of Fig. 5.2 summarizes the main steps executed by the vision processing pipeline. Once the raw images provided by the image sensors are sent to the FPGA, they are rectified in order to compensate for lens distortions. Moreover, the raw stereo pair is put in *standard form* (i.e., *epipolar lines* are aligned to image *scanlines*). Both steps require a *warping* for each image of the stereo pair, which can be accomplished by knowing the *intrinsic* and *extrinsic* parameters of the stereo system [31]. Both parameters can be inferred by means of an offline calibration procedure. Once the rectified images are in standard form, potential corresponding points are identified by the stereo matching module as will be discussed in the next sections. Unfortunately, since not all of the correspondences found by the previous module are reliable, a robust outlier detection strategy is crucial. This step typically consists of multiple tests aimed at enforcing constraints to the inferred disparity maps (e.g., left–right consistency check, uniqueness constraint, analysis of the cost curve, etc.), the input images, or the matching costs computed by the previous matching engine according to specific algorithmic strategy. The filtered disparity map is then sent to the Data/Video manager. This unit contains a small FIFO synthesized in the FPGA logic, and it is mainly focused on packaging selected video streams and other relevant data. This data is then sent to the communication front end implemented in the FPGA logic and directly connected to the external communication controller that in the current prototype is an USB 2.0 controller manufactured by Cypress.

The host computer, once it has received the disparity map, will compute depth by triangulation according to the parameters inferred by the calibration procedure. Although in this paper, we will focus our attention on the stereo matching module, the overall goal consists in mapping all the blocks depicted in Fig. 5.2 into a low-cost FPGA. As previously pointed out, a similar design would allow for small cost, size, weight, power requirements, and reconfigurability. Moreover, the upgrade of the whole project to newer FPGAs (typically cheaper and with better performance in terms of speed and power consumption compared to previous generation) is almost straightforward. Finally, we point out that, with the availability of integrated solutions based on reconfigurable logic, plus embedded processors such as the Xilinx Zynq [44], a self-contained FPGA module would make feasible the design of a fully embedded 3D camera with complete onboard processing without any additional external host computer.

5.4 Stereo Vision: Analysis of Memory Footprint and Bandwidth

Stereo vision algorithms are well-known for their demanding computational requirements that sometimes even do not enable their deployment in practical applications with real-time constraints. This limitation in standard computing architecture such as CPUs or GPUs is often concerned with *number crunching* capabilities. However, when it comes to consider highly constrained computing architectures such as that previously outlined, major limitations typically consist in the massive memory footprint and/or bandwidth requirements within the memory and the processing unit. Let us consider these facts by analyzing the simplest stereo matching algorithm that evaluates, within a prefixed disparity range D with disparity $d \in [d_{\min}, d_{\max}]$, the matching costs $C(x, y, d)$ computed, on a point basis, between each point in the reference image at coordinate $R(x, y)$ and each potential corresponding pixel $T(x - d, y)$, $d \in [d_{\min}, d_{\max}]$ in the target image. Many effective cost functions have been proposed in the literature and among these, the absolute difference of pixel intensity (AD) or its truncated version, often referred to as truncated absolute difference (TAD), that saturates the cost to an upper threshold T, Census transform coupled with Hamming distance [47] and its variants such as the mini-Census [4] or the more robust ternary based approach proposed [30] are widely adopted by algorithms implemented into FPGAs. In fact, AD- and Census-based approaches, compared to other cost functions such as squared differences (SD), normalized cross-correlation (NCC) or zero-mean normalized cross-correlation (ZNCC), robust cost functions computed on rectangular patches, or mutual information (MI) [41], are certainly less demanding in terms of reconfigurable logic required for their hardware implementation. In terms of robustness, the nonparametric local transform [47] makes this approach robust to strong photometric variations, although in its original formulation, it is quite noisy in uniformly textured region. Concerning AD, in order to increase its robustness to photometric distortions that frequently occur in practical application scenarios, a transformation that reduces the low-frequency components (e.g., LoG (Laplacian of Gaussian) or Sobel filter) is often applied to the stereo pair before AD computation. For the reasons outlined so far, AD- and Census-based approaches are frequently deployed by stereo vision algorithms implemented into FPGAs. Sometimes, such as in [22], different cost functions (in [22], AD and Census) are combined to increase robustness. Finally, there are approaches [37] that rely on direct edge detection mechanism to improve computational efficiency. An exhaustive review and evaluation of cost functions suited to practical stereo vision systems, not restricted to FPGA implementation, can be found in [14].

Considering the previous example, from the memory point of view, stacking each $C(x, y, d)$ for each point and for each disparity within the disparity range would result in the 3D memory structure depicted in Fig. 5.3 and often referred to DSI (Disparity Space Image). However, in most effective algorithms adopted in practical applications, the matching cost evaluated to determine the best disparity value consists in aggregated pointwise matching costs $C(x, y, d)$, accumulated costs along

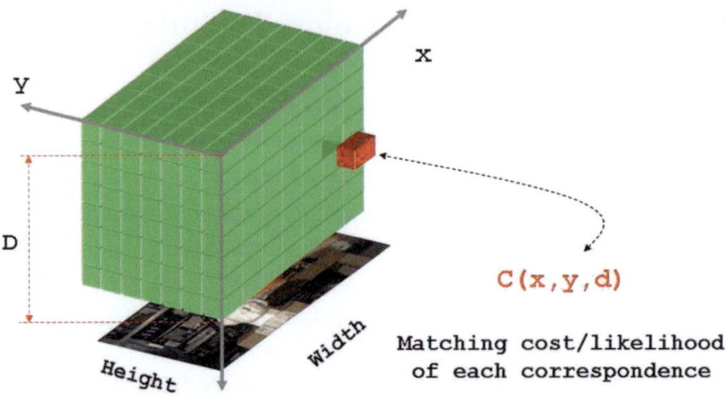

Fig. 5.3 Disparity Space Image, the 3D structure containing the pointwise matching cost $C(x, y, d)$ for each point and for each disparity value within the disparity range D

scanlines in order to enforce smoothing constraints on the disparity maps or by means of other strategies.

Some algorithms, as will be discussed in the remainder, require to store in a memory structure the whole DSI depicted in Fig. 5.3. Unfortunately, even with standard image resolution and disparity range, this is a significant amount of data that typically exceeds the memory available in most current FPGAs and for this reason, an external memory would be mandatory in these cases. For instance, by considering images at 752×480, a disparity range of 64 and 16 bit for each matching cost $C(x, y, d)$, the DSI consists of 44 MB. Although a similar amount of data seems not critical deploying external memory devices such as DDR memory or SRAM memory, there is a more critical constraint concerned with memory bandwidth. In fact, FPGAs, despite their reduced clock frequency, compared to other parallel computing devices such as GPUs, can be effective with respect to such devices by exploiting their potential massive parallel capabilities by means of tailored internal logic reconfigurations. Nevertheless, to this aim and in order to provide a throughput of (at least) one disparity per clock cycle to keep pace with the pixels provided by the imaging sensors, there is a strong memory pressure when intermediate results (for instance, as typically occurs, the D values concerned with the point under examination or D values for intermediate results (sometimes even $k \times D$ values) must be read within a single clock cycle. This case is summarized in Fig. 5.4.

For instance, by considering our previous configuration, D = 64 and size of each matching cost $C(x, y, d)$ 2 bytes, with a pixel clock frequency of 30 MHz (appropriate for imaging sensors similar to those deployed in our camera), the memory bandwidth required turns out to be higher than 3.5 GB/s. In most cases, for each clock, this amount of data must be read, processed/updated, and then written back to memory, thus doubling the overall required memory bandwidth highlighted. Of course, with higher resolution imaging sensors, typically clocked at higher frequency, moving data back and forth between FPGA and memory further emphasizes the memory bandwidth bottleneck.

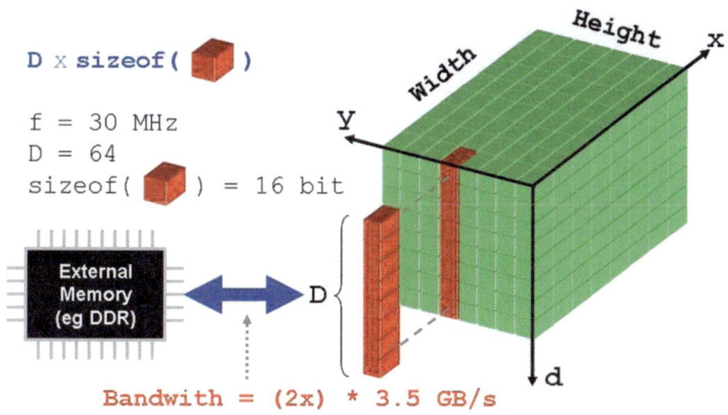

Fig. 5.4 Moving data back and forth between FPGA and external memory can easily lead to exceed the available bandwidth

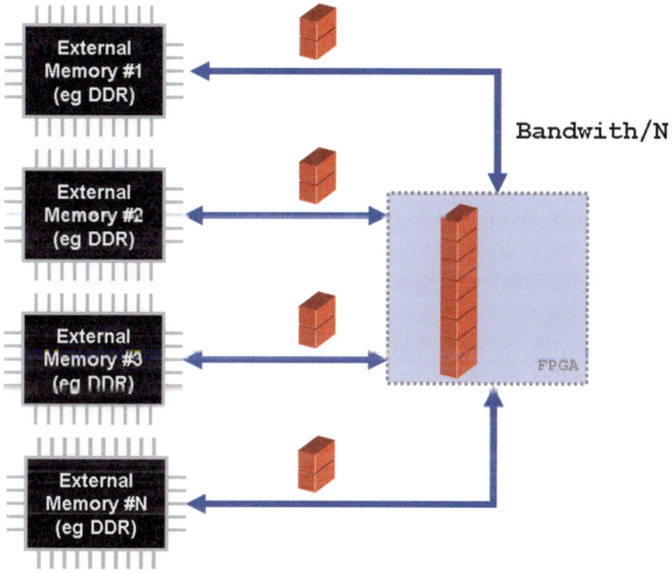

Fig. 5.5 The overall memory bandwidth can be increased by adding to the design multiple memory devices

According to the previous analysis, since the memory bandwidth required can exceed that available in current memory devices, a straightforward solution to overcome this problem would consist in using multiple memory devices as outlined in Fig. 5.5. However, although the strategy depicted in the figure could solve memory bandwidth issues, this strategy would have on the other hand some disadvantages. In particular, using multiple memory devices to increase the overall memory bandwidth would lead to increased costs, power consumption, overall complexity, and area. Moreover, such a solution would also increase the overhead, in terms of reconfigurable logic and memory controllers, required by the FPGA for handling multiple external memory devices.

For the reasons outlined so far, in our design, we decided to avoid external memory devices at all. Although this choice enables to overcome some of the problems previously outlined, it also means that we can rely only on the fast, yet small, memory available inside the FPGA. As should be clear, this choice imposes very strong constraints on the algorithms that can be implemented on such a computing architecture. Nevertheless, as we will show in the next sections, following specific algorithmic methodologies, very effective results can be obtained adopting this simplified design strategy.

5.5 Stereo Vision Algorithms Suited to the Constrained Computing Architecture

A computing architecture similar to that outlined in the previous section poses significant constraints to the computational structure of the algorithms that can be implemented. In fact, considering a representative case study of the Xilinx Spartan 6 FPGA family [44], we can see that the overall block memory available is about 261 KB for the Model 45 (and about 600 KB for the most powerful device of this family, the Model 150). In between models 45 and 150, there are two devices, 75 and 100, with an amount of logic cells close to, respectively, 75,000 and 100,000 and with an amount of block memory, respectively, of about 400 KB and 600 KB. This means that, ignoring other requirements, we would not even be able to store a stereo pair at WVGA resolution (about 720 KB) in the most complex 150 device. This observation, plus the limited overall reconfigurable logic available (about 43,000 and 147,000 logic cells for the Model 45 and 150, respectively), dictates that *stream processing* [2] is mandatory for our purposes. This technique consists of processing pixels as soon as they are available from the imaging sensors, with minimal buffering requirements. Of course, for the same reason, the resulting output cannot be entirely stored into the FPGA and must be sent to the communications controller as soon as it is made available by the processing pipeline. We also point out that other relevant constraints are concerned with the overall reconfigurable logic available for processing (e.g., about 55,000 flip-flops for the Model 45 and 185,000 flip-flops for the Model 150) and the maximum distributed RAM available (e.g., about 50 KB for Model 45 and about 17 KB for Model 150). More details concerned with these devices are available in [44].

In the next sections, we will consider some relevant stereo vision algorithms potentially suited to this constrained target architecture. For this purpose, we will adopt the classification proposed in [31], where algorithms are classified into two major categories, local approaches and global approaches, making a further distinction when dealing with approaches not completely described by these two broad categories.

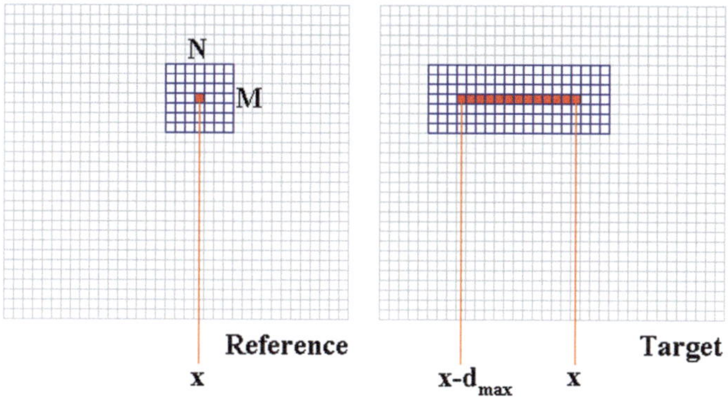

Fig. 5.6 Support windows, of size $M \times N$, for cost aggregation in local algorithms at disparity d. In the reference image, the support window is centered on point (x), while in the target image, the support windows are centered on points $[x, x - d_{\max}]$

5.5.1 Local Algorithms

Local algorithms process each point independently ignoring relationship between neighboring disparity values. For this reason, they do not enforce an explicit smoothness constraint on the target disparity map, and typically for each disparity candidate within the disparity range D, compute the matching cost by aggregating neighboring pixels (often on rectangular patches referred to as *support* windows, as depicted in Fig. 5.6). Cost aggregation is often explicitly obtained by summing up, according to different strategies, each pointwise matching cost within the support window, as depicted in Fig. 5.6. However, it is worth noting that some recent approaches implicitly aggregate costs in constant time, independently of the size of the support [7, 27].

More generally, cost aggregation performed by most local algorithms can be figured out, as depicted in Fig. 5.7, as a filtering [15] of the DSI data structure according to different strategies. Examples of filtering operations applied to the DSI are averaging/sum, bilateral filtering [46], approximated bilateral filtering [19], guided filter [12], etc. Since local algorithms completely ignore relationships between neighboring points and different disparity values within the disparity range, from the computational point of view, this means that D filtering operations can be applied in parallel to the DSI in order to aggregate matching cost for each disparity candidate. Adopting for the processing pipeline the same clock of imaging sensors, the computation of the D filtering operations for each point should hopefully finish within a single (pixel) clock cycle. This fact potentially enables a high degree of parallelism (multiplied by a factor D compared to the sequential case) but at the same time it imposes that all the data required in the DSI (highlighted in the DSI depicted in Fig. 5.7), or a subset of this data centered in the point under examination, must be accessed in parallel. Therefore, at least the portion of data highlighted in Fig. 5.7 should be carefully managed, by means of appropriate data structures and buffering

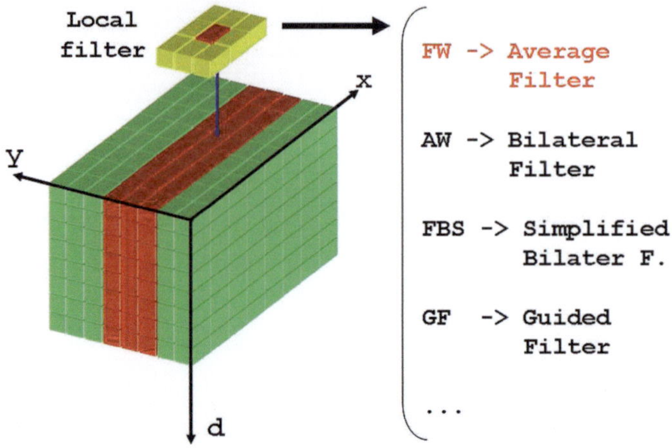

Fig. 5.7 In most local algorithms, cost aggregation is carried out by filtering the DSI according to different strategies

techniques implemented in the internal logic of the FPGA, in order to enable parallel access required to sustain parallelism. Of course, in the outlined constrained computing architecture, the overall portion of the DSI highlighted in the figure must be stored in the internal memory of the FPGA, typically in the block RAM. Nevertheless, with WVGA imaging sensors (even with imaging sensors at higher resolution) and typical disparity range deployed in practical applications, this amount of data becomes compatible with the internal memory made available by FPGAs similar to those previously examined.

In local algorithms, the best disparity for each point is often identified according to a simple *winner-takes-all* (WTA) strategy by finding the candidate with the best aggregated cost. For the reasons previously outlined, local algorithms are inherently parallel, and hence are ideal candidates for FPGA implementation. Detailed reviews and evaluations of local stereo algorithms can be found in [15, 31, 33, 36, 42].

5.5.1.1 Fixed Window Algorithm

In spite of their simplicity and intrinsic parallel nature of local algorithms, even the mapping of the simplest approach to the constrained target architecture outlined in previous sections should be carefully planned. The simplest local algorithm is often referred to as fixed window (FW) or *block matching* and simply sums up/averages all the matching costs within the support window. Although this algorithm has some well-known limitations, such as inaccurate depth reconstruction near depth discontinuities and, as most local algorithms, problems in uniformly textured regions of the sensed scene, it is often deployed in several practical applications, thanks to its overall robustness in determining the rough 3D structure of the scene and to its simple algorithmic structure.

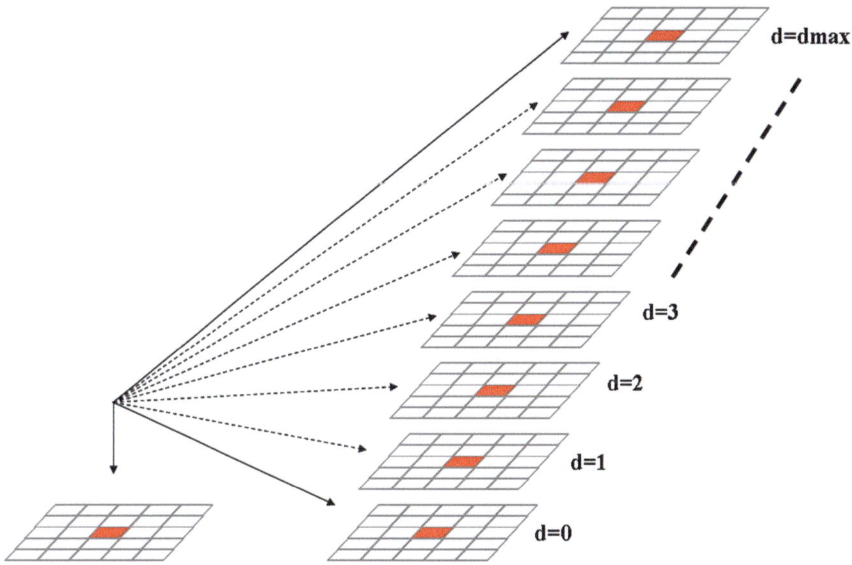

Fig. 5.8 Multiple filters applied to the reference and target images for cost aggregation. The number of filter is equal to the disparity range ($d_{max} + 1$ in the figure)

According to Fig. 5.7, in this case filtering consists in summing/averaging within the support, for each disparity value, the matching costs in the DSI. From a different point of view, this operation consists in applying multiple instances of the same filter (sum/average filter for FW) between reference and target image as illustrated in Fig. 5.8.

With a support of size $M \times N$ and a disparity range of $[0, d_{max}]$, the number of arithmetic operations for the brute force approach is proportional to $M \times N \times (d_{max} + 1)$. Considering that plausible values for these parameters could be $M = 15$, $N = 15$, and $d_{max} = 63$, the number of arithmetic operations required might exceed the hardware resources available in the target FPGA. Nevertheless, this number of operations can be significantly reduced by adopting well-known incremental calculation schemes such as *box-filtering* [21] or *integral images* [40]. The former in particular, as outlined in Fig. 5.9, is particularly suited for FPGA implementation of the FW algorithm.

The figure shows that the overall cost aggregation for the supports depicted in the upper side of the figure can be obtained more efficiently by deploying the 1D optimization depicted in the middle of the same figure. In fact, the aggregate costs required by the operations in the upper side of Fig. 5.9 can be reduced by observing that the overall cost for the central point can be obtained by updating the overall cost computed in the previous position along the scanline, adding the aggregated costs of the rightmost columns, and subtracting the aggregated costs of the leftmost columns.

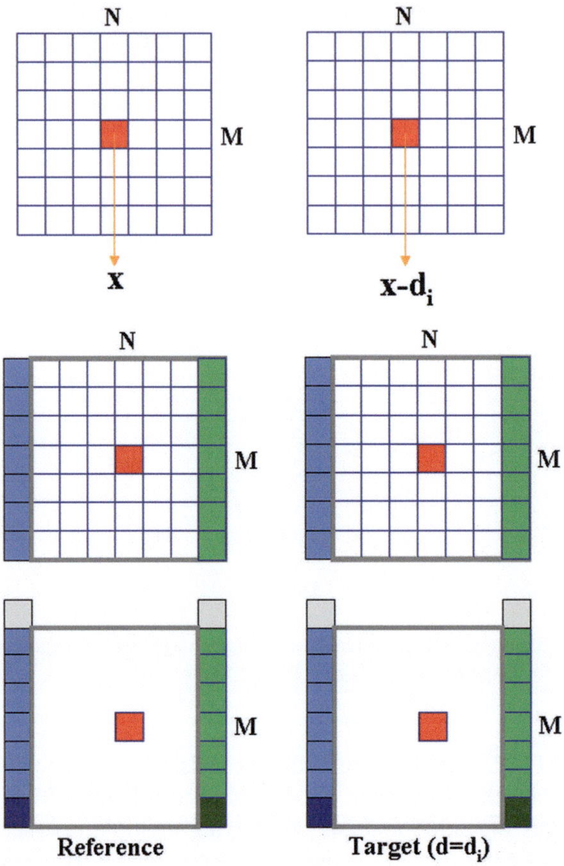

Fig. 5.9 Incremental techniques, referred to as box-filtering, aimed at reducing to a constant value the number of basic operations required for cost aggregation in fixed window. *Top*, full cost computation. *Middle*, incremental optimization along horizontal direction (number of elementary operations reduced by a factor N). *Bottom*, vertical optimization required to compute the sum of the vertical stripes shown in the middle of the figure. In this latter case, the full cost for each disparity value, is computed with a fixed number of operations involving the four points highlighted at the *bottom* of the figure in reference and target images

In deploying this 1D optimization strategy, the number of operations is reduced by a factor N, manageable with the logic included in most FPGAs. Nevertheless, a further reduction of operations can be obtained by deploying a 2D incremental scheme that stores intermediate results for each column as depicted in the bottom of the figure. In this case, the number of operations per window is constant and independent of the size of the support, though compared to the brute force approach depicted at the top of the figure, at the expense of a higher memory footprint for buffering intermediate results required to sustain the additional 2D incremental calculation.

Several implementations of the FW algorithm, and its variants, suited for FPGA were proposed in the literature with different degrees of algorithmic complexity and hence with different resources used. Some recent representative approaches in this field are [17, 39, 50]. In Sect. 5.6, we report experimental results concerned with our implementation of the FW algorithm on the constrained hardware architecture previously outlined.

5.5.1.2 Local Algorithms Based on Adapting Weights and Constrained Supports

Although the FW approach is widely used in many practical applications, it is clearly outperformed by more recent local approaches based on cost aggregation techniques that aggregate costs according to weights assigned by examining the image content [15, 19, 23, 36, 46]. In these approaches, differently by the simple average score computed by FW, the overall score is given by a weighted sum/average of the costs computed within each support window [18]. The key idea behind this strategy consists of weighting each cost according to its *relevance* with respect to the point under examination (i.e., the central points of the supports).

Many methodologies to assign weights have been proposed in the literature and an effective rationale is that inspired by bilateral filtering [26, 34] applied to the stereo matching by the AW (Adaptive Weights) algorithm [46]. That is, points with *similar* intensity with respect to the central point should be more influential in the weighted sum. Moreover, points *closer* to the central point should also be more relevant according to [46]. This strategy is similar to the weight computation strategy used by bilateral filtering and, in stereo, weights are often computed within the support window of reference and target images (this strategy is often referred to as *joint* or *symmetric*). In the strategy based on segmentation [35], the original bilateral filtering weight computation was relaxed by removing the proximity constraint.

A first optimization [15, 23] consists of asymmetrically computing weights, examining only the image points belonging to the reference image. Although this strategy significantly reduces weight computation by a factor of $d_{\max}$, the number of operations required for cost aggregation is always proportional to $M \times N \times (d_{\max} + 1)$ and may exceed the resources available in the target FPGA. However, simplified yet effective strategies based on the computation of weights and/or costs and/or overall weighted costs only in sampled points may help to further reduce the number of elementary operations per point, maintaining high accuracy. These approaches also exploit massively incremental calculation schemes for cost computation, similar to those outlined for FW. An approach that efficiently computes weights, on a sparse regular grid, and aggregated costs on a block basis, by means of [21], is the Fast Bilateral Stereo (FBS) algorithm [19]. This approach represents a link between the traditional fixed window approach and AW. Figure 5.10 shows for the Tsukuba stereo pair, the results obtained by FW, AW, and FBS. Compared to AW, FBS obtains equivalent results with a fraction (about 10 %) of operations making it suitable for hardware

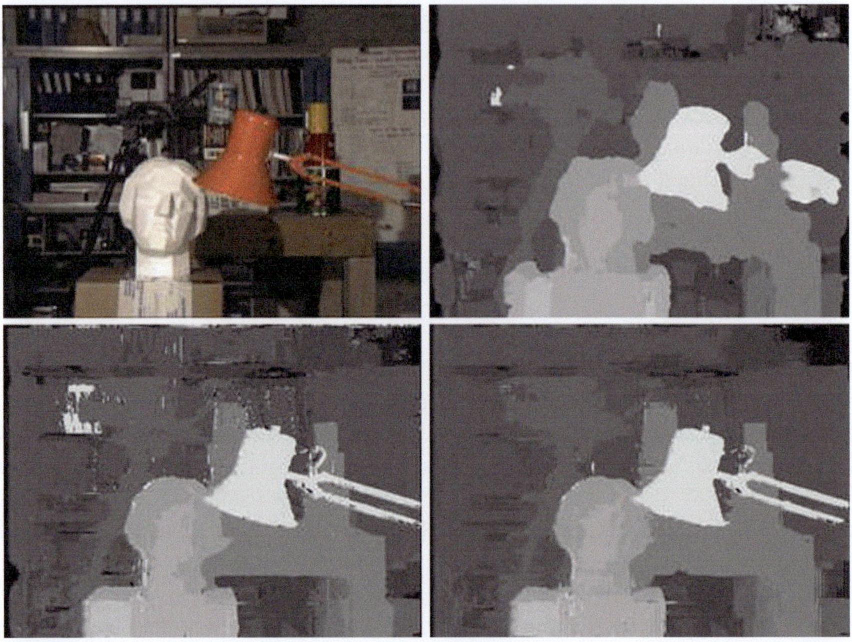

Fig. 5.10 *Top left*, original reference image of the Tsukuba stereo pair [28, 29]. *Top right*, disparity map obtained by the FW approach. *Bottom left*, disparity map obtained by the AW algorithm [46]. *Bottom right*, disparity map obtained by the Fast Bilateral Stereo algorithm [19]

implementation. Observing the figure, we can also notice that algorithms based on the adapting weights strategy are much more accurate near depth discontinuities.

In [23], further optimizations compared to FBS have been devised, including a *preselection* of potential candidate disparities and asymmetric weight computations making also this algorithm a candidate for hardware implementation.

Zhang et al. [48] described a different and effective strategy for cost aggregation based on two orthogonal cost aggregation phases. As for many previous methods, this approach heavily relies on incremental calculation schemes for fast cost aggregation.

A different two-phase strategy to reduce the computational burden of the original AW approach consists in the two-pass aggregation described in [43]. In this method, originally deployed within a Dynamic Programming framework, the nonseparable weighted cost computation of AW is approximated with a vertical cost aggregation, followed by an horizontal aggregation of the costs computed during the first phase (i.e., vertical cost aggregation). Compared to AW, this simplified strategy enables to obtain similar results reducing significantly the number of operations from $O(n^2)$ to $O(n)$, with n the cardinality of the support window.

Finally, it is worth noting that some recent local algorithms [7, 27] filter the DSI according to the guided filtering technique [12], thus enabling weighted cost aggregation in constant time. Such approaches massively exploit incremental calculation

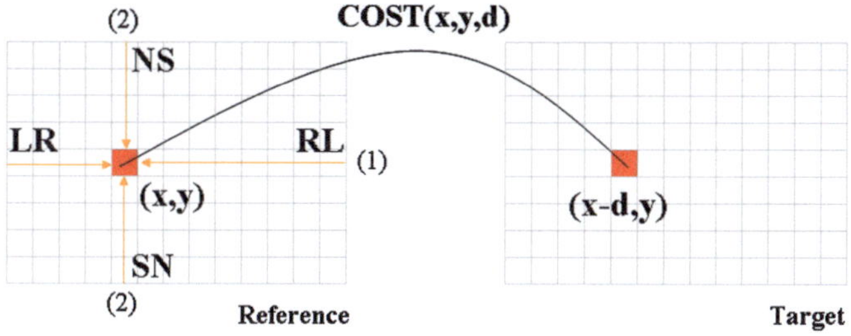

Fig. 5.11 The four paths used to compute permeability terms and aggregated cost for algorithm [5]

techniques [21] potentially suited to the constrained FPGA architecture, thanks to the reduced (and constant) number of operations required with respect to explicit cost aggregation approaches inspired by bilateral filtering. Despite these positive facts, the results provided by these constant time algorithms are comparable to those based on explicit cost aggregation, and hence these algorithms are potentially suited for implementation in the outlined target platform.

Concerning FPGA implementations based on adaptive weights strategy, [8] reported a hardware friendly implementation of the original AW approach [46]. In [24], a further simplification of the AW approach based on simpler binary weights was devised. A method based on the mini-census transform for cost computation and the two-pass approach [43] for cost aggregation is [4] while [49] used, with the same cost function, the two pass orthogonal cost aggregation strategy proposed in [48]. An FPGA implementation of a cost aggregation strategy based on segmentation is reported in [38]. Finally, an interesting method based on adaptive weight cost aggregation, identification of reliable points and disparity refinement, by means of an effective method aimed at enforcing local consistency [20] of the disparity field, was proposed in [16].

5.5.1.3 Algorithms Based on Unconstrained Supports

According to the taxonomy provided in [29], the algorithms reviewed in the previous sections clearly belong to the class of local algorithms. However, there are some local algorithms that significantly diverge from traditional approaches, in particular for what concerns the support regions used for cost aggregation.

An interesting local approach, referred to as Permeability, was proposed in [5]. This technique performs multiple 1D cost aggregations constrained by an *information permeability* term (see [5] for a detailed explanation) computed along horizontal or vertical scanlines, as shown in Fig. 5.11, without enforcing any explicit smoothness term. The permeability term, computed along the horizontal scanline from left to right is defined as follows:

$$W^{\mathrm{LR}}(x, y) = e^{-\frac{|I(x,y) - I(x-1,y)|}{\sigma}} \tag{5.1}$$

with $I(x, y)$ and $I(x-1, y)$ the pixel intensity at coordinate (x, y) and $(x-1, y)$, respectively, in the reference image and σ an appropriate empirically determined constant value. The aggregated cost computed along the same horizontal scanline and direction, from left to right in the considered example, is then computed according to:

$$C^{\mathrm{LR}}(x, y, d) = C(x, y, d) + W^{\mathrm{LR}}(x-1, y) \cdot C^{\mathrm{LR}}(x-1, y, d) \tag{5.2}$$

This strategy, applied to both horizontal directions depicted in Fig. 5.11 and along both vertical directions on horizontally aggregated costs, efficiently enables to adaptively perform cost aggregation on unconstrained 2D support windows. More precisely, cost aggregation is initially independently performed along horizontal scanlines (from left to right (LR) and right to left (RL)). Then, a similar approach is applied along vertical directions (from top to bottom (NS) and bottom to top (SN)) to the summed aggregated matching cost computed along horizontal paths. In practice, in this method, the support window implicitly consists of the entire image. Although this strategy requires us to store the entire image and matching costs, a simplification of the original approach restricted to a subset of scanlines (e.g., from left to right, from right to left, and from top to bottom) is certainly feasible for the constrained target computing architecture outlined. We report in Sect. 1.6, results concerned with our hardware friendly implementation of the Permeability algorithm based on two single directions. Another implementation suited to FPGAs was proposed in [1].

Finally, a different and effective algorithm that, similarly to the previous method, does not explicitly define a fixed support window was proposed in [45]. In this approach, the matching costs are aggregated using as weights the minimum intensity distance between any two points in the reference image. These weights are stored in a tree structure and, to this aim, a MST (Minimum Spanning Tree) containing a number of nodes equal to the number of image points is created. This enables to very efficiently and in constant time obtain for each point the aggregated weighted cost computed on the whole image. Nevertheless, although this method is very fast and effective on traditional CPU or GPU architectures, in its original formulation, it, due to the memory footprint required to store the MST, seems inappropriate to a target computing architecture without being provided with external memory devices, such as DDR memory.

5.5.2 Global and Semiglobal Approaches

Although local algorithms described so far yield excellent results, they are often outperformed by approaches that explicitly enforce a smoothness term on the resulting disparity map. These methods solve the correspondence problem in terms of a pixel-labeling assignment of disparities, determining the disparity field D that minimizes the energy term (5.3):

$$E(D) = E_{\text{data}}(D) + E_{\text{smooth}}(D) \tag{5.3}$$

The *data term* E_{data} in (5.3) encodes how well the disparity assignment fits with the stereo pair, and often it is the sum of per-pixel data costs $C(D(p))$ between one point in the reference image R and the supposed homologous point in the target image T:

$$E_{\text{data}}(D(p)) = \sum_{p \in R} C(D(p)) \tag{5.4}$$

In (5.3), the *smoothness term* $E_{\text{smooth}}(D)$ enables to enforce a piecewise disparity field D by modeling the interaction between each point p and its neighboring points $q \in \mathcal{N}(p)$. In fully global approaches, $\mathcal{N}(p)$ includes points in vertical and horizontal directions (typically, the four nearest neighbors of p on the pixel grid) while in 1D approaches, based on Scanline Optimization (SO) or Dynamic Programming, the smoothness term is enforced only in one direction (typically $\mathcal{N}(p)$ includes only one point along a scanline). The former disparity optimization methods are typically referred to as 2D. In general, 2D methods perform better as they enable the enforcement of *inter* and *intra* scanline smoothness assumptions.

Unfortunately, when deploying a 2D approach, minimization of (5.3) turns out to be an $\mathcal{NP}$-hard problem. Therefore, global approaches typically rely, under particular hypotheses [32] on (5.3), on efficient energy minimization strategies typically based on Graph Cuts (GC) or Belief Propagation (BP). However, the iterative nature of these energy minimization strategies and their high memory footprint typically render these approaches inappropriate for devices with limited resources such as for our target architecture.

Nevertheless, a subclass of these algorithms that enforces disparity constraints on 1D domains by means of dynamic programming such as [43] or multiple scanline optimization [13] represents, for the outlined target computing architecture, a viable and effective alternative to local approaches. In particular, the semiglobal matching algorithm [13] computes multiple energy terms by means of the SO technique [29], independently enforcing 1D smoothness constraints along different paths (typically 8 or 16 from all directions as depicted in Fig. 5.12 for 8 paths).

The 1D energy terms independently minimized by means of the scanline optimization approach are then summed up and the best disparity is determined by means of the same WTA strategy adopted by local algorithms. Figure 5.13 shows, at top and middle, the disparity maps concerned with two 1D minimizations, independently computed along paths 0 and 5, and, at the bottom of the figure, the result of the multiple 1D optimization computed along eight paths. Observing the figure, we can notice that, although single scanline optimizations are not very accurate, their combination by means of the method proposed in [13] turns out to be very effective as can be seen, using eight paths, at the bottom of Fig. 5.12.

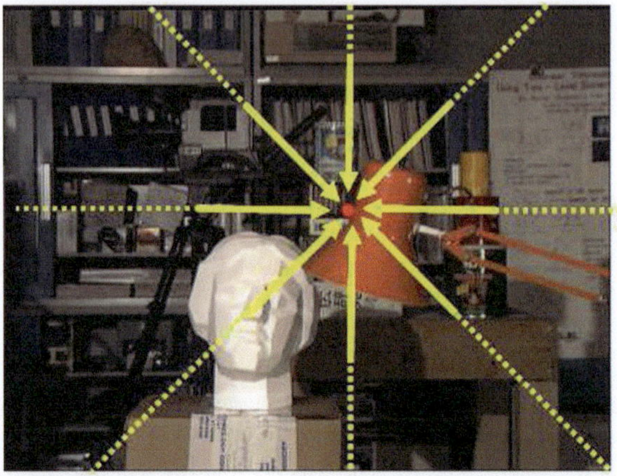

Fig. 5.12 The semiglobal algorithm [13], on each path, performs independent 1D disparity optimizations. The figure considers only eight paths

The strategy adopted by SGM enables fast implementations on CPUs and GPUs and it is very effective. For these reasons, SGM is frequently deployed in many practical applications. However, in its original formulation, due to its high memory footprint (it requires the entire DSI), it is not well suited to a computing architecture without a large amount of fast external memory. Moreover, in its original formulation, the SGM algorithm scans reference and target images two times (from top to bottom and then from bottom to top) making unfeasible the stream processing methodology required by our target architecture.

Nevertheless, by deploying a subset of the original paths (e.g., only four paths), the SGM algorithm becomes suitable with acceptable performance degradation for our target platform. We report in Sect. 5.6 experimental results concerned with our implementation of the SGM algorithms adopting this strategy.

Concerning FPGA implementations of the SGM algorithm, Gehrig et al. [9] implemented the original algorithm proposed in [13] by means of a two-pass approach on downscaled half resolution input images (originally at 680) using 8 paths. Differently, Banz et al. [3] proposed a simplified version of the SGM algorithm for hardware implementation aimed at reducing memory constraints using 4 paths (0, 4, 2 and 7 in Fig. 5.13).

5.6 Experimental Results

In this section, we report preliminary experimental results concerned with the implementation of three stereo vision algorithms—belonging to the three classes defined in the previous section—in the outlined computing architecture made of a single FPGA without additional external devices, with the exception of a high-speed

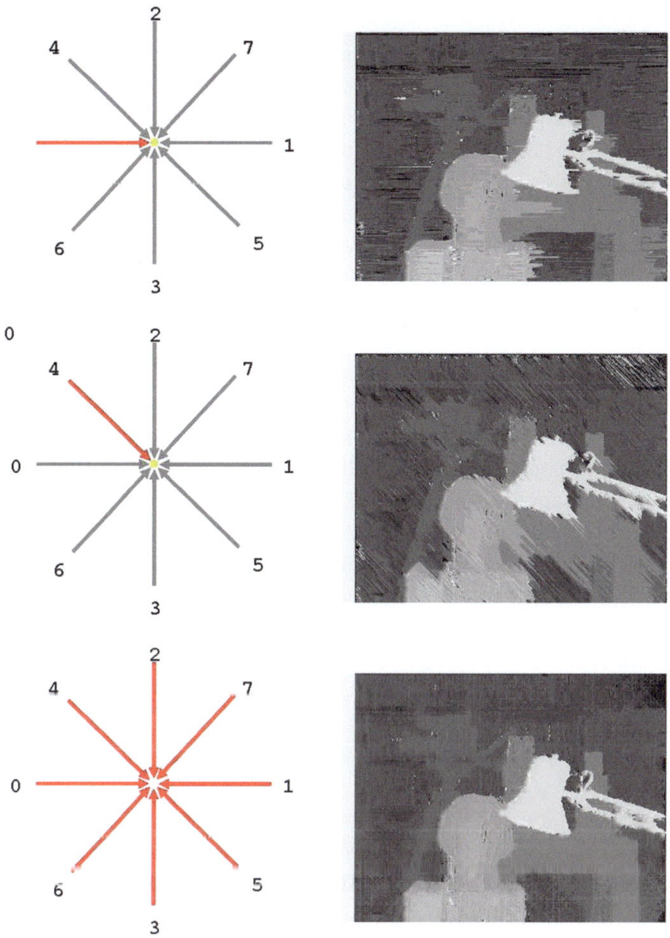

Fig. 5.13 *Top*, 1D scanline optimization along scanline 1—*Middle*, 1D scanline optimization along scanline 4—*Bottom*, result of the SGM algorithm performing multiple 1D scanline optimizations along the eight paths shown at the *left*

communications controller as depicted in Fig. 5.2. Each of these algorithms, as well as all of the other blocks depicted in the figure, was mapped on a Spartan 6 FPGA 45 and delivers depth maps at 30+ fps when processing stereo pairs at WVGA resolution as those deployed by our camera.

Specifically, the algorithms currently implemented in our target architecture are: FW using the optimization strategies previously outlined, a modified version of the Permeability algorithm [5] using two paths and a modified version of SGM [13] using four paths. Each implementation of these algorithms also includes image rectification, a prefiltering step based on the x-Sobel filter, and a postprocessing step aimed at filtering outliers by detecting uniformly textured regions as well as by detecting unreliable disparity candidates analyzing their local distribution. The design also mapped into the FPGA also includes the internal FIFO and all the other modules depicted in Fig. 5.2.

For evaluation purposes, we provide in Fig. 5.1 experimental results concerned with the three implemented algorithms processing frame ♯66 of the KITTI dataset [10]. Observing the figure, where in the disparity maps brighter greyscale levels encode closer points and darker levels farther points, we can see that all three algorithms enable us to obtain dense and fairly accurate disparity maps of this challenging stereo pair. Observing the trees in the right side of the reference frame, we can notice that the SGM algorithms seems less noisy compared to the two local algorithms. In the same figure, we can also notice the most unreliable (e.g., occlusions) and uniform regions (e.g., shadows) are correctly detected by the postfiltering modules.

At this link http://www.youtube.com/watch?v=KXFWIvrcAYo is available a video[2] concerned with an outdoor sequence processed by our modified version of the SGM algorithm implemented on the outlined constrained target architecture. In this case, the stereo camera, based on a Spartan 6 Model 75, was configured with a very short baseline of about 4 cm. Observing this video, we can notice that the camera provides, at high frame rate, very accurate and dense depth maps processing stereo pairs at 640×480 resolution. In the video, we can also notice that the outlier detection module implemented into the FPGA correctly detects most unreliable disparity measurements.

5.7 Conclusions

In this chapter, we have reviewed stereo vision algorithms that, with appropriate modifications, are suited for implementation on a basic computing architecture made of a single low-cost FPGA without additional external devices. Algorithms mapped on such architecture provide accurate and dense depth maps in real time enabling to obtain a small, low-power, and low-cost RGBD stereo vision sensor self-contained into an FPGA.

Acknowledgments I'd like to thank Ilario Marchio, Marco Casadio, Stefano Bruciati, Michael Cavina, Simone Calisesi and Marco Destro for the experimental results reported in this paper.

References

1. Aysu A, Sayinta M, Cigla C (2013) Low cost FPGA design and implementation of a stereo matching system for 3D-TV applications. In: VLSI-SoC, pp 204–209
2. Bailey DG (2011) Design for embedded image processing on FPGAs. Wiley, Asia

[2] Other videos available at:
http://www.youtube.com/channel/UChkayQwiHJuf3nqMikhxAlw.

3. Banz C, Hesselbarth S, Flatt H, Blume H, Pirsch P (2010) Real-time stereo vision system using semi-global matching disparity estimation: architecture and FPGA-implementation. In: ICSAMOS, pp 93–101
4. Chang NY-C, Tsai T-H, Hsu P-H, Chen Y-C, Chang T-S (2010) Algorithm and architecture of disparity estimation with mini-census adaptive support weight. IEEE Trans Circuits Syst Video Techn 20(6):792–805
5. Cigla C, Alatan AA (2011) Efficient edge-preserving stereo matching. In: ICCV 2001 workshops, pp 696–699
6. Mutto CD, Zanuttigh P, Mattoccia S, Cortelazzo G (2012) Locally consistent ToF and stereo data fusion. In: Proceedings of 2nd workshop on consumer depth cameras for computer vision, ECCV'12, pp 598–607
7. De-Maeztu L, Mattoccia S, Villanueva A, Cabeza R (2011) Linear stereo matching. In: ICCV: 2011, pp 1708–1715
8. Ding J, Liu J, Zhou W, Yu H, Wang Y, Gong X (2011) Real-time stereo vision system using adaptive weight cost aggregation approach EURASIP. J Image Video Process 1:1–19
9. Gehrig KS, Eberli F, Meyer T (2009) A real-time low-power stereo vision engine using semi-global matching. In: ICVS, pp 134–143
10. Geiger A, Lenz P, Urtasun R (2012) Are we ready for autonomous driving? the KITTI vision benchmark suite. In: CVPR 2012, Providence
11. Goldberg SB, Matthies LH (2011) Stereo and IMU assisted visual odometry on an omap3530 for small robots. In: ECVW 2011, pp 169–176
12. He K, Sun J, Tang X (2010) Guided image filtering. In: ECCV 2010, pp 1–14
13. Hirschmüller H (2008) Stereo processing by semiglobal matching and mutual information. IEEE Trans Pattern Anal Mach Intell 30(2):328–341
14. Hirschmüller H, Scharstein D (2009) Evaluation of stereo matching costs on images with radiometric differences. IEEE Trans Pattern Anal Mach Intell 31(9):1582–1599
15. Hosni A, Bleyer M, Gelautz M (2013) Secrets of adaptive support weight techniques for local stereo matching. Comput Vis Image Underst 117(6):620–632
16. Jin M, Maruyama T (2014) Fast and accurate stereo vision system on FPGA. ACM Trans Reconfigurable Technol Syst 7(1):3:1–3:24
17. Jin S, Cho J, Pham XD, Lee KM, Park S-K, Kim M, Jeon JW (2010) FPGA design and implementation of a real-time stereo vision system. IEEE Trans Circuits Syst Video Technol 20(1):15–26
18. Lan Z-D, Mohr R, Remagnino P (1995) Robust matching by partial correlation. In: BMVC, pp 1–10
19. Mattoccia S, Giardino S, Gambini A (2009) Accurate and efficient cost aggregation strategy for stereo correspondence based on approximated joint bilateral filtering. In: ACCV 2009, pp 23–27
20. Mattoccia S (2010) Fast locally consistent dense stereo on multicore. In: Sixth IEEE embedded computer vision workshop, San Francisco
21. Mc Donnel M (1981) Box-filtering techniques. Comput Gr Image Process 17:65–70
22. Mei X, Sun X, Zhou M, Jiao S, Wang H, Zhang X (2011) On building an accurate stereo matching system on graphics hardware. In: ICCV workshops, pp 467–474
23. Min D, Lu J, Do MN (2011) A revisit to cost aggregation in stereo matching: How far can we reduce its computational redundancy? In: ICCV 2011, pp 1567–1574
24. Motten A, Claesen L, (2010) A binary adaptable window SoC architecture for a stereo vision based depth field processor. In: VLSI-SoC, pp 25–30
25. Mutto CD, Zanuttigh P, Cortelazzo GM (2012) Time-of-flight cameras and microsoft kinect (TM). Springer Publishing Company, Incorporated
26. Paris S, Kornprobst P, Tumblin J (2009) Bilateral filtering. Now Publishers Inc., Hanover
27. Rhemann C, Hosni A, Bleyer MC, Gelautz M (2011) Fast cost-volume filtering for visual correspondence and beyond. In: CVPR 2011, pp 3017–3024
28. Scharstein D, Szeliski R, http://vision.middlebury.edu/stereo/

29. Scharstein D, Szeliski R (2002) A taxonomy and evaluation of dense two-frame stereo correspondence algorithms. Int J Comput Vis 47(1/2/3):7–42
30. Stein F (2004) Efficient computation of optical flow using the census transform. In: Rasmussen CE, Bülthoff HH, Schölkopf B, Giese MA (eds) Proceedings of the 26th DAGM symposium. Lecture Notes in Computer Science, vol 3175. Springer, pp 79–86
31. Szeliski R (2010) Computer vision: algorithms and applications. Springer New York Inc, New York
32. Szeliski R, Zabih R, Scharstein D, Veksler O, Kolmogorov V, Agarwala A, Tappen M, Rother C (2008) A comparative study of energy minimization methods for Markov random fields with smoothness-based priors. IEEE Trans Pattern Anal Mach Intell 30(6):1068–1080
33. Tippetts B, Lee DJ, Lillywhite K, Archibald J (2013) Review of stereo vision algorithms and their suitability for resource-limited systems. J Real-Time Image Process
34. Tomasi C, Manduchi R (1998) Bilateral filtering for gray and color images. In: ICCV98, pp 839–846
35. Tombari F, Mattoccia S, Di Stefano L (2007) Segmentation-based adaptive support for accurate stereo correspondence. In: Proceedings of PSIVT 2007
36. Tombari F, Mattoccia S, Di Stefano L, Addimanda E (2008) Classification and evaluation of cost aggregation methods for stereo correspondence. In: CVPR08, pp 1–8
37. Ttofis C, Hadjitheophanous S, Georghiades AS, Theocharides T (2013) Edge-directed hardware architecture for real-time disparity map computation. IEEE Trans Comput 62(4):690–704
38. Ttofis C, Theocharides T (2012) Towards accurate hardware stereo correspondence: a real-time fpga implementation of a segmentation-based adaptive support weight algorithm. In: DATE, pp 703–708
39. Villalpando CY, Morfopolous A, Matthies L, Goldberg S (2011) FPGA implementation of stereo disparity with high throughput for mobility applications. In: Proceedings of the 2011 IEEE aerospace conference, AERO'11DC, Washington, pp 1–10
40. Viola P, Jones MJ (2004) Robust real-time face detection. Int J Comput Vis 57(2):137–154
41. Paul V, Wells WM (1997) III. Alignment by maximization of mutual information. Int J Comput Vis 24(2):137–154
42. Wang L, Gong MW, Gong ML, and Yang RG (2006) How far can we go with local optimization in real-time stereo matching. In: Proceedings of the third international symposium on 3D data processing, visualization, and transmission (3DPVT 2006), pp 129–136
43. Wang L, Liao M, Gong M, Yang R, Nister D (2006) High-quality real-time stereo using adaptive cost aggregation and dynamic programming. In: Proceedings of 3DPVT 06, pp 798–805
44. Xilinx. www.xilinx.com
45. Yang Q (2012) A non-local cost aggregation method for stereo matching. In: CVPR 2012, pp 1402–1409
46. Yoon KJ, Kweon IS (2006) Adaptive support-weight approach for correspondence search. IEEE Trans PAMI 28(4):650–656
47. Zabih R, Woodfill J (1994) Non-parametric local transforms for computing visual correspondence. In: ECCV 1994. Springer, pp 151–158
48. Zhang K, Lu J, Lafruit G (2009) Cross-based local stereo matching using orthogonal integral images. IEEE Trans Circuits Syst Video Technol 19(7):1073–1079
49. Zhang L, Zhang K, Chang TS, Lafruit G, Kuzmanov GK, Verkest D (2011) Real-time high-definition stereo matching on FPGA. In: Proceedings of the 19th ACM/SIGDA international symposium on field programmable gate arrays, FPGA'11, pp 55–64
50. Zicari P, Perri S, Corsonello P, Cocorullo G (2012) Low-cost FPGA stereo vision system for real time disparity maps calculation. Microprocess Microsyst 36(4):281–288

Chapter 6
Plane Sweeping in Eye-Gaze Corrected, Teleimmersive 3D Videoconferencing

Maarten Dumont, Patrik Goorts and Gauthier Lafruit

Abstract A teleimmersive videoconferencing system for autostereoscopic 3D displays is presented. Eye contact between participants is restored by synthesizing novel, interpolated views from multiple surrounding cameras, effectively emulating a capturing camera position behind a virtually transparent display. Nonuniform, adaptive plane sweeping with dynamic workload balancing yields real-time performances on low-cost embedded GPU platforms.

6.1 Introduction

Imagine a world with perfect immersive teleconferencing, where people are able to communicate remotely with an intense sense of human awareness that would be virtually indistinguishable from real-life social communication. People would be able to communicate seamlessly with their friends and family thousands of miles away. Face-to-face meetings would be enabled without the need to travel, and telecollaboration would reach the holy grail of *The Office Of The Future* [22] with a high level of immersion.

And yet, in spite of all the work already done in immersive teleconferencing and the high level of quality reached in today's video capturing and rendering technology, this ultimate dream remains unrealized. What are the potential causes and how can technology provide a solution to this problem?

M. Dumont (✉) · P. Goorts · G. Lafruit
Expertise Centre for Digital Media, Hasselt University - TUL - IMinds, Wetenschapspark 2, 3590 Diepenbeek, Hasselt, Belgium
e-mail: maarten.dumont@uhasselt.be

P. Goorts
e-mail: patrik.goorts@uhasselt.be

G. Lafruit
e-mail: gauthier.lafruit@uhasselt.be

B. Kisačanin and M. Gelautz (eds.), *Advances in Embedded Computer Vision*, Advances in Computer Vision and Pattern Recognition,
DOI 10.1007/978-3-319-09387-1_6

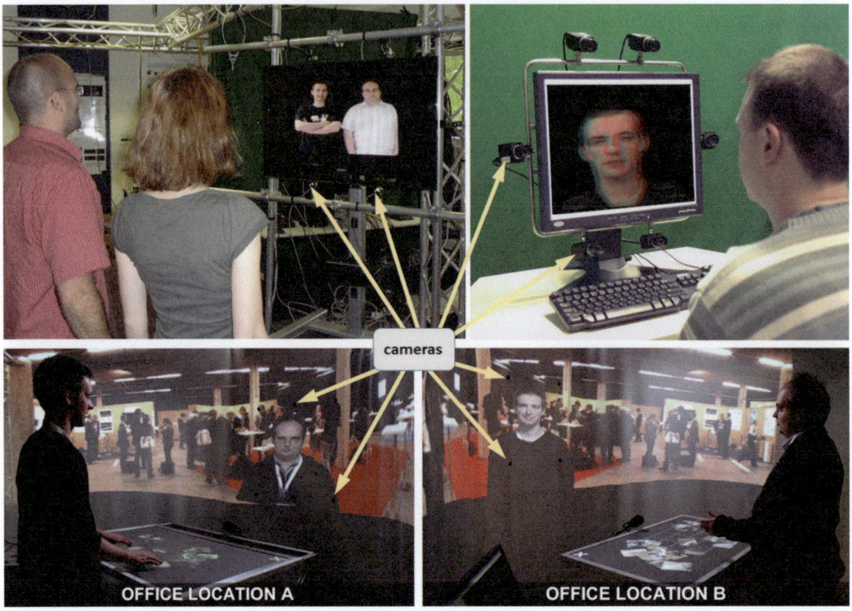

Fig. 6.1 Restoring eye contact by synthesizing a virtual view in between the surrounding camera views

Gaze awareness and stereoscopic perception are actually important factors to provide a high level of realism needed to feel oneself immersed in a natural social environment [33]. Unfortunately, since cameras and displays cannot possibly occupy the same spatial position simultaneously, videoconferencing participants are unable to look each other in the eyes: a person who stares at the display will be captured by the cameras as looking away at a slightly diverging angle.

An elegant way to solve this problem is to synthesize a virtual view in between the surrounding camera views, as if it would be rendered by a camera positioned right behind the screen, effectively restoring the correct head position and eye contact [25], as shown in Fig. 6.1.

Synthesizing a multitude of such nearby views even supports stereoscopic (Fig. 6.1, top right anaglyph) and glasses-free automultiscopic 3D displays (Fig. 6.2), where tens of nearby virtual views are projected in different directions, allowing the viewer's eyes to capture two parallax-correct images at any position in space for a natural 3D perception.

This chapter presents a robust method for multicamera view synthesis for eye-gaze correction and natural 3D video rendering, based on seminal work in plane sweeping [7, 8, 13, 14]. Important improvements are proposed to target embedded vision applications on GPU-accelerated platforms.

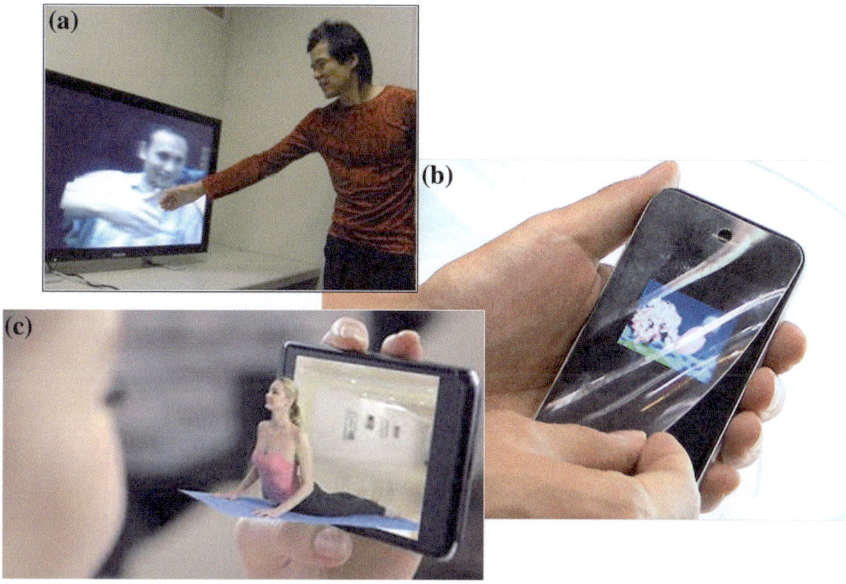

Fig. 6.2 A plethora of multicamera and lenticular display technology, providing all means to natural eye-gaze corrected and 3D video communication, is available on the market today. In automultiscopic 3D displays, tens of nearby virtual views are projected in different directions, so that the viewer's eyes always capture two parallax-correct images at any position in space, hence providing glasses-free, natural 3D perception

6.2 View Synthesis Prior Art

Early solutions in handling the problem of eye-gaze correction in videoconferencing applied model-based approaches [28, 31] using a detailed head 3D model, which is projected in the virtual viewpoint direction. This solution often lacks in natural impression with participants talking to humanoid-looking avatars.

More advanced techniques therefore focus on image-based rendering approaches (IBR) [1, 4], where a virtual view is synthesized with depth-based image warping and in painting techniques [20, 26]. Depth is hereby often recovered from stereo matching [24] on a pair of sanline rectified images. The limited amount of 3D scene parallax and associated depth information often results in visual artifacts in the synthesized views. Solutions such as the ones of [2, 25] overcome this limitation at the cost of using expensive dedicated hardware and/or unpractical camera setups.

On the other hand, plane sweeping is a method that uses a multitude of cameras and that by design is much more robust to camera illumination mismatches, misalignments, etc. It recovers scene depth by sweeping over multiple depth plane hypotheses for each pixel in the camera view that is to be reconstructed, hence its name *plane sweeping*. In principle, plane sweeping does not need to explicitly extract depth for handling view synthesis, though depth extraction helps in image postprocessing for boosting the natural perception of the virtual views.

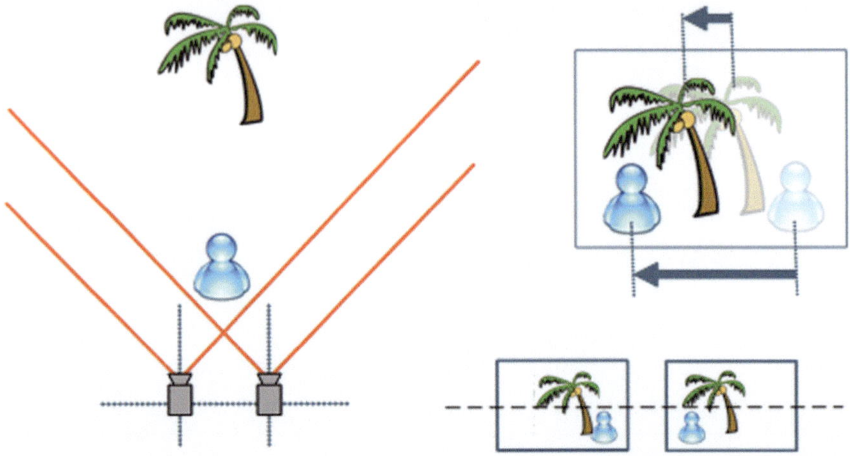

Fig. 6.3 Concept of stereo vision. A scene is captured using two rectified cameras. Stereo matching attempts to estimate the apparent movement of the objects across the images. A large apparent movement (i.e., parallax) corresponds to close objects (a low depth value)

Let's first introduce the high-level concepts of these techniques, in order to better understand the advantages of our full system prototype in Sect. 6.3.

6.2.1 Stereo Matching

Stereo matching uses a pair of images to estimate the apparent movement of the pixels from one image to the next. This apparent movement is more specifically known as the parallax effect as demonstrated in Fig. 6.3, where two objects are shown, placed at different depths in front of a stereo pair of cameras.

When moving from the left to the right camera view, an object undergoes a displacement—called the disparity—which is inversely proportional to the object's depth in the scene. Objects in the background (the palm tree) have a smaller disparity in comparison to objects in the foreground (the blue buddy). The goal of stereo matching is to compute a dense disparity map by estimating each pixel's displacement.

6.2.2 Plane Sweeping

To conceptually grasp the concept of plane sweeping, let us take a look at Fig. 6.4. Here, cameras C_1 to C_3 are real cameras in an arbitrary configuration, whereas camera C_v is the virtual camera view of which we wish to reconstruct the color image and the scene depth.

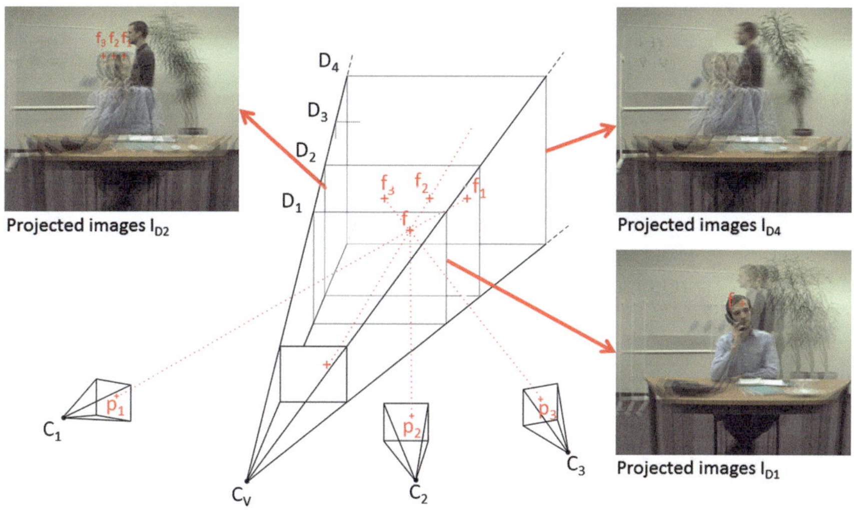

Fig. 6.4 Plane sweeping conceptually: deprojecting real cameras C_i ($i = 1 \ldots 3$) on different depth planes D_i for virtual camera C_v causes a nonfocused ghosting artifact, depending on whether or not the scene object in question is present at depth D_i

Any voxel f in 3D space at, e.g., depth plane D_1 is projected onto the 2D pixels p_i on the image plane of the respective camera views. Conversely, inversely projecting (i.e., deprojecting) the pixels p_i into 3D space will have them match at one single voxel f at the corresponding depth plane D_1. On all other depth planes D_j ($j \neq 1$) the pixels p_i deproject on points f_i that do not coincide, as illustrated on depth plane D_2. Visually, reprojecting these points f_i back into the virtual camera view C_v causes a nonfocused ghosting artifact in the resulting image, as can be observed in the projected images I_{D2}.

For instance, for the two-person scene of Fig. 6.4, the person answering the phone at the desk in the foreground is in focus at depth D_1 (as can be seen in the projected images I_{D1}), whereas the person walking by in the background is out of focus at the same hypothesized depth D_1. The background person in turn is in focus on depth plane D_2 (as can be seen in the projected images I_{D2}), hence suggesting that his corresponding voxels are indeed at depth D_2. Looking even deeper into the scene, the whiteboard in the far background is de- and reprojected in focus at its corresponding depth plane, say D_4, and is now in fact readable (projected images I_{D4}).

6.3 A System Prototype

We present a fully functional prototype that corrects the eye gaze of the videoconferencing peers by using multiple cameras, using the plane sweeping method reviewed in the previous section. The proposed sixfold camera setup is easily integrated into the monitor frame of Fig. 6.1 [7, 8].

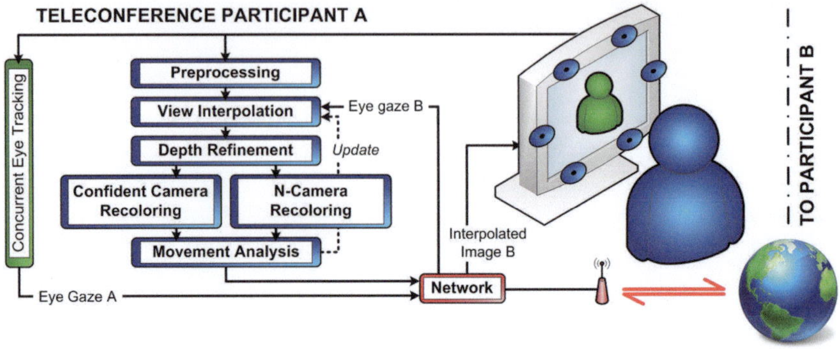

Fig. 6.5 Data flow and overview of our system architecture

Our software framework harnesses the powerful computational resources inside the Graphics Processing Unit (GPU), achieving over real-time performance for Full HD resolution images. Furthermore, although depicted as such in Fig. 6.4, the distribution of the depth planes is not required to be uniform, which we elaborate on in Sect. 6.4 for further computational complexity savings.

In comparison, competitive solutions such as the system of [6] implement their framework on commodity CPUs, resulting in a very low frame rate when sufficient visual quality is required. Others optimize only parts of the application, such as multicamera video coding [5, 16] for efficient data communication and real-time view synthesis [9, 21, 29] on graphics hardware, but neither of them integrate and optimize the end-to-end performance for eye-gaze corrected video chat.

The core functionality of our system is visualized in Fig. 6.5 and consists out of five consecutive processing modules that are completely running on the GPU. In an initial step (Sect. 6.3.1), the camera sensor Bayer patterns $\iota_1, \ldots, \iota_N$ are captured from a total of N cameras $C_1, \ldots, C_N$ that are fixed on a custom built metal frame which closely surrounds the screen (see Fig. 6.1). The first module computes the RGB-images $I_1, \ldots, I_N$, based on the method of [12, 19], and performs lens correction and image segmentation, as a form of preprocessing. The preprocessing module is specifically designed to enhance both the quality and speed of the consecutive view interpolation, and to ensure a high arithmetic intensity in the overall performance.

The second module (Sect. 6.3.2) interpolates an image I_v, as it would be seen with a virtual camera C_v that is positioned behind the screen. The image I_v is computed as if camera C_v captures the image through a completely transparent screen. Furthermore, the view interpolation module produces a joint depth map Z_v, providing dense 3D information of the captured scene.

The synthesized image still contains a number of noticeable artifacts in the form of erroneous patches and speckle noise. The third module (Sect. 6.3.3) is therefore specifically designed to tackle these problems by detecting photometric outliers based on the generated depth map.

Following the depth refinement, the image pixels are recolored using the filtered depth information (Sect. 6.3.4). Our system currently supports recoloring of the synthesized image using all N cameras, or selecting the color from the camera which has the highest confidence of accurately capturing the required pixel.

In a final step, the depth map Z_v is also analyzed to dynamically adjust the system and thereby avoiding heavy constraints on the user's movements. This optimization is performed in the plane distribution control module (*movement analysis*) and, as previously mentioned, discussed in its dedicated Sect. 6.4.

Besides the main processing on the graphics hardware that synthesizes I_v, the virtual camera C_v needs to be correctly positioned to restore eye contact between the participants. An eye tracking module (Sect. 6.3.5) thereby concurrently runs on CPU and determines the user's eye position that will be used for correct placement of the virtual camera at the other peer.

By sending the eye coordinates to the other peer, the input images $\iota_1, \ldots, \iota_N$ do not have to be sent over the network (Sect. 6.3.6), but can be processed at the local peer. This results in a minimum amount of required data communication—i.e., the eye coordinates and the interpolated image—between the two participants.

6.3.1 Preprocessing

Our system inputs Bayer patterns $\iota_1, \ldots, \iota_N$, i.e., the direct camera sensor inputs (see Fig. 6.6a). The RGB-colored images $I_1, \ldots, I_N$ are consistently computed by using the method of [19], which is based on linear FIR filtering. This is depicted in Fig. 6.6b. Uncontrolled processing that would normally be integrated into the camera electronics is therefore avoided, guaranteeing the system's optimal performance.

Camera lenses, certainly when targeting the low-budget range, induce a radial distortion that is best corrected. Our system relies on the use of the *Brown–Conrady* distortion model [3] to easily undistort the input images on the GPU.

Each input image I_i with $i \in \{1, \ldots, N\}$ is consequently segmented into a binary foreground silhouette S_i (see Fig. 6.6c), to allow the consecutive view interpolation to adequately lever the speed and quality of the synthesis process. Two methods of

Fig. 6.6 The preprocessing module performs demosaicing, undistortion, and segmentation of the input images

segmentation are supported; Green screening according to Eq. 6.1, where R_{I_i}, G_{I_i}, and B_{I_i} are the red, green, and blue components of I_i. For clarity the pixel location (x, y) has been omitted.

$$S_i = \begin{cases} 1 : G_{I_i} > \tau_g \cdot (R_{I_i} + G_{I_i} + B_{I_i}) \\ 0 : G_{I_i} \leq \tau_g \cdot (R_{I_i} + G_{I_i} + B_{I_i}) \end{cases} \tag{6.1}$$

The second method is able to subtract a real-life background [18] according to Eq. 6.2, where I_{B_i} is the static background picture and τ_g, τ_f, τ_b, τ_a are experimentally determined thresholds which are subjected to parameter fine tuning. For shadow removal, the cosine of the angle $\widehat{I_i I_{B_i}}$ between the color component vectors of the image pixel $I_i(x, y)$ and the static background pixel $I_{B_i}(x, y)$ is determined. As a final step, the silhouette is further enhanced by a single erosion and dilation [30].

$$S_i = \begin{cases} 1 : \left\| I_i - I_{B_i} \right\| > \tau_f & \text{or} \\ \quad\;\; \left\| I_i - I_{B_i} \right\| \geq \tau_b & \text{and } \cos(\widehat{I_i I_{B_i}}) \leq \tau_a \\ 0 : \left\| I_i - I_{B_i} \right\| < \tau_b & \text{or} \\ \quad\;\; \left\| I_i - I_{B_i} \right\| \leq \tau_f & \text{and } \cos(\widehat{I_i I_{B_i}}) > \tau_a \end{cases} \tag{6.2}$$

Both methods are evaluated on a pixel basis and require very little processing power, while still being robust against moderate illumination changes.

6.3.2 View Interpolation

To interpolate the desired viewpoint, we adopt and slightly modify a plane sweeping approach based on the method of [32]. As depicted in Fig. 6.7a, the 3D space is discretized into M planes $\{D_1, \ldots, D_M\}$ parallel to the image plane of the virtual camera C_v. For each plane D_j, every pixel f_v of the virtual camera image I_v is backprojected on the plane D_j by Eq. 6.3, and reprojected to the input images I_i according to Eq. 6.4. Here, $\mathbf{T}_j$ is a translation and scaling matrix that defines the depth and extent of the plane D_j in world space. The relationship between these coordinate spaces is represented in Fig. 6.7b.

$$f = \mathbf{V}_v^{-1} \times \mathbf{P}_v^{-1} \times \mathbf{T}_j \times f_v \tag{6.3}$$

$$f_i = \mathbf{P}_i \times \mathbf{V}_i \times f \tag{6.4}$$

Points on the plane D_j that project outside a foreground silhouette in at least one of the input images, are immediately rejected—e.g., point g in Fig. 6.7a—and all further operations are automatically discarded by the GPU hardware. This provides a means to lever both speed and quality because noise in the segmentation masks will, with a high probability, not be available in all N cameras. Otherwise, the mean

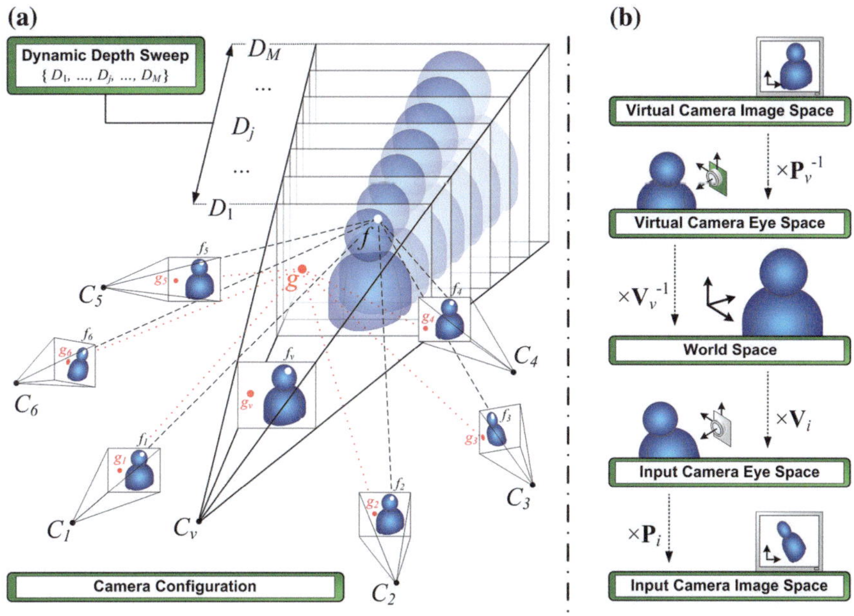

Fig. 6.7 Concept of the plane sweep algorithm

(i.e., interpolated) color ψ and a jointly defined custom matching cost κ are computed as in Eq. 6.5.

$$\psi = \sum_{i=1}^{N} \frac{I_\text{i}}{N}, \quad \kappa = \sum_{i=1}^{N} \frac{\|\psi - I_\text{i}\|^2}{3N} \tag{6.5}$$

As opposed to [32], we propose the use of all input cameras to compute the matching cost. The plane is swept for the entire search range $\{D_1, \ldots, D_M\}$, and the minimum cost—together with the corresponding interpolated color—is per pixel selected on a winner-take-all basis, resulting in the virtual image I_v (see Fig. 6.8a) and a joint depth map Z_v (see Fig. 6.8b).

6.3.3 Depth Refinement

The interpolated image calculated in the previous section still contains erroneous patches (see Fig. 6.9a) and speckle noise due to illumination changes, partially occluded areas, and natural homogeneous texturing of the face. These errors are

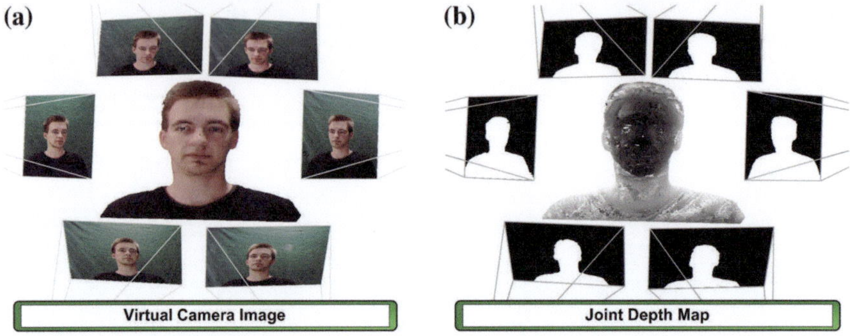

Fig. 6.8 The view interpolation module generates a virtual image and joint depth map

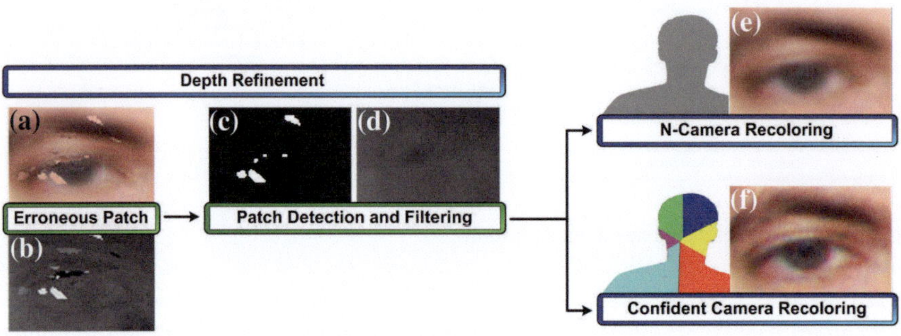

Fig. 6.9 Depth refinement and recoloring module concept

even more apparent in the depth map Z_V and we therefore propose a photometric outlier detection algorithm that detects and restores the patches in Z_V.

To suppress the spatial high frequency speckle noise, we finally run a low-pass Gaussian filter over the depth map.

6.3.3.1 Erroneous Patch Filtering

To detect erroneous patches, we propose a spatial filter kernel λ, as depicted in Fig. 6.10a. For every pixel z_V of depth map Z_V, a two-dimensional depth consistency check is performed according to Eq. 6.6, where ε is a very small constant to represent the depth consistency, λ thereby defines the maximum size of patches that can be detected.

$$\begin{aligned} \|Z_V(x-\lambda, y) - Z_V(x+\lambda, y)\| < \varepsilon \quad \text{or} \\ \|Z_V(x, y-\lambda) - Z_V(x, y+\lambda)\| < \varepsilon \end{aligned} \tag{6.6}$$

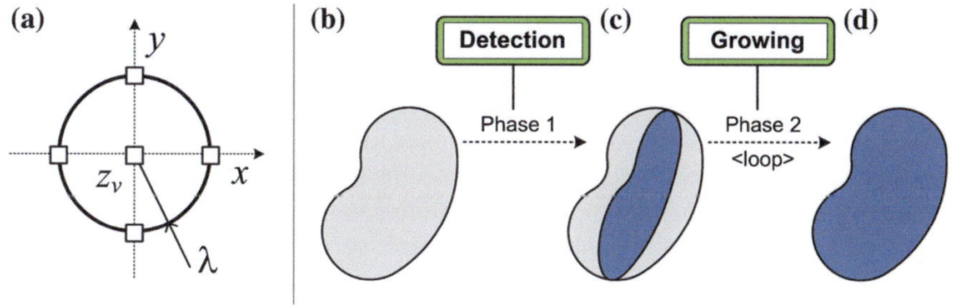

Fig. 6.10 **a** The proposed filter kernel, and **b**–**d** the outlier detection concept

If the area passes the consistency check in one of the dimensions, the depth pixel z_V—and therefore the joint image pixel f_V—is flagged as an outlier if z_V does not exhibit the same consistency by exceeding a given threshold τ_O. Equation 6.7 shows the outlier test when a depth consistency is noticed in the X-dimension, an analogous test is used in case of consistency in the Y-dimension.

$$\left\| Z_V(x, y) - \frac{Z_V(x - \lambda, y) + Z_V(x + \lambda, y)}{2} \right\| > \tau_O \tag{6.7}$$

After performing the proposed filter kernel, the patch centers are detected, as conceptually represented in Fig. 6.10b, c. Consistently, a standard morphological grow algorithm is executed, which causes the detected center to grow only if the neighboring pixels exhibit the same depth consistency as the initial outliers. As depicted in Fig. 6.9c, d, the complete patch is thereby detected. As a final step for the patch filtering, the morphological grow is reversed and the detected patch is filled with reliable depth values from its neighborhood. Since all of these operations are implemented on a pixel basis, they are inherently appropriate for implementation on a GPU, achieving a tremendous speedup compared to a generic CPU algorithm.

6.3.3.2 Speckle Noise Filtering

Due to the nature of the human face, a significant amount of large homogeneous texture regions are present. As indicated by [24], these areas cause the depth map to contain spatial high frequency speckle noise. The noise is most effectively filtered by a low-pass filter, but this eliminates the geometrical correctness of the depth map. A standard 2D isotropic Gaussian filter is applied on the depth map and thanks to its separable convolution properties, it can even be highly optimized on graphics hardware [11].

6.3.4 Recoloring

All of the previous refinement steps involve changing the depth map Z_v, which is normally—due to the plane sweep—jointly linked to the image color in I_v. To restore this link, the refined depth map is used to recolor the interpolated image with the updated depth values. As opposed to other more geometrically correct approaches [17], we thereby significantly enhance the subjective visual quality. The system is currently able to recolor the image in two different approaches, each having their particular effect on the resulting quality.

6.3.4.1 N-Camera Recoloring

The simplest and fastest recoloring solution is similar to the plane sweeping mechanism because it recomputes each pixel of the image I_v with an updated $\mathbf{T}_\text{j}$ matrix (Eq. 6.3) according to the refined depth information. The interpolated pixel color is then again obtained by averaging all N cameras.

This approach generates very smooth transitions of the input images in the synthesized result, at the expense of loss of detail (see Fig. 6.9e).

6.3.4.2 Confident Camera Recoloring

For each pixel f_v of the image I_v, the second recoloring solution determines which input camera C_i is closest in angle to the virtual camera C_v, and stores the camera index in a color map H_v according to Eq. 6.8, where $\mathbf{h}_\text{i} = \overline{fC_\text{i}}$ is the vector from f to C_i, and $\mathbf{h}_\text{v} = \overline{fC_\text{v}}$.

$$H_\text{v} = \arg \max_{i \in \{1 \ldots N\}} \cos(\widehat{\mathbf{h}_\text{v}\, \mathbf{h}_\text{i}}) \tag{6.8}$$

We assume C_i to represent the optical image center of the camera, and f is the image point f_v backprojected to world space according to Eq. 6.3, again with an updated $\mathbf{T}_\text{j}$ matrix. This recoloring scheme is illustrated in Fig. 6.9f, with depicted color map H_v.

Selecting the color from a single camera defined in H_v, ensures a sharply detailed synthesized image. However, the quality is sensitive to deviating colors between input cameras due to variations in illumination and color calibration (see Fig. 6.9f).

6.3.5 Concurrent Eye Tracking

To restore the eye contact between the video chat participants, the camera C_v needs to be correctly positioned. Eye tracking can be performed robustly and more efficiently on CPU, and is therefore executed concurrently with the main processing of the system.

The 3D eye position is then mirrored toward the screen, resulting in the correct virtual viewpoint that is needed to restore the eye contact between the system users. The two screens are placed in a common coordinate space, as if they were pasted against each other. Hence, this creates the immersive effect of a virtual window into the world of the other participant.

6.3.6 Networking

Our prototype system sends the eye coordinates over the network, and therefore the requested image I_v can be computed locally at the peer that captures the relevant images. These cross computations bring the required network communication to a minimum, by avoiding the transfer of N input images. The total peer-to-peer communication thereby exists out of the synthesized images and the eye coordinates.

6.4 Complexity Control

The previously discussed plane sweeping method is an efficient method to create novel viewpoints. Nevertheless, we can increase performance even more by reducing the number of depth hypotheses. We propose 2 methods: an adaptive uniform plane distribution method where the nearest and farthest depth values are adapted to the scene, and an adaptive nonuniform plane distribution method, where the depth planes themselves are redistributed in space to move computational power to the places where there are actually objects. Both methods have other applications besides videoconferencing and are discussed below.

6.4.1 Adaptive Uniform Plane Distribution

Most of the time, the head of a single person is visible in the camera views. To avoid heavy constraints on the participant's movement, a large depth range has to be scanned to keep the complete head in the virtual view. This actually infers a lot of redundant computations, since the head of the user only spans a small depth range. We therefore propose to dynamically limit the effective depth range to $\{D_{\text{min}}, \ldots, D_{\text{max}}\}$ (similar to [10, 23]) through a movement analysis on the normalized depth map histogram. This implicitly causes a quality increase of the plane sweep, as the probability of a mismatch due to homogeneous texture regions is significantly reduced. Moreover, all M depth planes can be focused as $\{D_1 = D_{\text{min}}, \ldots, D_M = D_{\text{max}}\}$, which leverages the dynamic range and thereby significantly increases the accuracy of the depth scan. Three separate cases can be distinguished, as the user moves in front of the screen:

- *Forward*: If the user moves forward, he will exit the active scanning range. Therefore, the histogram will indicate an exceptionally large number of detected depth pixels toward $D_{\min}$.
- *Stable*: The histogram indicates a clear peak in the middle, this resolves to the fact that the user's head remains in the same depth range.
- *Backward*: Analog to forward movement of the user, the depth histogram will indicate a peak toward $D_{\max}$.

As depicted in Fig. 6.11a, b, we fit a Gaussian distribution function $G(\mu, \sigma)$ with center μ and standard deviation σ on the histogram. The effective depth range is updated according to Eqs. 6.9 and 6.10, where b_1, b_2 are constant forward and backward bias factors that can be adopted to the inherent geometry of the scanned object. $D'_{\min}$ represents the previous minimal depth, and $\Delta = D'_{\max} - D'_{\min}$ for denormalization.

$$D_1 = D_{\min} = D'_{\min} + (\mu - b_1 \cdot \sigma)\Delta \tag{6.9}$$

$$D_M = D_{\max} = D'_{\min} + (\mu + b_2 \cdot \sigma)\Delta \tag{6.10}$$

As the user performs forward or backward movement, the center μ of the Gaussian fit changes and dynamically adapts the effective scan range of the system. The image will briefly distort in this unstable case, but will quickly recover as the depth scan is adapted for every image iteration. A real-time high frame rate therefore increases

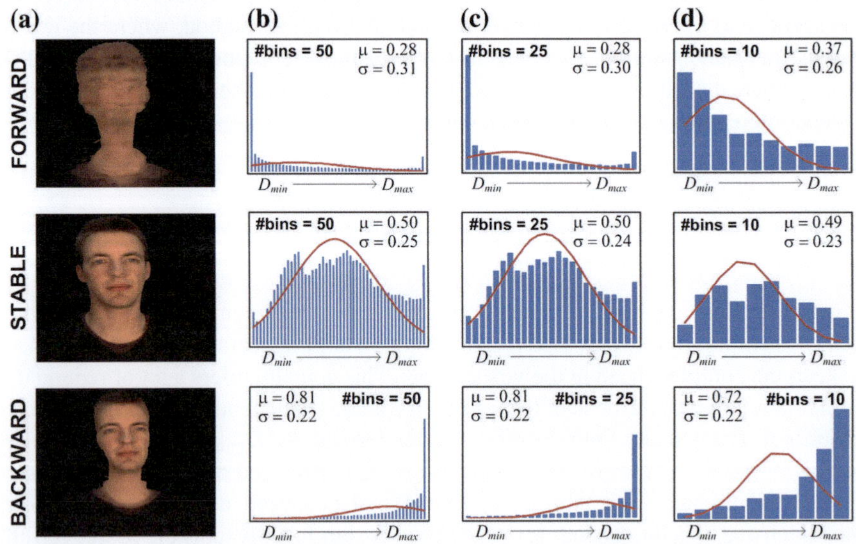

Fig. 6.11 The depth histogram-based movement analysis in normalized coordinates

the responsiveness of the system, and is able to achieve fast restabilization. Normal moderate speed movement will thereby not be visually noticed by the participants.

6.4.2 Adaptive Nonuniform Plane Distribution

This method of changing the nearest and farthest depth plane is very powerful for videoconferencing with one person. There are, however, situations where this method will not work, for example, when multiple people are standing and walking around. Therefore, we present an optimization where the distribution of the planes is adapted to the actual scene content, instead of only the nearest and farthest depth.

A histogram is calculated of the resulting depth map. This histogram guides the plane distribution for the next temporal frame. This will redistribute computational power to the more dense regions of the scene, and consequently increase the quality of the interpolation by reducing mismatches and noise.

When the scene consists of a limited range of depths between D_{min} and D_{max}, some processing resources are allocated to depth planes where no objects are present. This can be in between other objects. This is demonstrated in Fig. 6.12a. Here, a lot of planes are placed in the scene where no objects are positioned. This wastes resources and introduces more noise due to mismatches between the cameras. Therefore, we rearrange the distribution of the depth planes to provide less planes in depth ranges with less objects, and more, dense planes in scene regions with more objects. We determine the interest of a depth by analyzing the previous frame in a temporal sequence. The method works best when the movement of the scene is limited, such as moving people or scenes with many static objects.

After the interpolation step, we generate the histogram of the depth map using the well-known occlusion querying method [15] on GPU, allowing fast processing. The histogram can be seen in Fig. 6.12b. The occurrence of every depth value, as determined by the depth of the depth planes in the depth map, is counted. The histogram has discrete depth values between D_{min} and D_{max}, represented by the

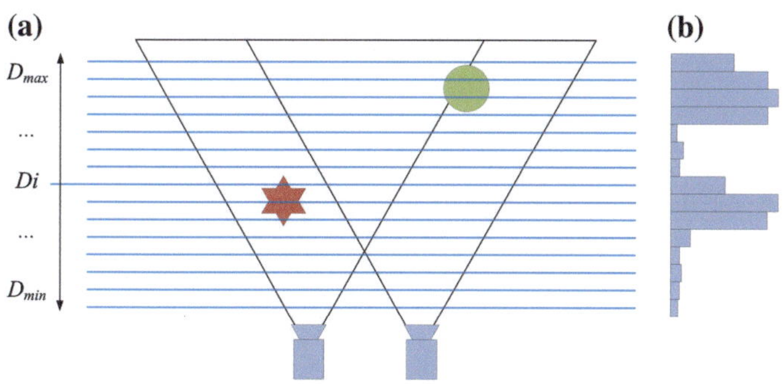

Fig. 6.12 **a** Uniform plane distribution. **b** Histogram of the depth values

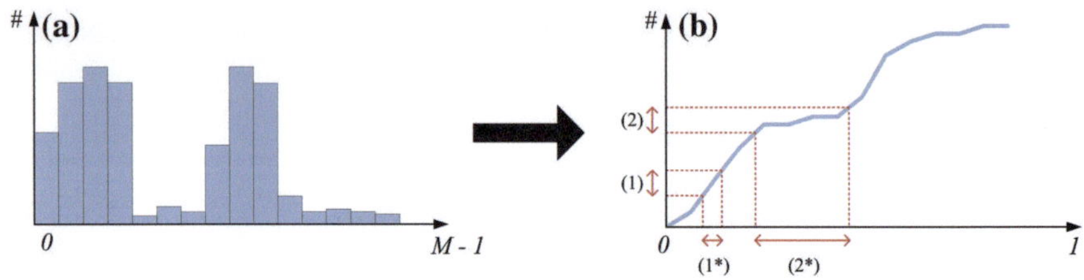

Fig. 6.13 **a** Resulting histogram. **b** Corresponding cumulative histogram $H(x)$

depth plane numbers. Scene depths of high interest will contain more depth values than depths of low interest. If there are depths in the scene where no objects are present, few of this depth values will be available in the depth map and this is reflected in the histogram. In the next frame, we want to provide more planes in depth ranges where a lot of depth values can be found, thus where there are large values in the depth histogram. The depth planes are not necessarily uniformly distributed, thus the histogram uses the depth plane number as the bin value, instead of the depth directly.

To use the depth distribution information, we convert the histogram to its cumulative version, as shown in Fig. 6.13. Here, we do not count the number of occurrences per depth value, but we rather include the number of occurrences lower than this depth. Furthermore, we rescale the depth values from $[D_{\min}, D_{\max}]$, as represented by the depth plane numbers, to $[0, 1]$. This transforms the nonuniform distribution of the depth planes to actual normalized depth values between 0 and 1. This transformation generates a monotonically increasing function $H(x) = y$, where $x \in [0, 1]$ is a normalized depth value and y is the number of values in the rescaled depth map smaller or equal to x. For values of x where there are a lot of corresponding values in the depth map, $H(x)$ will be steep. For values of x with a low number of occurrences, $H(x)$ will be flat. Because of the nonuniform depth plane distribution as input, $H(x)$ will be constant at some points where there were no depth planes for the corresponding normalized depth value.

We use the cumulative histogram to determine a mapping of a plane number m with $0 \leq m < M$ to a depth value D_m with $D_{\min} \leq D_m \leq D_{\max}$. For a uniform distribution, this would be:

$$D_m = D_{\min} + \frac{m}{M}(D_{\max} - D_{\min}) \tag{6.11}$$

We adapt this uniform distribution method. When using the cumulative histogram to determine the distribution, we calculate a fraction $\tau_m \in [0, 1]$ based on the plane number m, applied as follows:

$$D_m = D_{\min} + \tau_m(D_{\max} - D_{\min}) \tag{6.12}$$

The fraction τ_m is determined by the cumulative histogram. The Y-axis is divided in M cross sections, with a distance λ from each other, where $\lambda = \max(H)/M$. Each

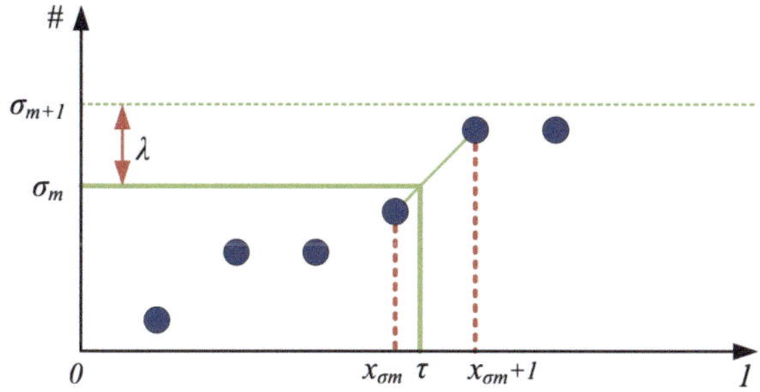

Fig. 6.14 Detail of the cumulative histogram with discrete values. τ is calculated by determining $x_{\sigma m}$ and $x_{\sigma m}+1$, such that $H(x_{\sigma m}) \leq \sigma_m$ and $H(x_{\sigma m}+1) > \sigma_m$, where σ_m represents a depth plane number

cross section represents a depth plane m. The actual depth fraction τ_m for each cross section σ_m , i.e., a depth plane, is calculated by first determining the depth value $x_{\sigma m}$ where $H(x_{\sigma m}) \leq \sigma_m$ and $H(x_{\sigma m}+1) > \sigma_m$. This is demonstrated in Fig. 6.14. Because the depth values x in the cumulative histogram are discrete, finding a value $x_{\sigma m}$ where $H(x_{\sigma m}) = \sigma_m$ is unlikely, and not desirable when generating planes that are dense, i.e., closer together, than the depth values provided in the cumulative histogram.

Once $x_{\sigma m}$ is determined, τ_m is calculated as follows:

$$\xi = \frac{m\lambda - H(x_{\sigma m})}{H(x_{\sigma m}+1) - H(x_{\sigma m})} \tag{6.13}$$

$$\tau_m = \xi(x_{\sigma m}+1) + (1-\xi)(x_{\sigma m}) \tag{6.14}$$

Figure 6.13b shows the transformation from a uniform depth plane distribution to a nonuniform distribution based on the cumulative histogram. In region (1), where the cumulative histogram is steep, there is a dense plane distribution, as can be seen at (1*). When the cumulative histogram is flat, a sparse plane distribution is acquired, as can be seen at (2*).

Using τ_m, an actual depth for every plane m ($0 \leq m < M$) is determined and used in the plane sweeping step:

$$D_m = D_{\min} + \tau_m(D_{\max} - D_{\min}) \tag{6.15}$$

This is depicted in Fig. 6.15. Here, the planes are redistributed using the cumulative histogram of Fig. 6.13b. More planes are available for determining the depth of the objects, and less planes are available in empty space. It is desirable to include some planes in the empty spaces between objects to allow the appearance of objects in dynamic scenes. To allow this, all the values in the histogram are increased with a fixed number, based on the number of pixels. This way, the cumulative histogram is less flat in less interesting regions, allowing some planes here.

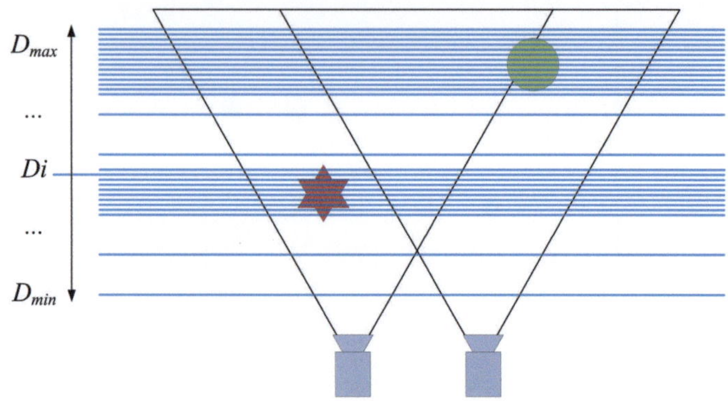

Fig. 6.15 Redistributed depth planes

6.5 Implementation and Optimizations

The use of carefully selected and adapted algorithms allows us to exploit the GPU for general-purpose computations, a technique that is often referred to as general-purpose GPU computing. Our framework harnesses the powerful computational resources of the graphics hardware, and maximizes the arithmetic intensity of the algorithm to ensure real-time performance.

The algorithm execution is further accelerated by elevating the processing granularity from pixels to tiles, configured in a set of well-defined granularity parameters. The processing is hereby only performed on the vertices (i.e., corner points) of the tiles, and therefore approximates—by inherent linear interpolation—the result of pixels inside the tile.

6.5.1 Improved Camera Data Transfer

Experimental profiling shows that downloading RGB-colored input images to the graphics card causes a threefold increase in the data transfer time due to the memory bandwidth bottleneck of PCI express, i.e., the bus connection between the motherboard northbridge controller and the GPU. This severely reduces the frame rate to two-third of its maximum capacity.

This bottleneck is effectively tackled by transferring Bayer-pattern images directly to the video memory. By inserting an additional demosaicing processing step, more computations are introduced, but only one-third of input image data has to be sent, effectively increasing the performance over 30 %. The reason is that graphics hardware benefit high arithmetic intensity kernels, as they process computations significantly faster than transferring data.

6.5.2 Acceleration by Elevated Granularity

By elevating the processing granularity from pixels to tiles, the algorithm execution speed can be drastically accelerated. In general, the computational complexity of the processing is inversely proportional to the granularity of the tessellation. If the tile size is chosen wisely, the speed can be significantly increased without noticeable visual quality impact. Our system uses three optimization schemes based on these speed versus quality trade-offs.

Tiled Undistortion Standard lens distortion is generally corrected on a pixel-basis level, but can be approximated by applying an equivalent geometrical undistortion to small image tiles using a resolution factor $0 < \rho_{tu} \leq 1$. Since a GPU pipeline exists out of a geometry and pixel processing stage, the lens correction can hence be ported from the pixel to the geometry stage. The pixel processing stage becomes clear to perform the consecutive segmentation processing in a single pipeline pass, which significantly leverages the GPU utilization.

Tiled Tallying in Reduced Bins For the movement analysis, the multiresolution capabilities of the GPU are used to tally tiles instead of pixels in the histogram bins. This sampling resolution is expressed by a factor $0 < \rho_s \leq 1$, where ρ_s is proportional to the granularity of the tiles.

Evidently, it is of no use to have more histogram bins than the number of planes in the sweep. However, the essential part is deriving the parameters μ and σ to adjust the dynamic range of the depth scan. As depicted in Fig. 6.11c, d, we are able to approximate the histogram by reducing the number of bins, without a large impact on the Gaussian parameters. Therefore, the number of bins are defined proportional to the number of planes M, with factor $0 < \rho_b \leq 1$. Heavily reducing the number of bins (see Fig. 6.11d) causes the center μ to become less accurate, as it is shifted toward the center of the effective scan range. An optimal trade off point can therefore be defined, since the accuracy loss will cause the responsiveness of the system to decrease.

Tiled Splatting Identical to the tiled undistortion, the depth map can be tessellated with a factor $0 < \rho_{ts} \leq 1$ to form a mesh for splatting tiles instead of pixels. This technique can significantly accelerate the confident camera recoloring, by interpolating angles between the tile corners.

6.6 Results

We demonstrate our previously discussed methods using a prototype setup. Our prototype setup is built with $N = 6$ auto-synchronized Point Gray Research Grasshopper cameras mounted on an aluminum frame, which closely surrounds the screen (see Fig. 6.1, top right). The presented camera setup avoids large occlusions, and has the potential to generate high quality views since no image extrapolation is necessary. We have used the *Multicamera Self-Calibration* toolbox [27] to calibrate the camera

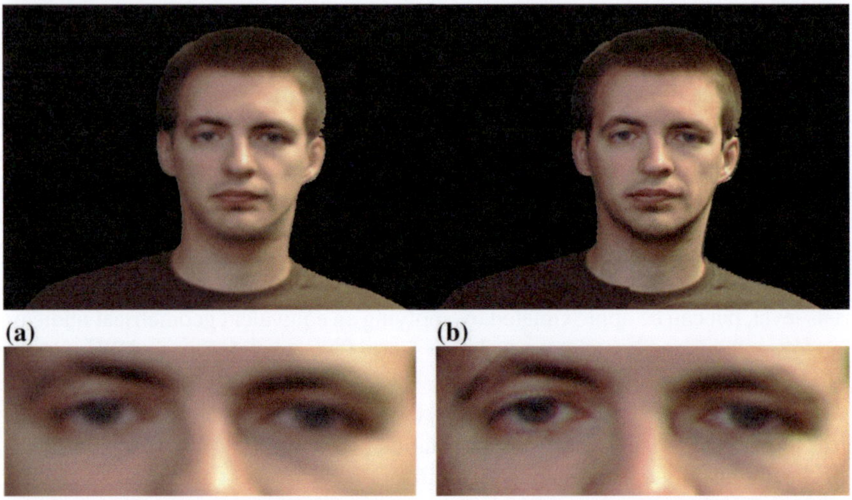

Fig. 6.16 Eye-gaze corrected images using **a** N-camera versus **b** confident camera recoloring

setup offline, but a built-in camera setup into the screen would avoid this procedure due to fixed calibration parameters. Our software framework runs on an Intel Xeon 2.8 GHz, equipped with 2 GB system memory and an NVIDIA GeForce 8800GTX graphics card. Communication with the GPU is done through OpenGL, and it is programmed with the high-level GPU language Cg.

6.6.1 Visual Quality

Final quality results using N-camera view recoloring are shown in Fig. 6.16a, and the results using confident camera recoloring are depicted in Fig. 6.16b. These results are generated under moderate variable illumination conditions, but with a fixed set of fine tuned practical system parameters summarized in Table 6.1. In Fig. 6.16a, some small artifacts along the ears and chin, together with minor ghosting around the neck, can still be noticed due to limitations of the depth refinement. The results generated with the confident camera recoloring are much more detailed and sharp, however some minor artifacts can be noticed due to abrupt camera transitions in the color map H_v. Nevertheless, the images maintain their integrity and are regarded as high subjective visual quality, while they convincingly seem to be making eye contact with the reader.

Table 6.1 Set of optimized system parameters

Module	Parameter	Value
Preprocessing	τ_g	0.355
	τ_f	0.010
	τ_b	0.002
	τ_a	0.998
	ρ_{tu}	0.2
View interpolation	N	6
	M	35
Depth refinement	λ	20
	ε	0.2
	τ_o	0.3
Confident camera recoloring	ρ_{ts}	0.2
Movement analysis	b_1	2.0
	b_2	2.0
	ρ_b	0.4
	ρ_s	0.5

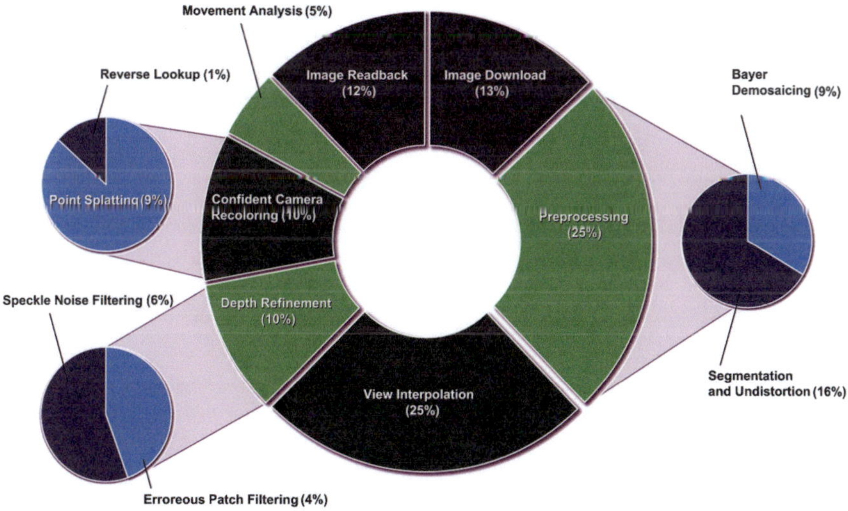

Fig. 6.17 Detailed workload profiling of the end-to-end optimized processing chain

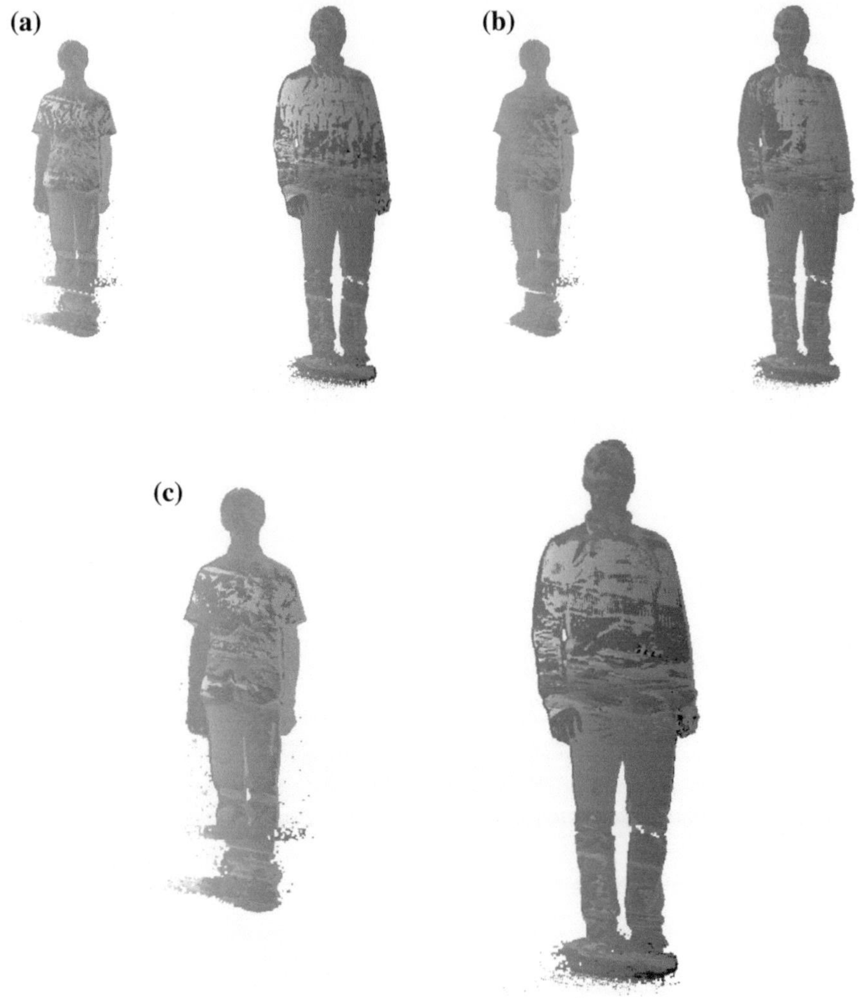

Fig. 6.18 **a** Depth map with a uniform depth plane distribution. A low number of planes (50) is used. **b** Depth map with a nonuniform depth plane distribution. A low number of planes (50) is used. **c** Depth map with a uniform depth plane distribution. A high number of planes (256) is used

6.6.2 Performance

A detailed workload profiling for the main processing modules—using confident camera recoloring—can be seen in Fig. 6.17, with input cameras and output resolutions of 800 × 600 pixels. By using online demosaicing, the arithmetic intensity can be kept relatively high, and even results in a higher execution speed than our previous implementation [7] using N-camera recoloring. The adaptive uniform plane distribution method was used to reduce computational complexity.

Summing up the different timings of the individual modules, we reach a confident speed of 27 fps for Full HD resolution, but our experimental setup is limited by 15 Hz support in the cameras and Firewire controller hardware. The current implementation speed allows for further quality optimization by advancing the algorithm and computational complexity.

6.6.3 Adaptive Nonuniform Plane Distribution

To demonstrate the validity of the adaptive nonuniform plane distribution system in multiple scenes, we created separate datasets with moving persons. We tested the method on different scenes and compared image quality and planes required.

The experiment shows that the quality is higher when a low number of planes is available, compared to the same number of planes using a uniform plane distribution. To increase the overall quality in both methods, we use foreground–background segmentation. Figure 6.18a shows the result for a uniform depth plane distribution. Artifacts caused by the sparse plane distribution can be clearly seen; the depth map shows clear outliers. The depth map when using a nonuniform plane distribution, based on the histogram of the first depth map, can be seen in Fig. 6.18b. Less noise and outliers in the depth values can be perceived. Furthermore, the silhouette is more distinct and the features of the persons are clearer. Using the nonuniform plane distribution increases the quality of the depth map using a low number of planes, therefore increasing overall performance.

Figure 6.18c shows the result for a high number of planes. Here, some noise and unclear edges can be perceived. These artifacts are effectively filtered out using the nonuniform plane distribution. The depth planes generating vague edges and noise are not used and cannot contribute to the depth map, and therefore to the noise and artifacts.

To demonstrate the effect of the cumulative histograms, Fig. 6.19 shows an input image of a video sequence (a), the corresponding cumulative histogram of the depth map of the preceding frame (b) and the corresponding fraction τ from Eq. 6.13 (c). When only one dominant depth can be perceived, such as in Fig. 6.19 (top), one steep section in the cumulative histogram is visible. This part is transformed to a flat value of τ, thus increasing the density of the planes in the corresponding region in the sweeping space. Flat sections of the cumulative histogram correspond to steep values in the graph of τ, resulting in a sparse plane distribution.

When multiple dominant depths are available in the scene, the cumulative histogram shows multiple steep sections (see Fig. 6.19, bottom). This results in multiple dense regions in the plane distribution, as reflected by the values of τ.

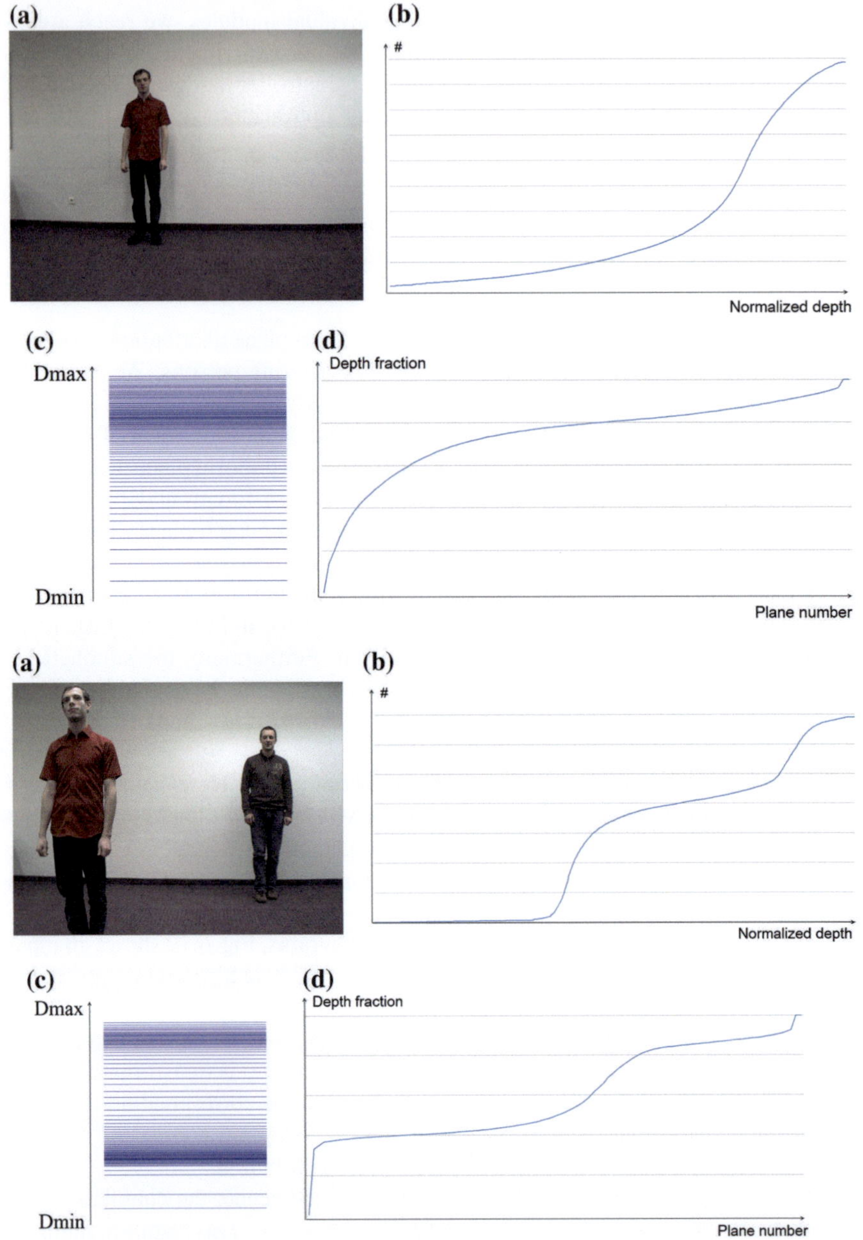

Fig. 6.19 Results for 1 person (*top*) and 2 persons (*bottom*). **a** Input image with one person. **b** Cumulative histogram of the depth map. **c** New depth plane distribution. **d** Corresponding fraction τ for a given plane number

6.7 Conclusions

In this chapter, we presented a prototype for 3D videoconferencing with eye-gaze correction. A virtual camera is placed behind the display, and its image is synthesized with image-based rendering from multiple real cameras around the display, using a modified plane sweeping algorithm. A GPU implementation yields real-time performances at high visual quality.

Performance is even further increased, thanks to algorithmic complexity reduction approaches. We presented a method to reduce the computational requirements by adapting the depth range and reducing the number of hypothesis depth planes in the search space, redistributing them to places with a high object density. This results in a substantial processing performance increase without impeding on the visual quality of the view synthesis.

References

1. Avidan S, Shashua A (1997) Novel view synthesis in tensor space. In: Proceedings of the conference on computer vision and pattern recognition (CVPR), Washington. IEEE, pp 1034–1040
2. Baker H, Bhatti NT, Tanguay D, Sobel I, Gelb D, Goss ME, Culbertson WB, Malzbender T (2002) The coliseum immersive teleconferencing system. In: Proceedings of the international workshop on immersive telepresence, Juan-les-Pins
3. Brown DC (1966) Decentering distortion of lenses. Photom Eng 32(3):444–462
4. Chen SE, Williams L (1993) View interpolation for image synthesis. In: Proceedings of the conference on computer graphics and interactive techniques (SIGGRAPH), Anaheim, 1993. ACM, pp 279–288
5. Chien S Y, Yu S H, Ding L F, Huang Y N, Chen L G (2003) Efficient stereo video coding system for immersive teleconference with two-stage hybrid disparity estimation algorithm. In: Proceedings of the international conference on image processing (ICIP), pp 749–752
6. Criminisi A, Shotton J, Blake A, Torr PHS (2003) Gaze manipulation for one-to-one teleconferencing. In: Proceedings of the ninth IEEE international conference on computer vision (ICCV), Washington. IEEE, pp 191–198
7. Dumont M, Maesen S, Rogmans S, Bekaert P (2008) A prototype for practical eye-gaze corrected video chat on graphics hardware. In: Proceedings of the international conference on signal processing and multimedia applications (SIGMAP), Porto, July 2008. INSTICC, pp 236–243
8. Maarten D, Sammy R, Steven M, Philippe B (2009) Optimized two-party video chat with restored eye contact using graphics hardware. Springer Comm Comput Inf Sci 48(11):358–372
9. Geys I, Gool LV (2004) Extended view interpolation by parallel use of the GPU and the CPU. In: Proceedings of the society of photo-optical instrumentation engineers (SPIE) conference: videometrics VIII, vol 5665, pp 96–107
10. Geys I, Koninckx TP, Gool LV (2004) Fast interpolated cameras by combining a GPU based plane sweep with a max-flow regularisation algorithm. In: Proceedings of the 2nd international symposium on 3D data processing, visualization, and transmission (3DPVT), Washington. IEEE, pp 534–541
11. Goorts P, Rogmans S, Bekaert P (2007) Optimal data distribution for versatile finite impulse response filtering on next-generation graphics hardware using CUDA. In: Proceedings of the

international conference on parallel and distributed systems (ICPADS), Shenzhen, December 2009, pp 300–307
12. Goorts P, Rogmans S, Bekaert P (2012) Raw camera image demosaicing using finite impulse response filtering on commodity GPU hardware using CUDA. In: Proceedings of the tenth international conference on signal processing and multimedia applications (SIGMAP), Rome. INSTICC
13. Goorts P, Ancuti C, Dumont M, Bekaert P (2013a) Real-time video-based view interpolation of soccer events using depth-selective plane sweeping. In: Proceedings of the eight international conference on computer vision theory and applications (VISAPP 2013), Barcelona. INSTICC, pp 131–137
14. Goorts P, Maesen S, Dumont M, Rogmans S, Bekaert P (2013b) Optimization of free viewpoint interpolation by applying adaptive depth plane distributions in plane sweeping. In: Proceedings of the tenth international conference on signal processing and multimedia applications (SIGMAP 2013), Reykjavik. INSTICC
15. Green S (2005) Image processing tricks in OpenGL. Presentation at GDC
16. Guo X, Gao W, Zhao D (2005) Motion vector prediction in multiview video coding. In: Proceedings of the 2005 international conference on image processing (ICIP), Genoa, pp 337–344
17. Lei BJ, Hendriks EA (2002) real-time multi-step view reconstruction for a virtual teleconference system. EURASIP J Appl Signal Process 2002(1):1067–1087
18. Magnor M, Pollefeys M, Cheung G, Matusik W, Theobalt C (2005) Video-based rendering. In: Cources of the conference on computer graphics and interactive techniques (SIGGRAPH cources), Los Angeles
19. Malvar HS, He L-w, Cutler R (2004) High-quality linear interpolation for demosaicing of bayer-patterned color images. In: Proceedings of the IEEE international conference on acoustics, speech, and signal processing (ICASSP), Montreal. IEEE, pp 485–488
20. McMillan L (1997) An image-based approach to three-dimensional computer graphics. PhD thesis, University of North Carolina
21. Vincent N, Sylvain M, Didier A (2006) Real-time plane-sweep with local strategy. J WSCG 14:121–128
22. Raskar R, Welch G, Cutts M, Lake A, Stesin L, Fuchs H (1998) The office of the future: a unified approach to image-based modeling and spatially immersive displays. In: Proceedings of the conference on computer graphics and interactive techniques (SIGGRAPH), New York. ACM, pp 179–188
23. Rogmans S, Dumont M, Cuypers T, Lafruit G, Bekaert P (2009) Complexity reduction of real-time depth scanning on graphics hardware. In: Proceedings of the international conference on computer vision theory and applications (VISAPP), Lisbon, February 2009, pp 547–550
24. Scharstein D, Szeliski R (2002) A taxonomy and evaluation of dense two-frame stereo correspondence algorithms. Int J Comput Vis 47(1):7–42
25. Schreer O, Brandenburg N, Askar S, Trucco M (2001) A virtual 3D video-conference system providing semi-immersive telepresence: a real-time solution in hardware and software. In: Proceedings of the eBusiness-eWork conference, Venice, pp 184–190
26. Seitz SM, Dyer CR (1997) View morphing: uniquely predicting scene appearance from basis images. In: Proceedings of the image understanding workshop, New Orleans, pp 881–887
27. Tomáš S, Daniel M, Tomáš P (2005) A convenient multicamera self-calibration for virtual environments. PRESENCE: Teleoperators Virtual Environ 14(4):407–422
28. Thomas V (1998) Synthesis of novel views from a single face image. Int J Comput Vis 28(2):103–116
29. Yang R, Pollefeys M (2003) Multi-resolution real-time stereo on commodity graphics hardware. In: Proceedings of the conference on computer vision and pattern recognition (CVPR), Madison, June 2003. IEEE, pp 211–220
30. Yang R, Welch G (2002) Fast image segmentation and smoothing using commodity graphics hardware. J Gr Tools 7(4):91–100
31. Yang R, Zhang Z (2002) Eye gaze correction with stereovision for video-teleconferencing. In: Proceedings of the 7th European conference on computer vision part II (ECCV), London. Springer, pp 479–494

32. Yang R, Welch G, Bishop G (2002) Real-time consensus-based scene reconstruction using commodity graphics hardware. In: Proceedings of the 10th pacific conference on computer graphics and applications (PG), Washington. IEEE, pp 225–234
33. Yang Z, Yu B, Wu W, Diankov R, Bajscy R (2006) Collaborative dancing in tele-immersive environment. In: Proceedings of the 14th annual ACM international conference on multimedia. ACM, pp 723–726

Chapter 7
Challenges in Embedded Vision for Augmented Reality

Rajesh Narasimha, Norbert Stöffler, Darko Stanimirović, Peter Meier and Markus Tremmel

Abstract Augmented Reality (AR) applications hold great promise for mobile users in the near future, but mobile devices cannot yet deliver on this promise. Even the quite substantial processing capabilities of modern mobile devices are not at the level needed for running the latest object recognition, tracking, or rendering methods. Furthermore, the resultant power consumption drains the battery fast. To ensure a great user experience, AR algorithms have to cope with real-world conditions like illumination, jitter, scale, rotation, and noise. The fusion of different optimized AR technologies like 2D or 3D feature tracking, edge detection, gravity awareness, or SLAM should be able to handle these issues to the satisfaction of the end-user but current mobile devices cannot handle these complex algorithms running in real-time and in an "always on–always Augmented mode". With the "always on–always Augmented" scenario, AR applications need to work on various devices such as smartphones, tablets, PC, etc., and at different form factors such as wearables and head mounted displays. Additionally, technology enablers such as dedicated hardware to accelerate feature tracking and matching that keep the power consumption to an acceptable level, along with easy-to-use software tools and user interfaces designed for non-experts would be the key to provide a low-cost and high volume AR solution. The "always on–always Augmented" scenario also needs considerable cloud support to offload computations and provide a seamless AR experience. To implement these technologies, hardware (HW) architectures have to evolve in parallel to provide efficient resources that can keep power consumption at an acceptable level.

R. Narasimha (✉) · P. Meier · N. Stöffler · D. Stanimirović · M. Tremmel
Metaio GmbH, Hackerbrücke 6, 80335 Munich, Germany
e-mail: Rajesh.Narasimha@metaio.com

P. Meier
e-mail: Peter.Meier@metaio.com

N. Stöffler
e-mail: Norbert.Stoffler@metaio.com

D. Stanimirović
e-mail: Darko.Stanimirovic@metaio.com

M. Tremmel
e-mail: Markus.Tremmel@metaio.com

B. Kisačanin and M. Gelautz (eds.), *Advances in Embedded Computer Vision*,
Advances in Computer Vision and Pattern Recognition,
DOI 10.1007/978-3-319-09387-1_7

In this chapter we discuss the challenges and solutions in embedded processing for a seamless AR user experience in the context of the "always on–always Augmented" use case.

7.1 Introduction to Augmented Reality (AR)

7.1.1 Definition of Augmented Reality (AR)

Augmented Reality (AR) deals with adding virtual content into the real world and aims to develop new user interfaces that combine the real world and the user interfaces in a natural way. AR places the data where it actually belongs—into the real world, rather than showing information on isolated displays. This allows for the creation of simple yet intuitive user interfaces for complex use cases. According to the Reality–virtuality continuum proposed by Milgram [14] as shown in Fig. 7.1, AR is one possible manifestation of Mixed Reality (MR), which brings together real and virtual within a single display.

According to the definition provided by Azuma [1] an AR system has to fulfill three requirements:

1. Combine the real and virtual
2. Be registered in the real world in 3D
3. Be interactive in real-time.

The first requirement is a fundamental concept of AR, where in it is combined the real world with virtual content. The second requirement requires that the virtual content being rendered must be registered in 3D within the real world and thus separates AR from the more general concepts of mixed Reality. The third and final requires the system to react to the user and update in real-time, distinguishing AR from all offline augmentation scenarios.

In this chapter we focus on how AR can be made suitable as a mass-market user interface and hence we focus on the challenges and possible solutions to make this happen. We highlight the requirements for AR to be a mass commodity as follows:

Robust Tracking: This is one of the basic requirements of any AR system. The tracking should be simple, fast, and robust to illumination, jitter, noise, scale, and rotation which are the important real-world parameters the AR system has to tackle.

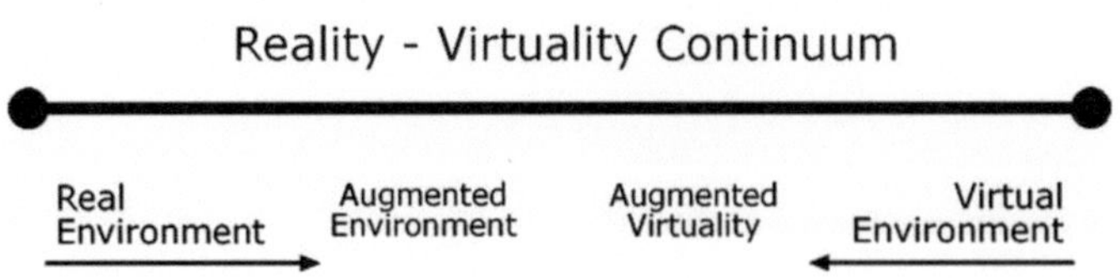

Fig. 7.1 Milgram's Reality–virtuality continuum

Virtual Content Creation: The AR system needs to have an easy-to-use and intuitive content creator engine with plenty of assets for various use cases. Also, with intuitive interface and development tools, it should enable rapid prototyping capabilities for the developer community so the time to market for the apps can be minimal.

Always On Always Augmented: This means that the AR solution should work on various devices such as smartphones, tablets, PC, etc., and at different form factors such as wearables and head mounted displays.

Additionally, for AR to reach a mass market, the applications should be able to run on mobile devices that invariably would need dedicated hardware to accelerate feature tracking and matching to keep the power consumption at an acceptable level. Moreover, the success and adaptability of AR depends on easy-to-use software tools and user interfaces designed for non-experts. All the above factors would be key to providing a low-cost and high volume AR solution. The "always on always Augmented" needs to access data continuously and save battery power by offloading expensive computations. Therefore, AR coupled with cloud technology can provide a seamless AR experience.

7.1.2 Short Evolution of AR

Although AR appears to be a recent phenomenon, it has been an active area of research and application for decades now. There is a plethora of information on the web on AR (please see [3] and the references therein). Hence we provide a brief history of AR in this chapter. AR has been a staple of sci-fi films throughout the first decade of the twenty-first century, but has much deeper roots than that. The birth of AR could be considered to be in 1962, when the Sensorama Stimulator (thc so-called "Experience Theatre") was patented. Researchers had already begun investigations into augmenting Reality in the 1950s, but this invention in particular provided a simulation of an experience by using visual images, breezes, and vibrations.

"There are increasing demands today for ways and means to teach and train individuals without actually subjecting the individuals to possible hazards of particular situations," the inventor Morton Heilig wrote in his patent application [8]. Further into the 1960s, Ivan Sutherland invented "The Sword of Damocles," the first head-mounted display system. Suspended from a ceiling, the device fed the viewer (rudimentary) computer generated graphics. Subsequent gradual developments occurred over the years until the 1990s when the term "Augmented Reality" was first coined, and virtual Reality was brought to television audiences through popular media. In 1994 the article "Augmented Reality: A class of displays on the Reality–virtuality continuum" was published by Milgram and associates [14] and in 1999 Hirokazu Kato's ARToolkit [5] sparked great interest in the research community.

In early 2000, the first commercial spinoffs such as from Boeing [19] and dedicated AR companies were founded like Metaio [22] and Total Immersion [9]. All early AR

Fig. 7.2 Example of marker based augmentation

applications were PC-based and highly specialized, often using markers as shown in Fig. 7.2 or expensive tracking systems from Virtual Reality.

The varied uses of Augmented Reality-in manufacturing, research and development, medical, and mechanical operations as well as in entertainment were further manifested later that decade. The first Augmented Reality software was invented in Japan in the 2000s and combined virtual graphics with real-life imagery, using video tracking to overlay computer graphics onto a video feed.

In 2005, Metaio [22] built the first commercial marker-less 3D tracking system published at ISMAR 2006. In 2008, AR went mobile for the first time as documented in the PhD dissertation of Daniel Wagner "Handheld Augmented Reality" [4]. In 2009, Augmented Reality Browsers emerged such as Wikitude [23], Layar [21] and Junaio [20]. The first two browsers focused on location-based AR using 2D tracking and Junaio featured location-based AR using both 2D and 3D tracking.

In recent years, Augmented Reality has become a playground for enthusiastic developers from all over the world. The technology has emerged from the "test phase" and is now a serious field with numerous applications across a wide variety of industries. The wide variety of the latest camera form factors, screens, CPUs, GPUs, and sensors sparked new innovations and a massive increase in data traffic and usage. In 2011, Metaio [6] published "Gravity-Aware Handheld Augmented Reality" [12] that used an inertial sensor for the first time to improve the performance of 3D tracking. Today, AR is used in print, automotive manufacturing, trade fair exhibitions, and in advertisement to name just a few applications of the technology. Next, we discuss the various AR use cases in detail.

7.2 Augmented Reality Use Cases

AR use cases can be divided into two broad categories—micro and macro. Micro covers the recognition and tracking of smaller rigid objects and superimposing small areas around you with virtual content. Macro, on the other hand, deals with the

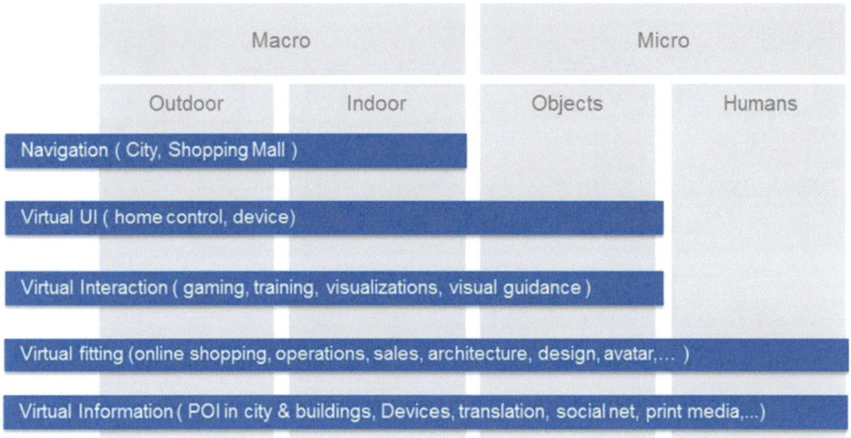

Fig. 7.3 Augmented Reality use cases starting at the *bottom* from simplest to complex on the *top*

identification, tracking, and mapping of an indoor or outdoor environment. This use-case is gaining immense interest because 3D depth cameras are being introduced at smaller form factors. As in the figure, from bottom to top we have the main use case segments in AR. Starting with the most basic one is "*Virtual Information*," the overlay of text, graphics, or video onto real objects like a virtual instruction manual. This currently is the most common AR use case (Fig. 7.3).

Examples of *Virtual Information overlay* are in print media, where the documents and manuals are overlaid with virtual content. Several examples are shown in Fig. 7.4 and in the top left image of Fig. 7.5. The AUDI Interactive manual from Metaio [6] provides information about the operation when a smartphone is pointed

Fig. 7.4 Examples of overlaying text, graphics and video using AR marker

Fig. 7.5 Virtual information overlay, virtual fitting, and retail AR applications

at a dashboard component. The app snapshot shown in the top right image of Fig. 7.4 recognizes over 300 individual elements of Audi A3, from the insignia on the windshield wipers and entertainment system to actual engine components under the hood. It also returns relevant how-to information or even virtual overlays of maintenance instructions, animated in real-time and in 3D [15]. Cloud-based architecture pushes digital information directly to the device, meaning the user will never have to update the app. Using 2D and 3D tracking technology, the user positions the camera of the mobile device directly over the individual vehicle elements, instantly detecting and returning information on the desired subject. For example, after scanning the engine compartment, the app returns information and an animated overlay showing how to locate the engine coolant and refill it to the appropriate level.

One step up in complexity is *Virtual Fitting* like apps where the augmentation has to be really precise and to scale. Examples are shown in Figs. 7.5, 7.6 and 7.7. To fit 3D furniture models to scale into a real home environment 3D feature tracking and monocular SLAM is used as shown in the third image in the top row of Fig. 7.5. With the inclusion of 3D depth cameras this application will be better and precise due to the accurate scale and occlusion information as shown later in Fig. 7.12. The application shown in the bottom left image of Fig. 7.5 relies on 2D image tracking approach to recognize the different LEGO boxes and visualizes the 3D animations to the corresponding LEGO model. Children can now hold LEGO packaging up to the "digital box" and watch a 3D animation of the product from any angle and in every detail—all in their hands. The technology not only creates a fascinating technical experience, but also gives retailers a unique selling pitch while helping to inform interested customers. Examples of car maintenance applications are shown in Fig. 7.6. For reliable project planning, the installation of the new engine needs to be simulated in advance, saving time and money. Using AR visualization in the virtual positioning and mounting of the new engine as shown in the top right image in Fig. 7.7 is based

Fig. 7.6 Industrial AR application examples based on markers

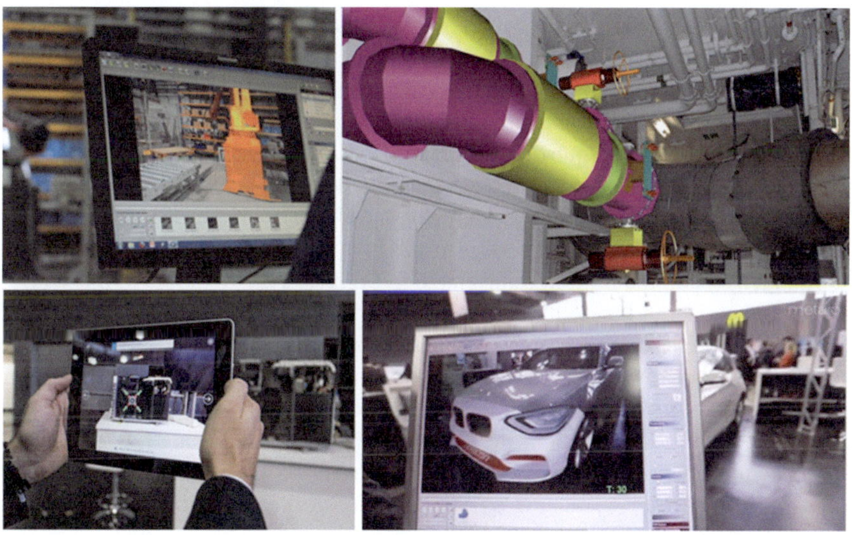

Fig. 7.7 Industrial AR application examples based on markers. Examples include factory floor planning, maintenance, and remodeling

on the images of the current factory environment. Engineers simulate the geometric bonding between the engine and gear using Augmented Reality. Furthermore, the spatial requirements for maintenance can be evaluated and different concepts for the installations of exhaust gas treatment can be visualized.

In the automotive industry, robot facilities have been growing in use. As it happens, up to 10 different car models are integrated in a facility during a span of 15–20 years. The required modifications need to be realized "within runtime." This means that the integration work takes place within the short downtime on weekends or company holidays, while the production continues as usual and without incidents. But the quality of the related CAD documentation at the beginning of every project can be unreliable, creating a risk. If plans are based on incorrect data, significant issues will appear during a new car model's integration. In worst case scenarios, production has to be moved. To minimize this risk, data verification takes place in preparation of the planning. The current status of a facility is analyzed and compared to existing virtual information with the goal of verifying positions of equipment within the workspace. The superimposition of images in the facility with the related CAD models enables a visual comparison as depicted in the top left image in Fig. 7.7. Based on the alignment data, quality can be determined immediately. The biggest challenge is to find a common coordinate system which is overcome in the following manner. A special adapter is used to set the master marker in direct relation to a known coordinate system of the analyzed facility. With the measurement the deviations between real and virtual equipment are determined and transferred into the CAD software. This eliminates the need for 3D scanning when evaluating the current status of facility.

In recent years, the complexity of maintenance and service operations in the automotive industry has risen significantly. A wide variety of cars partly exist with a small number of copies, which usually require specific maintenance processes based on abstract and complex user manuals. One key to increase the efficiency of service and maintenance procedures is to support the technicians effectively during task performance. This requires an improvement of traditional repair instructions, which guide the technician step-by-step through the maintenance task while providing all necessary information (e.g., description of task, tools to use). A use case of air conditioner maintenance is shown in the bottom left image in Fig. 7.7 and for car maintenance in the bottom right image in Fig. 7.8. The "Window to the World" application shown in the bottom right image in Fig. 7.7 combines the physical and the virtual world in a very precise way. The system consists of a movable Augmented Reality screen between the user and the object to be analyzed. Variants can be shown or virtual parts not yet produced can be added to the physical prototype. The visualization is even more realistic if the CAD model is enhanced using lighting effects and reflections. In order to achieve very high and robust tracking, the system needs to be based on the Infrared Tracking System, within flexible and high-volume working spaces. A precisely calibrated camera is placed behind a monitor, in such a way that the user literally looks through the monitor into the real-world.

Due to the need for shorter product life cycles and the rising complexity in automotive construction and design, ease of comparison between actual prototypes and CAD 3D models is key to reducing time and cost. Using AR as shown in the top row of Fig. 7.8, one can superimpose virtual 3D models directly onto the related prototype. The camera system is calibrated optically and mounted directly to the measuring arm. By knowing the position of the camera and aligning the measuring arm with the prototype, an accurate superimposition of the CAD data and 3D model can be created. Examples of AR in education are shown in Fig. 7.9.

Fig. 7.8 Examples of CAD model-based AR and car maintenance applications

Fig. 7.9 Examples of AR applications in Education

For all the above-mentioned purposes an Augmented Reality solution can provide advanced support for the employee. 3D contents, such as CAD models or animations, are visualized in superimposition with real objects—directly at the location of interest. Thus, objects can be highlighted or actions to perform can be shown. While superimposed 3D animations show the employee directly which action to perform and how to do it, further descriptions, warnings, and hints are provided for the technician in the form of text, images, and drawings.

Fig. 7.10 AR navigation examples

Thus, an Augmented Reality solution can improve traditional service and maintenance processes by providing the following features:

- Interactive and intuitive step-by-step guidance through maintenance and service procedures.
- Superimposition of 3D models to highlight construction parts on the real object.
- Superimposition of 3D animations to show tasks to perform on the real object.
- Attachment of annotations and digital labels (e.g., pictures, sketches) to real components in order to provide object-specific information and hints.
- "Maintenance and employee generated" marking of regions on real assemblies to support textual instructions and warnings.
- Linking of comments, hints, and warnings to specific construction parts.

One more level up in complexity is the *Virtual Interaction* (Fig. 7.3) which enables the user to touch, speak, or otherwise interact with the virtual objects to enable multiple levels of augmentation. The *Virtual UI* establishes an Augmented UI which can be interacted with and also controls the real object via a Bluetooth or Wifi backchannel. *AR Navigation* shown in Fig. 7.10 is the final vision where every real object will have associated virtual content, which will teach and guide us. Examples of Augmented city/navigation are shown in Fig. 7.10.

7.2.1 Tracking

A typical AR pipeline performs either marker-based tracking or feature-based tracking and is ideal for mobile platform since they include advanced graphics rendering and high definition displays, computation and memory, various sensor support, and wireless capabilities for cloud content access. The caveat is that the AR application needs to run at real-time frame rates and with the "always on–always Augmented" use case, the power usage of the mobile device becomes a major challenge since the battery may drain out within approximately one hour. Next we look into some of the AR technologies that are commonly used.

Marker-based Tracking: In order to obtain the camera pose in real-time, marker-based techniques are used. One example of marker-based tracking is the IKEA app from Metaio that uses tracking and monocular simultaneous localization and mapping (SLAM) algorithms. The marker is used to obtain the scale of the room. Markers are easily detected in the image due to their unique color and pattern. The high contrast combination of black-and-white square block pattern used along with four known marker points provides accurate calculation of camera pose. The issue is that the marker should always be visible in the camera frame of view and is susceptible to illumination variation.

Marker-less Tracking: The typical "marker-less" pipeline takes a video frame, extracts features like corners, describes them in a descriptor vector, and matches them against a database of reference object descriptors, which have been previously recorded. After the objects are detected they are tracked frame by frame. The key for a robust, accurate and fast 3D feature tracking pipeline is to find the right balance between number of features, pyramid scaling, and recording the 'right' information in the descriptors. This task requires a lot of experience, real-life expertise, and validation. Thus, not many really good 3D feature trackers are available in the market. The amount of detected feature points depends on the size and complexity of the object or environment to be detected and tracked. Typically, for a single 3D object, the algorithm has to deal with 1,000–2,000 feature points, for small rooms about 5,000 features, and for outdoor scenarios 10,000–20,000 features. These reference features have to be matched with all the new detected features estimated every at 30 fps, resulting in more than 200 GOPS for the detection or initialization phase, whereas the tracking phase is less demanding. SLAM on the other hand tries to localize the camera in the mapped environment and then estimates the camera pose relative to the mapped environment. The better we can map the environment, the more precise is the camera pose and vice versa. The common feature detectors can extract corners, blobs, patches, and edges and only a few feature detectors such as FAST [16] are suitable for embedded real-time processing. In some scenarios, dense tracking is needed to compute structure from motion and Lucas Kanade feature tracking is widely used. Feature matching is performed from frame to frame or key to frame to frame using template-based or feature descriptors. These algorithms require a large amount of computation and memory bandwidth which has a direct impact on the power requirement.

Edge-based Tracking: Currently, tracking and mapping approaches based on distinctive feature points are the most common algorithms employed for AR purposes. Usually, 2D points in images are selected and represented using the standard computer vision detector-descriptor scheme. Positive features of point-based tracking approaches are the following:

- high level of invariance to rotation and translation;

- moderate level of invariance to illumination changes and perspective distortion;
- availability of point matching algorithms based on extracted descriptors, facilitating automatic camera pose initialization.

These advantageous properties drove the adoption of point-based tracking algorithms in a wide range of AR scenarios.

However, point-based approaches do not perform well with sparsely textured or specular objects. Further, a high level of illumination changes could lead to the inability to correctly establish correspondences between previously mapped feature points and currently observed points. Moreover, any significant change in texture will also lead to failed correspondence search. The reason for this is that the feature point description most often relies exclusively on surrounding texture in the image. In order to overcome these problems, edge-based approaches can be utilized for camera pose initialization and tracking. The benefit of using edges is their stability in the image with regard to illumination changes, existence of specular reflections, and texture changes, given the assumption that edges originating from textures are used for neither initialization nor tracking.

Next, we provide details on edge-based camera pose initialization use case. A goal of this algorithm is to establish a pose of the camera with regard to a known 3D object. It is required to provide an accurate edge model of the 3D object, which contains the most distinctive 3D lines of the object that are visible in the images. Further, it is also necessary to provide a surface model of the 3D object. Due to the low level of information contained in simple 3D lines, as opposed to the rich descriptions of texture available in the state of the art, it is often necessary to provide an approximate initial pose of the camera. For e.g., in the outdoor case, the initial pose can be computed using the GPS, compass and gyroscope, assuming availability of these sensors. Once the camera pose is successfully initialized, it is possible to proceed with camera pose tracking, with regard to the 3D object. Camera pose tracking can be performed using only edges, only feature points, or combining both information cues in a hybrid approach. Further, tracking can be performed on a single-frame basis, with or without bundle adjustment of camera poses, and mapped edge or point features. Alternatively, it can be performed in a filter-based SLAM framework.

The main challenge inherent to state-of-the-art edge-based approaches is the camera pose limited convergence basin. This implies that to correct camera pose can be computed only when the initial pose is similar enough. The maximal pose difference, allowing for accurate camera pose initialization depends mostly on the 3D model appearance characteristics, the edge-model accuracy, and "distinctiveness". This leads to another disadvantage of edge-based approaches, which is strict edge-model requirements. First, extracted edges should be visible in the image in a wide range of illumination intensities, and also from a wide range of viewpoints. Further, since the majority of edge-based approaches determine correspondences between edges based on the image gradient magnitude and orientation, extracted edges should preferably be unique with regard to their spatial surroundings. In most cases, an edge-model is extracted using the provided surface model, which

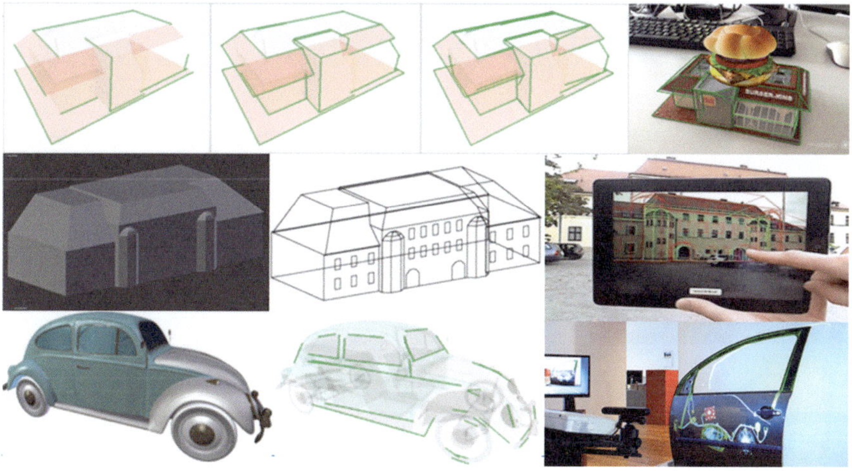

Fig. 7.11 Edge-based tracking examples

also includes texture information. However, even in this case, for many objects it is difficult to extract an edge-model that will guarantee good camera pose initialization in the wide range of initial viewpoints. *The tracker requires two models to work: a surface model and an alien model as shown in Fig.* 7.11. *The surface model (left-most image in the center row) is required for occlusion tests and for initialization and assisting the Markerless 3D tracking. The line model (green lines in top row images) is what is used to determine the correct pose in the camera image. The more distinctively the lines of the model can be found as edges in the image, the better the initialization will be. Surface model and line model, before (red) and after initialization (green) are shown in Fig.* 7.11 *(rightmost image in the center row).*

7.2.2 3D Vision and Augmented Reality

In all the above cases, real-world parameters such as illumination, jitter, noise, scale, and rotation play a vital role in the quality of user AR experience. The end-user/consumer, however, expects that an AR application works all the time without the need of any special knowledge or complex user interface. To achieve this there is a need for additional technologies that help to improve accuracy of the AR experience. The AR application can render virtual objects onto a plane and hence real-world objects need precise scale, distance from camera, and occlusion information for seamless AR experience. 3D sensing with depth cameras can help to get AR technology over this hurdle. Kinect [7] has already shown that depth information can be used robustly for detecting and tracking of humans and the Kinect Fusion project has demonstrated the capabilities for the reconstruction of rooms and objects

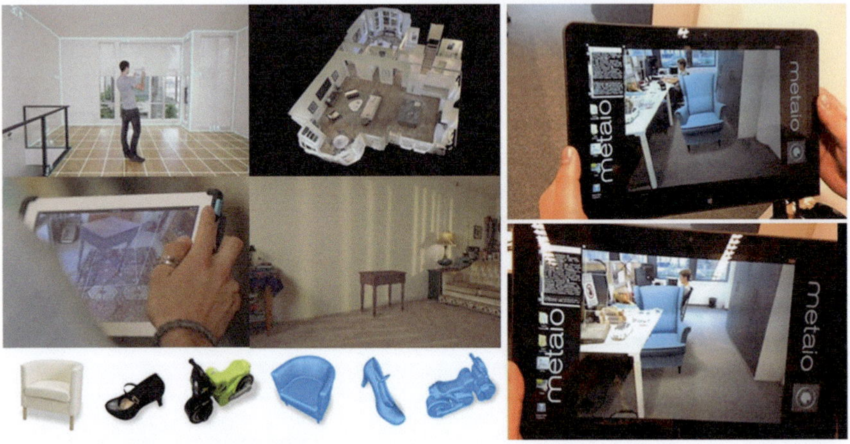

Fig. 7.12 Examples where 3D depth sensing would improve AR applications. *Image sources* structure.io

as shown in Fig. 7.12. With 3D depth sensing readily available one can perform (a) precise measurements of the environment, (b) creation of a 3D model of the physical spaces, (c) extract accurate object scale and shape information, (d) occlusion handling so that AR content can be seamlessly integrated into the physical world, (e) generation of CAD models for 3D printing, and (f) easy content generation for the cloud in the form of cad models to perform 3D object recognition, matching, tracking, rendering, etc. As discussed above, depth cameras will enable three major features for seamless AR experience:

1. *Easy content generation*
2. *Easy mapping and measurement of the real world*
3. *More robust detection and tracking of the real worlds.*

In the coming years, multiple 3D sensors will be introduced in the mobile space similar to Kinect-like cameras for smartphones and tablets and the benefits of this technology will then be available for an average user. The Google "project Tango" is one of the examples [10]. The arrival of depth-based cameras in a mobile device will enable a quantum leap in AR user experience. The next interesting sensor technology that comes right after depth cameras are array cameras. Arrays of CMOS image sensors, either in a 2×2 form factor at the beginning, and 4×4 or more as the technology matures will enable computational photography in really tiny form factor featuring all focus, low light, and depth video streams which can further enhance AR use experience. Unfortunately, point cloud processing has a large footprint in terms of memory, power, and computation. Power consumption, in particular, of 3D depth sensing and of those arrays, together with the required additional image processing will be a major challenge that needs to be addressed and hence hardware acceleration of key hot spots in the depth sensing pipeline would help in alleviating this challenge (Fig. 7.13).

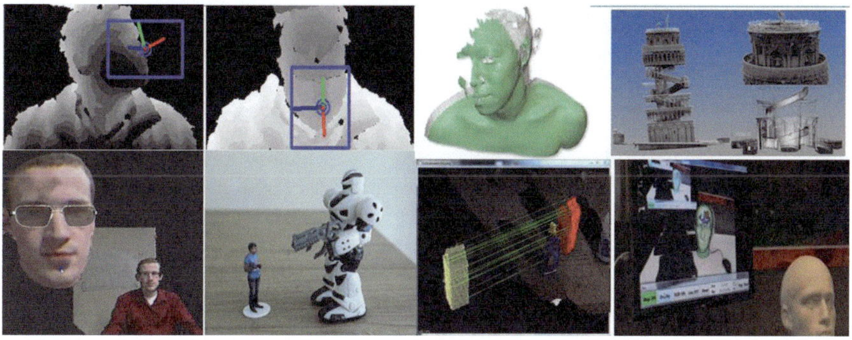

Fig. 7.13 Future AR application using 3D sensing. *Image sources* www.hao-li.com, www.pcl.org and www.3ders.org

7.3 Challenges in AR

As described in the earlier sections, AR applications hold great promise for mobile users in the near future but mobile devices cannot yet deliver on this promise. But to implement the technologies discussed earlier, hardware (HW) architectures have to evolve in parallel to provide efficient resources that can keep power consumption at an acceptable level. One answer is an embedded heterogeneous system (HMP) with highly specialized HW blocks and dedicated data buses and memory architectures, like the AR Engine, hardware IP designed by Metaio [6, 17, 18]. Although an HMP is a great solution on the HW level, it has to be complemented by intelligent programming frameworks for scheduling and resource management. Combining optimized tracking technologies with efficient HW IP and easy to use software development tools is the foremost challenge of the decade for AR, and has to be solved to ensure seamless application development for various AR applications and across multiple mobile platforms.

7.3.1 AR Hardware IP (AR Engine)

As shown in Fig. 7.14, feature extraction, descriptor building, matching, and tracking are the key hotspots in the AR pipeline. The most critical prerequisite for any AR application is the exact knowledge of the camera pose (pose being the combination of position and viewing direction, together 6 degrees of freedom (DOF)). This pose defines a fixed coordinate system in the real world that can be used for seamless rendering of content from the virtual world. If the camera pose is not known from other sources, it has to be determined by computer vision techniques. Figure 7.14 shows a typical AR pipeline. In the first half of the pipeline, the captured images are processed for camera pose estimation. In the second half, the camera pose is used

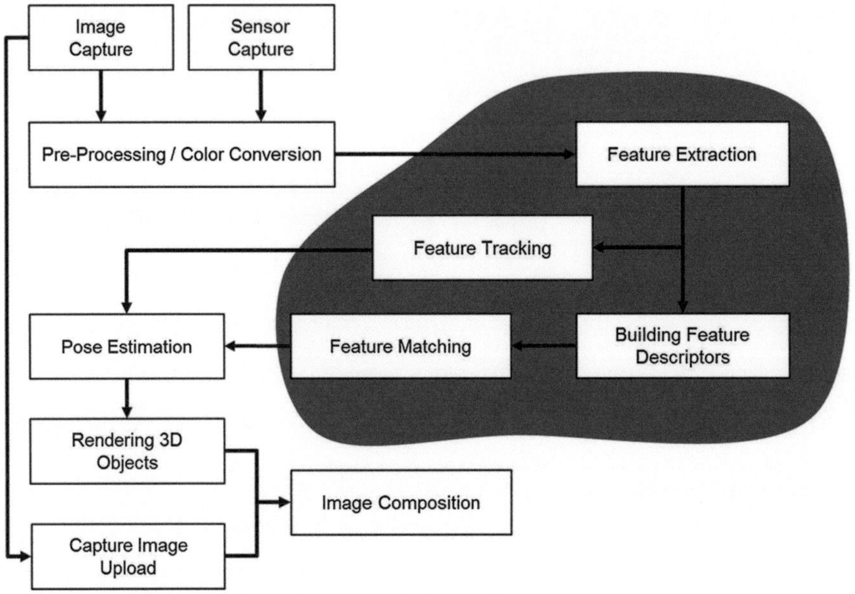

Fig. 7.14 Key hotspots highlighted in the tracking pipeline

for rendering. The captured images are stored together with other available sensor information. These additional sensors can provide initial estimates for the camera orientation and position. Examples would be inertial sensors and GPS. Then images are preprocessed and converted to a suitable color space. Although color is a very useful source of information, most feature-based systems such as SIFT [13], SURF [2], etc., use only the image intensity today, i.e., gray value images. The blocks highlighted in the figure are computationally the most expensive steps in the algorithm. Feature points are extracted from the entire image or in a scale space consisting of several images of different resolution.

Next, a descriptor is calculated that can be used to identify the features in databases or key frames. Features are also tracked from frame to frame by KLT-tracking or other tracking algorithms. Finally, all the recovered information is used for pose estimation. Now that the world coordinate system is available, 3D objects (i.e. the virtual objects) can be rendered with a standard rendering pipeline, e.g., utilizing a GPU and OpenGL ES. The captured images are reused for image composition, leading to the final "Augmented Reality" impression. The augmentation is performed by rendering the virtual world superimposed on the real images. This can be accomplished by two approaches. Typical display controllers already offer a blending of several layers during display. The blending factor is determined by a global or pixel-wise "alpha" blending. If this type of blending is unavailable, OpenGL itself can also be used. Finally, the captured image is uploaded as a "texture" that is placed onto a virtual background polygon. If scene models or depth maps are available, occlusions between real and virtual world can also be handled with ease.

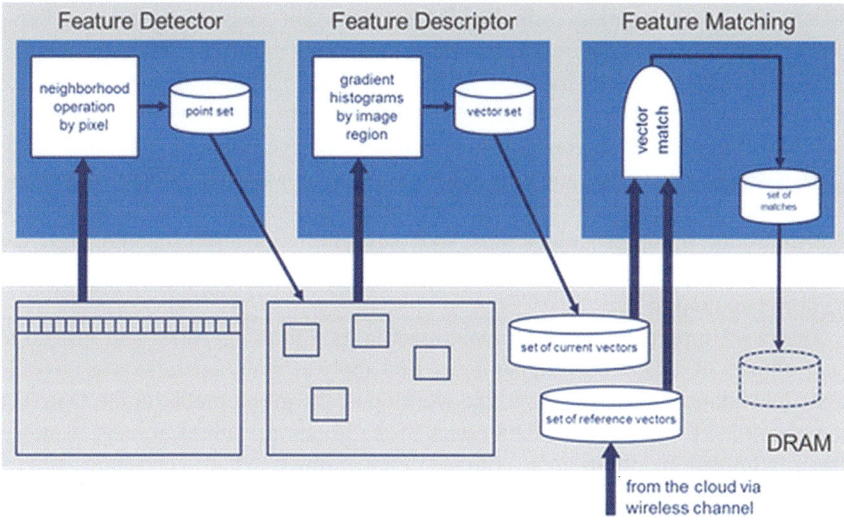

Fig. 7.15 Data locality of the feature tracking pipeline

Figure 7.15 shows the data locality in parts of the feature tracking pipeline shown in Fig. 7.14. Feature points are extracted from the entire image using a small neighborhood that can be either (n+1)*(n+1), where n is an even number. For e.g., in a 3×3 neighborhood case every image line contributes three times to the calculation, once as upper line, once as center line, and once as lower line. For an implementation that is efficient in terms of external memory bandwidth, four line buffers should be kept in local memory and operated as a ring buffer. Three lines contribute to the current calculation and the fourth line is fetched in parallel by a DMA controller. Feature descriptor calculations require a lot of random accesses in a larger area of pixels around the feature point of interest. Here, the most effective implementation is to store entire regions in local buffers. As the set of points is previously known from the earlier step, the region that will be processed can be preloaded into an available free buffer. Also, the memory accesses during full search in a database are deterministic and can be exploited for effective prefetching of data by a DMA controller. This means while comparing query to *entry[i]* one can already prefetch *entry[i+1]*. When this data management is implemented properly, all the data are accessed once, and thus computations will never have to be in the wait state for the data.

7.3.2 Memory Complexity

The memory subsystems of mobile system on chip (SoCs) are limited in terms of bandwidth, due to limited pin count to connect to the external SDRAMs and due to the priority to save power, which is mainly achieved by lower clock rates to external

DRAM ICs. The complexity of application processor SoCs with many internal clients 'competing' for external memory resources slows down the access. The large amount of client memory requests has to be buffered and has to go through multi-level of interconnect networks to ensure consistency and arbitration. As a result there is a long latency for fetching data from external memory into the processing engines. Thus while designing and implementing AR and CV functions one should understand the bottlenecks and reduce bandwidth as much as possible. Hence, AR and CV algorithms and implementations must take these limitations into account. Next, we highlight some of the rules that can be followed to improve throughput and reduce memory bandwidth.

The most important rule is to avoid reading data multiple times and instead to move chunks of data into local memories, and apply as many operations as possible to the local data. This is similar to the working of the graph model in the OpenVX framework [11]. Intermediate data nodes in the graph are stored in local memory. Other optimization options are to compress data during transfer to and from external SDRAM or to hide large latencies by prefetching data. In case deterministic access is mandatory, double buffered data transfers by DMA are performed into local memory. The first buffer waits for data and the other buffer is processed without wait-states. When moving from 2D or 3D sparse features to full 3D dense point clouds, databases are huge and hence more effort is required to manage external memory access efficiently. Matching or comparison of one large database (e.g., point cloud) against another (e.g., using Iterative Closest Point (ICP)) cannot be performed by exhaustive search since it would lead to $O(n^2)$ complexity. This will need index structures such as binary trees to reduce the complexity to $O(n \log(n))$. But this leads to another challenge: the data access becomes non-deterministic and prefetching is not possible anymore. This can be solved using another method which is implemented by GPUs. The GPUs make use of caches and run a large number of tasks in parallel. Tasks that have to wait while their data are fetched from external memory pass their computation unit to the next task that is ready. If enough tasks are initiated, the memory latencies become hidden and all available computation units can be fully utilized.

Figure 7.17 shows the architecture of the Metaio AR Engine. According to the considerations stated in previous sections, accelerator blocks only access local memory. Ideally, they can be accessed with zero cycle delay. The buffers are prefilled and emptied by an autonomous DMA controller. As the matcher typically runs in parallel to other algorithms and has to access big databases in external memory, it has its own interface to the memory controller. To keep the maximal flexibility in streamlining data flows for the individual application, a programmable core has been added as embedded control unit. It is software programmable and sets up all the individual operations and data transfers. This flexibility also allows the implementation of an OpenVX-like graph model of the data flow between the individual units. The engine can operate completely autonomously. It communicates with the host CPU (an ARM core typically) by interrupts and through a dedicated host interface. The host can access parts of the internal memories of the engine to set up parameters and commands. To get to an optimum AR user experience, HW and SW have to evolve so that they cause all processing resources available on an application processor. For

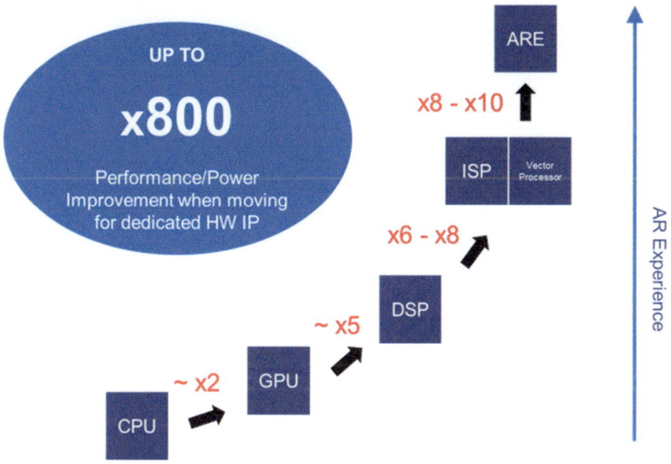

Fig. 7.16 Processor architecture gains in performance per power consumption

AR, the most performance-consuming algorithms, as we have seen before, are related to 3D object detection, matching, and tracking, which highly benefits from parallel processing. Different processor architectures enable different gains in performance per power consumption (MIPS/mW) as shown in Fig. 7.16. It is highly desirable to have a SIMD Vector processor or a dedicated HW engine available for AR algorithm processing to get to the needed performance/power level and to keep the GPU free for rendering the virtual overlays (Fig. 7.17).

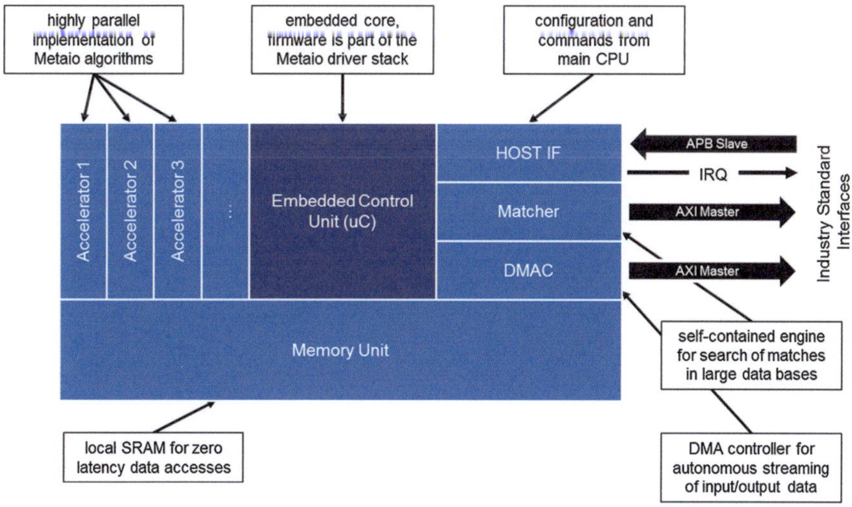

Fig. 7.17 Architecture of the Metaio AR Engine

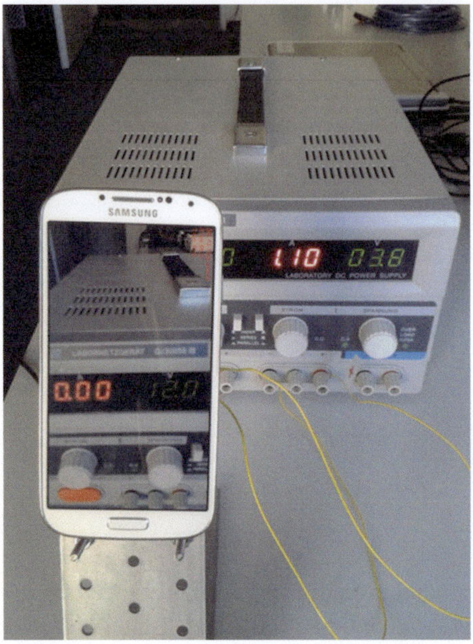

Fig. 7.18 Power consumption for a tracking application on Samsung Galaxy S4

7.3.2.1 Processor Architecture

The dedicated AR HW acceleration engine discussed above is a small HW IP module that is less than 1 mm^2 in size at 28 nm CMOS technology, and runs the full AR 3D pipeline at 30 fps. The module consumes less than 10 mW, compared to an ARM CA15 CPU running at 4–5 fps consuming around 1 W as shown in Fig. 7.18. The figure depicts a tracking application on a Samsung Galaxy S4 that drains roughly in the order of $\sim$1 A at 3.8 V leading to a power consumption of 3.8 W. Subtracting the 1.8 W that the camera app consumes results in 2 W for processing on the ARM (also includes rendering one polygon with the camera image as texture). This example clearly shows the need for HW acceleration of the key hotspots of the AR pipeline for a longer battery life, which enables the always on always augmented use case.

7.4 Concluding Remarks

AR will be the digital User Interface of choice for everybody in the future as it will bridge the gap between real world and digital world more efficiently than any other technology. AR will be "See it—understand it—control it," the perfect self-contained UI. It launches itself when needed; it can explain itself on the fly and offers the appropriate controls in real time-Instant seamless and relevant! But to make this happen, AR, especially the CV part of AR, needs to be available all the

Fig. 7.19 Augmented city

time with outstanding user experience, running 24/7 on your personal mobile device. On current mobile devices this is not possible due to limited performance and battery resources. Dedicated HW resources for CV and AR are required to get to the needed performance and power efficiency. Additionally, they would offload the CPU to make it available for pure application-related tasks. Running AR with instant and robust recognition and tracking at 30 fps at around 10 mW will enable full day AR use cases, which are needed to make AR applications like visual navigation, AR gaming, and real-time AR UI useful to the end-user. To reach this goal, the full AR detection and tracking pipeline needs to be fully implemented in HW and optimized at system level. The AR engine from Metaio [6] is an early example for such optimization and acceleration (Fig. 7.19).

References

1. Azuma RT (1997) A survey of augmented reality. Presence: Teleoperators Virtual Env 6(4):355–385 (Earlier version appeared in Course Notes #9: Developing Advanced Virtual Reality Applications, ACM SIGGRAPH '95 (Los Angeles, 6–11 August 1995), 20–1 to 20–38.)
2. Bay H, Ess A, Tuytelaars T, Van Gool L (2008) SURF: speeded up robust features. Comput Vis Image Underst (CVIU) 110(3):346–359
3. http://en.wikipedia.org/wiki/Augmented_Reality
4. http://studierstube.icg.tugraz.at/thesis/Wagner_PhDthesis_final.pdf
5. http://www.hitl.washington.edu/artoolkit/
6. http://www.metaio.com
7. http://www.microsoft.com/en-us/kinectforwindows/
8. http://www.mortonheilig.com/SensoramaPatent.pdf
9. http://www.t-immersion.com/
10. https://www.google.com/atap/projecttango/#project
11. https://www.khronos.org/openvx

12. Kurz D, Benhimane S (2011) Gravity-aware handheld augmented reality. In: Proceedings of the IEEE and ACM International symposium on mixed and augmented reality (ISMAR2011). Basel, Switzerland, pp 111–120
13. Lowe DG (2004) Distinctive image features from scale-invariant keypoints. Int J Comput Vis 60(2):91–110
14. Milgram P, Kishino F (1994) A taxonomy of mixed Reality visual displays. EICE Trans Inf Syst E77-D(12):1321–1329
15. Platonov J, Heibel H, Meier P, Grollmann B (2006) A mobile markerless AR system for maintenance and repair. In: The fifth IEEE and ACM International symposium on mixed and augmented reality, Santa Barbara, 22–25 October 2006
16. Rosten E, Drummond T (2006) Machine learning for high-speed corner detection. In: European conference on computer vision, vol 1. pp 430–443
17. Wilson T, Dipert B (2013) Embedded vision on mobile devices. IEEE J. http://www.eejournal.com/archives/articles/20130731-embvision/
18. Wilson T, Dipert B, Jacobs M, Droz T (2014) Augmented reality: a compelling mobile embedded vision opportunity. IEEE J. http://www.eejournal.com/archives/articles/20140401-Augmented
19. www.boeing.com
20. www.junaio.com
21. www.layar.com/
22. www.metaio.com
23. www.wikitude.com/

Chapter 8
Tic-Tac-Tandroid: A Tic-Tac-Toe Mobile Vision App that Can "See" and "Think"

Milena Djordjević-Kisačanin, Vinjai Vale and Branislav Kisačanin

Abstract We present our work on a mobile Android app that can play the game of tic-tac-toe by using (1) computer vision to "see" the current situation on the hand-drawn board and (2) artificial intelligence to "think" of the best next move. The app displays the next best move on the device display. In order for the app to be usable on mobile devices, such as smart phones and tablets, the vision part of the app uses computationally and power-efficient version of gradients of the camera image to determine the location of the tic-tac-toe board and the cells within it. We then use averages of gradients in the cells as well as in much smaller boxes around the centroids to determine whether the contents of the cells are empty, X, or O. After this our AI algorithm analyzes the situation on the board and determines the next best move. In both the vision and the AI part of the app we could have used a variety of approaches to achieve the same goal. In order to get the best possible performance, we determined through experimentation which particular approaches work best. We document the limitations of the system, discuss similarities and differences between embedded and mobile vision, and look at how this and other mobile vision apps will benefit from mobile vision accelerators and developments in OpenVX.

8.1 Introduction

The game of tic-tac-toe is played on a 3×3 grid. Players can chose to be "X" or "O" and place their symbols in one of the "cells" of the grid. Tic-tac-toe has been popular throughout history. An early variant called *Terni Lapalli* was played in Ancient Rome around the 1st century BC [1]. Here is the version of the rules that we used (Fig. 8.1):

- X always goes first
- The players alternate placing their symbols
- The objective of the game is to get three symbols in a row (vertically, horizontally, or diagonally)

M. Djordjević-Kisačanin · V. Vale · B. Kisačanin (✉)
Fermat School of Math and Science, Plano, TX, USA
e-mail: b.kisacanin@yahoo.com

B. Kisačanin and M. Gelautz (eds.), *Advances in Embedded Computer Vision*, Advances in Computer Vision and Pattern Recognition,
DOI 10.1007/978-3-319-09387-1_8

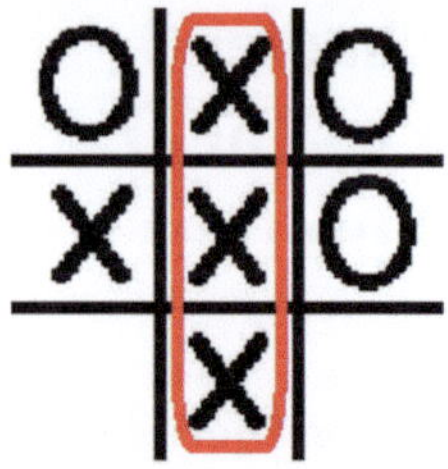

Fig. 8.1 A sample tic-tac-toe game in which X wins

Tic-tac-toe has been the topic of choice for many interesting projects in the past. In 1952, it became one of the first video games—the EDSAC computer could play it flawlessly against a human opponent. In 1975, MIT students created a tic-tac-toe computer [2] almost entirely out of Tinkertoy pieces (a type of wooden construction set for children) that could play a perfect tic-tac-toe game. As far as we know, there has been no prior work to combine vision and AI for a game of tic-tac-toe.

The objective of this project was to create an Android app that plays tic-tac-toe against an opponent or against itself. The app should be able to do the following:

- "See" the tic-tac-toe board hand-drawn on a sheet of paper
- "Understand" the visual input
- "Think" of the most optimal next move
- Report the result to the user

The human user then writes the move on the game paper and the game goes on.

8.2 Vision Algorithms with a Mobile Twist

In this section, we explain how our choice of vision algorithms for the Tic-Tac-Tandroid app was influenced by mobile environment constraints.

In many ways, the mobile environment is more restrictive for vision applications than the embedded vision in general. This is because in embedded vision, we generally have at least some control over which processor is used for vision, how much memory, what kinds of optics are designed in, etc. In mobile environment, we are constrained by what processor is the common denominator for all supported platforms, such as smart phones and tablets, and have to rely on operating systems to assign memory to our app. Considering how data-intensive vision is, these can be serious impediments in achieving real-time operation. There are not many high-profile mobile vision apps around, so it may be worth mentioning a few:

- Sudoku Grab [3], which reads a Sudoku puzzle before solving it.
- EyesOnRoad [4], an app that can assist drivers and improve road safety.
- Many developments around the Google Project Glass [5], a platform that opens up many possibilities for using vision for augmented reality and human-computer interaction.

As the mobile platform in this project we use the HTC Inspire 4G, a smart phone with a single core, 1 GHz Qualcomm Snapdragon S2 MSM8255 application processor. Its main CPU has Qualcomm's Scorpion architecture, similar to the ARM Cortex-A8 and Cortex-A9 CPU cores. The device is running Android version 2.3.3. While its camera produces images with 8 mega pixel resolution, we used the preview images which are 240×320.

8.2.1 Edge Detection

Inspired by biological vision [6–8], in which edge detection has a fundamental role [9], we started by looking at the ways we could apply gradients to accomplish our goal of giving our app the power of "seeing." Since we were focusing on a mobile implementation, we started with the computationally least expensive implementation of gradients. If the camera image is given by matrix A, its x- and y-gradients are conveniently defined as [10]:

$$G_x(i, j) = A(i, j+1) - A(i, j-1)$$
$$G_y(i, j) = A(i+1, j) - A(i-1, j)$$

In order to continue the analysis with the minimum computational complexity, instead of the standard L_2 gradient magnitude (which involves square roots, which are computationally expensive on a mobile device and use more power than necessary), we focused on an alternative, L_1 magnitude gradient:

$$G_m = |G_x| + |G_y|$$

Another approximation we applied in order to save on computations and battery life was the use of the green image component provided by the camera instead of calculating the luminance. This approximation works well as long as the ink in the game is not bright green and thus, practically indistinguishable from the white background in the green channel.

8.2.2 Tic-Tac-Tandroid Vision

Board detection. The first vision block specific to tic-tac-toe is the detection of the game board, which is composed of four lines—two vertical and two horizontal. This simple arrangement, along with manageable camera distortion and nicely thick (but not too thick) lines, allowed us to locate the tic-tac-toe board and its cells in a fairly simple manner, as illustrated in the screenshot in Fig. 8.2:

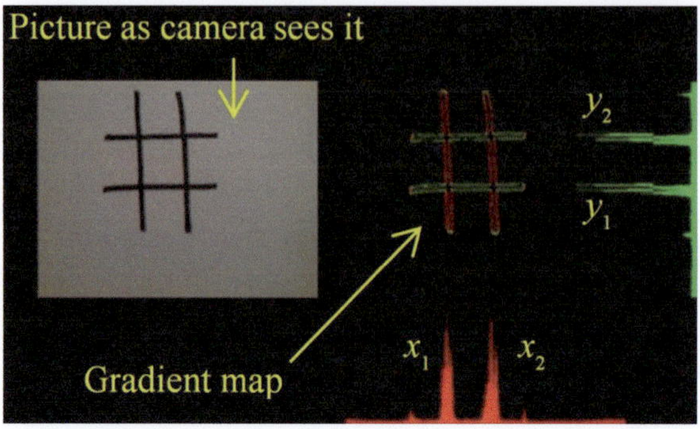

Fig. 8.2 Segmentation in action

1. Sum all of the gradients in the x-direction and find the two maximum values. The two greatest horizontal gradient sums indicate where the horizontal lines are located and we label these locations y_1 and y_2. To find these two maximum gradient sums, we use non-maximum suppression: after finding the first maximum, we zero out the values next to the first maximum. This allows us to accurately find the second peak, corresponding to the second horizontal line. By zeroing out the pixels around the first maximum, we can prevent the issue of accidentally mistaking a double peak as the second line.
2. Similarly, sum up all the gradients in the vertical-direction to obtain the two maximum vertical sums (again using non-maximum suppression) so that, we know the location of the vertical lines. We name the lines x_1 and x_2.
3. Finally, we find the intersections of the four lines and can now access the contents of the board cells.

Cell locations. Once we determine the location of the four lines, we can use their intersection points to find the nine cells. We first look at the central cell, with x_1, x_2, y_1, and y_2 as its four bounding lines. We then find the rest of the tic-tac-toe cells around the central cell.

"Empty" versus "full" detection. Before we determine if a cell contains an X or an O, we have to determine if it is empty or full. To that goal, we average the gradients in each cell separately. If the gradient average is greater than an experimentally determined threshold, the box must be full. If not, it is empty. We use gradients instead of luminance in order to improve the robustness to global illumination changes. If luminance was used for this purpose, the threshold would have to change as illumination changes (Fig. 8.3).

"X" versus "O" detection. Once we determine that a cell is full, we need to know which symbol is inside it. We do this by determining where its centroid is (represented by a blue dot on the display). Then, after we find the centroid, we consider a small box around it, and average the gradients inside that box. The centroid, naturally, appears close to the center of the shape, whether the box contains an X or an O, because both

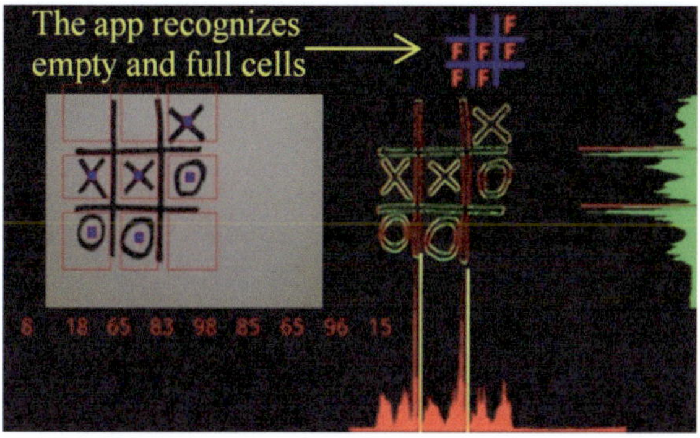

Fig. 8.3 "Empty" versus "full" detection

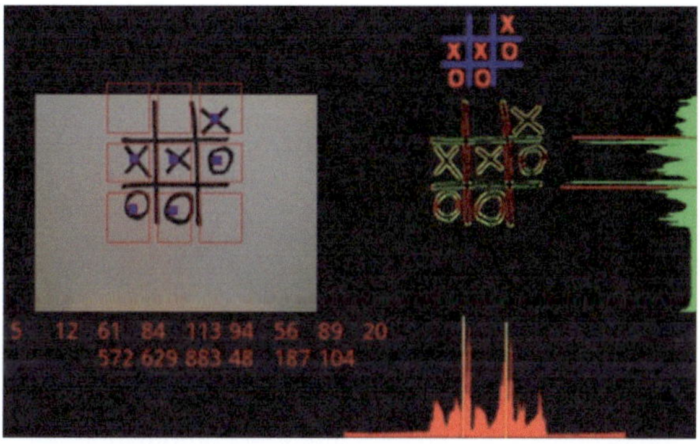

Fig. 8.4 "X" versus "O" detection

shapes are symmetric. So we recognize an X if the box is full of gradients, or an O if it has little or no gradients (Fig. 8.4).

8.2.3 *Tic-Tac-Tandroid AI*

Priority-based algorithm. In order to compute the best next move from the information deduced by the vision block, we devised a priority-based algorithm. The first step in any zero-sum game like tic-tac-toe is to check if someone is about to win. If the computer is about to win, then its first priority should be to play the winning move. If it is not about to win, but the opponent is, it should try to block the opponent. If neither the computer nor the opponent is about to win, we need a third option. The computer should not just play randomly; then it is possible for the opponent to force a win. To do this systematically, we dynamically assign a "priority number" to each cell in the grid, and we pick the one with the highest priority to play in.

Fig. 8.5 The cell numbering

0	1	2
3	4	5
6	7	8

Before we can define the priority number of a cell, we must first define the cell layout and what a winning combination is. The cells are labeled as shown (Fig. 8.5):

Note that there are eight winning combinations on the board—that is, eight three-in-a-rows:

- 0, 1, 2 (top row)
- 3, 4, 5 (middle row)
- 6, 7, 8 (bottom row)
- 0, 3, 6 (left column)
- 1, 4, 7 (middle column)
- 2, 5, 8 (right column)
- 0, 4, 8 (main diagonal)
- 2, 4, 6 (other diagonal)

One possible approach to determining the priority number of a cell labeled n, P_{n}, is to add the number of winning combinations that share cell n, W_{n}, and the number of tokens currently on the board that share a winning combination with cell n, T_{n}:

$$P_{\mathrm{n}} = W_{\mathrm{n}} + T_{\mathrm{n}}$$

This is a plausible approach because:

- The number of winning combinations that share cell n indicates the overall "usefulness" of the cell
- The number of tokens that share a winning combination with cell n indicates the current usefulness of the cell, for both forming 3-in-a-row and for blocking the opponent's 3-in-a-row

Alternatively, we wanted to try a weighted formula which would play more aggressively, in which the alternate priority number of cell n, denoted by Q_n, is the weighted sum of the number of 'my' tokens currently on the board that share winning combinations with cell n, M_{n}, and the number of opponent's tokens currently on the board that share winning combinations with cell n, denoted by O_{n}:

$$Q_{\mathrm{n}} = 2M_{\mathrm{n}} + O_{\mathrm{n}}$$

This approach is plausible because:

- The "winning potential" of the cell, the number of CPU tokens currently on the board that share winning combinations with the cell, is weighted so the algorithm favors cells that contribute to a win.
- The "blocking potential" of the cell, the number of player tokens currently on the board that share winning combinations with cell n, is unweighted so that the algorithm pays less attention to a block, but still counts it in the overall priority number.

8.3 Experimental Evaluation

In this section, we present the results of experimental determination of the optimal cell detection box size in the vision block and evaluation of the two AI approaches described above.

8.3.1 Vision Experiments

Although we tried to minimize detection error in our vision block, the performance was still less than perfect. We found the major culprits to be the following:

- If outer cell boxes are too small, they sometimes cut off parts of the cell content
- If outer cell boxes are too big, they can accidentally capture parts of the grid, causing incorrect results

In order to determine the optimal outer cell size, we devised an experiment that would find what cell detection box size would yield the most accurate results. For each of five different scale factors (the center cell scaled up by 1, 1.125, 1.25, 1.375, or 1.5) we made a separate app and tuned its thresholds on a set of five tic-tac-toe boards written in different styles and handwritings. Then we used additional ten tic-tac-toe boards, not seen by the app during the tuning process, to evaluate the detection error as a function of the scale factors.

In Table 8.1, we present the number of errors for each cell size: V1, V2, V3, V4, and V5 denote the app version with outer cell scale factors 1, 1.125, 1.25, 1.375, and 1.5, respectively.

We see that the scaling factor of 1.25 used in V3 can be chosen as the optimal value which is neither too big nor too small.

Table 8.1 Vision block accuracy with different cell sizes

Number of errors	V1	V2	V3	V4	V5
X detect	2	0	0	4	2
O detect	0	1	0	4	2
E detect	0	0	0	0	0

Table 8.2 AI block accuracy with different priority number approaches

Algorithm type	Unweighted	Weighted
Number of correct answers	17	20

8.3.2 AI Experiments

In order to evaluate which priority number approach produces better results we collected 20 tic-tac-toe situations to use as test input. As a reference, we manually determined the optimal moves for each situation. We presented the test inputs to both approaches and compared their results to the reference results. Table 8.2 lists the number of correct results produced by the two AI algorithms.

We see that the weighted algorithm worked the best. In the cases where only the weighted algorithm worked properly, the app had multiple options. One option allowed the program to possibly win while the other always resulted in a draw. So, the more "aggressive" weighted approach chose the winning moves and won those games.

8.4 App Integration and Testing

We integrated our app using standard Java SDK tools for Android development [11]. As a starting point we used the Stanford EE368 Viewfinder [12], which provided us with the code for using the Android camera and the images in the memory. The Viewfinder also demonstrates a few useful techniques: how to access the image in the memory and how to display graphics on the screen. We added our vision and AI code to the Viewfinder and modified its display routines to accommodate our needs. The result can be seen in our YouTube video [13].

We played with the app extensively, identified and fixed a number of small bugs, and concluded that the app is fairly robust to global illumination changes. In fact, in our regional science fair demonstration we had to work in very dark conditions and our app still worked great.

In Fig. 8.6 we show the final appearance of the device display when our app is running. As indicated by the yellow circle, the recommended next move is X in the lower right corner. It is a good move because it blocks O from winning and opens up the opportunity to win on that diagonal.

A video demonstration of our app can be found on YouTube:
www.youtube.com/watch?v=TCoBJy_W1ms.

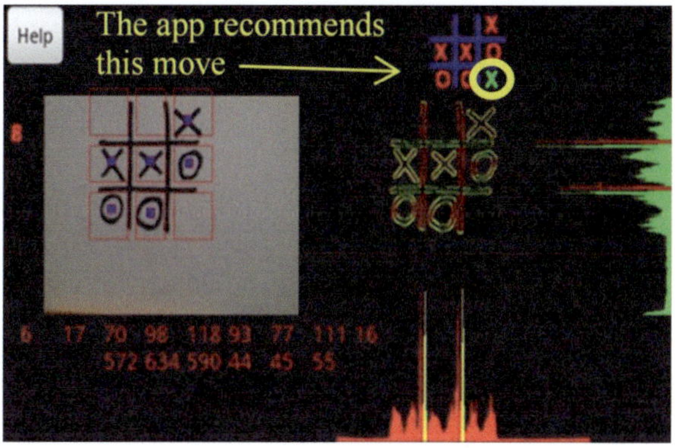

Fig. 8.6 The final app making the next move recommendation

8.5 Vision Acceleration on Mobile Devices

In this section, we describe what we learned about acceleration of vision algorithms on mobile devices, such as smart phones and tablets. Our app, as written in Java, runs at around five frames per second, fast enough to allow seamless user interface. Therefore, we can say we achieved real-time operation. However, we can imagine that other, more complex vision apps with more stringent real-time requirements, would have much more difficulty achieving real-time operation, so we wanted to learn about how vision apps can be accelerated on mobile devices. We used the Tic-Tac-Tandroid as a proxy application—our experience can be extrapolated to other vision apps.

Mobile devices, such as smart phones and tablets, commonly have application processors based on ARM Cortex architecture, which includes a SIMD (single instruction multiple data) media accelerator called Neon [14]. Particular devices commonly have other processors, such as DSPs and GPUs, however, at this time the mobile operating systems such as Android, do not offer access to them because each of these accelerators requires special-purpose code, contrary to the expectation of writing code once and running it on any device. Therefore, we focused on acceleration using Neon.

Acceleration with Neon. All ARM Cortex-A8 devices and many Cortex-A9 devices, commonly used on recent smart phones and tablets, include a media accelerator known as Neon [14]. It is a 16-way SIMD (single instruction multiple data) accelerator that can perform 8-, 16-, 32-, and 64-bit integer operations as well as 32-bit (single precision) floating-point operations. Having Neon available on most Android smartphones opens up the possibility to accelerate many low-level vision operations [15]. These include lens distortion correction, color conversion, image filtering, pyramid building, gradient computations, etc.

Code Profiling. In order to decide where to start with vision optimization, we first measured the execution times of various parts of our code as they executed in

Table 8.3 Tic-Tac-Tandroid code profiling

Tic-Tac-Tandroid code blocks	Average execution times in Java [ms]
Image color formatting	18.0
Luma extraction (Green)	3.3
Gradients (Sobel, L_1)	25.6
Board segmentation	7.5
Symbol detection	8.5
AI	0.1
Graphics and display	4.1
Other	145.5

Java. Table 8.3 contains the results of code profiling, presenting the averages over 100 frames of steady-state operation. The camera images we use have a resolution of 240 × 320.

From this information we concluded that the best candidate for initial experiments with Neon vision acceleration is the block that calculates gradients, because this block is SIMD-friendly and is the longest pole in the tent among vision blocks.

UncannyCV Neon Library. In order to avoid reinventing the wheel, we looked for available vision libraries for Neon and found the UncannyCV library by UncannyVision [16]. We obtained an evaluation copy and learned that this library offers a wide range of low-level vision functions accelerated on Neon: convolution kernels for various data types, morphological operations, image resizing, rotation, and transpose, color conversions, integral image, Sobel and Canny edge detection, lens distortion correction, Hough transform for lines, Harris corners, etc.

Comparing Performance on ARM and Neon. Next we present the measurement results of average and minimum execution times for the edge detection kernels processing a 240 × 320-pixel image. The reason we include the minimum times is to provide additional data to those researchers who may be able to prevent the operating system from interrupting the image processing tasks. We also present the average execution times for each video frame at the app level. We called UncannyCV functions using the Java SDK tools, which is different from what was originally intended—to be called from the Android NDK tools. This probably explains the difference between the anticipated execution time of Sobel on a 240 × 320 image (0.5 ms) [16] and the execution times we measured: on average 11.4 ms, and the minimum was 1.9 ms. In the following tables we present the results of our measurements. We measured the performance of Roberts and Sobel edge detection in Java SDK on ARM and Sobel and Canny edge detection using UncannyCV Neon code when called from Java SDK. We measured average execution times (Table 8.4), minimum execution times (Table 8.5), and average app execution times (Table 8.6) as the app uses different approaches and different cores to calculate the results.

In conclusion, thanks to the generous support from Uncanny Vision, we were able to demonstrate the benefits of implementing gradients on Neon instead on the

Table 8.4 Average kernel execution times (ms)

	Roberts	Sobel	Canny
Java on ARM	15.2	25.6	–
Uncanny CV on Neon (called from Java)	–	11.4	15.4

Table 8.5 Minimum kernel execution times (ms)

	Roberts	Sobel	Canny
Java on ARM	11.0	19.5	–
Uncanny CV on Neon (called from Java)	–	1.9	4.4

Table 8.6 Average application execution times (ms)

	Roberts	Sobel	Canny
Java on ARM	202.6	212.6	–
Uncanny CV on Neon (called from Java)	–	198.2	202.4

main CPU. On average, the gradients block executes more than two times faster, and sometimes up to 10 times faster, while the acceleration at the app level was, on average, 7 %.

This conclusion naturally extends to other low-level vision blocks, such as filtering, color space conversions, and image pyramid calculation, all of which are SIMD-friendly.

Another important realization we had about vision on Android is that the operating system interrupts the processor frequently and execution time measurements show a lot of variability. This leads to another advantage of using Neon—it is not interrupted by the operating system and can give faster and more reliable real-time guarantees.

Other accelerators. Most application processors used in smart phones and tablets have additional processing elements that can be used to accelerate vision operations. They include DSP and GPU processors which offer a lot of computational horsepower particularly useful for acceleration of low-level vision. The problem, however, is that these accelerators are specific to chip manufacturer and currently cannot be efficiently used by Android apps, which are written in hardware-agnostic fashion. It is possible to circumvent the Android protection mechanisms and to write efficient code that uses these accelerators, but that code will run only on devices that have the same accelerator, not on all smart phones and tablets as preferred by Android.

The promise of OpenVX. This issue will be addressed by the OpenVX initiative by Khronos, which aims to standardize the APIs for many commonly used vision functions. The implementation on the accelerator that is available on a particular device will be provided by chip manufacturers so the same code will efficiently run regardless of the underlying hardware specifics, thus achieving the hardware-agnostic coding typical for Android apps (Figs. 8.7 and 8.8).

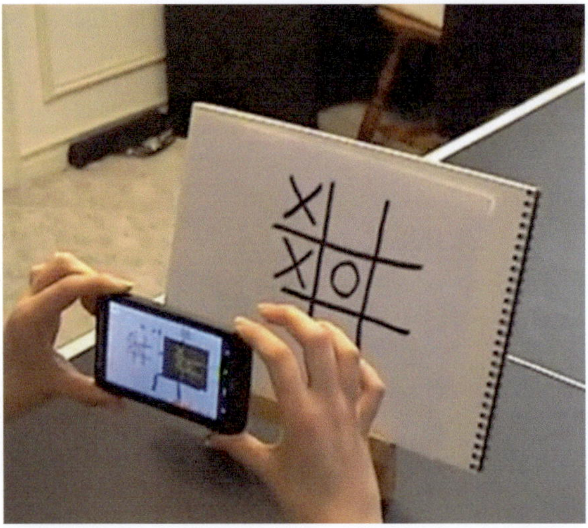

Fig. 8.7 Our app "looking" at a tic-tac-toe board

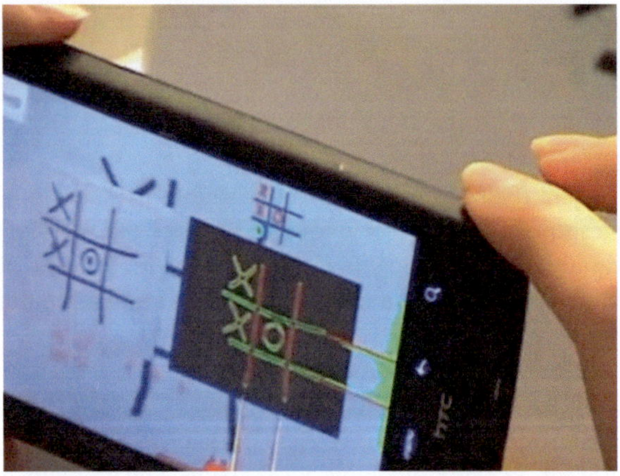

Fig. 8.8 Our app making a recommendation

8.6 Conclusions

Our contributions. Our project turned out to be a great combination of engineering and scientific methods. We started from the Stanford EE368 Viewfinder (it gave us Android camera access), but the rest of the code, both computer vision and AI, is a novel contribution. We had a great presentation at our regional science fair and have qualified to the state competition.

Robustness. We are very happy with our Android app and its performance. We played with it a lot to ensure that it runs robustly (and it does!). For example, it does not require special illumination—it works well in a variety of lighting conditions as long as there are no sharp shadows on the board.

Real-time operation. Although it was written in Java under Android and runs on an ARM (a small processor in a smartphone), our app runs at about five frames per second. This is fast enough to ensure smooth interaction with the user and so we can call it a "real-time" operation.

Limitations. We tested our app in many situations and found that the major drawbacks are:

- The phone must be held carefully to capture only the tic-tac-toe board and nothing else
- The phone must be held at a distance of about 10–30 cm from the tic-tac-toe board because the app does not have auto-focus. This distance dictates that the size of the board needs to be about 10 cm on a side
- The lines must be drawn almost entirely straight, otherwise the cells may be incorrectly detected
- The X's and O's must be fairly symmetric because the algorithm relies on the centroids of these symbols
- The app works well despite global illumination changes (we tried it in low and high room light) but if there are local illumination changes (such as sharp shadows), the system may give incorrect results.

Acknowledgments Many thanks to Drs. Darnell Moore and Rajesh Narasimha for their valuable comments during our school science fair, to Stanford University for open-sourcing their EE368 Viewfinder Android app and to Ranjith Parakkal, Takashi Nishizaki, and Dossan George, all from Uncanny Vision, for their generous support with Neon evaluation and their UncannyCV library.

References

1. de Praves D, Terni Lapilli. http://www.latinpraves.blogspot.com
2. Dewdney K (1993) A Tinkertoy computer that plays tic-tac-toe. http://www.rci.rutgers.edu/~cfs/472_html/Intro/TinkertoyComputer/TinkerT
3. Sudoku Grab. http://sudokugrab.blogspot.com/2009/07/how-does-it-all-work.html
4. Eyes On Road. http://www.eyesonroad.co.il
5. Google Project Glass. http://www.google.com/glass
6. Quiroga RQ, Fried I, Koch C (2013) Brain cells for grandmother. Sci Am 308(2):30–35
7. Park D (1997) The fire within the eye. Princeton University Press, Princeton
8. Rock I (1995) Perception. Scientific American Library, New York
9. Zeki S (1992) The Visual Image in Mind and Brain. In: Special issue of scientific American on mind and brain
10. Forsyth D, Ponce J (2011) Computer vision: the modern approach, 2nd edn. Prentice Hall, New Jersey
11. Android Developers. http://developer.android.com
12. Stanford EE368. http://www.stanford.edu/class/ee368
13. Tic-Tac-Tandroid on YouTube. http://www.youtube.com/watch?v=TCoBJy_W1ms

14. Neon Media Accelerator. http://www.arm.com
15. Kisačanin B, Nikolić Z (2010) Algorithmic and software techniques for embedded vision on programmable processors. Signal processing: image communication. Elsevier Science Inc., New York
16. Uncanny Vision. http://www.uncannyvision.com

Chapter 9
Vehicle Detection Onboard Small Unmanned Aircraft

Mathias Kölsch and Robert Zaborowski

Abstract This book chapter presents a system and experiments for on-aircraft detection of ground vehicles. The focus is on the steps for creating an embedded real-time system that met operator desires despite the limitations of the computer vision methods, the communication network, and the small flight platform. Detailed experimentation was essential for planning and coordinating the hardware and software components to achieve real-time performance and the most benefit to the operators. A fast object detection method was repeatedly trained and evaluated until it achieved the desired speed and accuracy. The fault-tolerant client–server architecture delivered the most relevant information even despite severe netword degradation. The demonstrated content-aware filtering of imagery elevated the human analyst's task from vehicle detection to detection verification, presumably a much less repetitive, fatiguing, and error-prone task. The system was successfully demonstrated as part of a Search And Rescue operation.

9.1 Essential Embedded Analysis

Old wisdom in project management says that you can have it done fast, well, or inexpensively, but never all three of those. Obtaining imagery from an unmanned aerial vehicle (UAV, also called "drone") in real-time apparently follows a similar law: you can stream high quality video, fly a small and inexpensive communication package, or transmit further than about a kilometer, but never all three of those. Directed antennae or satellite radios allow high bandwidth links for tens of kilometers or even globally, but they come at a cost of increased payload size, weight, and expense. Signals in the 0.3–30 MHz range can be sent beyond line of sight, but the available bandwidth is grossly insufficient for image transmission. However, if the quality of

---

M. Kölsch (✉) · R. Zaborowski
Naval Postgraduate School, Monterey, CA, USA
e-mail: kolsch@nps.edu

B. Kisačanin and M. Gelautz (eds.), *Advances in Embedded Computer Vision*,
Advances in Computer Vision and Pattern Recognition,
DOI 10.1007/978-3-319-09387-1_9

Fig. 9.1 Picture of the Sig Rascal 110 ARF remote-controlled aircraft and a view into the payload bay with the PC-104 board

the transmission can be improved without increasing the bandwidth, then payload cost and communication distance do not have to be sacrificed. Aggressive image and video compression already reduce the bandwidth dramatically, but depending on the application, further reduction by several orders of magnitude is possible.

This chapter describes a UAV system that produced "actionable information" through embedded computer vision where a traditional system would have been limited by image quality or operating range. Figure 9.1 shows the UAV with its commercial off-the-shelf (COTS) and custom payload (see Sect. 9.2.1). The embedded video analysis (see Sect. 9.3) prioritized image regions of interest (ROI) for transmission based on content and thereby reduced the bandwidth requirements by a factor of 500 without impeding its operational "quality" (see Sect. 9.5.6). This was possible because searching for a specific object—vehicles—was the primary goal for flying the UAV. This is a common need during desaster recovery, for search and rescue, and in military operations: operators are searching for people, vehicles, or ships lost at sea, for example. If likely image areas of such objects can be identified on the aircraft or satellite, these areas of interest can be transmitted with higher priority and/or with higher resolution (see Wilcox [1]) than the rest of the image.

It might even suffice to merely send the coordinates of a detection, a tiny fraction of the size of an image. In tactical military operations, timeliness of "actionable" information determines the usefulness of a UAV sensor and can determine the success of a mission. Yet the above-stated "law" limits either availability (due to cost, size, or logistics), range of operation, or image quality. Additionally, to benefit from technological improvements to the sensors (camera resolution and speed are increasing rapidly), the downlink bandwidth would have to keep pace. Storing data on the UAV is an option for some applications, but when timeliness or information sensitivity (in case the UAV is lost) are issues, streaming is preferable over storing.

Most remote-controlled aircraft for hobby use differ in several ways. Most importantly, they do not send high-resolution imagery or video to the operator, only what's required for navigation and control. That is, an operational restriction that the system described here attempts to remove: images had to either be small, low resolution, or be transmitted with growing latency or even downloaded after UAV recovery.

The experience was often frustratingly slow transmission of the large image files, which resulted in a continuously growing backlog of imagery waiting to be transmitted. The ground station computer that processed (or merely displayed) the imagery was often waiting while the UAV continued to collect more imagery.

9.2 Embedded System Overview

The embedded system consisted of hardware and software components, some COTS and some custom-built. Only the tight coupling of these components permitted efficient and fault-tolerant operation in face of large amounts of imagery data, intermittent and weak connectivity, and low-latency requirements for getting crucial information to the operators.

9.2.1 System Architecture

The ground control station (GCS) desktop computer (Windows XP, Intel Core 2 Quad Core, 2.40 GHz, 3 GB RAM) was connected to the UAV via a Wave Relay[1] mobile ad hoc network, specifically, through several low-gain sector antennae on the ground (approx. 9 dBi, 2.3–2.5 GHz, 600 mW) and low-gain (approx. 1.8 dBi), omnidirectional antennae on the aircraft. The UAV was a customized Sig Rascal 110 ARF remote-controlled aircraft, shown in Fig. 9.1, and maintained by the Center for Autonomous Vehicle Research (CAVR) at the Naval Postgraduate School. A separate VHF control and navigation link were dedicated to the Piccolo flight control system.

Prior to this configuration, the compute-payload consisted of two PC-104 boards (ADL MSM800XEV, 500 MHz AMD processor, 256 MB memory), where one PC-104 board was dedicated to flight and navigation tasks, and the other performed all camera operations [2]. Careful requirements analysis suggested that a single-board solution is more capable yet consumes less battery than two boards (see Sect. 9.5.4). Some services had to be ported from Windows to a Linux OS.

Hence, the payload consisted of a powerful PC-104 board (Advanced Digital Logic ADL945PC-T7400 with Intel Core 2 Duo, 2.16 GHz, 4M cache) and a Cannon G9 PowerShot still image (12MP) camera, mounted on a custom-built 2-DOF gimbal (two degrees of freedom: pitch and roll). The gimbal pointed the camera straight down irrespective of aircraft attitude in order to collect nadir imagery.

Payload capabilities had to be carefully balanced: aircraft jitter, gimbal stability, and image sensor sensitivity determined exposure time and image resolution. Higher resolution is advantageous for detection, but also requires more memory and processing resources, and in turn more battery, more weight, more heat dissipation, and reduced flight time. The chosen boards were selected for their sweet spot in terms

---

[1] www.persistentsystems.com.

of computational power and power consumption: for further CPU speed increase, the increase in power consumption was significantly larger. The optimal solution was found to be a PC-104 board with a dual-core CPU. Its power consumption was less than that of a single-core CPU board that offered a marginal increase in CPU speed.

9.2.2 Software Architecture

The PC-104 hardware was booted into a Linux operating system (OS) via a solid-state USB hard drive (SSD). Several modules ran independently and communicated via custom network messages: navigation, flight control (autopilot), GPS, camera sensor, and gimbal control. Some of the modules needed to be time-synchronized or perform timestamp interpolation for data fusion. The sensor module talked to the camera via another USB connection. It controlled several camera parameters, released the shutter, processed the images, and fused the metadata from GPS and gimbal information.

The communication to the GCS relied on a standard web server and HTTP messages. A dynamic page at a fixed address contained status information including the available imagery data, which was also pulled via HTTP. The client initiated download of cropped areas and full-size imagery based on a priority queue that could be modified through user input. The cropped areas from the vehicle detection process were given higher priority than the full-size imagery, unless preempted by an explicit full-size image request by a human operator. Within each priority group, the most recent images were given the highest priority. The server was state-free with respect to the GCS client, which permitted easy restart of the service since no state information had to be saved.

The time- and compute-intensive image analysis was performed in a separate process to permit load balancing with the navigation process and the image capture process. While not strictly a real-time system on a real-time OS, this division into processes along with process prioritization (with `nice`) proved effective in maintaining system responsiveness and to give sufficient cycles often enough to the navigation and capture processes. The image analysis task was optimized with the Intel Thread Building Block (TBB) library to implement thread safe containers and control the processing.

For development and troubleshooting purposes, clients could connect to the plane via SSH connection and perform in-flight software maintenance, power cycle the camera, and so forth.

The Ground Control Station (GCS) also ran several processes: A downloader sequentialized the image pull requests to avoid link overload. A standard Windows (File) Explorer served as a COTS user interface display that presented all vehicle detections to a human operator who would drag positive detections into a dedicated file folder. Another process listened on this folder for confirmations of objects-of-interest and triggered Search and Rescue actions based on the location information of the target (metadata) [3].

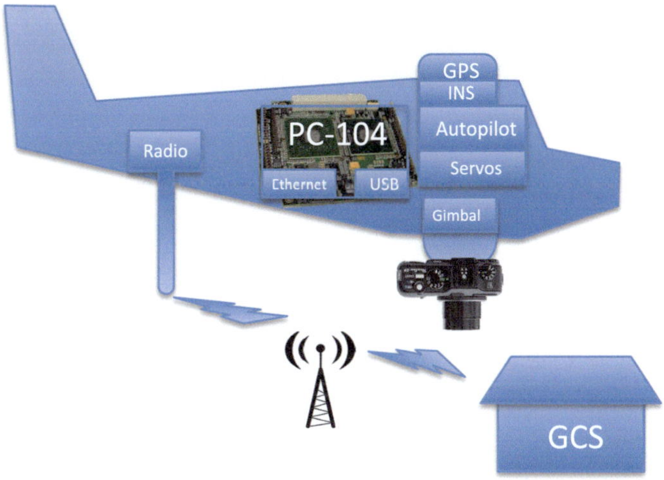

Fig. 9.2 Overview of the aircraft systems and the multihop communication link to the ground control station (GCS)

9.3 Object Detection

Key to the success of the embedded image analysis was the careful crafting to its operational objective that required a vehicle detector that was invariant to illumination, background, motion, scale, and in-plane rotation, that was flexible with the types of vehicles found, and that could analyze the images fast enough on the available hardware. Feature-based methods (e.g., SIFT and SURF, [4, 5]) are invariant to rotation, but not general enough for detecting vehicles, and also not particularly fast. This section briefly introduces the vision method used, then describes two approaches for overcoming the method's inherent shortcomings and how the operational requirements were met (Figs. 9.2 and 9.3).

9.3.1 Viola–Jones Style Detector

Cascaded detectors in the style of Viola and Jones [6] are fast, sufficiently generic, and can be tuned for the desired recall or precision, but they are not rotation invariant. Their proven performance with objects with rather uniform appearance [7] stems from multiple processing stages, each composed of several weak classifiers, can improve object discrimination while maintaining recall performance. The detectors for these experiments were trained on human-annotated positive (near-nadir vehicles) and negative images (no vehicles) that were previously collected Rascal UAV imagery.

Fig. 9.3 Partial training set for OpenCV's Viola–Jones style training algorithm for the "aligned" cascade

A common obstacle is rotational invariance, because the positive images are typically aligned in the same direction to allow for the most representative features to be extracted by the training software. For this detector this means that all cars would be facing the same direction. Vehicles appearing in the near-nadir aspect, as they will be in the images obtained by the UAV, can be in any orientation in the image plane. Two methods of overcoming this obstacle were examined, the faster of the two was used for the ground station and onboard processing experiments.

9.3.2 Rotation Invariance Through Image Rotation

The first method trains a detector on vehicles in one orientation and detects rotated vehicles by repeatedly rotating the image before applying the detector. For the machine learning to focus on similarities, the training set was resized with the same margin by percentage of the detection's dimensions for all positive training images. The training set was aligned with all vehicles facing left to standardize all images.

With the aligned training detector the vehicles need to be facing the same direction. To achieve rotational invariance during detection time, all test images had to be rotated within the functional tolerance of the trained detector before the detector is applied to search for vehicles. This real-time process incurs additional processing time.

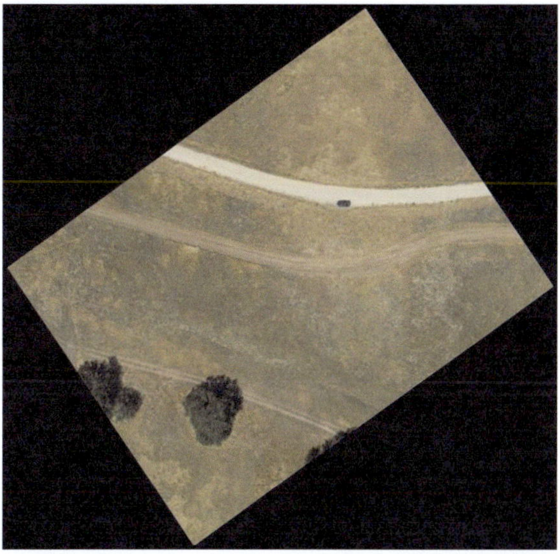

Fig. 9.4 This shows one of the rotated test images as provided to the detector trained with the "aligned" training set

Figure 9.4 shows the rotated image as it is applied to the aligned detector. This enlarges the size of the image, increases the number of search windows, and increases the computational cost of vehicle detection by adding the step of several image rotations before applying the detector repeatedly.

9.3.3 Rotation Invariance Through Rotated Training Set

The second method attempts to learn a detector that is rotationally invariant so that the detector has to be applied only once, irrespective of vehicle orientation. The rotated training set consists of multiple transformations of each image in the aligned training set: each image is rotated through 360° in 5° increments. To maintain a consistent size for all rotational increments during detector training, all images are the same square dimensions.

Figure 9.5 shows an example of the rotation performed for one of the training set images. This increased the size of the positive training image set from 200 images to 14,400 images.

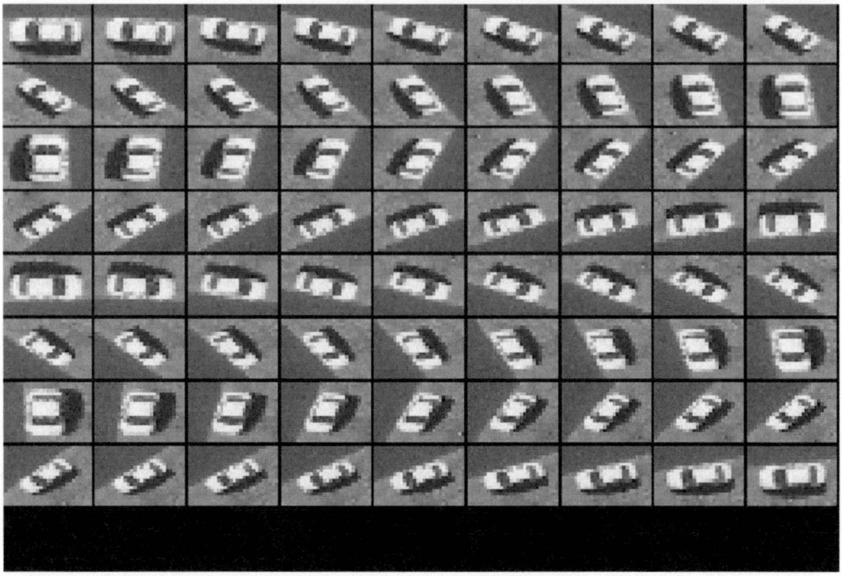

Fig. 9.5 An example of one positive image rotated in 5° increments

9.3.4 Vision Algorithm Tuning

The hardware specifications including camera optics, gimbal specifications, and flight altitude were chosen at a sweet spot of resolution on the ground, seamless area coverage, and motion blur. The core computer vision method placed additional constraints on the required number of pixels on target, view angle (close to nadir), and processing time. Sufficiently fast processing speeds and robust accuracy were achieved through cascade tuning, incremental training with negative images, tuning of detector parameters on a desktop computer, and scale restrictions at runtime.

Aside from the previously discussed orientation experiments, the detection method was trained with several sets of training data representing different mixes of natural environments (dirt roads with vegetation around) and city streets (pavement and buildings nearby). These data were presented to the training algorithm at various (cascade) stages in an attempt to optimize the speed performance while achieving the same accuracy. Proper selection of the positive training set improved recall, and with experimentation it was seen that the negative training set required additional samples to reduce the false positives. The object size was also varied during training and subsequent evaluation before settling on 30×30 pixels.

The runtime restrictions amounted to specifying the minimum and maximum scale values and the size-increment factor between scales for the scanning window detection approach. This reduced the false positive rate and processing times for each image. These parameters were set in a configuration file which allowed settings to be modified on the UAV while it was in flight. (This could be automated by calculating the expected pixel size of vehicles based on camera parameters and altitude. Still, as GPS is not without error, and small UAVs are subject to environment and control system complications, additional experimentation was needed with real-life test data to select the optimal minimum and maximum scale factors and the step size over which to move between the factors.)

9.4 Parts-Based Detection

One notices that the different vehicle corners look very similar to each other (see Fig. 9.5). To capitalize on this similarity for speed reasons, a separate detector was built that first detects any of the corners, or "parts," in any orientation and then looks for part "constellations" (orientations and locations) that are indicative of an entire vehicle. (For more details, see Zaborowski [8]). Parts-based detection has several benefits: the parts are faster to detect than the whole object, parts can be detected even if the object is partially occluded, and multiple parts can be detected in parallel, possibly even in hardware.

Parts were detected with a modified Viola–Jones method. Instead of binary results, it scored detections as the number of successfully passed stages divided by the total number of cascades of the detector.

After nonmaximum suppression, the scored locations of part detections were then analyzed with a structural model that was trained on pairwise combinations of part detections. The pair detectors were binary weak classifiers, but with a learned part score threshold. A second iteration over all training samples determined the predicted result of every weak classifier for all samples. These predictions were the input to an AdaBoost algorithm that generated a decision tree.

Figure 9.6 shows detection scores for four parts. The bottom part are the discretized maps, and highlighted with a pair of circles is one feature of the structural model. Detection is done in a multiscale scanning window approach.

9.5 Experiments and Results

Several experiments addressed the following questions:

1. Verification: Does the algorithm work as expected, in terms of accuracy and speed?
2. Which rotation-invariant method works better?
3. What is the usable throughput of the Wave Relay radios?
4. Is the PC-104 board fast enough to keep up with the computer vision tasks along with the normal aviation workload?

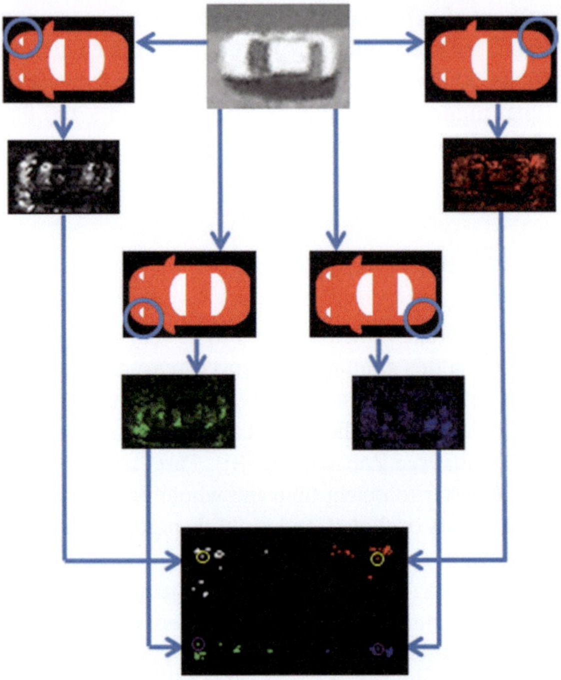

Fig. 9.6 Graphical illustration of how the four corner detectors are applied to an image

5. Does the algorithm integrate well into the rest of the system? Is the system architecture (hardware and software) able to produce the expected data, at the expected quality?
6. Validation: Is the produced information (vehicle detections with the actual, not ideal, performance) of value to the operators?

After preliminary tests in the lab, all actual flight tests were performed at the Camp Roberts US Army base in California. Six flights were made in total over five days, with a gap of several months between the first four and the last two flights. Over 3,100 images were taken that contained over 2,600 depictions of vehicles. Vehicles present in more than one image were counted each time. Those were manually annotated with bounding boxes around the vehicles ("ground truth"). A detection was scored a match only if at least 50 % of the respective bounding boxes overlapped.

9.5.1 Vehicle Detection in Aerial Imagery

The goal of this experiment was to demonstrate the feasibility to recognize vehicles in aerial imagery with a Viola–Jones style detector as described in Sect. 9.3.3 (trained

Table 9.1 Detector performance on four flights, with true positives P_T, false negatives N_F, false positives P_F, and the false positive rate (FPR) per image

Flight	Images	Vehicles	P_T	N_P	P_F	Recall	FPR
2010-08-08	714	715	433	282	321	0.6056	0.4496
2010-08-11a	760	95	82	13	69	0.8632	0.0966
2010-08-11b	719	19	16	3	59	0.8421	0.0826
2010-08-12	414	9	7	2	147	0.7778	0.2058
Overall	2,607	838	538	300	596	0.7721	0.2086

with rotated positive samples). Table 9.1 shows the results of processing the images from four flights on the GCS. All flights are designated by the date they were flown in year–month–day format. In the case of multiple flights on the same day, the first flight is denoted as "a" with the second flight on that day denoted as "b".

Postprocessing combined nearby detections, so any one reported area may be a collection of multiple detections. Therefore, detection areas containing multiple vehicles were counted as the number of vehicles they contained. Recall R is the ratio of true positives P_T to vehicles present V, $R = \frac{P_\mathrm{T}}{V}$ and was found to be 77.21%. The average false positive rate (FPR) per image was 0.21. Flights 2010-08-11a and 2010-08-11b had significantly lower false positive rates and higher recall compared to the other two flights; it is unclear why.

Reading an image from disk on the GCS took, on average, 514.89 ms (±64.12 ms), the vehicle detection algorithm itself about 1,487.50 ms (±166.77 ms). Over 14 GByte of jpg-compressed images were captured and processed in four flights. The cropped areas from detections amounted to just under 30 MByte (see also Table 9.3)

9.5.1.1 Discussion

Although the time of day, above ground level altitude, and detector settings were constant across all pictures, the UAV itself does not always exhibit consistent flight and camera platform parameters. For example, the gimble may be in motion while a picture is being taken, which could result in both blur and a viewing aspect that is not consistent with the training samples provided to the detector.

The observed recall and FPR are not as good as recent face detectors including the method this implementation was based on [6]. However, recall much better than chance (realize there are 10,000 s of areas tested with scanning window approach), and FPR low enough to not swamp network connection. The measured speed showed a limit of processing an image about every other second.

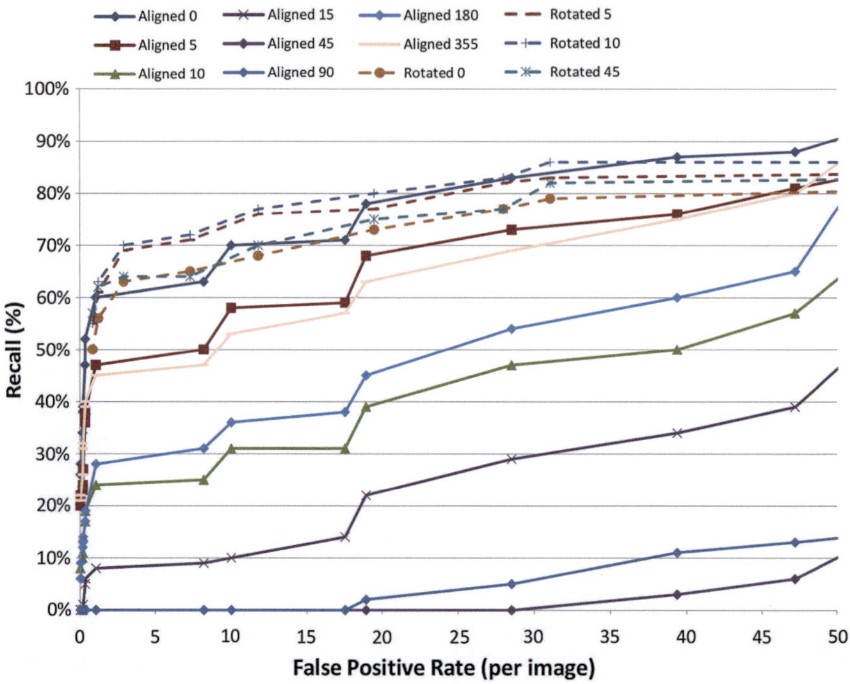

Fig. 9.7 The graph above shows the performance as test images are rotated in 5° increments. *Solid lines* represent the detector trained with an aligned positive imagery set, *dashed lines* represent the detector trained with a rotated positive imagery set

9.5.2 *Performance of Rotation Invariance*

Comprehensive evaluation determined the two detection methods' invariance to in-image-plane rotations. 100 images from the four flights were annotated with vehicle rotation information and subsequently rotated in 5° increments for a total of 7,200 test images. Figure 9.7 shows the results of processing these 72 series of images with the detector that had been trained on aligned training images (see Sect. 9.3.2) and with the detector trained on rotated training images (Sect. 9.3.3).

9.5.2.1 Discussion

Vehicles rotated beyond 5° in either direction cannot be detected well with the "aligned" detector (Fig. 9.7, solid lines), confirming prior analysis of the Viola–Jones method [9]. This suggests that a training set rotated in 5° increments would yield superior results. Indeed, the detector trained on rotated images is significantly more robust toward rotated vehicle detections (dashed lines in Fig. 9.7).

Training a detector with the additional samples (14,400 positive samples in 72 orientations versus the 200 positive samples used for the aligned detector) results in a modest increase in off-line training time. This training technique produces classifiers with more features, and therefore requires more CPU cycles to process an image. However, the dashed ROC curves in Fig. 9.7 indicate that the recall across the range of in-plane rotations was consistently higher compared to that of the aligned training set. The rotated training set enabled building a rotation-invariant detector, meaning it can find vehicles in all orientations in only one pass, thereby eliminating the need to perform multiple passes over incrementally rotated test images. Given the computational runtime expense of image rotation, the possible introduction of artifacts caused by the interpolation method, and the increased pixel count from the additional black areas (see Fig. 9.4), the rotated training set yielded the preferred method.

9.5.3 Bandwidth Performance of Wave Relay

The available bandwidth between the Rascal UAV and the GCS over Wave Relay varies with the number of network users, with vehicle distance, altitude, and the exact relative orientation of the (omnidirectional) antenna. In tests with few users the throughput for a realistic data set (sending a large, JPG-compressed images to the GCS) was determined to be around 200 kB/s typically. Throughput decreased roughly linearly with altitude. At that rate, a 12 MPixel image, compressed to 4 MB, took about 20 s to download.

9.5.3.1 Discussion

For the desired coverage and ground resolution, given jitter and vehicle speed, the sweet spot for vehicle altitude and focal length identified 0.5 Hz as the necessary shooting speed. The download speed therefore is one order of magnitude too slow to keep up with a high-resolution image every other second.

9.5.4 From GCS to Embedded Processing

After profiling and parameter evaluation with existing systems, and after procurement of appropriate embedded hardware, the performance of the algorithms was evaluated on the embedded hardware during a live flight. Between experiments, a new detector had been trained with an increased negative training set to reduce false detections that frequently occurred on the runway and other rectangular objects. Both detectors had been trained with rotated imagery.

Table 9.2 gives the detection results. The average recall was 47.02 % at a FPR of 50.17 %. There were large differences between the two flights. While the four flights

Table 9.2 Detector performance during testing at Camp Roberts in conjunction with TNT 11-3

Flight	Images	Vehicles	P_T	N_P	P_F	Recall	FPR
2011-05-06	113	461	339	122	291	0.7354	0.2051
2011-05-07	398	1,414	290	1,124	570	0.2051	0.7983
Overall	511	1,875	629	1,246	861	0.4702	0.5017

Table 9.3 Detector speed performance on the ground station (top, GCS), and the embedded PC-104 (bottom)

Flight	Image size	Cropped size	μ (σ) access		μ (σ) processing	
2010-08-08	3,914,757	18,656	504.40	(46.17)	1,494.11	(149.55)
2010-08-11a	4,242,232	4,198	542.70	(122.92)	1,532.57	(156.56)
2010-08-11b	4,165,580	2,394	500.65	(41.36)	1,473.77	(155.13)
2010-08-12	2,532,752	4,589	511.79	(46.04)	1,449.56	(205.83)
Overall GCS	14,855,321	29,839	**514.89**	**(64.12)**	**1,487.50**	**(166.77)**
2011-05-06	472,171	17,167	548.73	(73.98)	3,020.46	(353.45)
2011-05-07	2,015,450	20,700	667.02	(551.67)	3,093.87	(395.62)
Overall PC-104	2,487,621	37,867	**607.87**	**(312.82)**	**3,057.16**	**(374.54)**

Image sizes are cumulative for the entire flight and measured in kB. Times are reported in ms

from TNT 10-4 (Table 9.1) and the first flight from TNT 11-3 were performed at the same altitude with only small deviations, the second flight from TNT 11-3 exhibited frequent and pronounced altitude changes. The raw images of the second flight had more blur, probably partially due to crosswinds and partially due to the rapid position and attitude changes of the aircraft during image exposure. Additionally, there was no feedback from the gimbal to the PC-104 so the camera would only take a picture when the gimbal is stable. Changing altitudes was an attempt to find reduced crosswinds to stabilize the flight and to reduce the blur. As the UAV flew higher, the vehicle images were smaller, and smaller vehicles reduce the number of features available to the detector. This leaves less room for error and causes a reduction in detection performance.

For the purpose of comparison, the same parameters were used for all test flights. However, reducing the required number of neighboring detections or scaling the scanning window with a smaller scale factor (closer to 1) could improve performance. Naturally, this would increase the total number of windows searched and hence the processing time. This time might be reduced by accounting for the smaller detection sizes and reducing the maximum detector scale. The implementation tested here did not incorporate a feedback for UAV altitude into the detector settings.

Table 9.3 shows the speed performance for embedded vehicle detection. The mean processing time was 3,057 ms, with no large discrepancy between the mean processing time of the two flights. The mean access time was 607.87 ms.

9.5.4.1 Discussion

Embedded processing achieved accuracy performance in the same rough order of magnitude as GCS processing. The file access time was unchanged, but the image processing time approximately doubled. The PC-104's reduced on-chip cache size is a probably culprit for this unsurprising increase. The PC-104 also performed both flight control and detection.

Reviewing the imagery, there appears to be some halo and blurring around the edges of the vehicles that was not present to the same extent on the first five flights. Object boundaries and edges contain a lot of information, and many potential features for a haar-like feature-based detector to utilize. This, combined with additional blurring of the imagery, is most likely the cause of the reduced recall.

9.5.5 Embedded System Operation

The overall system as described in Sect. 9.2.1 worked as desired: the sensors reported to software processes which were granted sufficient resources by the hardware platform to effectively act as a true real-time system. Combining flight control and payload processing on the same PC-104 board resulted in space and power savings without incurring negative effects. The CPU load was measured in two instrumented flights. As expected, the image analysis task was demanding on the CPU, but only intermittently. Presumably, image transfer and load operations alternated with processing on the CPU, giving other processes sufficient time to run.

9.5.6 Operational Results

The embedded image analysis enabled longer range communication, continued operation despite severely degraded network performance, more rapid availability of critical information, and filtering of excessive data. Had the network bandwidth been sufficient to transmit all images at full resolution, a single human operator likely would not have been able to thoroughly search a 4,000 $\times$ 3,000 pixel image every other second for tiny vehicles. A person reviewing these images would have to zoom in and pan over the 12-megapixel images as each is larger than the screen size. The repetitious task also bears the danger of operator fatigue and complacency. Without embedded analysis, most images would not be available until after landing the aircraft. With embedded analysis, only the most pertinent information was immediately downloaded, which at the same time reduced the human operator load to a very manageable level: inspect a few cropped areas every few seconds. Compared to downloading full-size images, embedded processing yielded a bandwidth reduction by a factor of 500. The reduced bandwidth and reduced operator load meant that the embedded analysis system met the operational objectives–directing search and rescue efforts [3].

While full motion video (FMV) offers more fidelity, it is currently not possible to recover the data lost during a network outage until after the UAV has landed. When sending cropped detections, on the other hand, the data is small enough that a small backlog from network congestion or outage can be overcome. Embedded, onboard processing "at the edge" of the network facilitates more efficient network utilization by passing limited amounts of processed information in place of large amounts of raw data.

9.6 Conclusions

Embedded, onboard analysis of imagery presents a solution to the bandwidth limitations of small unmanned vehicles and their steadily improving camera capabilities. Prerequisites are an automated detection method for the object or scene of interest and the ability to discard unimportant image or full motion video (FMV) areas. Still, adopting a computer vision algorithm for use in an embedded environment involved detailed planning and customizations:

- Analysis of flight and platform characteristics (nadir shooting possible, flight altitude, jitter, required image resolution, available bandwidth, etc.),
- Selection of a suitable computer vision method, based on speed and accuracy,
- Method training, modifications, and tuning (e.g., for rotation invariance),
- Selection of embedded hardware that meets payload demands (USB ports, power consumption, heat dissipation, CPU speed, memory),
- System integration (connections to hardware and software components), including adaptations for the specific hardware and operating system, and
- Validation of the entire system as part of the operational workflow.

While smaller bandwidth needs are advantageous even in a fully functional and reliable network, onboard processing dramatically increases *information throughput* when the network is only intermittently available, and preserves the real-time value of the UAV.

The advantages of the described system extend beyond network aspects into human performance. The human image analysts' responsibility changes from a repetitive, error-prone detection task to a lower volume, less taxing detection *verification* task. The demonstrated prefiltering elevates the operator to make decisions based on the information passed from the UAV. While these experiments took place on a UAV in still video, this could easily be extended to embedded analysis of full motion video.

Acknowledgments We would like to thank the contributions of the NPS unmanned systems community for their help and support, particularly Prof. Tim Chung, Prof. Kevin Jones, and Prof. Vladimir Dobrokhodov.

References

1. Wilcox J (2013) Content-aware adaptive compression of satellite imagery using artificial vision. Master's thesis, Naval Postgraduate School
2. Jones KD, Dobrokhodov V, Kaminer I, Lee DJ, Bourakov E, Clement MR (2009) Development, system integration and flight testing of a high-resolution imaging system for small UAS. In: 47th AIAA aerospace sciences meeting including the new horizons forum and aerospace exposition, American Institute of Aeronautics and Astronautics
3. Chung TH, Kress M, Royset JO (2009) Probabilistic search optimization and mission assignment for heterogeneous autonomous agents. In: International conference on robotics and automation
4. Bay H, Tuytelaars T, Van Gool L (2006) Surf: speeded up robust features. Comput Vis-ECCV 2006:404–417
5. Dorkó G, Schmid C (2008) Selection of scale-invariant parts for object class recognition. In: Ninth IEEE international conference on computer vision, 2003. Proceedings ICCV'03. IEEE pp 634–639
6. Viola P, Jones M (2001) Rapid object detection using a boosted cascade of simple features. In: IEEE computer society conference on computer vision and pattern recognition, vol 1. Citeseer
7. Viola P, Jones MJ, Snow D (2003) Detecting pedestrians using patterns of motion and appearance. In: Proceedings international conference on computer vision, October 2003, pp 734–741
8. Zaborowski RM (2011) Onboard and parts-based object detection from aerial imagery. Master's thesis, Naval Postgraduate School
9. Kölsch M, Turk M (2004) Analysis of rotational robustness of hand detection with a Viola-Jones detector. In: IAPR international conference on pattern recognition

Chapter 10
Vision-Based Lane Analysis: Exploration of Issues and Approaches for Embedded Realization

Ravi Kumar Satzoda and Mohan M. Trivedi

Abstract Vision-based lane analysis has been investigated to different degrees of completeness. While most studies propose novel lane detection and tracking methods, there is some research on estimating lane-based contextual information using properties and positions of lanes. According to a recent survey of lane estimation in [7], there are still open challenges in terms of reliably detecting lanes in varying road conditions. Lane feature extraction is one of the key computational steps in lane analysis systems. In this paper, we propose a lane feature extraction method, which enables different configurations of embedded solutions that address both accuracy and embedded systems' constraints. The proposed lane feature extraction process is evaluated in detail using real-world lane data to explore its effectiveness for embedded realization and adaptability to varying contextual information such as lane types and environmental conditions. Accuracy of more than 90 % is obtained during the evaluation of the proposed method using real-world driving data.

10.1 Introduction

Intelligent driver assistance systems (IDAS) are increasingly becoming a part of modern automobiles. Reliable and trustworthy driver assistance systems require accurate and efficient means for capturing states of vehicle surroundings, vehicle dynamics as well as state of the driver in a holistic manner [23].

Trivedi et al. [23] describe a Looking-in Looking-out (LiLo) framework for computer-vision-based active vehicle safety systems, which aim at bringing together the three components of overall IDAS, which are the environment, the vehicle, and the driver. It is shown that sensing and contextualizing all the three components together is critical and efficient in an IDAS. The role of vision sensors, complemented by

R.K. Satzoda (✉) · M.M. Trivedi
Laboratory of Intelligent and Safe Automobiles, University of California San Diego, La Jolla, CA 92093, USA
e-mail: rsatzoda@eng.ucsd.edu

M.M. Trivedi
e-mail: mtrivedi@ucsd.edu

B. Kisačanin and M. Gelautz (eds.), *Advances in Embedded Computer Vision*, Advances in Computer Vision and Pattern Recognition,
DOI 10.1007/978-3-319-09387-1_10

other sensors such as vehicle controller area network (CAN) data, etc., in such a framework is explained in detailed in [23], wherein vision systems that enhance safety of the driver by looking-in and looking-out of the vehicle are proposed. It is established that it is not only important to sense the environment outside the vehicle such as obstacles (vehicles, pedestrians), but also monitor the dynamics of the driver (and possibly other passengers) inside the vehicle. Having such a holistic sensing would also enable in predicting driver intentions and take the necessary control/alarm actions well in time and mitigate dangerous situations [4].

The vehicle surround analysis modules include operations such as lane analysis [19] and vehicle detection [20], which are the front end modules in terms of capturing and analyzing the vehicle surroundings. The information from these modules are then further analyzed to assess the criticality of the situation and predict driver intentions and behavior before the driver takes any decision or maneuver [21, 22] This assessment and prediction can either be used to warn/alert the driver of any unsafe maneuvers or otherwise, or input to automatic control systems such as Adaptive Cruise Control (ACC) systems. Therefore, the vehicle surround analysis modules play a vital role in deciding the effectiveness of the IDAS because they are the primary modules that sense and analyze data from outside and inside the vehicle to extract meaningful information for the rest of the IDAS.

Among the different modules for active driver safety framework, lane analysis using monocular cameras contributes to its efficiency in multiple ways. Firstly, lane analysis, i.e., lane estimation and tracking, aids in localizing the ego-vehicle motion, which is the one of the very first and primary steps in most IDAS such as lane departure warning (LDW), lane change assistance, etc. [11, 23]. Next, lane analysis is also shown to aid other vehicle surround analysis modules. For example, in [17], lanes are used to detect vehicles more robustly because vehicles are assumed to be localized to their ego-lanes. Similarly, lane detection is shown to play a significant role in predicting driver intentions before lane changes occur [11, 23], etc.

By lane estimation, we refer to the process of detecting and tracking lane markings that define the lanes in a road scene. A detailed survey of various lane estimation techniques is presented in [7, 10]. Though a number of lane estimation methods have been proposed in literature [1, 2, 5, 7, 8, 10, 16], the variations in the road scene makes lane estimation a challenging process [5, 7, 10] such as shadows from trees, vehicles, etc., presence of skid marks, varying tar color and road surfaces, varying ambient lighting conditions, etc. Figure 10.1 shows some of these challenging scenarios.

The lane estimation methods in [1, 5, 7, 8, 10, 16] usually comprise three main steps: (1) lane feature extraction, (2) outlier removal, and (3) lane tracking [10]. Lane feature extraction techniques are usually based on the properties of lanes like directionality, intensity gradients, texture, and color. Techniques like steerable filters [3, 10, 16], adaptive thresholding [1, 12], Gabor filters [8], etc. are used to extract lane features. Learning based approaches are also employed in [5] to extract lane features. The detected lane features are further filtered for outliers in the second step of lane estimation process. This step usually involves fitting the detected lane features into a known road/lane model, thereby eliminating nonlane features. This

Fig. 10.1 Challenging road scenes to detect lanes: different types of lane markings—dashed lanes and circular reflectors, tar color changes, tire skid marks, shadows of trees, vehicles, infrastructure, etc.

step includes algorithms such as RANSAC [1, 16], Hough transform [1, 10, 14], etc. Finally trackers like Kalman filters [10] or particle filters [5] are used to model the tracking of lanes. This is inspired from the fact that there is a predictability of the lane positions in every frame based on the information from past frames and the knowledge of the vehicle dynamics.

The computing algorithms in these methods can be closely related to some aspects of the human visual system's (HVS') perception of lanes. In [10, 16], lane features are extracted using steerable filters, which detect directional gradients. This can be related to the HVS' perception of lanes as being directionally pointed toward the vanishing point and having higher intensities than the background. Similar reasoning is used to extract lane features using Gabor filter kernels in [8]. Another way that the HVS uses is the changes in the gray level intensities of the lane markings. This kind of perception is used in [12] to extract lanes where lanes are detected as straight lines of constant width and having a specific range of gray level intensities. Though this model works well for lanes in near-view, the straight model of the lanes may fail to capture lanes in far-view of the ego-vehicle. However, the work presented in [12] uses other modalities like stereo vision, GPS, etc., to model the digital map of the ego-vehicle. A more general model using the same gray level perception property is employed by Borkar et al. in [1], in which an adaptive thresholding method is proposed to extract the brighter lanes from darker road surface. A temporal averaging is also employed in [1], which averages the dashed lane markings over time, so that a continuous line is seen in every frame instead of dashed lanes. This follows from the HVS' perception that the lanes are actually straight lines but spatially sampled along the road, which gives a dashed appearance. In addition to these methods based on perception of visual properties of lanes, a learning-based approach is presented in [5], wherein an Adaboost-based learning algorithm is used to extract lane features in challenging road scenarios.

The detected lane features are further sent for outlier removal. This is done by employing road models and clustering algorithms on the lane features extracted from the first step, and are applied on two different domains. Firstly in the image domain with perspective effect, HVS perceives lanes as usually straight (and then curved if they are curving in far-view from the host vehicle), and are directed toward a vanishing point. Second domain is the inverse perspective map (IPM) view, which is the top view of the road, where the lanes are perceived to be parallel lines which are either straight or following a clothoid model [10]. These visual perceptions are translated into computer vision algorithms such as Hough transform, which is a straight line detector [1, 10], and RANSAC, which is a outlier detection algorithm based on a road model [1]. The third step in lane estimation process is lane tracking, which is usually performed using techniques like Kalman filters and particle filters [1, 5, 10, 16]. Lane tracking follows the HVS' perception that positions of lanes can be predicted in the current frame based on the history of lane positions in the previous frames and the vehicle dynamics. In addition to these three steps, other visual perception cues are also used for efficient lane estimation. For example, in [16], vehicle detection was used to robustly locate lanes as an additional cue. This is inspired from the HVS' perception process that vehicles are expected to be in lanes and hence lanes could be localized nearby the vehicles.

Although there are a number of computer-vision-based lane analysis methods reported in literature as shown in recent works [1, 5–7, 10], most of these works address the robustness of the vision algorithms in different road scenarios. However, as pointed by Stein in [18] titled, "The challenge of putting vision algorithms into a car," there is a need to explore lane analysis approaches for embedded realization. Attempts have been made to realize embedded solutions for lane estimation and tracking [9, 15], etc., but as indicated in [9], most of them have been architectural translations of *some parts* of existing lane detection algorithms.

In this paper, we propose a lane feature extraction method that addresses some of these issues related to embedded realization.

10.2 Lane Analysis and Embedded Vision

Different variants of lane analysis techniques have been proposed in literature such as [1, 5, 10] as shown in (Table 10.1). A detailed survey of lane analysis methods is presented in [10] and [7]. An effective lane analysis method [7, 10] comprises of three main steps: (1) lane feature extraction, (2) outlier removal or postprocessing, and (3) lane tracking. Pixel level filtering operations such as steerable filters, etc., are applied on the entire image or regions of interest (usually the lower half of the input image) to extract lane features. A further postprocessing and outlier removal is performed using techniques like RANSAC [1], Hough transform [13], etc., in order to improve the robustness. Inverse perspective mapping (IPM) of the input image is

Table 10.1 Lane analysis: Illustrative research studies

	Lane Analysis Framework	
	Basic formulation	Algorithms
McCall [10] 2006	Directionality coupled with intensity transitions of lanes	Steerable filters for lane feature extraction
		Hough transform, IPM &Road model for outlier removal
	Lane positions can be predicted over time based on vehicle movement	Steerable filter response to differentiate lane markings and circular reflectors
	Lane markings show directionality, circular markers do not	Kalman filtering for lane tracking
		Ego-vehicle position estimation using lane positions
Cheng [3] 2007	Extension of formulation as in [10] to omnidirectional cameras	Extension of lane estimation methods in [10]
		Ego-vehicle position estimation using lane positions
Borkar [1] 2012	Dashed lanes when averaged can give continuous lanes	Temporal blurring for lane feature extraction
	Lanes are brighter than lanes, especially at night	Adaptive thresholding
	Lanes have two different gradients	Gaussian kernel template matching and RANSAC for outlier removal
	Lane positions can be predicted over time based on vehicle movement	Kalman filtering for lane tracking
Gopalan [5] 2012	Lanes have predetermined properties which can be learnt	Learning based method for lane feature extraction
	Lane positions can be predicted over time based on vehicle movement	Particle filtering for lane tracking
Nedevschi [12] 2013	Lanes are brighter than road, have constant width	Gray level based feature extraction
	Movement of lane markings is periodic across time	Periodic histograms for lane boundary classification
		Double lanes detection
		Ego-vehicle global localization using visual and GPS data

(continued)

Table 10.1 (continued)

	Lane Analysis Framework	
	Basic formulation	Algorithms
Sivaraman [16] 2013	Directionality coupled with intensity transitions of lanes	Steerable filters for lane feature extraction
		IPM, road model and RANSAC for outlier removal
	Lane positions can be predicted over time based on vehicle movement	Kalman filtering for lane tracking
		Lane localization using vehicle detection
		Ego-vehicle position estimation using lane positions
		Vehicle detection using lane detection

also performed to transform the input image into world coordinate system (WCS) [10]. In addition, lane models and vehicle dynamics from CAN data are used to track lanes across time using Kalman filtering, etc.

Considering that IDAS are implemented on battery-powered embedded platforms inside a car, attempts have been made to implement lane detection systems on embedded platforms in [9, 15], etc. However, as indicated previously, most of these are partial systems with the exception of the full system implemented in [9]. For example, in [15], lane detection is implemented using steerable filters on an FPGA platform. However, this is only the lane feature extraction module of a comprehensive and robust lane analysis method called VioLET in [10]. One of the very few complete lane analysis systems is reported in [9], which includes a pipelined architecture for lane feature extraction, lane model fitting and tracking, and implemented on an FPGA platform using DSP48 cores of Spartan FPGAs.

In [18], different kinds of embedded constraints are elaborated that decide the feasibility of employing a computer vision task in a car, which is an excellent example of a complex embedded system. These constraints bring together the requirements from two different disciplines—computer vision and embedded engineering. In other words, robustness is the key performance index for a computer vision algorithm but real-time operation, limited hardware resource utilization, energy efficiency are the key metrics for embedded realization. With the two together in active driver safety framework, the reliability and dependability of computer vision algorithms that run on resource constrained computing platforms is another challenge that needs to be satisfied.

10.3 Feature Extraction Method for Context-Aware Lane Analysis

Lane feature extraction is one of the key steps in real-time lane analysis, which includes both lane estimation and tracking. The robustness of the entire lane analysis system depends directly on reliable lane features that need to be extracted from the road scene. This also implies that there is a direct relationship between the efficiency of lane feature extraction process and the robustness of the system. Adding more computer vision algorithms for lane feature extraction in order to improve robustness can directly impact the efficiency of the system. Also, the robustness, and hence the efficiency, of this feature extraction step is dependent on vehicle surround conditions like road types, weather conditions such as fog, wet roads etc., environmental changes in road scene like shadows, road surface, etc., and the availability of other data sources like road maps, etc. These factors—application requirements (e.g., safety critical systems demand higher robustness), environmental and weather conditions, road information, lane types, etc., constitute the context in which lane analysis is to be performed. Therefore, this context plays an important role in the robustness and efficiency of the lane feature extraction step. A detailed exploration of the lane feature extraction step that can cater to such contextual information is worthy of further study.

It can be seen that E_+ and E_- have nonlane features also. We now propose *shift and match* technique to extract lane features and eliminate nonlane features from each band. In order to do this, we compute the horizontal projection vectors $\mathbf{p}_+$ and $\mathbf{p}_-$ for E_+ and E_- as shown in Fig. 10.3. Peaks are formed in these projection vectors where there are clusters of pixels in E_+ and E_-. Since the dark→light and light→dark transitions in a lane marking are separated by δ pixels in the IPM image I_W, the peaks corresponding to the lane edges in $\mathbf{p}_+$ and $\mathbf{p}_-$ are also separated by a small δ. In order to capture these pairs of transitions of lanes, $\mathbf{p}_+$ is shifted by δ places to the left and multiplied with $\mathbf{p}_-$ resulting in the vector $\mathbf{K}_{\mathrm{B}_i}$ for scan band B_i, i.e.,

$$\mathbf{K} = (\mathbf{p}_+ \ll \delta) \odot \mathbf{p}_- \tag{10.1}$$

where $\odot$ represents pointwise multiplication. Figure 10.3 shows the result of the shift and match operation performed on $\mathbf{p}_+$ and $\mathbf{p}_-$ for the upper band selected in Fig. 10.2. It can be seen that we get peaks in $\mathbf{K}_{\mathrm{B}_i}$ in Fig. 10.3 at the same locations as the left edge of each lane marking in the upper band in Fig. 10.2. The locations of the peaks in $\mathbf{K}_{\mathrm{B}_i}$ for each scan band B_i are then used along with the road model to eliminate outliers.

In this paper, for the sake of illustration and simplicity, we limit the discussion to a simple straight road model in the IPM domain, i.e., we assume the road is straight (deviated only by a few pixels). Considering that input images are calibrated with WCS in IPM image, the lane marking positions can be predicted in a deterministic manner. Let us take the case of ego-lane. After calibration, if x_{L} and x_{R} correspond to the lane positions of the left and right lane markings of the ego-lane, the lane markings are expected to be in the vicinity of these lane positions. The peaks positions in $\mathbf{K}_{\mathrm{B}_i}$ from each scan band are mapped to the predicted lane markings x_{L} and x_{R}. This

Fig. 10.2 Generating steerable filter output from bands

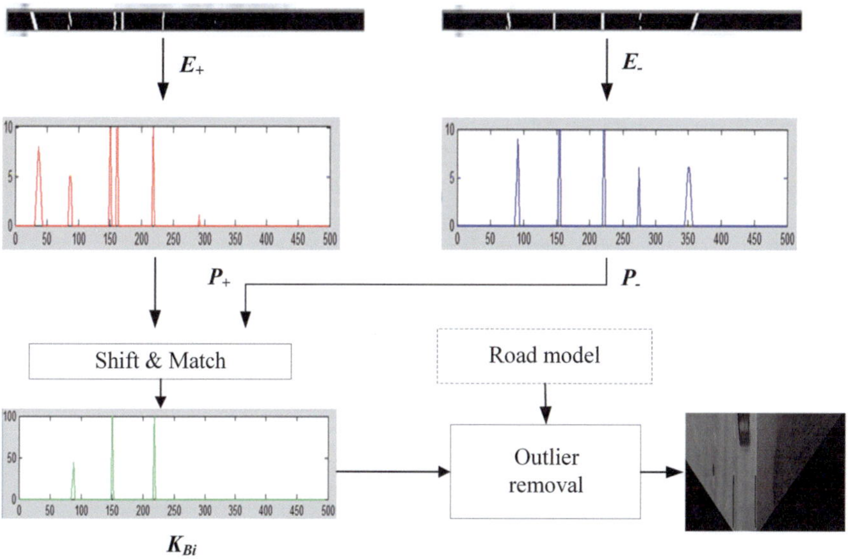

Fig. 10.3 Illustrating shift and match operation for band B_i

mapping will eliminate any outliers that may be picked during the shift and match operation. The lane estimation output is shown in Fig. 10.3.

In order to cater for higher curvatures of the lanes, lane models such as clothoid model can be also be used on the peak positions obtained in $\mathbf{K}_{B_i}$ to estimate curved lanes and also eliminate the outliers. Furthermore, lane tracking using Kalman filters using vehicle dynamics like yaw rate and steering angle information [10] increases the robustness of outlier removal tremendously.

Figure 10.4a shows the overall lane analysis method using the proposed lane feature extraction method. Figure 10.4b, c show two possible design options enabled by the proposed scan band based lane feature extraction. The filtering operation and shift-match operation that are applied on each scan band can be ported as a processing element (PE). A parallel architecture with each scan band being processed by one PE gives a parallel design option as shown in Fig. 10.4b.

The second option shown in Fig. 10.4c is a pipelined option, which can offer a wide variety of design implementations. If one PE is used, we get a serial implementation, where each band is processed serially. The number of pipeline stages can be increased depending on the number of PEs that are used. This pipelined design option can also be used to control/predict the lane feature positions in each subsequent PE. In other words, if PE_0 detects lane features at specific positions, this information can be relayed to the PE_1 as positions around which lane features are expected. Vehicle dynamics and road model information can further aid in the overall robustness and efficiency of this implementation.

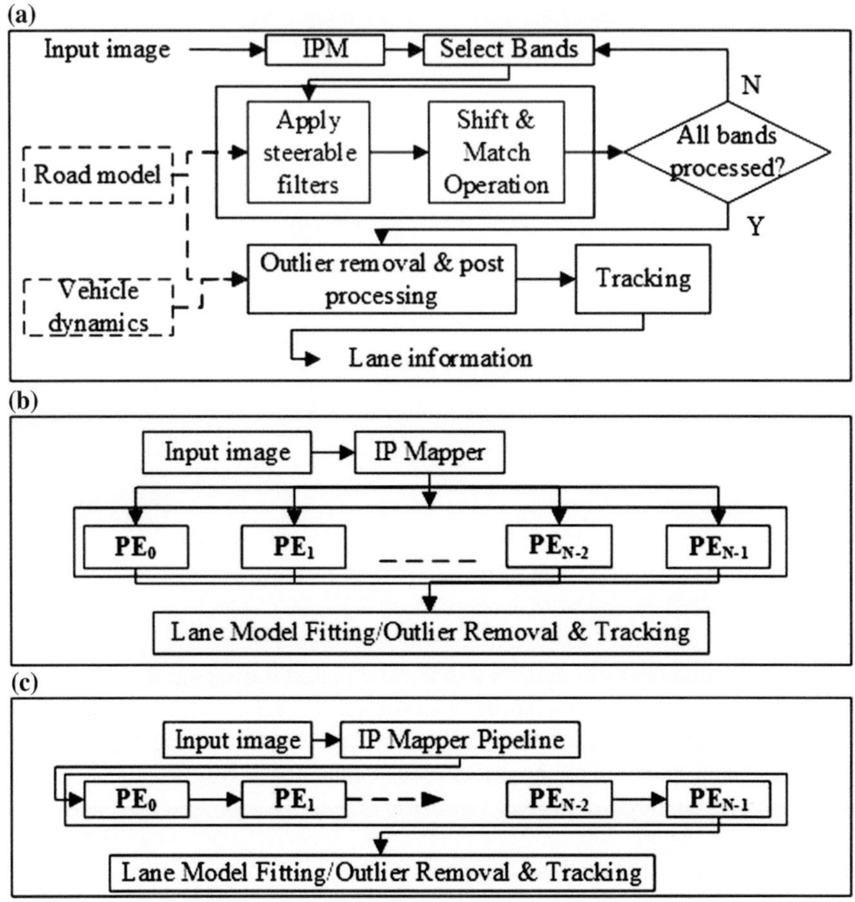

Fig. 10.4 Design options possible for the lane analysis method: **a** lane analysis using the proposed scan band based lane feature extraction method, **b** parallel architecture with each PE catering to each scan band and extracting from all scan bands in parallel, **c** pipelined architecture with each PE also acting as a controller to predict positions in the next PE

10.4 Experimental Studies

In this section, we present a detailed study of the proposed lane feature extraction method to address robustness and the constraints posed by embedded platforms [18]. We present the possible scenarios and trade-offs between robustness and metrics for embedded realization that are possible using the proposed technique. We also present the different configurations that can be explored for different conditions and user requirements. As indicated previously, lane tracking is not considered in the scope of evaluations and is considered for future work. Therefore, for the study presented in this paper, lanes are assumed to be detected if the lanes are present in the ground

Table 10.2 Dataset description

Set 1	Freeway lanes		Set 2	Freeway with vehicles	
Set 3	Freeway concrete surface		Set 4	Freeway circular reflectors	
Set 5	Urban road with shadows				

truth and the proposed technique is able to determine the lane features in "correct" positions in the frame. The proposed technique is evaluated using the test video datasets obtained by LISA-Q testbed [10]. The results are presented for five different test image sequences that are listed in Table 10.2, each dataset having a minimum of 250 image frames that are captured at 10–15 frames a second.

10.4.1 Accuracy Analysis

First, Fig. 10.5 shows some sample images with lanes that are extracted from complex road scenes by applying the proposed lane feature extraction method on input images from the datasets listed in Table 10.2. It can be seen that the proposed algorithm is able to extract lanes in varying lane conditions, such as cracks (Fig. 10.5a–d), presence of vehicles (Fig. 10.5e), presence of strong shadows (Fig. 10.5e–h). The proposed method is also able to extract lanes with circular reflectors as shown in Fig. 10.5f, g.

Figure 10.6 shows detection accuracy results of the lanes in datasets 1, 2, and 3, in which we are evaluating the detection of dashed lane markings (i.e., no circular reflectors or solid lane boundaries). The effect of changing the number of scan bands and the scan band width on detection accuracy is shown in Fig. 10.6. It is evident that reducing the number of scan bands will reduce the detection accuracy of the lane features because depending on the position of the lane marker and the speed of the vehicle, the scan band at a particular coordinate may fail to detect the lane marking

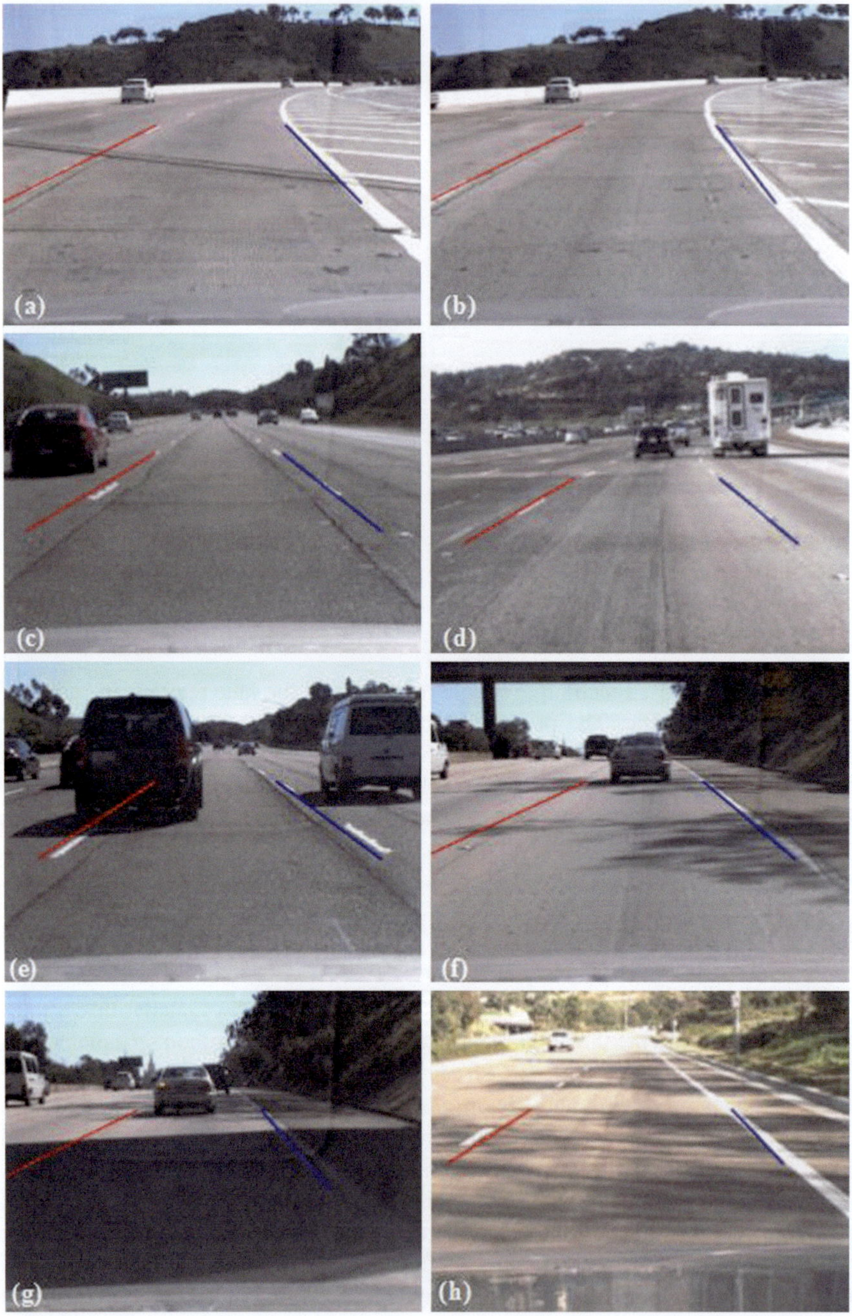

Fig. 10.5 Sample results of the proposed lane analysis method showing lane detection is the complex road scenes: **a** and **b** curved road with linear edges and lane like markings, **c** and **d** uneven road surface with linear features along the lane markings, **e** presence of overtaking vehicles, **f** circular reflectors and shadows, **g** circular reflectors and faint lanes under heavy shadow, **h** lanes on urban roads with frequent shadows

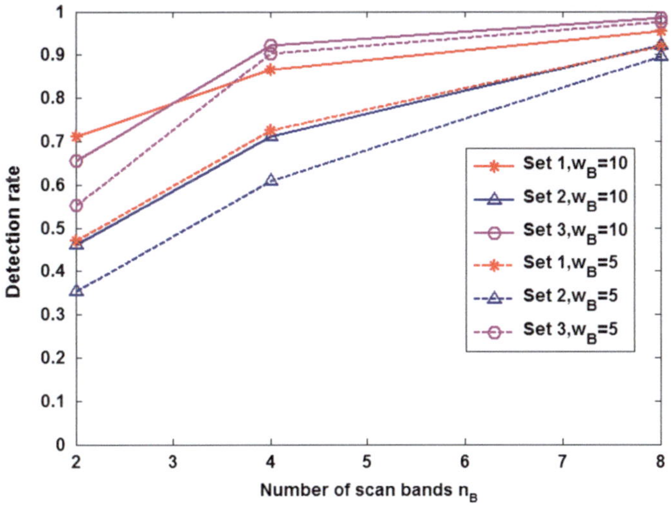

Fig. 10.6 Detection rate versus number of scan bands for scan band width = 10 and 5

(which we consider as failed detection). Therefore, having more scan bands increases the detection rate as seen in Fig. 10.6 for both cases of the scan band width, i.e., 10 and 5 pixels. The detection accuracy with 8 scan bands is over 90 % in all test datasets. This is an important observation because this implies that for the IPM images of size 360 × 500, processing just 8 scan lines with 10 pixels each is sufficient to get a detection rate of 95 %, instead of processing the entire 360 × 500 sized image (which is usually the case in most conventional methods). This figure also plots the detection accuracy for varying scan band width, i.e., $w_B = 10$ and 5 in Fig. 10.6. A higher scan width captures more information, implying better detection rate. Therefore, it is expected that bands with width of 5 pixels have lesser detection rate. However, it is noteworthy that as the scan lines increase to 8, the detection rate is nearing 90–95 % in both the cases of scan band width. The implication of this on computation cost will be discussed later.

It can also be seen that for a band width of 10 pixels, the difference in accuracy between $n_B = 8$ and 4 is less than 20 % in each dataset. Therefore, one can decide to go for 4 scan bands instead of 8, trading off accuracy by less than 20 % for half the number of processors.

10.4.2 Computational Complexity Analysis

Let us now consider the main operations involved in the proposed method. Each $k \times k$ filtering operation involves k^2 multiplications, $k^2 - 1$ additions and 1 comparison. Assuming all operations are of equal complexity (simplified model), the total number operations in filtering n_B scan bands of width w_B each and length N_w is equal to $2n_B w_B N_w k^2$. The next step involves horizontal projections in each band, which is $w_B N_w n_B$ addition operations. The shift and add operation involves N_w multiplications and comparisons per band resulting in a total of $2N_w n_B$ operations. Therefore, the total number of operations for lane feature extraction in the proposed method is given by

$$N_{prop} = 2n_B w_B N_w (k^2 + 1) \tag{10.2}$$

This is a simplified model but it is sufficient to evaluate qualitatively the effect of scan bands on the overall computation cost efficiency. Figure 10.7 shows a scatter plot between number of operations N_{prop} and the detection rate for different possible number of scan bands and scan band widths. The top left corner in the graph, i.e., high accuracy but less number of operations, is the ideal place to be in and we can see in Fig. 10.7 that using eight scan bands of width $w_B = 5$ gives similar detection rate as eight bands of $w_B = 10$ but at 50 % lesser number of operations. Also, when compared to conventional methods wherein the entire image is processed for filtering alone, the proposed method gives orders of magnitude savings in the number of operations. Other constraints for embedded realization such as total computation cycles, latency, energy cost, total memory accesses, etc., are also directly related to the number of operations by different factors.

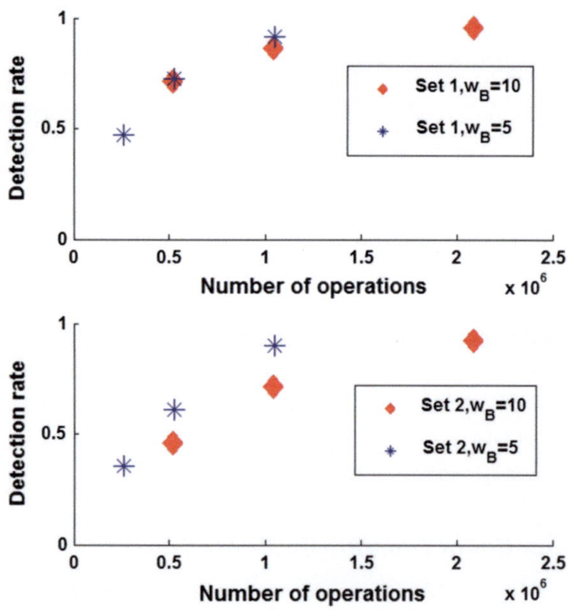

Fig. 10.7 Number of operations versus detection rate for different scan band widths in Set 1 and Set 2

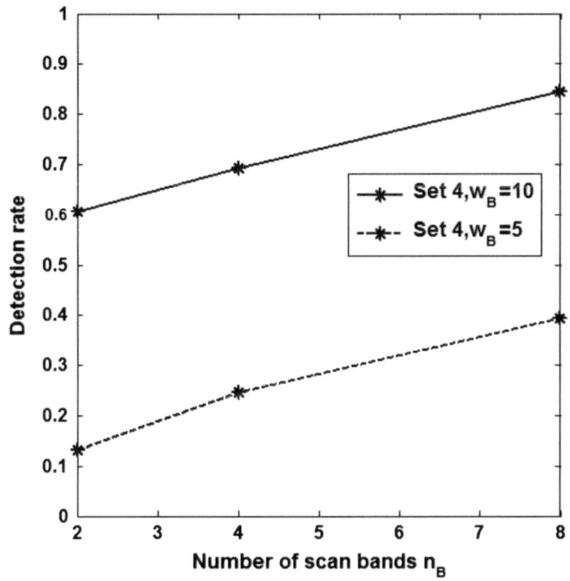

Fig. 10.8 Detection rate versus number of scan bands for Set 4 with circular reflectors

The effectiveness of the proposed technique to detect circular reflectors using the proposed scan band based lane feature extraction is illustrated in Fig. 10.8. It can be seen that a detection accuracy of 85 % is obtained using 8 scan bands with each band of 10 pixels. A comparison on the effect of reducing the scan bands and their width is also shown in Fig. 10.8. It can be seen that reducing the scan band width also reduces the detection rate. For the same number of scan bands but scan band width reduced to 5 pixels, the detection rate has been reduced to about 40 %. This is because thinner scan bands fail to completely and conclusively capture the circular reflectors. Therefore, having wider scan bands and more number of scan bands to sample as many reflectors as possible is desirable to get higher accuracy.

An experiment was also conducted to see the effect of changing the scan band sizes across different scan bands in a single frame. The scan bands nearer to the ego-vehicle were given higher weight by having thicker bands ($w_B = 10$) as compared to farther scan bands with $w_B = 5$. Different permutations were used to find if such hybrids can give better detection accuracy for lesser number of operations. Figure 10.9 shows the scatter plot with some of these varying options. The option VARY_5_5_5_10_10_10 is one particularly interesting design option. It gives a detection accuracy of nearly 90 %, which is the same as design options with $n_B = 8$ processors for scan band widths $w_B = 5$ and 10 both. However, it uses only 6 processors instead of 8. In terms of number of operations, the design option with $w_B = 5$ is better, but this varying scan band width design option is better choice if we want to reduce the number of processors.

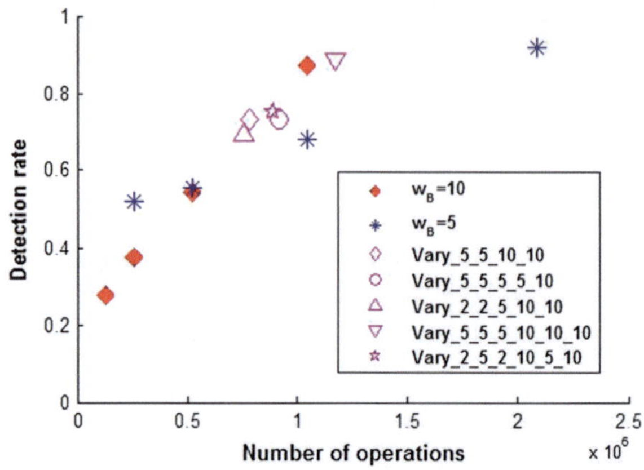

Fig. 10.9 Detection rate versus number of operations with varying band sizes of different scan bands in the same frame

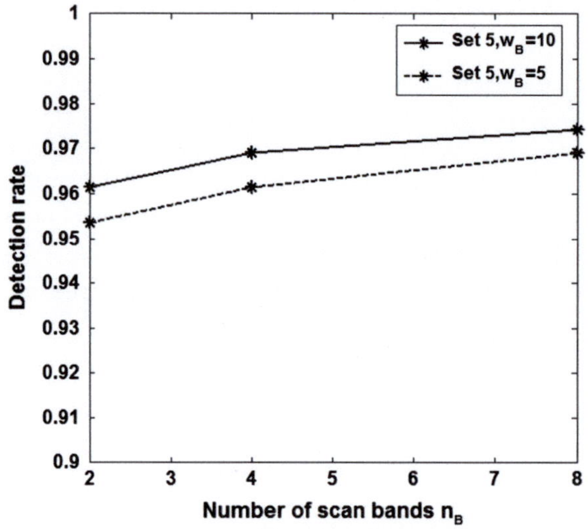

Fig. 10.10 Detection rate for urban lane scenario with solid lane in Set 5

Figure 10.10 shows the detection rates for varying scan bands to detect solid right lane in urban road context (Set 5). It can be seen that detection rates of over 90 % are achieved for all band widths and any number of scan bands. Also, the dataset was chosen such that there are heavy shadows of trees in the images (which usually is the case in most urban road scenarios). These detection rates imply that it is an overkill if more than 2 processors are running when the system is detecting solid lanes.

In Table 10.3, we present possible recommendations of the different configurations that are possible based on the user requirements, road and environmental conditions.

Table 10.3 Design configurations by varying n_B and w_B

	$n_B \downarrow$ $w_B \downarrow$	$n_B \downarrow$ $w_B \uparrow$	$n_B \uparrow$ $w_B \downarrow$	$n_B \uparrow$ $w_B \uparrow$
Lane types				
Solid	√	√		
Dashed		√ ↔	√	
Circular reflectors bot dots				√
Environmental				
Sunny day	Depends on lane types above			
Night scene				√[a]
Foggy conditions		√[a]		
Rainy conditions		√[a]		
Embedded constraints				
Parallel processing			√	√
Low area constraint	√	√		
Pipelining			√	√
Low memory resources	√		√	
Timing	Depends on hardware configuration			

[a] This also depends on placement of scan bands

First, we consider the types of lane markings and what combination of scan band size w_B and number n_B could give acceptable detection rates. For example, solid lanes require minimal number of scan bands and can also work with smaller band sizes. However, circular reflectors need higher number and wider band sizes also. Similarly, certain combinations of n_B and w_B are suited for specific environmental conditions. For example, in foggy and rainy conditions, it is desirable to extract lanes from the road surface closest to ego-vehicle. Therefore, lesser number of bands but wider bands closer to the vehicle are sufficient for robust extraction.

In the next part of Table 10.3, we consider the different configurations for n_B and w_B that comply with certain embedded constraints/requirements. A combination of the selections between the different categories can be used to give a user-constrained embedded realization of an accurate lane feature extraction system.

10.5 Conclusions

In this paper, we proposed a lane extraction method that is shown to provide a way to explore the different configurations for embedded realization, based on the user requirements and the context in which the lane analysis is to be done. It is shown that the two design parameters, i.e., number of scan bands and width of scan bands can be used to get an embedded vision system that caters to robustness as well as computation cost efficiency. The proposed technique enables to further study a possible adaptable lane analysis solution that takes into account the road and environmental conditions.

References

1. Borkar A, Hayes M, Smith MT (2012) A novel lane detection system with efficient ground truth generation. IEEE Trans Intell Transp Syst 13(1):365–374
2. Cheng H-Y, Jeng B-S, Tseng P-T, Fan K-C (2006) Lane detection with moving vehicles in the traffic scenes. IEEE Trans Intell Transp Syst 7(4):571–582
3. Cheng SY, Trivedi MM (2007) Lane tracking with omnidirectional cameras: algorithms and evaluation. EURASIP J Embed Syst 2007:1–8
4. Doshi A, Morris BT, Trivedi MM (2011) On-road prediction of driver's intent with multimodal sensory cues. IEEE Pervasive Comput 10(3):22–34
5. Gopalan R, Hong T, Shneier M, Chellappa R (2012) A learning approach towards detection and tracking of lane markings. IEEE Trans Intell Transp Syst 13(3):1088–1098
6. Hautière N, Tarel JP, Aubert D (2007) Towards fog-free in-vehicle vision systems through contrast restoration. In: 2007 IEEE computer society conference on computer vision and pattern recognition (CVPR), pp 1–8
7. Hillel AB, Lerner R, Levi D, Raz G (2012) Recent progress in road and lane detection: a survey. Mach Vis Appl 23:1159–1175
8. Kim ZW (2008) Robust lane detection and tracking in challenging scenarios. IEEE Trans Intell Transp Syst 9(1):16–26
9. Marzotto R, Zoratti P, Bagni D, Colombari A, Murino V (2010) A real-time versatile roadway path extraction and tracking on an FPGA platform. Comput Vis Image Underst 114(11):1164–1179
10. McCall JC, Trivedi MM (2006) Video-based lane estimation and tracking for driver assistance: survey, system, and evaluation. IEEE Trans Intell Transp Syst 7(1):20–37
11. McCall JC, Trivedi MM, Wipf D (2005) Lane change intent analysis using robust operators and sparse bayesian learning. In: 2005 IEEE conference on computer vision and pattern recognition (CVPR'05)—workshops, vol 3, pp 59–59
12. Nedevschi S, Popescu V, Danescu R, Marita T, Oniga F (2013) Accurate ego-vehicle global localization at intersections through alignment of visual data with digital map. In: IEEE transactions on intelligent transportation systems, pp 1–15
13. Sathyanarayana SS, Satzoda RK, Srikanthan T (2009) Exploiting inherent parallelisms for accelerating linear hough transform. IEEE Trans Image Process 18(10):2255–2264
14. Satzoda RK, Sathyanarayana S, Srikanthan T (2010) Hierarchical additive hough transform for lane detection. IEEE Embed Syst Lett 2(2):23–26
15. Shang E, Li J, An X, He H (2011) Lane detection using steerable filters and FPGA-based implementation. In: 2011 sixth international conference on image and graphics, August 2011, pp 908–913
16. Sivaraman S, Trivedi MM (2013) Integrated lane and vehicle detection, localization, and tracking: a synergistic approach. IEEE Trans Intell Trans Syst 11(4):1–12
17. Sivaraman S, Trivedi MM (2010) Improved vision-based lane tracker performance using vehicle. In: 2010 IEEE intelligent vehicles symposium, pp 676–681
18. Stein F (2012) The challenge of putting vision algorithms into a car. In: 2012 IEEE conference on computer vision and pattern recognition workshop on embedded vision, June 2012, pp 89–94

19. Satzoda RK, Martin S, Ly MV, Gunaratne P, Trivedi MM (2013) Towards automated drive analysis: a multiomdal synergistic approach. In: 2013 IEEE Intelligent Transportation Systems Conference, pp 1912–1916
20. Satzoda RK, Trivedi MM (2013) Selective salient feature based Lane Analysis. In: 2013 IEEE Intelligent Transportation Systems Conference, pp 1906–1911
21. Satzoda RK, Trivedi MM (2014) Drive analysis using vehicle dynamics and vision-based Lane Semantics. IEEE Trans Intell Transp Syst (99), In press
22. Satzoda RK, Trivedi MM (2014) Efficient lane and vehicle detection with integrated synergies (ELVIS). In: 2014 IEEE Computer Vision and Pattern Recognition Workshops on Embedded Vision, pp 708–713
23. Trivedi MM, Gandhi T, McCall J (2007) Looking-in and looking-out of a vehicle: computer-vision-based enhanced vehicle safety. IEEE Trans Intell Transp Syst 8(1):108–120

Part III
Future Challenges

Chapter 11
Distributed Smart Cameras in the Age of Cloud Computing and the Internet-of-Things

Marilyn Wolf

Abstract This chapter considers the implications of cloud-oriented, Internet-of-Things systems for distributed smart cameras. Advances in smart camera design enable new applications and capabilities. Advances in middleware and software support for distributed algorithms on smart camera networks have resulted in improved software platforms, but work still needs to be done. A variety of network-level algorithms and services are now possible and are starting to be developed.

11.1 Introduction

The term *Internet-of-Things* (IoT) has become current as an overarching term for physical objects that have cyber identities. A variety of specific meanings have been applied to IoT, ranging from simple tagging, through inventory management, through active sensing. One of the enablers of IoT is cloud computing—cloud databases and computing services tie together individual things into a coordinated system.

Smart camera networks can play several roles in the IoT universe. On the one hand, smart camera networks can be used to observe physical objects and systems; they can provide either primary or corroborative information about the state of the physical objects. On the other hand, a smart camera network itself is an IoT. Smart camera systems can leverage IoT and cloud technology to improve the performance, reliability, and scalability of their services. A network of smart cameras can also provide useful IoT services, such as crowdsourced news or physical location scouting.

In this chapter, we consider several technological trends that contribute to the move toward cloud-oriented IoT architecture for distributed smart cameras. We start with potential improvements in camera nodes. Smaller, cheaper, lower-energy, and higher performance smart cameras can open up new deployment opportunities. We

M. Wolf (✉)
Georgia Institute of Technology, Atlanta, GA, USA
e-mail: wolf@ece.gatech.edu

B. Kisačanin and M. Gelautz (eds.), *Advances in Embedded Computer Vision*,
Advances in Computer Vision and Pattern Recognition,
DOI 10.1007/978-3-319-09387-1_11

survey recent results in both high-performance and low-power camera nodes. We also look at distributed middleware for distributed camera networks that provide a more powerful platform for smart camera developers. Finally, we consider algorithms and services at the network level.

11.2 High-Performance Camera Nodes

Multimedia has been a major driver for system-on-chip development for several decades; this effort has served as a foundation for embedded vision platforms. A CV-aware platform is traditionally designed with several goals in mind. High throughput is important, not just on integer data but also on floating-point operations. Numerical precision is also an important characteristic, with some interesting trade-offs possible between accuracy and other system objectives. Low energy operation is a critical parameter for modern SoCs, which must operate without fans and may operate on battery power. These platforms are also engineered for relatively low cost compared to desktop processors. The combination of low energy and low cost has driven many platform designs to heterogeneous multiprocessors [31].

Small form factor cameras open up a wide range of new applications. Small cameras can fit into a variety of physical positions that provide new views of the subject, particularly if the camera does not require cables. Retail is one example of a field that can use cameras installed in product displays to monitor customer behavior. Low-power cameras are often cheap, which puts them into the budgets of more potential users. However, cameras designed to fit into small spaces must operate at low power levels to avoid generating excessive heat. Many users also appreciate the privacy gained by performing in-camera analysis and not transmitting video.

We now know a great deal about how to accelerate video compression, but we still have something to learn about accelerating computer vision algorithms. Vision algorithms differ from compression algorithms in that they generally require higher numerical precision. Numerical representations provide a rich set of trade-offs between algorithmic accuracy, energy consumption, and area but these trade-offs need careful evaluation by the designer. Like compression, vision algorithms often have complex control flows. However, while many compression algorithms are pixel-oriented, many later-stage vision algorithms make greater use of data structures.

Semiconductor manufacturers continue to refine the design of hardware platforms for vision applications, many of which are heterogeneous multiprocessor systems-on-chips (MPSoCs). EVE (embedded vision/vector engine) [25] is a co-processor for embedded vision. It includes a RISC core, a vector core, a DMA engine, a custom memory switch, and several specialized memories. The DMA engine supports ping-pong buffering in which the DMA engine fills one side of the buffer for the next round of operations, while the processors operate on the other side of the buffer. The vector unit provides scatter/gather memory access to provide additional flexibility for mid-level vision algorithms with data-dependent regions. The fact that computer vision systems have not been standardized in the way that video compression has been makes it more difficult for chip manufacturers to identify accelerators for vision processors—different software implementations may want to see different interfaces to the accelerator. A number of semiconductor manufacturers are now creating vision accelerators. In addition, the semiconductor intellectual property (IP) providers are developing vision accelerators that can be integrated into new designs. We should expect to see a great deal of innovation in MPSoCs for vision over the next few years. OpenVX (http://www.khronos.org/openvx) is being developed as a standard API for hardware accelerators for computer vision.

GPUs are widely used in desktop and laptop systems; smaller GPUs are now common in cell phones. Some work has explored the use of GPUs for computer vision. Fung et al. [14] developed the OpenVIDIA library for nVidia-based GPU-based computer vision. Their library map the GPU's vertex processor, rasterizer, and fragment processor onto various vision kernels. Their approach takes advantage of fragment shader programs, which can be used to perform filtering on pixels; the results of one filtering pass can be saved as a texture and used to perform another filtering pass. Nagendra [24] developed an automotive vision system using GPUs. The GPU implementations of the vision system, which used Viola and Jones object detection as well as morphological filters, showed speedups of several times over a 3 GHz CPU, but noted the significant power consumption of the GPUs used for the experiment. Li et al. [17] implemented Haar transform-based face detection on an Intel Sandy Bridge processor, which combines CPU cores and a GPU. Their results showed an average speedup for the CPU-GPU combination of 3X over the CPU-only implementation.

FPGAs provide powerful capabilities for the design of customized hardware platforms for computer vision. Matai et al. [20] designed a complete face detection and recognition system on an FPGA. The first stage of processing performed face detection using a design by Cho et al. [4]. That architecture is based on AdaBoost and computes Haar classifiers to detect faces. Jacobsen et al. [21] designed an FPGA-based system for accelerating online boosting for multi-target tracking. At each tracking step, a region around the last known location is searched to find a new location and new positive and negative training examples are selected. The classifier is used to generate training data for the next step. This approach requires sequential passes through the image data to first find the new location, then identify training examples. Classification is performed using Haar-like features that consist of between two and six non-adjacent rectangles. The FPGA implementation could track 57 independent targets at 30 frames/s. Gudis et al. [11] built FPGA-based vision systems based on a crossbar-connected set of accelerators, a DRAM controller, and an ARM host processor. The accelerators can be accessed via a C++ API.

Floating point is an important aspect of any embedded vision platform. Floating point computation is used in higher level classifiers and also in some more pixel-oriented algorithms such as optical flow. It is particularly important for FPGA-based systems because floating point is one of the aspects that provides the biggest cost/accuracy/performance trade-offs. IEEE compliant floating-point is not always necessary and not always an asset. The ability to control the accuracy of number representation is a basic consideration in platform design. The algorithm used to

Table 11.1 Comparison of vision processor approaches

Architecture	Pros	Cons
GPU	Good floating-point performance	Specialized programming model, complex memory system
MPSoC	High performance at low power	Can't mix and match pieces
FPGA	High performance, leverages specialized numerical designs	Requires hardware expertise

compute division can play a key role in the cost/accuracy/performance trade-off analysis. The VFloat library [28] provides a library of configurable floating-point units for reconfigurable computing fabrics. The modules parameters can be used by the designer to vary the accuracy and implementation cost of the generated module.

Table 11.1 summarizes some of the key differences between these approaches. GPUs have high performance, particularly for floating-point algorithms, but have a non-standard programming model and complex memory systems. MPSoCs have good performance/power but the system designer must choose among platforms that may vary widely in the accelerators they offer. FPGAs provide high performance, particularly for specialized numerical algorithms, but their design requires hardware expertise.

Platform design also needs efficient and scalable ways to integrate accelerators and processors. Networks are required for high-performance physical transport that meets the high bandwidth demands of computer vision. Firmware and software interfaces are crucial to the development and portability of systems based on such platforms. Gudis et al. [11] developed a service-oriented framework for integrating accelerators into heterogeneous processors. Video devices are connected by a crossbar. Vision accelerators shared the same memory space with the ARM host processor. A vision service framework provides abstractions for the accelerators and managing their communication. Farabet et al. [9] used a dataflow style for accelerators connected in a 2-D mesh. It uses a smart DMA unit as a memory controller.

11.3 Low-Power Camera Nodes

Low-power, small form factor cameras are increasingly available. The camera modules for hobbyist platforms such as Raspberry Pi are examples of the impressive combinations of optics, image sensors, computers, and networks that we can build. Researchers are also developing self-powered image sensors that can operate from scavenged energy. Low-power camera nodes have several characteristics that influence the vision algorithms deployed on them. They may provide relatively low resolution. They will almost certainly operate at small apertures to avoid focusing; this in turn limits their low-light capabilities. They may have relatively simple processors, largely due to limitations on the amount of heat they will be allowed to dissipate. If they are self-powered, they will not always be on.

The sensor network community has developed several camera nodes. Rahimi et al. [23] describe the Cyclops imager for wireless sensor networks. The image sensor provides a maximum resolution of CIF quality (352 × 288). The camera module can perform demosaicing, image scaling, color correction, tone correction, and color space conversion. An 8-bit ATMEL ATmega128L processor controls the camera. A Xilixn CPLD operates as a lightweight, low-power frame grabber. Cyclops provides 64 kB of SRAM and 512 kB of flash. Chen et al. [3] designed the CITRIC camera for low-bandwidth wireless sensor network applications. The device includes a 1280 × 1024 pixel image sensor, a mono microphone with sample rates ranging of 8–48 ks/s, an Intel XScale PXA270 processor with scalable clock frequencies, 64 MB RAM and 16 MB ROM; it is designed to connect to the TelosB sensor node board with dimensions of about 2″ × 2″. They measured the power consumption of CITRIC running a background substraction algorithm at 970 mW at a clock speed of 520 MHz. They reported the execution time of several vision algorithms: 340 ms for a Canny edge detector using the Intel Integrated Performance (IPP) primitives; 140 ms for a median filter not using IPP and 34 ms for a median filter using IPP.

Several sensors have been developed with on-sensor image analysis. These analysis circuits are generally analog functions that perform simple, relatively fixed operations at very low energy and high speed. Liu et al. [16] describe a CMOS image sensor with on-chip motion detection. Their sensor operates in three modes. Event generation mode identifies events by computing frame-to-frame luminance differences; a given number of pixels exceeding a difference threshold generates an event. Motion tracking mode uses 1-D Gaussian filters to smooth the image to generate row and column events. Video output mode provides full-resolution and compressed image output of the region of interest. Dubois et al. [6] designed a 64 × 64 CMOS image sensor that can perform high-speed gradient analysis. They designed an octagonal photodiode to reduce wire lengths to adjacent pixels. The area between sets of four adjacent pixels is occupied by an analog multiplier that performs the function $V_1 \cos(\beta) + V_2 \sin(\beta) - V_3 \sin(\beta) - V_4 \sin(\beta)$. They showed how to use the function to implement the Sobel operator and Laplacian.

Several groups have also designed ultra low-power image sensors. These sensors generally offer lower resolution but at extremely low energy levels. Energy harvesting has been successfully applied to a variety of ultra low-power systems and some recent work has explored energy harvesting for image sensors. Hanson and Sylvester [12] describe an ultra-low power sensor. Their test chip provides 128 × 128 pixels and is designed to operate over a range of power supply voltages from 0.45 to 0.7 V. It consumes 140 nJ per frame at 8.5 frames/s. Tang et al. [8] describe a CMOS image sensor with an energy harvesting mode. The imager has two modes, one for imaging and the other for harvesting energy from light using the pixels. In energy harvesting mode, the sensor can harvest 80 nA at 350 lux and 9.7 μA at 3,500 lux. Their sensor has a resolution of 128 × 96 pixels and consumes 10 μW at 10 frames/s. At these rates of energy harvesting and usage during imaging, the energy required to capture one frame can be provided through 200 ms of energy harvesting.

11.4 Middleware for Distributed Systems

Distributed computer vision systems are complex systems. As such, they need sophisticated software support. Dynamic management of resources is essential to correct and efficient utilization of computational and memory resources. Middleware also abstracts important operations such as communication and hides their details from application developers. Middleware allows computer vision developers to concentrate on vision algorithms. System-on-chip platforms for video computing generally provide reasonable middleware to support on-chip computation, communication, and storage. But middleware for computer vision systems still requires further development.

Why do we need middleware for distributed smart cameras? A well-defined middleware API provides useful services that allow vision algorithm designers to build complex algorithms without worrying about certain details. Middleware for vision systems should provide at least two types of services that cover the sorts of things many vision algorithm designers do not want to worry about. First, it should provide a simple mechanism for a set of camers to share data. Distributed algorithms inherently require sharing data; the communication protocols can require complex code sequences, particularly when real-time or timeout-sensitive performance is required. Second, middleware should allow one camera to request another camera to perform a task, a different type of service from communication. Moving data is part of a service, but you also need to schedule the set of processes required to perform the task. You may also have some freedom as to which node performs the task, in which case the middleware should choose a server based on loads, battery lifetime, bandwidth, etc.

MPI [10] is a message passing system that is widely used to build parallel and distributed computing applications. However, it has not received wide adoption in embedded systems despite several efforts to develop versions of MPI for embedded computing. McMahon and Skellum [22] developed a subset of MPI for memory-constrained embedded systems. Their design experiment completed two different approaches to embedded MPI subsets, which they compared in terms of code size, development effort, and flexibility. Agbaria et al. [1] developed a lightweight version of MPI known as LMPI. Kanevsky et al. [15] took a somewhat different approach, developing MPI/RT to add quality-of-service requirements to the MPI model. Ly et al. [18] developed an FPGA version of MPI that allowed interactions with hardware accelerators as well as software modules.

Doblander et al. [5] developed a SmartCam framework that operates as middleware on top of standard operating systems. SmartCam abstracts lower level communication services by providing a publish-subscribe model by which applications can communicate. Applications use mailboxes to distribute data; in the case of large video objects, the data are identified by reference. The DSP framework abstracts the hardware and communication, supports dynamic loading/unloading of tasks, and management of on-chip and off-chip resources.

11.5 Peer-to-Peer Distributed Algorithms

Client-server architectures do not scale for a wide range of vision problems. The community has now developed a range of distributed algorithms for important vision tasks, but we still have much to learn.

Long-term tracking using cameras with nonoverlapping views has received a great deal of attention. Kim and Wolf [13] developed a distributed algorithm for Markov chain Monte Carlo tracking. Cameras estimate local paths based on local communications; the local paths are then transmitted through the network and concatenated to build longer tracks of the target. Esterle et al. [7] use autonomous self-interested agents to learn the vision graph during operation. The algorithm does not require multi-camera calibration since it does not rely on a priori camera topology information. Cameras bid for the right to track an object; the utility of a tracked object to a camera depends on the visibility of the target to the camera and its confidence in its tracking estimate. Sales of a target from one camera to another are used to build the structure of the vision graph. As the system makes more observations, the communications between cameras can become more targeted based on their understanding of the vision graph structure. Wan and Li [27] formulated an online algorithm for associating observations with targets; at each new observation, nodes trade information with neighbors on observations and networks, then update their inferences.

Sek Chai [26] describes a distributed smart camera system based on smartphone processors called visual sensor networks (VSNs). Nodes distribute metadata for search purposes while video data remains on the local nodes. Metadata is organized into a video catalog accessible using key search indices including time, location, and object description. Nodes decide when to activate their cameras in order to manage their energy consumption; a node may be turned on at a predefined time or by an external event such as sound or vibration detection. Their implementation on a Qualcomm Snapdragon MSM8960 used 1.6 W for capture, processing, and storage of compressed video, with motion tracking and analytics generation requiring an additional 0.4 W.

An early example of in-network search was provided by Yan et al. [32], who developed a distributed image search system for a sensor network based on iMote2 sensor nodes. Their system uses SIFT to generate feature vectors that are clustered into visterms (representation of an image feature). They optimized both their vocabulary tree and inverted index for flash memory. They used buffered lookup to reduce the performance penalty of storing the vocabulary tree in flash, which has much longer access times than RAM. The read the tree in subtree increments that fit into ram, then buffer a collection of SIFT vectors for lookup in the subtree. Optimizations for the inverted index were designed to compensate for the write characteristics of flash: writes are slower than reads, and an entire block must be erased and rewritten to change any value in the block [19]. They stored the inverted index in a log-structure, which uses an appended log to record changes to the file, which requires multiple file reads for a data access. They minimize read overhead by writing only visterms with many associated image IDs to flash; Zipf's Law predicts that a small number of visterms will have very long image chains. They also performed distributed search: queries were distributed to the nodes, which computed a local ranking of search results; these results were sent back to the proxy, which normalizes the local search results by adjusting based on the number of images in which each visterm occurs and the total number of images in the database.

11.6 Cloud-Aware Systems

Although peer-to-peer is the clear choice for many algorithms, cloud-based computer vision also makes sense in other applications. Both online analysis and search are potentially amenable to the cloud. This is particularly true when we see peer-to-peer and cloud as part of a continuum. Our challenge is to partition an algorithm between camera nodes, the network, and the cloud. A variety of commercial services provide cloud-based online analysis. Several retail customer analysis companies, for example, use network cameras to ship video to the cloud for analysis. Widen [30] surveys U. S. law on privacy and surveillance.

Law enforcement has received a great deal of attention as an application of both online analysis and search. An episode of Nova [29] surveyed the various technologies, including video search, used to track down the Boston Marathon bombing suspects. Much of the video used in the initial analysis was gathered by detectives going door-to-door to local businesses. They also described New York City's Domain Awareness System, which analyzes in real-time video from 4,000 video cameras as well as environmental sensors and license plate readers. The system reads license plates in every lane of the bridge and tunnel connections into lower Manhattan and compares them to terror watch lists. It analyzes video for suspicious behavior in real time; it can also perform query-based search.

We are also starting to see computer vision implemented as cloud applications. CloudCV [2] provides a library of computer vision algorithms as a cloud service. It provides Matlab and Python interfaces to its services. At the time of this writing, it implements image stitching and object detection.

11.7 Conclusion

Advances in camera platforms are driving important new applications of distributed smart cameras. Moore's Law provides not only high-performance computing nodes but also advanced image sensors. FPGAs also provide rich platforms for the development of custom vision platforms. Middleware can allow vision algorithm designers to concentrate on vision without worrying about managing communication, memory, and processors. Peer-to-peer algorithms provide a powerful mechanism for the design of ubiquitous smart camera networks. Cloud-aware vision systems complement peer-to-peer algorithms.

References

1. Agbaria A, Kang Dong-In, Singh K (2006) Lmpi: Mpi for heterogeneous embedded distributed systems. In: Parallel and distributed systems, 12th international conference on ICPADS 2006, vol 1, p 8
2. Batra D, Agrawal H, Banik P, Chavali N, Alfadda A (2013) Cloudcv: Large-scale distributed computer vision as a cloud service
3. Chen P, Hong K, Naikal N, Shankar Sastry S, Tygar D, Yan Posu, Allen Yang Y, Chang L-C, Lin L, Wang S, Lobatón E, Oh S, Ahammad P (2013) A low-bandwidth camera sensor platform with applications in smart camera networks. ACM Trans Sen Netw 9(2):21:1–21:23
4. Cho J, Benson B, Mirzaei S, Kastner R (2009) Parallelized architecture of multiple classifiers for face detection. In: Application-specific systems, architectures and processors 20th IEEE international conference on ASAP 2009, pp 75–82
5. Doblander A, Zoufal A, Bernhard R (2009) A novel software framework for embedded multiprocessor smart cameras. ACM Trans Embed Comput Syst 8(3):24:1–24:30
6. Dubois J, Ginhac D, Paindavoine M (2007) A single-chip 10000 frames/s CMOS sensor with in-situ 2d programmable image processing. In: Computer architecture for machine perception and sensing international workshop on CAMP 2006, pp 124–129
7. Esterle L, Peter Lewis R, Yao X, Rinner B (2014) Socio-economic vision graph generation and handover in distributed smart camera networks. ACM Trans Sen Netw 10(2):20:1–20:24
8. Fang T, Yuan C, Bermak A (2010) An ultra-low power current-mode cmos image sensor with energy harvesting capability. In: 2010 Proceedings of the ESSCIRC, pp 126–129
9. Farabet C, Martini B, Corda B, Akselrod P, Culurciello E, LeCun Y (2011) Neuflow: A runtime reconfigurable dataflow processor for vision. In: 2011 IEEE computer society conference on Computer vision and pattern recognition workshops (CVPRW), pp 109–116
10. Gropp W, Lusk EL, Skjellum A (1999). Using MPI, portable parallel programming with the message-passing interface, 2nd edn. MIT press, Cambridge
11. Gudis E, Lu Pullan, Berends D, Kaighn K, van der Wal G, Buchanan G, Chai Sek, Piacentino M (2013) An embedded vision services framework for heterogeneous accelerators. In: 2013 IEEE conference on computer vision and pattern recognition workshops (CVPRW) , pp 598–603
12. Hanson S, Sylvester D (2009) A 0.45 μm 0.7v sub-microwatt CMOS image sensor for ultra-low power applications. In: 2009 symposium on VLSI circuits, pp 176–177
13. Honggab K, Marilyn W (2010) Distributed tracking in a large-scale network of smart cameras. In: Proceedings of the fourth ACM/IEEE international conference on distributed smart cameras, ACM Press, p 816
14. James F, Steve M (2005) OpenVIDIA: parallel GPU computer vision. In: Multimedia '05: proceedings of the 13th annual ACM international conference on multimedia
15. Kanevsky A, Skjellum A, Rounbehler A (1998) MPI/RT-an emerging standard for high-performance real-time systems. In: Proceedings of the thirty-first Hawaii international conference on system sciences, vol 3, pp 157–166
16. Liu Xilin, Zhang Milin, Van der Spiegel J (2013) A low power multi-mode CMOS image sensor with integrated on-chip motion detection. In: 2013 IEEE international symposium on circuits and systems (ISCAS), pp 2416–2419
17. Li E, Wang Bin, Yang Liu, Peng Ya ti, Du Yangzhou, Zhang Yimin, Chiu Yi-Jen (2012)GPU and CPU cooperative accelaration for face detection on modern processors. In: 2012 IEEE international conference on multimedia and expo (ICME), pp 769–775
18. Ly DL, Saldana M, Chow P (2009) The challenges of using an embedded MPI for hardware-based processing nodes. In: International conference on field-programmable technology, FPT 2009, pp 120–127
19. Marilyn W (2012) Computers as components: principles of embedded computing system design, 3rd edn. Kauffman Morgan
20. Matai J, Irturk A, Kastner R (2011) Design and implementation of an FGPA-based real-time face recognition system. In: 2011 IEEE 19th annual international symposium on field-programmable custom computing machines (FCCM), pp 97–100

21. Matthew J, Pingfan M, Siddarth S, Ryan K (2014) Hardware accelerated online boosting for multi-target tracking. In: Proceedings, FCCM'14. IEEE
22. McMahon TP, Skjellum A (1996) eMPI/eMPICH: embedding MPI. In: Proceedings second MPI developer's conference, pp 180–184
23. Mohammad R, Rick B, Obimdinachi I, Garcia Juan C, Jay W, Deborah E, Mani S (2005) Cyclops: In Situ image sensing and interpretation in wireless sensor networks. In: Proceedings of the 3rd international conference on embedded networked sensor systems, SenSys'05. ACM, pp 192–204
24. Nagendra P (2011) Performance characterization of automotive computer vision systems using graphics processing units (gpus). In: 2011 international conference on image information processing (ICIIP), pp 1–4
25. Sankaran J, Hung C-Y, Kisacanin B (2014) Eve: a flexible simd coprocessor for embedded vision applications. J Sign Process Syst 75:95–107
26. Sek C (2014) Distributed smart cameras using smartphone processors. IEEE Comput
27. Wan J, Liu L (2014) Distributed data association in smart camera networks using belief propagation. ACM Trans Sen Netw 10(2):19:1–19:24
28. Wang X, Leeser M (2010) Vfloat: a variable precision fixed- and floating-point library for reconfigurable hardware. ACM Trans Reconfigurable Technol Syst 3(3):16:1–16:34
29. WGBH. Nova: Manhunt-boston bombers, 2013
30. Widen WH (2008) Smart cameras and the right to privacy. Proc IEEE 96(10):1688–1697
31. Wolf W, Jerraya AA, Martin G (2008) Multiprocessor system-on-chip (MPSoC) technology. IEEE Trans Comput Aided Des Integr Circuits Syst 27(10):1701–1713
32. Yan T, Ganesan D, Manmatha R (2008) Distributed image search in camera sensor networks. In: Proceedings of the 6th ACM conference on embedded network sensor systems, SenSys'08. ACM, New York, pp 155–168

Chapter 12
Data-Driven Stream Mining Systems for Computer Vision

Shuvra S. Bhattacharyya, Mihaela van der Schaar, Onur Atan, Cem Tekin and Kishan Sudusinghe

Abstract In this chapter, we discuss the state of the art and future challenges in adaptive stream mining systems for computer vision. Adaptive stream mining in this context involves the extraction of knowledge from image and video streams in real-time, and from sources that are possibly distributed and heterogeneous. With advances in sensor and digital processing technologies, we are able to deploy networks involving large numbers of cameras that acquire increasing volumes of image data for diverse applications in monitoring and surveillance. However, to exploit the potential of such extensive networks for image acquisition, important challenges must be addressed in efficient communication and analysis of such data under constraints on power consumption, communication bandwidth, and end-to-end latency. We discuss these challenges in this chapter, and we also discuss important directions for research in addressing such challenges using dynamic, data-driven methodologies.

12.1 Introduction

In this chapter, we address challenges involving the development of algorithms, models, and design methods for distributed and adaptive real-time knowledge extraction of information from high volume image streams. We focus on an important emerging class of "big data" systems called *adaptive stream mining* (*ASM*) systems,

S.S. Bhattacharyya (✉) · K. Sudusinghe
University of Maryland, College Park, MD, USA
e-mail: ssb@umd.edu

K. Sudusinghe
e-mail: kishans@umd.edu

M. van der Schaar · O. Atan · C. Tekin
University of California, Los Angeles, CA, USA
e-mail: mihaela@ee.ucla.edu

O. Atan
e-mail: oatan@ucla.edu

C. Tekin
e-mail: cmtkn@ucla.edu

B. Kisačanin and M. Gelautz (eds.), *Advances in Embedded Computer Vision*,
Advances in Computer Vision and Pattern Recognition,
DOI 10.1007/978-3-319-09387-1_12

and discuss the state-of-the-art and challenges in design and implementation of effective ASM systems for embedded computer vision. ASM systems can be viewed as real-time data mining systems that operate on streams of data and are constructed as topologies (directed graphs) of classifiers, where parameters associated with the topologies and constituent classifiers may be manipulated dynamically based on changes in data characteristics, operational constraints, and other relevant run-time considerations.

Intended applications of ASM systems for embedded computer vision are very diverse, ranging from medical services, to dynamic management of vehicular traffic, to real-time detection of events in home-based health-care, to many kinds of surveillance and environmental monitoring applications. Each of these applications requires a topology of classifiers (such as a chain or "pipeline" configuration) that analyzes streaming data (which dynamically changes over time) from a set of raw data sources to extract valuable information in real time.

The need for adaptivity in ASM systems is inherent in almost all practical knowledge extraction application areas as data characteristics and operating conditions often exhibit uncertain or time-varying behavior. Accurate assessment, understanding, and optimization of ASM systems generally requires extensive experimentation of how algorithms for data classification and classifier adaptation interact with the characteristics of input data, and how scheduling and buffer management for such algorithms should be performed to satisfy real-time constraints subject to given resource constraints.

Decomposing applications as topologies of distributed processing operators has merits that transcend the scalability, reliability, and performance objectives of large-scale, real-time stream mining systems [1, 11, 18, 27]. Specifically, many stream classification and mining applications implement topologies (ensembles such as trees or cascades) of low-complexity binary classifiers to jointly accomplish the task of complex classification [24]. Such a structure enables the successive identification of multiple attributes in the data, and also provides significant advantages in terms of reduced resource consumption through appropriate dynamic data filtering, based on the incrementally identified attributes.

It has been shown that using a tree of binary classifiers can achieve better performance compared to other techniques such as support vector machines or SVMs (e.g., see [10]), rule-based techniques, and neural nets for some applications [6, 11, 19, 26, 28, 31, 42]. Furthermore, using classifiers operating in series with the same model (boosting [31]) or classifiers operating in parallel with multiple models (bagging [19]) has resulted in improved classification performance.

12.2 ASM System Example

Consider the surveillance application depicted in Fig. 12.1. A straightforward approach to dealing with this application requires the cameras to acquire the images on a continuous basis with the highest resolution, and send them to a central processing unit that is responsible for analyzing the images with complex data analytics.

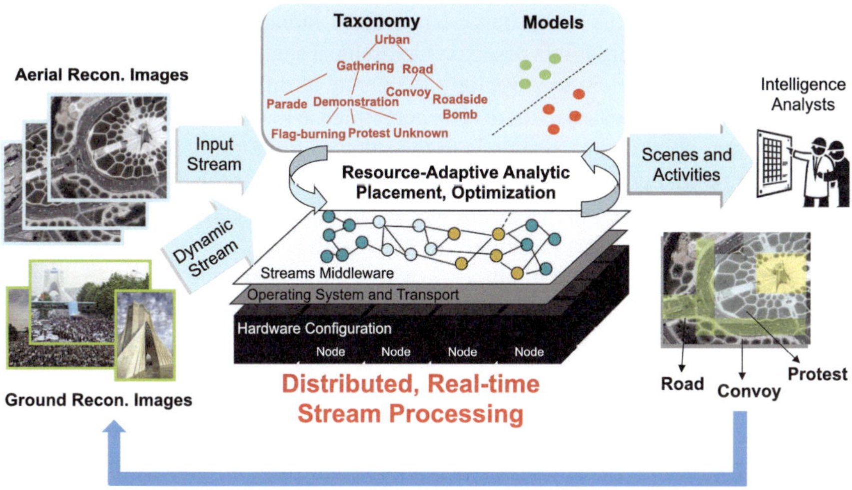

Fig. 12.1 An example of an ASM system for surveillance

Unfortunately, this approach is infeasible because it requires large communication bandwidths and energy consumption, and long transmission and processing delays. A feasible approach involves classifiers—localized in the same processing node of a camera—that are in charge of preprocessing the images. Based on the results of such preprocessing, the classifiers decide: (1) at which rate to acquire images, (2) whether or not to discard a specific image, and (3) in case the image is not discarded, the node to which the image must be sent for further processing and the resolution at which the image must be transmitted. Then the results of image processing can be exploited to trigger actions that modify the environment under observation (e.g., some roads are opened or closed) and even the stream mining system itself (e.g., additional cameras are turned on).

12.3 Challenges in ASM System Design

Key challenges in distributed real-time stream mining systems arise from the need to cope effectively with system overload due to large data volumes and limited system resources. There is a large computational cost incurred by each classifier (proportional to the data rate) that limits the rate at which the application can handle input video. Commonly used approaches to dealing with this problem in resource constrained stream mining are based on *load-shedding*, where algorithms determine when, where, what, and how much data to discard given the observed data characteristics, e.g. burst, desired Quality of Service (QoS) requirements [4, 5, 37–41], data value or delay constraints [12, 15].

An alternate approach to resource-constrained stream mining involves constructing topologies of classifiers based on hierarchical semantic concepts, and allowing individual classifiers in the topology to operate at different performance levels given the resources allocated to them. The performance level is determined by a classifier operating point that corresponds to the selected trade-off between probability of detection p_D and probability of false alarm p_F. Here, the probability of detection is defined as $p_D = p_{tp} + p_{tn}$, where p_{tp} and p_{tn} denote, respectively, the probability of a true positive, and the probability of a true negative.

This approach is illustrated in Fig. 12.2, where the curve on the right side shows a profile of the classifier accuracy in terms of the *detection error trade-off* (*DET*)—i.e., the trade-off of p_D versus p_F. Examples of operating points include decision thresholds for likelihood ratio tests or SVM normalized scores. Hence, instead of deciding on what fraction of the data to process, as in load-shedding approaches, such an approach determines *how* the available data should be processed given the underlying resource allocation. A solution based on this approach for configuring filtering applications that employ binary classifier chains has been proposed [14, 16–18].

Nevertheless, general binary tree topologies go significantly beyond linearly cascaded classifiers by providing greater flexibility in data processing, while also posing different challenges in terms of resource-constrained configuration. Specifically, while excess load can be easily handled within the optimization framework for a binary classifier chain, using a single operating point for each classifier in a tree generates two output streams with a total sum output rate that is fixed. Hence, it may not be possible to simultaneously meet tight processing resource constraints for downstream classifiers along both output edges when using only one operating point.

12.4 Dynamic, Data-Driven ASM Systems

Building on the conceptual framework of dynamically reconfigurable topologies of classifiers introduced in Sects. 12.1 and 12.3, an important direction for further work on stream mining for computer vision systems is in the rigorous integration of Dynamic Data Driven Applications Systems (DDDAS) into all aspects of processes for design and implementation. A significant class of future challenges for embedded computer vision therefore involves what may be referred to as *DDDAS-enabled ASM systems*.

12.4.1 DDDAS-Enabled ASM Systems

DDDAS is a paradigm that rigorously integrates application system modeling, instrumentation, and dynamic, feedback-driven adaptation of model and instrumentation parameters based on measured data characteristics [13]. DDDAS methods are

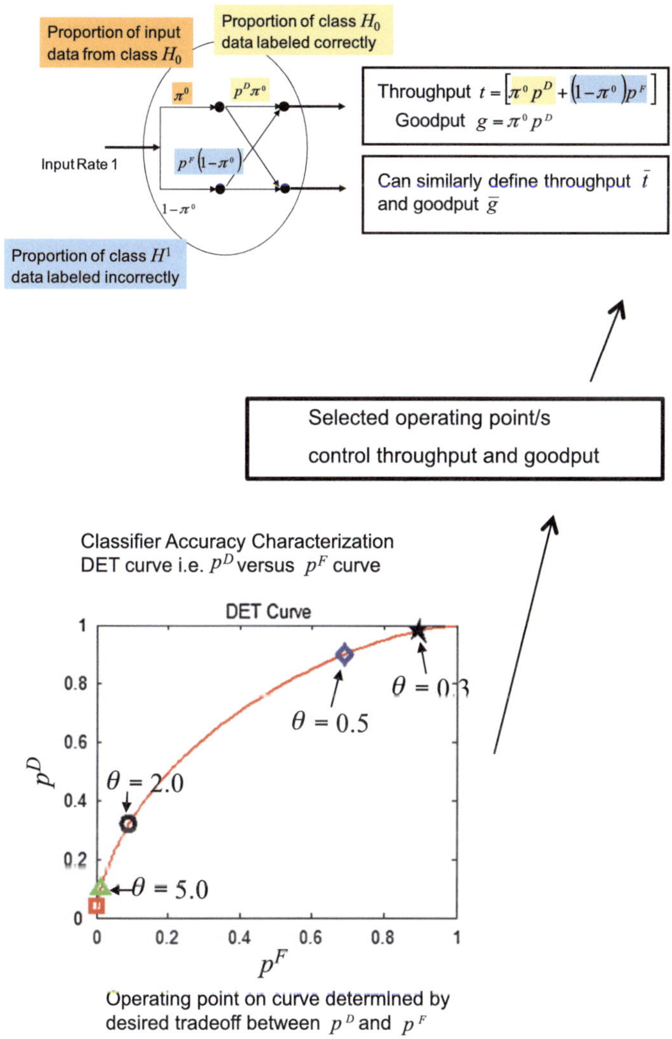

Fig. 12.2 An illustration of an adaptive and scalable classifier

highly relevant to design and implementation of ASM systems because they enable techniques for exploiting characteristics of the currently arriving set of image streams as well as characteristics of the overall operating environment to dynamically optimize critical trade-offs among key execution metrics, including power consumption, communication bandwidth, knowledge extraction accuracy, and end-to-end latency.

In ASM systems for embedded computer vision, DDDAS can be employed, for example, at network edges to systematically filter out image features that are not relevant to the current operational scenario or to adjust the resolution or frequency of captured images based on the type of object or amount of motion detected.

Such preprocessing at the network edges can help to reduce communication with a back-end server, and to improve overall system accuracy under communication and computation constraints. DDDAS techniques can also be employed at the server side. An example of such an application would be to dynamically determine the set of cameras at the network edges that should be active at a given time—e.g., to optimize trade-offs among energy efficiency, communication bandwidth requirements, and accuracy for the current image analysis scenario. In Sect. 12.5, we provide a detailed case study of DDDAS methods applied to a relevant application in embedded computer vision.

Use of DDDAS design techniques involves tightly integrated feedback from instrumentation. Use of DDDAS design techniques also involves application of dynamic parameters that are adapted based on such feedback, and that also control how subsequent rounds of instrumentation are performed. Figure 12.3 illustrates an abstract view of DDDAS as it relates to the class of stream mining systems addressed in this chapter.

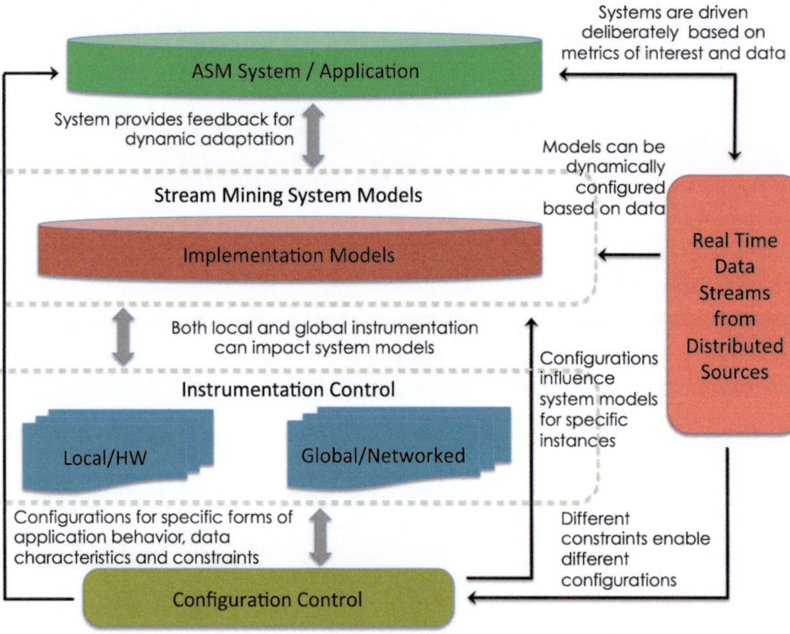

Key challenges in integrating DDDAS principles into stream mining systems include the following.

- Development of abstract models for stream mining systems that can compactly and accurately represent the underlying design space of topological and classifier configurations. For this purpose, signal-processing-oriented dataflow models of computation are a promising starting point [8, 35].
- Development of methods to steer parameters of image stream acquisition (e.g., to select specific subsets of cameras or frame rates and resolutions for activated

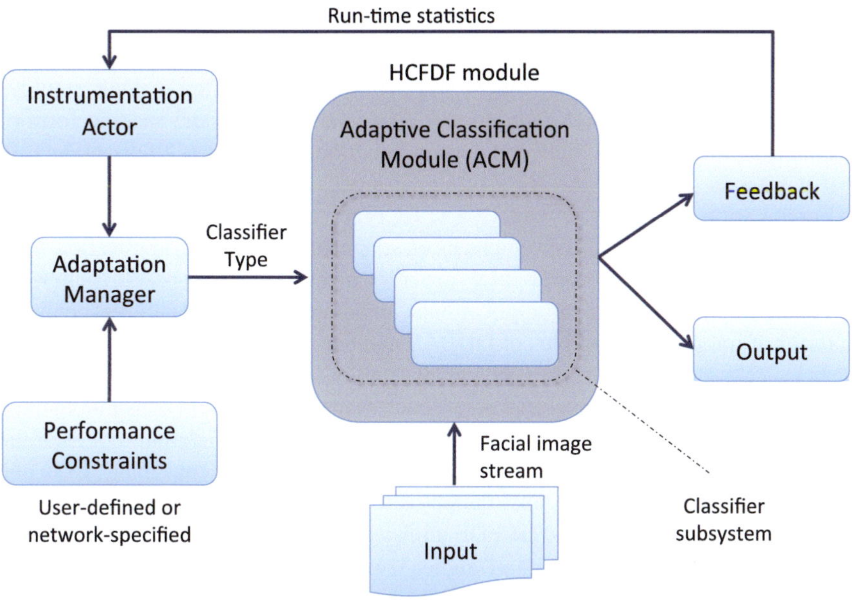

Fig. 12.3 An illustration of the LiD4E design tool and its application to DDDAS-enabled, multimedia, stream mining system design

cameras) based on the currently active regions of the stream mining design spaces, as estimated, for example, with the help of the abstract models described above.

- Development of methods to dynamically optimize the mapping of ASM topologies onto the targeted hardware platforms based on current configurations for the topologies, and their constituent classifiers. This mapping process may be especially challenging due to dynamics in stream mining topology characteristics, resource constraints on the target platforms or severe application requirements in terms of the volume of image data that needs to be processed, real-time constraints, etc.

Lightweight Dataflow for Dynamic Data-Driven Application Systems Environment (*LiD4E*) is a recently-developed design tool to help in the investigation of these challenges and other aspects of DDDAS-enabled stream mining systems. We discuss LiD4E next, in Sect. 12.4.2.

12.4.2 LiD4E

In this section, we provide an overview of LiD4E, which is a design environment that has been developed to facilitate experimentation with methods for DDDAS-enabled ASM system design, with emphasis on multimedia ASM systems [35].

A key feature of LiD4E is the provision for signal processing pipelines (i.e., chains of signal processing modules, such as classifiers, digital filters and transform operators) that can be data-dependent and dynamically changing. LiD4E employs *hierarchical core functional dataflow* (*HCFDF*) semantics as the specific form of dynamic dataflow [35]. HCFDF and the core functional dataflow (CFDF) model [29] that it extends belong to the class of signal-processing-oriented dataflow models of computation described in Sect. 12.4.1. HCFDF can be viewed as a hierarchical extension of CFDF. Through its emphasis on supporting structured, application-level dynamic dataflow modeling, HCFDF provides a formal, model-based framework through which stream mining applications can be designed and analyzed precisely in terms of integrated principles of DDDAS and dataflow.

In HCFDF graphs, actors are specified in terms of sets of processing modes, where each mode has static *dataflow rates*—i.e., each mode produces and consumes a fixed number of data values (tokens) on each actor port. However, different modes of the same actor can have different dataflow rates, and the actor mode can change from one actor execution (*firing*) to the next, thereby allowing for dynamic dataflow behavior (dynamic rates). Additionally, HCFDF allows dataflow graphs to be hierarchically embedded (nested) within actors of higher level HCFDF graphs, thereby allowing complex systems to be constructed and analyzed in a scalable manner. The design rules prescribed for hierarchical composition in HCFDF graphs ensure that actors at each level in a design hierarchy conform to the semantics of HCFDF or some restricted subset of HCFDF semantics, such as cyclo-static dataflow or synchronous dataflow (SDF) [9, 23]. For further details on HCFDF semantics, we refer the reader to [35].

As demonstrated in [35], HCFDF modeling enables run-time adaptation of signal processing topologies, including dataflow graphs that are constructed using arbitrary combinations of classifiers, filters, and transform units. Through the inclusion of a special HCFDF design component called an *adaptive classification module*, the designer can invoke multiple operating modes at run-time, and selection of such operating modes can be driven based on system feedback—e.g., based on instrumentation that monitors data characteristics, and guides selection based on desired trade-offs among performance, accuracy, and energy consumption.

Figure 12.3 provides an illustration of the LiD4E design tool and its application to DDDAS-enabled, multimedia, stream mining system design. For more details on LiD4E, we refer the reader to [35]. Extensions of the design principles in LiD4E to handle multi-mode stream mining systems are discussed in [34].

12.5 Case Study: Learning Based on Multi-armed Bandits

In this section, we present a case study in data-driven ASM techniques that are relevant for the emerging class of a ASM-enabled, embedded computer vision systems introduced in Sect. 12.1 through Sect. 12.4. The methods presented in the case study can be viewed as representative of the kinds of advances that are needed to address the challenges in providing robust, efficient, and integrated stream mining solutions for next-generation embedded computer vision systems.

The methods discussed in this section were originally presented in [2]. In this section, we provide a concise summary of the developments in [2] in the context of ASM systems for embedded computer vision. For full details on these methods, we refer the reader to [2].

12.5.1 Overview

In most video-based object or face recognition services on mobile devices, each device captures and transmits video frames over a wireless channel to a remote computing service (a.k.a. the "cloud") that performs the heavy-duty video feature extraction and recognition tasks for a large number of mobile devices. The major challenges of such scenarios stem from the highly-varying contention levels in the wireless local area network (WLAN), as well as the variation in the task-scheduling congestion in the cloud.

In order for each device to maximize its object or face recognition rate under such contention and congestion variability, a systematic learning framework based on *multi-armed bandits* has been developed [2]. Unlike well-known reinforcement learning techniques that exhibit very slow convergence rates when operating in highly-dynamic environments, this bandit-based, systematic learning approach quickly approaches the optimal transmission and processing-complexity policies based on feedback on the experienced dynamics (contention and congestion levels). The case study presented in this section centers on this bandit-based, systematic learning approach.

Many of the envisaged applications and services for wearable sensors, smartphones, tablets or portable computers in the next ten years will involve analysis of video streams for event, action, object or user recognition [21, 32]. In this process, they experience time-varying channel conditions, traffic loads and processing constraints at the remote cloud-computing servers where the data analysis takes place. Examples of early commercial services in this domain include Google Goggles, Google Glass, Facebook automatic face tagging [7], and Microsoft's Photo Gallery face recognition.

12.5.2 Application Example

Figure 12.4 presents an example of such deployments. Video content producers include several types of sensors, mobile phones, as well as other low-end portable devices, that capture, encode (typically via a hardware-supported MPEG/ITU-T codec) and transmit video streams to a remote computing server for recognition or authentication purposes. A group of M devices in the same WLAN comprises a

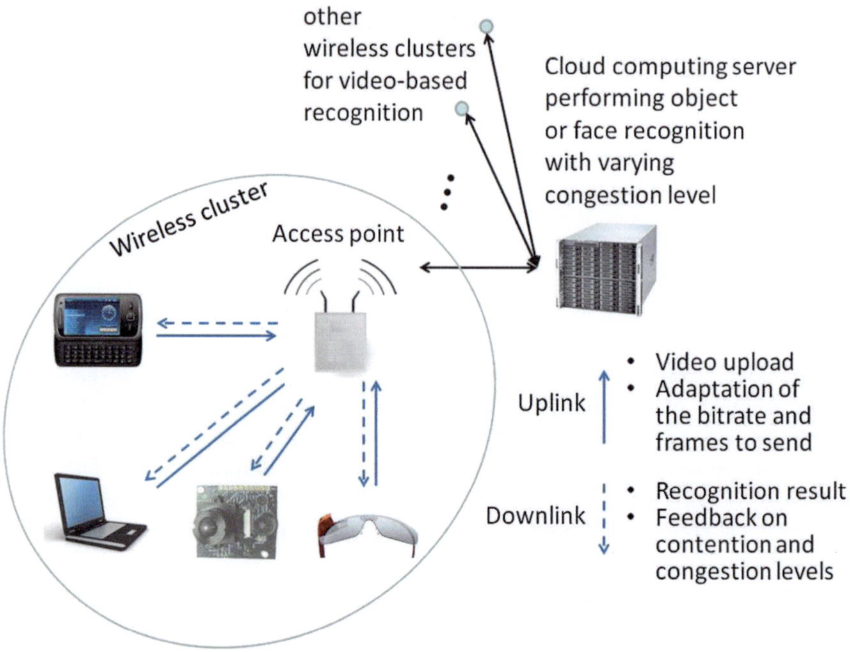

Fig. 12.4 Illustration of object or face recognition via adaptive wireless video transport to a remote computing server

wireless cluster. A server running openstack or Hadoop (or a similar runtime environment suitable for cloud computing) [25] is used for analyzing visual data from numerous wireless clusters, as well as other computing tasks unrelated to object or face recognition.

Each device can adapt the encoding bitrate, as well as the number of frames to produce (with the ensemble of N such settings comprising the set $\mathscr{A} = \{a_1, a_2, \ldots, a_N\}$), in order to alleviate the impact of contention in the WLAN. At the same time, the visual analysis performed in the cloud can be adapted to scale the required processing time to alleviate the impact of task scheduling congestion in the cloud [25, 30], with the sets of contention and congestion levels represented by the discrete sets $\mathscr{T}$ and $\mathscr{G}$, respectively. In return, each device receives from the cloud a label that describes the recognized object or face (e.g., the object or person's name), or simply a message that the object or person could not be recognized. In addition, each device or wireless cluster can also receive feedback on the experienced WLAN medium access control (MAC) layer contention and the cloud task scheduling congestion conditions.

Thus, the "reward" for each device is the recognition result at each time step. Given that each wireless access point and the cloud computing infrastructure serve many more requests than the ones from a given cluster of devices (as illustrated in Fig. 12.4), we can safely assume that for each device, the wireless contention and cloud congestion levels are both independent of the actions taken by the devices within their clusters. This makes each device independent, since the decisions made by other devices do not affect the reward.

12.5.3 Relation to Prior Work

Each mobile device of Fig. 12.4 seeks to maximize its own expected recognition rate at the minimum possible cost in terms of utilized wireless resources (i.e., MAC superframe transmission opportunities used). To this end, several approaches have been proposed that are based on reinforcement learning [36], such as Q-learning [30]. In these, the goal is to learn the state-value function, which provides a measure of the expected long-term performance (utility). However, they incur large memory overheads for storing the state-value function, and they are slow to adapt to new or dynamically changing environments. A better approach is to intermittently explore and exploit when needed, in order to capture such changes. Index policies for multi-armed bandit (MAB) problems, contextual bandits [22, 33], or epsilon-decreasing algorithms [3] can be used for this task. However, all existing bandit frameworks do not take into consideration the contention and congestion conditions as contexts in the application under consideration.

12.5.4 Learning Based on Multi-user Bandits

Motivated by the lack of efficient methods that fully capture the problems related to online learning in multi-user wireless networks and cloud computing systems with uncertain and highly-varying resource provisioning, an online systematic learning theory based on multi-user contextual bandits has been developed. This learning theory can be viewed as a natural extension of the basic MAB framework. Analytic estimates have been derived to compare its efficiency against the complete knowledge (or "oracle") benchmark in which the expected reward of every choice is known by the learner. Unlike Q-learning [36] and other learning-based methods, it is proven that the regret bound—the loss incurred by the algorithm against the best possible decision that assumes full knowledge of contention and congestion conditions—is logarithmic if users do not collaborate and each would like to maximize the user's own utility. Finally, the contextual bandit framework discussed here is general, and can be used for learning in various kinds of wireless embedded computer vision applications that involve offloading of selected processing tasks. Henceforth in this chapter, we refer to the contextual bandit framework by the abbreviation *CBF*.

Table 12.1 Average attempts (with the oracle bound given in parentheses) to obtain a recognition rate of 0.9 with 2D-PCA

Method	Iteration			
	$T = 50$	$T = 100$	$T = 250$	$T = 1{,}000$
CBF	3.3 (1.7)	3.1 (1.6)	2.4 (1.5)	1.9 (1.5)
CBF no context	3.1 (1.7)	2.8 (1.6)	2.6 (1.6)	2.4 (1.6)
Q-learning	3.5 (1.7)	2.8 (1.6)	2.7 (1.5)	2.2 (1.5)

12.5.5 Numerical Results

The CBF has been evaluated by simulation. The simulation environment comprises four mobile devices connected via an IEEE 802.11 WLAN to a cloud-computing server. Videos of human faces are produced by random images of persons taken from the extended Yale Face Database B (39 cropped faces of human subjects under varying illumination) [20]. Each video comprises 34 images from the same person, and is compressed to a wide range of bitrates via the H.264/AVC codec (x264 codec, crf $\in \{4, 14, 24, 34, 44, 51\}$). The 2D PCA algorithm [43] is used at the cloud side for face recognition from each decoded video (with the required training done offline as per the 2D PCA setup [43]). More than 80 % of the video frames have to match to the same person in the database to declare a given video as "recognized". There is a time window set for recognition, which limits the number of frames received by the cloud under varying WLAN contention levels (delay is increased under contention due to the backoff and retransmissions of IEEE 802.11 WLANs). Similarly, because of randomly varying congestion in the cloud, only a limited number of the received video frames is actually used by 2D PCA, thereby affecting the recognition rate.

Table 12.1 presents the average number of retries performed per recognition action by the CBF method (with and without using the cloud congestion information as context) in order to achieve a recognition rate of 90 %. Results are also presented in the following ways.

- An optimal solution that selects the transmission setting yielding the highest expected recognition rate [2]. This solution is defined as the *oracle solution*, since it assumes that all conditions for each case are precisely known beforehand.
- Q-learning [36, 44], as discussed in Sects. 12.5.3 and 12.5.4.

The results indicate that after 250 recognition attempts (each attempt comprises the retries listed), the CBF method approaches the oracle bound, and for the same recognition rate, incurs less retries per attempt in comparison to Q-learning.

12.5.6 Summary

In this section, we have examined in some detail a concrete case study of emerging methods for data-driven, ASM system design targeted to embedded computer vision. In particular, we have discussed a contextual bandit framework (CBF) for learning contention and congestion conditions in object or face recognition via wireless mobile streaming and cloud-based processing. Analytic results show that the CBF framework converges to the value of the oracle solution (i.e., the solution that assumes full knowledge of congestion and contention conditions). Simulations within a cloud-based face recognition system demonstrate that the CBF approach outperforms Q-learning, as it quickly adjusts to contention and congestion conditions. For more details on the CBF approach, we refer the reader to [2].

12.6 Future Directions in Stream Mining Systems for Computer Vision

Most existing solutions for designing and configuring computer vision and stream-mining systems based on the extracted visual data offload their processing to the cloud and assume that the underlying characteristics (e.g., visual characteristics) are either known, or that simple-yet-accurate models of these characteristics can be built. However, in practice, this knowledge is not available and models of such computer vision applications or the associated processing mechanisms are very difficult to build and calibrate for specific environments, since these characteristics are dynamically varying over time. Hence, despite applying optimization, these solutions tend to result in highly sub-optimal performance since the models they use for the experienced dynamics are not accurate. Hence, reinforcement learning (i.e., learning how to act based on past experience) becomes a vital component in all such systems. Some of the best-performing online reinforcement learning algorithms are Q-learning and structural-based reinforcement learning. In these, the goal is to learn the state-value function, which provides a measure of the expected long-term performance (utility) when it is acting optimally in a dynamic environment. It has been proven that online learning algorithms converge to optimal solutions when all the possible system states are visited infinitely often [36].

However, these methods have to learn the state-value function at every possible state. As a result, they incur large memory overheads for storing the state-value function and they are typically slow to adapt to new or dynamically changing environments (i.e., they exhibit a slow convergence rate), especially when the state space is large—as in the considered wireless transmission and recognition problem of Sect. 12.5. These memory and speed-of-learning deficiencies are alleviated in structural-based learning solutions. Despite this, a key limitation still remains: *all these schemes provide only asymptotic bounds for the learning performance—no speed-of-learning guarantees are provided.* Nevertheless, in most computer vision and recognition systems, users are interested in both short-term performance and long-term performance.

12.7 Conclusion

In this chapter, we have introduced the emerging area of adaptive stream mining systems for embedded computer vision, and we have discussed important research challenges in this area. We have emphasized key challenges in integrating methods of Dynamic Data Driven Applications Systems (DDDAS) rigorously in the design and implementation process for the targeted class of embedded computer vision systems. We have discussed the Lightweight Dataflow for Dynamic Data-Driven Application Systems Environment (LiD4E) as a recently-introduced design tool for experimenting with DDDAS-enabled stream mining methods. As a concrete example of recent advances in DDDAS-enabled adaptive stream mining, we have presented a case study involving learning based on multi-armed bandits. As motivated in this chapter, addressing the future challenges of adaptive stream mining systems for embedded computer vision will require interdisciplinary advances in areas that include machine learning, DDDAS design methods, and distributed embedded systems.

Acknowledgments This work is supported by the US Air Force Office of Scientific Research under the DDDAS Program.

References

1. Amini L, Andrade H, Eskesen F, King R, Park Y, Selo P, Venkatramani C (2005) The stream processing core. Technical Report RSC 23798
2. Atan O, Andreopoulos Y, Tekin C (2014) Bandit framework for systematic learning in wireless video-based face recognition. In: Proceedings of the international conference on acoustics, speech, and signal processing
3. Auer P, Cesa-Bianchi N, Fischer P (2002) Finite-time analysis of the multiarmed bandit problem. Mach Learn 47(2–3):235–256
4. Babcock B, Babu S, Datar M, Motwani R (2003) Chain: operator scheduling for memory minimization in data stream systems. In: ACM SIGMOD
5. Babcock B, Datar M, Motwani R (2003) Cost-efficient mining techniques for data streams. In: Proceedings of the workshop on management and processing of data streams
6. Balazinska M, Balakrishnan H, Madden S, Stonebraker M (2005) Fault tolerance in the borealis distributed stream processing system. In: Proceedings of the international conference on management of data
7. Becker BC, Ortiz EG (2008) Evaluation of face recognition techniques for application to facebook. In: Proceedings of the IEEE international conference on automatic face and gesture recognition, pp 1–6
8. Bhattacharyya SS, Deprettere E, Leupers R, Takala J (eds) (2013) Handbook of signal processing systems, 2nd edn. Springer, New York. http://dx.doi.org/10.1007/978-1-4614-6859-2. ISBN: 978-1-4614-6858-5 (Print); 978-1-4614-6859-2 (Online)

9. Bilsen G, Engels M, Lauwereins R, Peperstraete JA (1996) Cyclo-static dataflow. IEEE Trans Signal Process 44(2):397–408
10. Burges CJC (1998) A tutorial on support vector machines for pattern recognition. Knowl Discov Data Min 2(2):121–167
11. Cherniack M, Balakrishnan H, Carney D, Cetintemel U, Xing Y, Zdonik S (2003) Scalable distributed stream processing. In: CIDR
12. Chi Y, Yu PS, Wang H, Muntz RR (2005) Loadstar: a load shedding scheme for classifying data streams. In: Proceedings of the SIAM conference on data mining
13. Darema F (2005) Grid computing and beyond: The context of dynamic data driven applications systems. Proc IEEE 93(2):692–697
14. Ducasse R, Turaga D, van der Schaar M (2010) Adaptive topologic optimization for large-scale stream mining. IEEE J Sel Top Sign Proces 4(3):620–636
15. Eide V, Eliassen F, Granmo O, Lysne O (2003) Supporting timeliness and accuracy in distributed real-time content-based video analysis. In: Proceedings of the ACM international conference on multimedia
16. Foo B, van der Schaar M (2010) A distributed approach for optimizing cascaded classifier topologies in real-time stream mining systems. IEEE Trans Image Process 19(11):3035–3048
17. Foo B, Turaga D, Verscheure O, Amini L, van der Schaar M (2011) Configuring trees of classifiers in distributed multimedia stream mining systems. IEEE Trans Circuits Syst Video Technol 21(3):245–258
18. Fu F, Turaga D, Verscheure O, van der Schaar M, Amini L (2007) Configuring competing classifier chains in distributed stream mining systems. IEEE J Sel Top Sign Process 1(4):548–563
19. Garg A, Pavlovic V (2002) Bayesian networks as ensemble of classifiers. In: Proceedings of the international conference on pattern recognition, pp 779–784
20. Georghiades AS, Belhumeur PN, Kriegman D (2001) From few to many: illumination cone models for face recognition under variable lighting and pose. IEEE Trans Pattern Anal Mach Intell 23(6):643–660
21. Girod B, Chandrasekhar V, Chen DM, Cheung N, Grzeszczuk R, Reznik Y, Takacs G, Tsai SS, Vedantham R (2011) Mobile visual search. IEEE Signal Process Mag 28(4):61–76
22. Langford J, Zhang T (2008) The epoch-greedy algorithm for multi-armed bandits with side information. In: Platt JC, Koller D, Singer Y, Roweis S (eds) Advances in neural information processing systems. Curran Associates, New York, pp 817–824
23. Lee EA, Messerschmitt DG (1987) Synchronous dataflow. Proc IEEE 75(9):1235–1245
24. Lienhart R, Liang L, Kuranov A (2003) A detector tree for boosted classifiers for real-time object detection and tracking. In: Proceedings of the IEEE international conference on multimedia and expo
25. Li A, Yang X, Kandula S, Zhang M (2010) CloudCmp: comparing public cloud providers. In: Proceedings of the ACM SIGCOMM conference on internet measurement, pp 1–14
26. Ntoulas A, Najork M, Manasse M, Fetterly D (2006) Detecting spam web pages through content analysis. In: Proceedings of the international conference on world wide web
27. Olston C, Jiang J, Widom J (2003) Adaptive filters for continuous queries over distributed data streams. In: ACM SIGMOD
28. Pang S (2004) SVM classification tree algorithm with application to face membership authentication. In: Proceedings of the international joint conference on neural networks
29. Plishker W, Sane N, Kiemb M, Anand K, Bhattacharyya SS (2008) Functional DIF for rapid prototyping. In: Proceedings of the international symposium on rapid system prototyping, Monterey, California, pp 17–23
30. Ren S, van der Schaar M (2013) Efficient resource provisioning and rate selection for stream mining in a community cloud. IEEE Trans Multimedia 15(4):723–734
31. Schapire RE (2003) The boosting approach to machine learning: an overview. In: Denison DD, Hansen MH, Holmes C, Mallick B, Yu B (eds) Nonlinear estimation and classification. Springer, New York
32. Siewiorek D (2012) Generation smartphone. IEEE Spectr Mag 49(9):54–58

33. Slivkins A (2011) Contextual bandits with similarity information. In: Proceedings of the conference on learning theory
34. Sudusinghe K, Cho I, van der Schaar M, Bhattacharyya SS (2014) Model based design environment for data-driven embedded signal processing systems. In: Proceedings of the international conference on computational science, Cairns, Australia, pp 1193–1202
35. Sudusinghe K, Won S, van der Schaar M, Bhattacharyya SS (2013) A novel framework for design and implementation of adaptive stream mining systems. In: Proceedings of the IEEE international conference on multimedia and expo, San Jose, California, pp 1–6. http://ieeexplore.ieee.org
36. Sutton RS, Barto AG (1998) Reinforcement learning: an introduction. MIT Press/Bradford Books, Cambridge
37. Tatbul N (2002) Qos-driven load shedding on data streams. In: XML-based data management and multimedia engineering
38. Tatbul N, Etintemel UC, Zdonik SB (2007) Staying fit: efficient load shedding techniques for distributed stream processing. In: Proceedings of the international conference on very large databases
39. Tatbul N, Etintemel UC, Zdonik SB, Cherniack M, Stonebraker M (2003) Load shedding in a data stream manager. In: Proceedings of the international conference on very large databases, pp 309–320
40. Tatbul N, Zdonik SB (2006) Dealing with overload in distributed stream processing systems. In: Proceedings of the IEEE international workshop on networking meets databases
41. Viglas S, Naughton J (2012) Rate-based query optimization for streaming information sources. In: Proceedings of ACM SIGMOD
42. Wu JRSY, Tseng B (2004) Ontology-based multi-classification learning for video concept detection. In: Proceedings of the IEEE international conference on multimedia and expo
43. Yang J, Zhang D, Frangi AF, Yang J (2004) Two-dimensional PCA: a new approach to appearance-based face representation and recognition. IEEE Trans Pattern Anal Mach Intell 26(1):131–137
44. Zhu X, Lan C, van der Schaar M (2013) Low-complexity reinforcement learning for delay-sensitive compression in networked video stream mining. In: Proceedings of the IEEE international conference on multimedia and expo

Chapter 13
Designing Vision Systems that See Better

Sek Chai, Sehoon Lim and David Zhang

Abstract This chapter introduces computational sensing and imaging—a branch of computer vision that deals with embedded processing for capturing higher quality imagery, to the embedded vision developer. In this research domain, issues such as exposure, motion blur, and dynamic range are addressed by fundamentally changing how light is sensed, captured, and made available for downstream semantic processing. Some important applications enabled are in digital photography and situational awareness. We present several design examples on these camera platforms where modifications of the image-capture process result in significant improvements in image quality, allowing downstream vision analysis to perform better. Motivated by example applications, we then describe the basic architecture of an embedded vision system that dynamically tunes and adapts to the task at hand.

13.1 Computational Imaging Overview

Computational imaging refers to the capture, processing, and manipulation techniques that improve or extend the quality of an image. Beyond just image enhancements such as basic image processing, this field has evolved to include techniques from computer vision, graphics, and applied optics to affect the output from a traditional camera. Also commonly referred to as computational photography [1], in this chapter we would adopt the term computational imaging instead because the applications using this technology can extend beyond photography.

This growing area of research is important for embedded vision because it provides higher quality image data for downstream semantic processing, such as object detection, tracking, and recognition. Very often semantic processing fails because image quality is poor, noisy, blurry, or simply lacking desired features to segment

S. Chai (✉) · S. Lim · D. Zhang
SRI International, Menlo Park, USA
e-mail: sek.chai@gmail.com

B. Kisačanin and M. Gelautz (eds.), *Advances in Embedded Computer Vision*,
Advances in Computer Vision and Pattern Recognition,
DOI 10.1007/978-3-319-09387-1_13

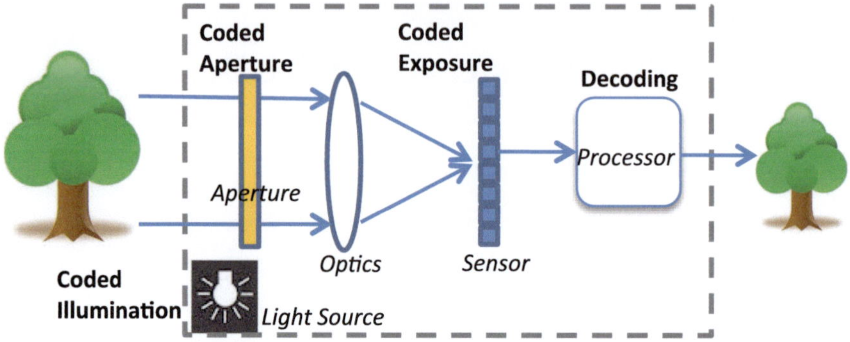

Fig. 13.1 Generic block diagram of a Computational Imaging system consisting of light source, aperture, optics, sensor and processor

the scene and detect an object in the first place. By creating a better camera system that sees better, we enable more robust embedded vision systems to be built in the future.

The field of computational imaging comprises more than just basic image processing where traditional pixel manipulation techniques such as filtering, color interpolation, image compression, and digital watermarking are applied. Techniques for image effects for artistic output such as tone mapping, color negatives, and distortion correction are not included because they deal only with direct pixel manipulation. In contrast, computational imaging considers a holistic view of the illumination, optics, sensor, and processing to effect the output of image [2].

Next, we will discuss the elements of the computational imaging system (Fig. 13.1). We provide a random sampling of current, published approaches, and we note that an exhaustive survey of the entire landscape is beyond the scope of this one chapter. Our intent is to provide sufficient background of the area in order to better appreciate the computational imaging platform, its embedded framework, and overall design implications.

13.1.1 Illumination

A computational imaging system can take into consideration how a scene is illuminated in order to improve the capture process. For example, with active illumination, coded lighting at different intensity and angle can produce strong features and responses to calculate a BRDF (bidirectional reflection distribution function) of an object, which can be applied for material classification in a recycling plant so that valuable materials are sorted during processing [3].

A computational imaging system may also detect the spectral responses of an object's material emissive properties. For example, ultraviolet lighting is provided so that a spectral response in near infrared can be detected based on the material luminance properties. Applications such as forensic criminal investigation may utilize such a system to detect fingerprints and bodily fluids left in a crime scene [4].

Structured illumination is also commonly used for geometry recovery. The basic principle involves projecting a narrow band of light onto a 3D shaped object such that the reflected illumination on the surface appears distorted. By analyzing the distortion from various perspectives, the geometric surface shape can be reconstructed. The Kinect Camera from Microsoft is one of the first consumer grade camera-system that uses a pattern of projected infrared light points to generate a dense 3D image [5]. Other computational imaging applications where illumination is controlled include image deblurring and object relighting.

13.1.2 Optics and Sensors

The optical elements in the camera systems are used to channel light into the image sensor. While the most basic function would be to focus light using a lens, other elements can be used to split, block, smear, or divert light accordingly to the proper physical sensor arrangements. Careful attention is paid to the spectral phenomenology of these optical elements to ensure proper transitivity of light.

In coded aperture imaging, for example, a mask is applied so that certain amount of light is captured at each location. Example applications include imaging spectroscopy where a 3D spectral datacube (a three-dimensional data array) is mapped to a 2D focal plane sensor [6]. In coded exposure imaging, the on/off state of the shutter is purposefully manipulated in certain patterns and at a high rate. Example applications include motion deblur in high frame rate processing [7, 8].

In sparse aperture imaging, an array of lenses or sensors is used to capture light field information of a scene. Each light measurement can be used to calculate the distance and phase in order to reconstruct the high-resolution image. For example, in a light-field camera, also known as a plenoptic camera, an array of microlenses is used to simultaneously capture all light field information of a scene. Scene reconstruction is possible, by analyzing the corresponding measured light properties of each pixel. Because distance and optical wavefront can be estimated, the camera can, from a single shot, produce multiple images refocused at different distances. In some recently announced light-field cameras [9, 10], a mask-based design is used based on a principle of optical heterodyning, where a printed film is placed close to the image sensor. In others, such as [11], a plenoptic camera system with n-lens array camera is proposed for use in smartphones, replacing the normal camera module and achieving much thinner overall form factor.

In these examples, the captured images are optically coded, requiring computational decoding to produce new images. More specifically, in computational imaging, light is manipulated and mapped to the sensor to offer fundamentally new ways to produce higher quality images beyond the capability of a standard lens and an image sensor.

13.1.3 Processing

With new mapping of how light is captured and coded through the optics and sensor, and also through various illumination techniques, a decoding step is required to "re-create" the image from raw sensor data. Very often, compressive sensing (CS for short) decoding algorithms provide a formalism in which a physical sampled data set is analyzed to generate data in a different domain. For example, 3D spectral datacube is physically mapped to a 2D focal plane sensor, in which the decoding process will recreate the 3D datacube with certain fidelity [6].

Efficient CS decoding algorithms will take advantage of the sparse nature of the mapping matrix that is used to translate raw sensed data to the final domain. CS decoding algorithms fall into two main categories: *convex optimization* and *greedy* algorithms. The former cast the problem into a linear program and apply efficient algorithms to its solution; the latter refine an initial estimate one element at a time. Compared to greedy algorithms, convex optimization algorithms tend to produce more accurate results but require higher computational complexity. Examples of two convex optimization algorithms that are reasonably efficient and produce good results for datacube reconstruction are TVAL3 [12] and TwIST [13]. TVAL3 is a decoding algorithm that can take advantage of a sparse sensing matrix and a signal that is dense in its native sampling domain. It is also optimized to work with *images*, since it implicitly performs Total Variation (TV) minimization—it searches for a solution with a sparse 2D *gradient*. TwIST is another decoding algorithm that has been optimized for image reconstruction. It is somewhat more flexible than TVAL3 but can take slightly more time to produce a result. Like TVAL3, it is a convex optimization algorithm.

13.1.4 Putting Everything Together

There is not a common camera architecture for computational imaging as there is much research left to explore before arriving at any optimal configuration of optics, sensor and processor. While there are camera platforms such as the Frankencamera [14] that exposes internal processing chain to allow for developers to create applications in this area, the field is a wide research territory to arrive at different configurations suitable for many embedded vision application domains, including face recognition [15], multivariate optical computing in spectroscopy [16], image sensing [17], material classification [18], and compressive video reconstruction [19].

Specific to the discussion about optimization for computational imaging, we advocate an alternative approach to directly capture only useful *features* (e.g., some key spectral bands) that are critical to perform a specified task. Known as *feature-specific imaging* [20, 21], this technique employs novel optical modulators to measure *linear projections* of incoming radiance. Depending on the nature of the given tasks, such computational imaging systems can be optimally designed by maximizing *task-specific information* [22] to measure projections for either reconstruction [17, 19, 20, 23] or classification [15, 16, 18]. Since the aim is to perform high-level computer vision tasks directly on compressed measurements, such systems can dramatically reduce the amount of data for a given SNR compared to traditional imaging architectures.

One major limitation of feature-specific imaging, however, is that the measured data is only useful for a specific task at any given moment. Thus it is nearly impossible to reuse the data for any other purposes such as updating statistical models of objects. This limitation is especially severe in spatial dimensions since many scene structures will be lost. What is needed is a unified, extensible framework for task-specific imaging systems that integrally performs detection, classification, tracking, and *learning directly on compressive measurements*. This approach is favorable because we are no longer dependent on the quality of the decoded imagery.

In the rest of this chapter, we will describe two examples of computational imaging solutions to motivate the application areas and to reinforce the advantages of this research area. Then we present the architectural framework of an adaptive task-specific imaging system, optimized for the embedded vision task at hand.

13.2 Multi Spectral Coded Aperture Camera

Multispectral imaging (MSI) enables recovery of spectral properties of material in a scene, based on the material's spectral responses to current illumination (e.g., reflection, absorption, fluorescence). In this section, we describe a key development towards a small form-factor imaging spectrometer that can enable instantaneous capture and analysis of the spectral signatures of all objects in the scene. This spectral classification system is achieved by combining a coded aperture snapshot spectral imager (CASSI) with a multispectral detection algorithm. We further improve the signal to noise ratio with temporal analysis enabled with image registration of captured images. The spectral datacube is captured and encoded simultaneously into a 2D image using a code aperture, and later decoded by sparsity-based computational framework. An adaptive-cosine estimator (ACE) is used to quantitatively detect and classify the target objects from the decoded spectral cube [24, 25]. We present details about our optical design, algorithm, and selected results of our camera system.

13.2.1 Computational and Optical Co-design

CASSI was first presented in [26] for a snapshot MSI. The optical encoding with a static coded aperture and a dispersive element enables the system to compressively record the spectral datacube and the computational decoding reconstructs the datacube from the compressed measurement. With respect to computational imaging, the optical measurement is formulated by a linear model and the input data is

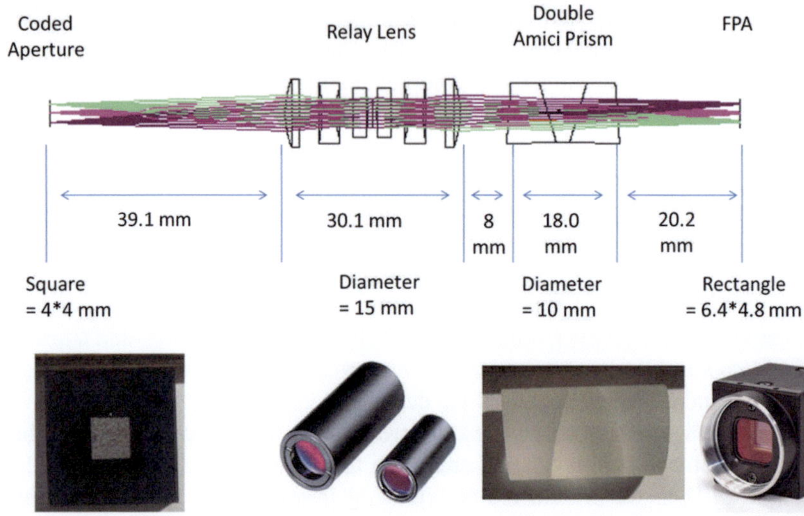

Fig. 13.2 CASSI's optical design and components: coded aperture with 200 by 200 pixels, relay lens, double amici prism, and FPA

reconstructed by computationally inverting the linear model. A binary random pattern is used to encode the spectral datacube into 2D imagery without critical information loss. To decode the compressed datacube, a sparse optimization is used to alleviate the underdetermined problem. The sparse optimization imposes spatial and spectral sparsity constraints on plausible solutions, resulting in the most optimal among them.

CASSI is optically designed and implemented to support the computational design. In Fig. 13.2, a collected optical field is modulated by the coded aperture in the frontend and the modulated field is one-to-one imaged onto the focal plane array (FPA) by a microscopic relay lens. In the optical path, a double amici prism disperses the spectral channels simultaneously. The coded aperture is designed by 200 by 200 pixels with 19.8 μ feature size resulting in 4 by 4 mm field-of-view (FOV). The double amici prism is used as an aberration free dispersive element to transform the spectral distribution to the spatial distribution. The double amici prism is composed of two different optical materials which compensates the nonlinearity of spectral dispersion. The total length of the system is 115.4 mm whose compactness is advantageous for compact video imaging.

In the computational design, the measurement model expresses the relationship between the measurement g and the spectral datacube f. Since the system matrix H is underdetermined, far away from the square form, the condition number of H is very large. The bad condition number makes the inverse problem hard. The sparsity constraints of CS make the inverse problem well conditioned in the proper basis such as total variation (TV) [27, 28]. The backward model is the transpose of the measurement model H and the transpose system matrix H^T estimates the spatial distribution of the coded aperture in g and combines the multiple estimates f^*.

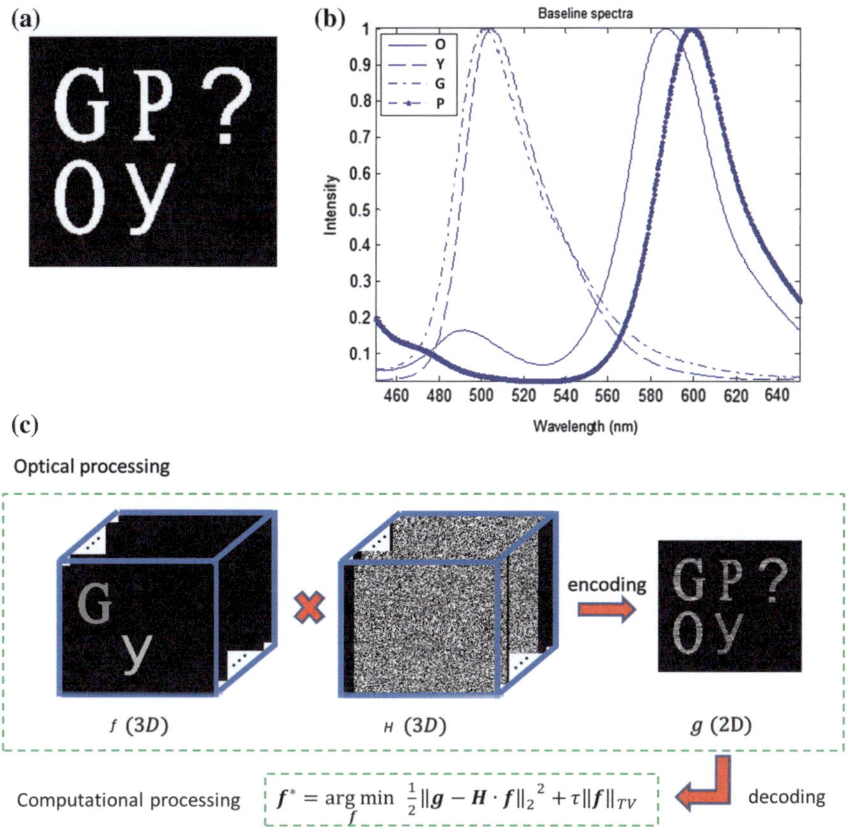

Fig. 13.3 CASSI simulation. **a** image of datacube, **b** spectral signatures of datacube, and **c** computational and optical flow describing the numerical processes from the computational and optical co-design

CASSI reconstruction in Fig. 13.3. The spectral datacube f consists of alphabet letters "G", "P", "Y", "O" in 2D space and 1D spectrum data. The individual letters have different intensity distributions in the spectral dimension. In the optical processing, the datacube f is encoded by the system matrix H, then the CASSI measurement g is obtained by summing the element-wise multiplied cube over the spectral dimension.

13.2.2 Image Registration

The goal of high frame rate image (video) stabilization is to remove motion blur while maintaining high SNR (Signal to Noise Ratio). In practice this can be achieved by utilizing robust image registration and motion compensation to align successive image frames that may have random inter-frame motion due to camera movement and/or object motion. In our CASSI system if the captured images are well aligned, then averaging N images will not only reduce blur, but will also increase the SNR by a factor of N as compared to a single capture with limited exposure time.

Image registration (e.g., motion estimation) methods can be broadly grouped into: feature based motion estimation and global motion estimation. Feature based methods [29, 30] use features extracted by image processing (corners, oriented edges, and so on) to find correspondences in successive images and hence solve for a motion model between these images. Global motion estimation [31] uses the intensity information from all the pixels in the image to directly recover the motion between successive image frames.

In our CASSI system the coded aperture (CA) introduces a fixed pattern in the image (before datacube reconstruction) which masks any structure of objects in the scene. Hence it is impossible to extract features from the scene that are suitable for motion estimation. The global methods, on the other hand, use all the pixels in the image. If the effect of the CA pattern can be averaged out and only the contributions from the signals in the scene remain, then this method would be a solution to the problem. We choose this approach since we can compensate for the known CA pattern in every captured frame while maintaining a reasonable SNR by normalization.

Our choice for global motion estimation method is the hierarchical model-based motion estimation [31] for which SRI has a real-time implementation. The estimation process involves Sum-of-Squared-Difference (SSD) minimization using a motion model between image frames, with Gauss-Newton minimization employed in a final refinement process.

13.2.3 CASSI Based Spectral Classification

An experiment was designed to demonstrate the CASSI-based spectral classification. A CASSI system (Fig. 13.4a) was used to measure the fluorescent visible colors illuminated by an UV light source. Four highlighter colors were used to generate green, pink, orange, and yellow alphabet letters in Fig. 13.4b. A single frame of CASSI measurement was shown in Fig. 13.4c for the datacube reconstruction. In the measurement, the "G" letter at the second row did not interact with the UV illumination because the letter was marked by a non-fluorescent green Sharpie pen. Two spectral channels of the CASSI reconstruction are compared at Channel 12 and 18 (Fig. 13.4d, e) from 20 channels. At Channel 12 the "G" letter is dominant and at Channel 18 the "O" and "?" letters are dominant. The question mark "?" was added in the object scene to demonstrate a multi-target classification. The question mark has the same spectrum with the "O" letter because "?" was marked by the orange highlighter color. In the datacube, the "G", "P", "O", and "Y" letters have different intensity distributions along the spectral channels.

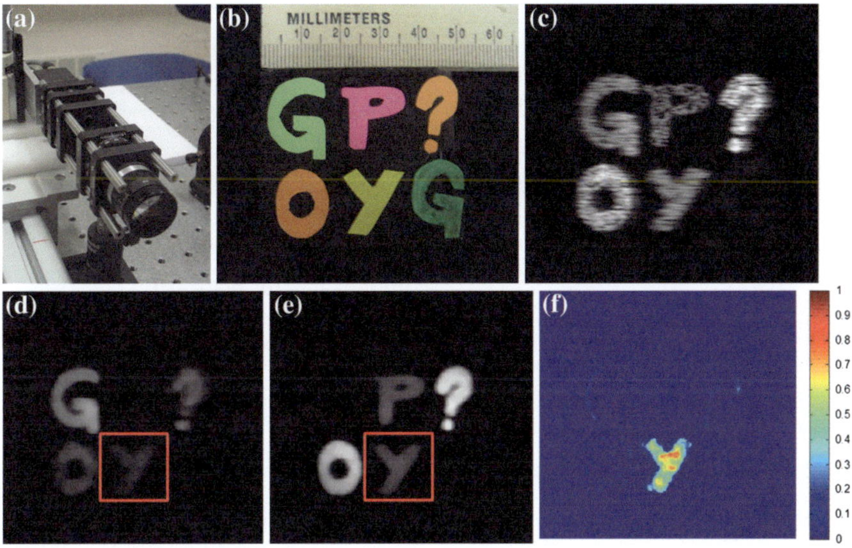

Fig. 13.4 CASSI-based spectral classification in the experiment: **a** photo of CASSI system, **b** photo of objects, **c** CASSI measurement, **d** Channel 12, **e** Channel 18, and **f** ACE scores of 1, 2, 14, 7, and 425 for the "G", "P", "?", "O", and "Y" letters by referencing the "Y" letter's spectrum. Note: the color range is shown as a score of spectral similarity

In the reconstruction, the datacube was decoded by using the measurement model of the computational design and the TV-based TwIST [13] was used to search the solution with parameters of 20 spectral channels and 200 iterations. Note 20 frames were used to reconstruct the datacube from CASSI measurements. In Fig. 13.4f, the ACE scores are visually shown to quantify the performance of CASSI-based spectral classification and the ACE scores are obtained by using ACE algorithm on the CASSI reconstruction. In the detection, some partial pixels of the "Y" letter were referenced to detect the rest of the "Y" letter. The true positive score was returned as 425 and the false positive score is 24, resulting in the ratio of 18. In the result, the pixels with the target spectrum are highly scored keeping the other pixels relatively low. Thus, the CASSI-based spectral classification effectively detects and classifies the desired pixels with a single frame in the scene.

13.3 Motion Compensation Coded Exposure Camera

In a traditional single-exposure camera system, the camera shutter opens and closes for a fixed amount of time. This means that the corresponding exposure time is static, and fast moving objects or camera motion can cause motion blur. This is because the exposure time defines a temporal period where light from a moving

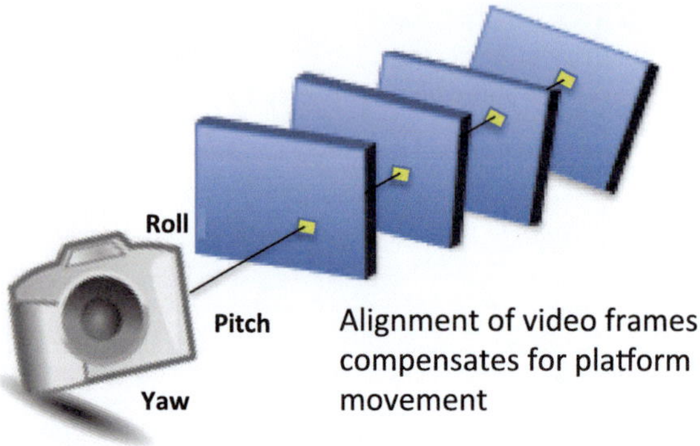

Fig. 13.5 Light collected over multiple frames is fused after alignment of video frames to compensate for platform motion

object is smeared across the image. Processing steps to deblur the image, e.g., by deconvolution, is near impossible because it is an ill-posed problem with uncertainty in both object and platform motion. In a computational imaging framework, a coded exposure approach would vary the period of time when the shutter is open during a chosen exposure time. This "flutter shutter" approach changes the ways in which the light is captured on each pixel, and preserves the high-frequency spatial details. To that end, deblurring through deconvolution becomes a solvable solution, and has been demonstrated for several challenging cases of motion-blur including large motion, textured backgrounds, and partial occlusions [8].

Another approach for motion deblurring relies on alignment and fusion of the coded exposure images. That is, by removing camera motion through video stabilization of images, light can be "collected" appropriately by summing the proper pixels associated with a particular part of the scene and object, as shown in Fig. 13.5. Light from the "same location" will be fused or summed across temporal frames, and as such, the described motion compensated system would generate video at a lower rate based on a higher rate input source (e.g., output at 60 Hz based on an input at 240 Hz frame rate). With this approach, the deblurring problem is once again a solvable problem, and the video frames contain light intensity information across multiple frames.

In this approach, images captured with low exposure would be less blurry but would be noisy because the sensor does not have time to capture sufficient amount of light. Dark current noise from each sensor pixel would dominate the signal produced from captured light, similar to low-light conditions where images are speckled with random salt-and-pepper noise. Images captured with high exposure would be less noisy but would be susceptible to blur because light is smeared across the image. Combining both low and high exposure image would produce both a low blur and low noise, with high dynamic range.

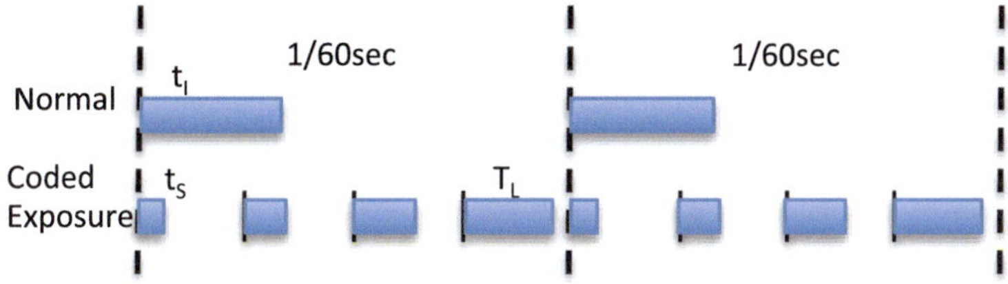

Fig. 13.6 The *top row* is the input rate and integration time from a commercial camera. The *bottom row* is the coded-exposure sampling rate with varying exposure times

13.3.1 Coded Exposures

In the approach based on frame alignment, multiple low dynamic range (LDR) images of varying exposure times are integrated to form a high dynamic range (HDR) image. Figure 13.6 provides an illustration of this approach. The shortest exposure LDR subframe image is called the 'seed' image; its exposure time is given as t_S. Other images are exposed for longer and can be regarded as the combination of the unit images with motion. Using this seed image approach, we do not require an optimized shutter open/closed pattern, and as such, it works with different camera speed and scene luminance. Using t_S as the unit exposure time, $T_2, T_3, \ldots, T_L$ as the subsequent exposure times, we ensure that all of the images with longer exposures are multiples of t_S.

For the general case in which motion blur is significant due to long exposure times, we create the output image by aligning and combining the short-exposure-time LDR sub-frame images. Based on our experience in low light imaging, it is more difficult to align the subframe images due to their unequal exposure times. Instead, our approach is to first align images with equal exposure times, and then interpolate the motions of other images of different exposure times. When there are multiple exposure patterns involved in the capturing, or when there is a need to have higher precision of motion interpolation, an accelerometer can be used to aid in motion estimation and interpolation.

To further improve the quality of the output HDR image, we generate a map of weighted values based on the camera's photopic response curve, and apply the weights to pixel values of the LDR images. This is done to normalize and blend the pixels, and the processing is done after alignment of the LDR images. This weight function gives less weight to pixels with values close to both 0 and the pixel maximum value, and more weight to pixels with midrange values. This mapping works well in cases where the scene has well-defined spatial features, which need to be preserved during fusion of LDR images.

13.3.2 Motion Compensation

The signal-to-noise (SNR) improvements and motion blur reduction comes directly from the alignment of LDR images to produce an HDR image. Without motion compensation, each pixel would integrate the captured light much like a camera with long exposure. There are many methods to enable image alignment. For example, one can use a gyro and accelerometer to detect camera motion and align image frames. However, this approach requires good initial calibration, precise timing, and drift adjustment to work accurately. We advocate further sub-pixel accuracy in alignment using image-based analysis.

In image-based alignment, feature based registration methods [32] work well to achieve this if each LDR image has sufficient SNR. However, global methods are preferred in SNR-limited low light conditions. Zhang et al. [33] have shown that a hierarchical motion estimation algorithm using Laplacian pyramid methods exhibits robust behavior for extremely low SNR ($\sim$1.0) imagery. For our approach, this robust motion estimation is applied to each LDR image. We also reduced processing latency by having the first captured LDR image from a subgroup (typically in a group of four images) used as the reference. The estimated true image is thus the weighted average of these four aligned LDR images.

13.4 Contrast Enhancements

To improve the feature feasibility on a display or downstream video analytics, we apply global and local contrast enhancement to the output HDR image. This would also ensure better contrast and full range display on monitors or displays which typically have low color range. For example, when we fuse LDR images (8–10 bits per pixel, we can generate a HDR scene with higher dynamic range (10–14 bits per pixel) and yet standard displays provide only 8 bit color depth. Using our contrast enhancement step, we can automatically scale different regions of the image to fit the highest dynamic range within the low color depth, while preserving the contrast.

Our global contrast enhancement is based on a logarithmic and exponential mapping function [34]. The processing would map the HDR image to the globally compressed image based on the average of both the logarithmic and exponential mapping functions. Our local contrast enhancement technique boosts the weak high spatial frequency contrast features of an image while reducing the gain of its low spatial frequency features in local regions. The source image is first decomposed into a Laplacian pyramid [35]. Then the local contrast and a contrast map pyramid are generated. At each pyramid level, this map is multiplied with the source pyramid to create a normalized pyramid. Finally, the Contrast Normalized image is obtained by the inverse transform of the pyramid. To ensure the best display, the output image is typically gamma corrected, either by the algorithm or the monitor itself.

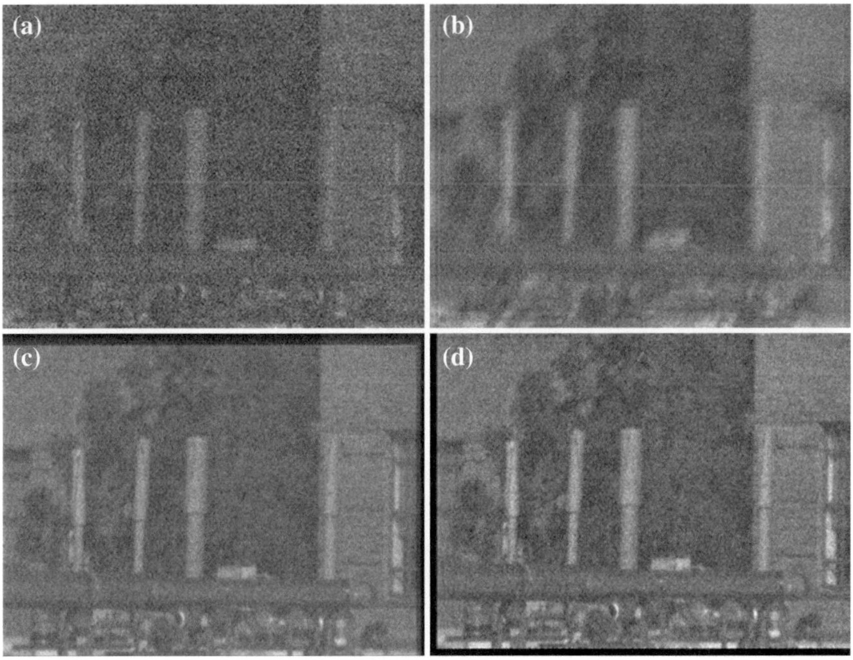

Fig. 13.7 The effect of coded exposure to deblur live 30 Hz video. **a** *Top left* a sample frame with short integration time minimizes motion blur at the expense of low SNR. **b** *Top right* maximizing the integration time improves SNR at the expense of motion blur. **c** *Bottom left* processing applied to eight subframe images maintains the SNR of (**b**) while giving the deblur performance of (**a**) at the same 30 Hz frame rate. **d** *Bottom right* video (**c**) following contrast normalization

13.4.1 High Dynamic Range Video in Low Light Conditions

We show the HDR output using the coded exposure approach described in this section. The source images shown in Fig. 13.7 were taken from a 30 Hz video stream in limited light with a large aperture and a relatively short integration time. The video is taken with slow panning motion, which adds to pixel blur with long exposures. The original video (top left) taken under these conditions thus contains significant thermal noise from the camera. To improve the SNR with a traditional approach, the camera exposure can be increased by changing the camera integration time, e.g., to 33.3 ms, the frame-rate-limited maximum value (top right). However, large amounts of motion blur are evident using this approach.

The coded exposure method is generated under the same illumination conditions and with the same camera motion. The output is at the same 30 Hz output frame rate, which is produced by aligning and combining eight LSR subframe images. Each LSR image is exposed for one-eighth of the frame-rate-limited integration time (i.e., 4.17 ms). The contrast-enhanced version of this image is shown at bottom right of Fig. 13.7, and a decrease in motion blur is evident.

In the HDR output, we are able to increase the effective dynamic range of 8- to 12-bit cameras by up to four bits (24 dB), allowing simultaneous dark and light areas in scenes to be accurately captured with little or no loss of information due to saturation. We run the video camera at frame rates four times faster than the image display rate while varying integration times from very short (to "freeze" scene motion) to "as long as possible" (to maximize SNR). Through processing, we produce an HDR image with significant blur reduction while simultaneously increasing the effective dynamic range of the sensor. Furthermore, we perform contrast enhancements on the HDR image to allow its high dynamic representation on 8-bit displays with virtually no loss of visual information.

This coded exposure method enables high performance video to be captured from any rapidly moving platform in real-world conditions (e.g., bright sunlight with deep dark shadows) and displayed in low-latency real-time. It can be used in embedded vision applications in the automotive and surveillance domains. In low light conditions with significant motion blur, this system enables considerable improvements in Detection, Recognition and Identification performance, demonstrated in real-time in a prototype described in [36] using an FPGA.

13.5 Adaptive Task-Specific Imaging System

To conclude this chapter, we present an architectural framework for a camera system that bridges the front-end computational imaging subsystem to the back-end semantic reasoning. We have motivated this framework by providing two examples of computational imaging solutions, and what is left is to make the connection to the traditional computer vision processing that deals with detection, classification, tracking, and learning. Our goal here is to reinforce the notion that computational imaging functions can be made optimized for the embedded vision task at hand.

One main difference is that our framework is based on performing adaptive feature-specific imaging directly on compressed measurements. This aspect is similar to visual sensor networks [37] where processing is performed at the camera so that video does not need to be transmitted. Without requiring the decoding step, we can enable lower latency processing. In our proposed framework, we do not require that the image be generated first, but instead, we perform some aspect of detection, classification, tracking, and learning directly on compressive measurements. These four components interact with each other, as shown in Fig. 13.8. For example, tracking results are fed into the learning module to update models to improve detection and classification, which in turn re-initializes tracking when tracks are lost in some frames. In spirit, our idea is similar to that in [20] where tracking, learning, and detection/classification are co-trained to support each other. Specifically, the four components are implemented as follows:

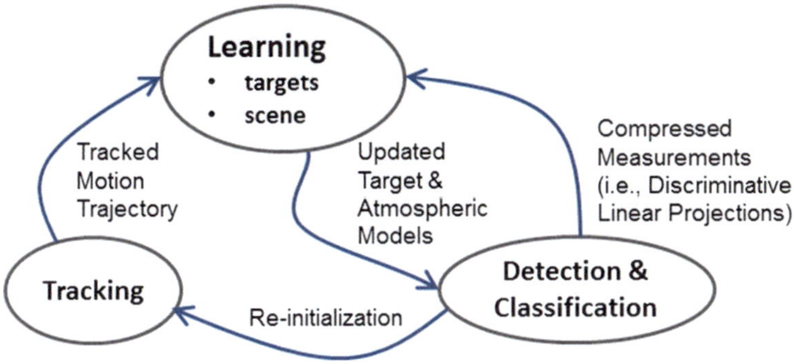

Fig. 13.8 Task interaction and data flow, showing tasks performed on compressed measurements

- **Detection/Classification**: Implement discriminative modulator patterns and directly measure linear projections of incoming radiance for detection and classification. Learn discriminative patterns via offline training and online update.
- **Tracking**: Use a Kalman filter to track the detected objects-of-interests. In case of a missing track, the detector finds the object and reinitializes tracking.
- **Learning**: The detection results (i.e., the measured discriminative linear projections), after being verified with tracked frames, are used to update the posterior probability distribution and the modulator patterns, and to improve the atmospheric models (e.g., fog, haze, heat scintillations).

The key enabler for this architecture framework is to identify functions that can be implemented with tight coupling between algorithms for *feature and semantic* analysis with lower *level computational imaging parameters* for coded illumination, aperture, and exposure. This coupling creates a feedback loop between application task and sensor, allowing for increased sensitivity and potentially lowered power operation by not following typical methods of just running the processing pipeline faster.

While current camera systems already have feedback mechanisms that allow the image capture subsystem to adapt based on the image processing system, there is a significant level of feedback latency that limits the effectiveness of the system. Very often, many multiple image frames have elapsed before any dynamic settings can be calculated because there is a long processing chain from raw pixels to detection/tracking/classification of objects. Furthermore, the settings are often for the entire frame and not at a finer grain level because there are no effective algorithms that consider region of interest control of sensor parameters. Here, we are exploring a camera system in which two subsystems (image capture and processing) are tightly coupled at a very fine grain, resulting in low latency level control at the sub-frame level. Such a system would be analogous to current auto-focus functionality, but instead, such a mechanism would be driven from needs of the feature and semantic analysis.

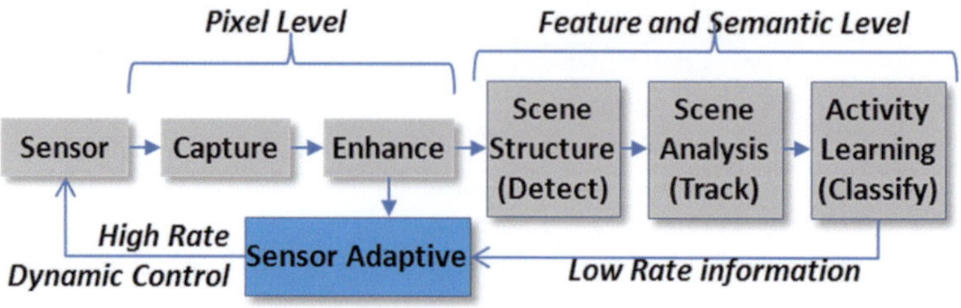

Fig. 13.9 Sensor adaptive algorithms in the pixel domain can more actively control the sensor without the latency to process feature and semantic level processing. Key elements of the detect-track-classify algorithms provide cues to the task-specific model to enable high rate sensor control based on scene understanding

Our proposed architecture revolves around selecting pieces of object detection, tracking, and classification algorithms to process earlier in the image processing pipeline. As shown in Fig. 13.9, this approach will offer a **sensor adaptive module** with tight coupling between feature-semantic-level processing to camera control. This approach is radically different than the traditional approach of simply speeding up the entire image processing pipeline to enable a faster control loop. Motion and other semantic cues are evaluated at a high sub-frame rate to reduce the latency for sensor control. The needs of feature and semantic processing for object detection, tracking and classification are evaluated quickly to provide near-instant feedback to the sensor. By being **task-adaptive**, this approach can improve image quality and SNR on target objects for higher quality actionable intelligence.

Sensor adaptive algorithms can improve the overall sensitivity of the camera system for dynamic task-specific needs. That is, by adapting sensor parameters to the dynamic understanding of the scene and targeted objects, the capture process can be made more efficient to capture the desired signal at the appropriate time, duration, and location.

The proposed architecture requires the mapping of sensor parameters to video analytic parameters within the developed simulation framework. It is important to explore sensor control parameters such as frame rate, resolution, exposure, and read-out times, and how they can be tuned based on video analytic parameters, such as the type of detected objects, number of salient targets, and predicted motion of targets. With a semantic understanding of the scene and detected objects, the capture process can adapt accordingly to the scene content.

The key to effectively migrating feature and semantic level algorithms into the "front end" pixel processing domain is to maintain a low-latency control loop at the sub-frame level such that sensor control can adjust quickly. This means that we will algorithmically make an inference on detected objects based on low-level analytics. While we efficiently and intuitively bridge the semantic gap between higher-level algorithms and sensor controls, we must maintain the robustness of the camera system to mission-specific functions.

Let us consider the technical challenges for feature- and semantic-level algorithms. Challenges in detecting moving objects include: (1) stabilization of jittery or on-the-move video for reliable detection of independently moving entities, and (2) eliminating false alarms due to extraneous factors, e.g., swaying trees, shadows and other illumination changes. Challenges for tracking objects include: (1) handling objects that come to a stop and blend into the background, and (2) predicting object movement for partial and full occlusions. Challenges for object classification include: (1) distinguishing objects with similar features, and (2) having sufficient views of the same object to extract distinguishing features. All of the algorithms would benefit from increased sensor sensitivity spatially, spectrally, and temporally, in order to reduce the false alarms caused by semantic inference from processing the video.

13.5.1 Sensor Adaptive Algorithms

Detection, classification, tracking, and classification algorithms directly interact with each other in order to formulate an output result based on an understanding of the scene. For example, a detection algorithm would provide motion and location parameters to a tracking algorithm. The tracking algorithm would sort among the detected objects to associate a label or track identification. It would maintain a history of tracks and other features with the object so overcome occlusion. The track and feature information is used by the classification algorithm to infer object type based on a trained database of features and activities.

We will leverage our understanding of interactions within feature- and semantic-level processing to create low-latency sensor adaptive algorithms. In Fig. 13.9, we show small elements of the detect-track-classify algorithms within the sensor adaptive algorithm module that drives input into a Sensor Control block. Each of the feature-semantic level algorithms has needs with respect to imagery to improve its tasks, but not all can be satisfied concurrently. For example, a detection algorithm typically wants a global view of the scene because it is tasked to find all moving targets. This means that imagery captured within a single frame will equalize the importance among all pixels in the field of view. In contrast, a tracking algorithm is focused a single object, so it would prefer to allocate more resources (time, power, dwell time) on a particular region of interest. Similarly, classification algorithms would prefer to remove spurious data points (e.g., noisy sampled features), so it might prefer to collect more data points around a particular modality (e.g., longer exposure for higher dynamic range to gather more distinguishing features).

Running concurrently, the Sensor Control block contains an **Adaptive Task-Specific Model** that organizes the inputs from the detect-track-classify algorithms to maintain a consistent and robust control loop with the imager. The task-specific model can be reinitialized based on different tracks, or when tracks are lost in some frames. Lower rate information from the back-end processing chain (see Fig. 13.9) can also feed into the task-specific model to enhance the robustness by prioritizing among multiple tracked objects.

The proposed algorithmic framework also allows for new algorithms to be created and integrated. For example, as part of the detection task, we can include a filter that detects the level of motion blur. Since blur can imply object motion, we can use it to infer the object type in the scene. As such, the algorithm can feed input into the task-specific model to decrease integration time for that region of interest because of anticipated needs for the tracking task. The use of motion blur is improved from typical optical flow analysis methods because the algorithm would measure the level of blur of several pixels, and not need to find correspondence between pixels in different frames.

13.6 Conclusion

Traditional embedded vision systems are bounded in performance because they are limited by the quality of images they can work with. With a computational imaging approach, these vision systems can "see" better because they are no longer limited to the single-lens to focus light onto a focal plane image sensor. In this chapter, we provide an overview of the research elements of computational imaging. We showed two example applications of this technology area using coded aperture and coded exposure. We then show a proposed architectural framework for a computational imaging system that is adaptive and task specific for back-end video analytics processing.

There is certainly a lot more work left to do as there are many technical challenges in low latency, high robustness, and low power. All of these can be addressed as we can readily adapt our understanding in accelerating embedded vision algorithms to hardware such as GPUs, FPGAs, and DSPs. The vision community in both academia and industry are already starting to head towards this path to reach significant gains in image quality and performance in analytics. Are you doing the same with your vision system?

References

1. Raskar R, Tumblin J (2009) Computational photography: mastering new techniques for lenses, lighting, and sensors. AK Peters Ltd, Wellesley
2. Nayar SK (2006) Computational cameras: redefining the image. IEEE Comput 39(8):30–38
3. Jinwei G, Liu C (2012) Discriminative illumination: per-pixel classification of raw materials based on optimal projections of spectral BRDF. In: 2012 IEEE conference on Computer vision and pattern recognition (CVPR). IEEE
4. Lim S, Berends D, Das A, Isnardi M, Chai S (2014) Forensic prescreening system using coded aperture snapshot spectral imager. SPIE defense, security, and sensing. international society for optics and photonics

5. Lu X, Chen C-C, Aggarwal JK (2011) Human detection using depth information by kinect. In: 2011 IEEE computer society conference on Computer vision and pattern recognition workshops (CVPRW). IEEE
6. Gehm ME et al (2006) Static two-dimensional aperture coding for multimodal, multiplex spectroscopy. Appl Opt 45(13):2965–2974
7. Zhang DC, Piacentino M, Chai S (2012) Extended motion adaptive signal integration technique for real-time image enhancement. SPIE defense, security, and sensing. international society for optics and photonics
8. Raskar R, Agrawal A, Tumblin J (2006) Coded exposure photography: motion deblurring using fluttered shutter. ACM Trans Gr (TOG), 25(3). ACM
9. Veeraraghavan A, Raskar R, Agrawal A, Mohan A, Tumblin J (2007) Dappled photography: mask enhanced cameras for heterodyned light fields and coded aperture refocusing. ACM Trans Gr 26(3)
10. Ren N et al (2005) Light field photography with a hand-held plenoptic camera. Computer Science Technical Report CSTR 2.11
11. Lumsdaine A, Georgiev T (2009) The focused plenoptic camera. In: 2009 IEEE international conference on Computational photography (ICCP). IEEE
12. Li C, Yin W, Zhang Y (2009) User's guide for TVAL3: TV minimization by augmented lagrangian and alternating direction algorithms. CAAM report
13. Bioucas-Dias J, Figueiredo M (2007) A new TwIST: two-step iterative shrinkage/thresholding algorithms for image restoration. IEEE Trans Image Process 16(12):2992–3004
14. Adams A et al (2010) The Frankencamera: an experimental platform for computational photography. ACM Trans Gr (TOG) 29(4):29
15. Baheti PK, Neifeld MA (2008) Adaptive feature-specific imaging: a face recognition example. Appl Opt 47:B21–B31
16. Nelson MP, Aust JF, Dobrowolski JA, Verly PG, Myrick ML (1998) Multivariate optical computation for predictive spectroscopy. Anal Chem 70.73–82
17. Duarte-Carvajalino JM, Yu G, Carin L, Sapiro G (2013) Task-driven adaptive statistical compressive sensing of gaussian mixture models. IEEE Trans Signal Proc 63(3):1
18. Gu J, Liu C (2012) Discriminative illumination: per-pixel classification of raw materials based on optimal projections of spectral BRDFs. IEEE CVPR
19. Hitomi Y, JinweiGu MG, Mitsunaga T, Nayar S (2011) Video from a singe coded exposure photograph using a learned over-complete dictionary. IEEE ICCV
20. Neifeld MA, Shankar P (2003) Feature-specific imaging. Appl Opt 42(17):10
21. Dinakarababu DV, Golish DR, Gehm ME (2011) Adaptive feature specific spectroscopy for rapid chemical identification. Opt Express 19:4595–4610
22. Neifeld MA, Ashok A, Baheti PK (2007) Task-specific information for imaging system analysis. J Opt Soc Am A 24(12)
23. Baheti PK, Neifeld MA (2006) Feature-specific structured imaging. Appl Opt 45:7382–7391
24. Manolakis D et al (2009) Is there a best hyperspectral detection algorithm? SPIE defense security, and sensing. international society for optics and photonics
25. Kraut S, Scharf LL (1999) The CFAR adaptive subspace detector is a scale-invariant GLRT. IEEE Trans Signal Process 47:2538–2541
26. Kittle D, Choi K, Wagadarikar A, Brady DJ (2010) Multiframe image estimation for coded aperture snapshot spectral imagers. Appl Opt 49:6824–6833
27. Donoho DL (2006) Compressed sensing. IEEE Trans Inf Theory 52(4):1289–1306
28. Candes E, Romberg J, Tao T (2006) Robust uncertainty principles: exact signal reconstruction from highly incomplete frequency information. IEEE Trans Inf Theory 52(2):489–509
29. Lowe D (2004) Distinctive image features from scale-invariant keypoints. Int J Comput Vis 60(2):91–110
30. Dalal N, Triggs B (2005) Histograms of oriented gradients for human detection. In: CVPR, pp 886–893
31. Bergen J, Anandan P, Hanna K, Hingorani R (1992) Hierarchical model-based motion estimation. In: Sandini G (ed) Computer vision ECCV'92. Lecture Notes in Computer Science, vol 588. Springer, Berlin Heidelberg, pp 237–252

32. Fonseca LMG, Manjunath BS (1996) Registration techniques for multisensor remotely sensed imagery. PE RS-Photogramm Eng Remote Sens 62(9):1049–1056
33. Zhang DC, Piacentino M, Chai S (2012) Motion compensation for low light and high motion imaging. Military sensing symposium
34. Burt P, Zhang C, van der Wal G (2007) Image enhancement through contrast normalization. Military sensing symposium
35. Burt PJ, Adelson EH (1983) The Laplacian pyramid as a compact image code. IEEE Trans Commun 31(4):532–540
36. Piacentino MR et al (2013) Motion adaptive signal integration-high dynamic range (MASI-HDR) video processing for dynamic platforms. SPIE Defense, security, and sensing. international society for optics and photonics
37. Winkler T, Rinner B (2009) Power aware communication in wireless pervasive smart camera networks. IEEE International conference on intelligent sensors, sensor networks and information processing (ISSNIP)

Index

B. Kisačanin and M. Gelautz (eds.), *Advances in Embedded Computer Vision*, Advances in Computer Vision and Pattern Recognition,
DOI 10.1007/978-3-319-09387-1

MIX
Papier aus verantwortungsvollen Quellen
Paper from responsible sources
FSC® C105338

If you have any concerns about our products,
you can contact us on
ProductSafety@springernature.com

In case Publisher is established outside the EU,
the EU authorized representative is:
Springer Nature Customer Service Center GmbH
Europaplatz 3, 69115 Heidelberg, Germany

Printed by Libri Plureos GmbH
in Hamburg, Germany